BLASTED ALLEGORIES

INTERNATIONAL
Tribune
10 Said Slain in Soweto
Black Strike Holds
In Britain, Some Ideas
To Combat the Drought
UN Defers Vietnam's Application
China Rejects Condolences
From Soviet Bloc Red Parties
CLASSIFIED
Youths Swell Ranks of Argentine Terrorists

An Anthology of Writings
by Contemporary Artists

B L A S T E D A L L E G O R I E S

Edited by Brian Wallis
Foreword by Marcia Tucker

The New Museum of Contemporary Art, New York
The MIT Press, Cambridge, Massachusetts;
London, England

The New Museum of Contemporary Art, New York
Documentary Sources in Contemporary Art
Series Editor: Marcia Tucker

Volume 1. *Art After Modernism: Rethinking Representation*
Edited by Brian Wallis
Volume 2. *Blasted Allegories: An Anthology of Writings by Contemporary Artists*
Edited by Brian Wallis

This volume is made possible through a generous grant from The Henry Luce Fund for Scholarship in American Art.

Photographs selected and arranged by Barbara Bloom
Endpapers: Richard Prince, *Jokes*, 1987
Printed by Halliday Lithograph Corp., West Hanover, Mass.
Designed by Katy Homans and Bethany Johns, Homans Design, Inc.

Library of Congress Cataloging-in-Publication Data
Main Entry under title:
Blasted allegories.
(Documentary sources in contemporary art)
Bibliography: p. 417
1. Postmodernism–United States–Themes, motives.
2. Arts, American–United States–Themes, motives.
3. Arts, Modern–20th century–United States–Themes, motives.
I. Wallis, Brian, 1953– . II. Series.
NX504.B5 1987 700′.973 87-42766

ISBN 0-262-23128-X (hardcover)
0-262-73086-3 (paperback)

First paperback edition, 1989

The New Museum of Contemporary Art,
583 Broadway, New York, N.Y. 10012

The MIT Press, Massachusetts Institute of Technology,
55 Hayward Street, Cambridge, Mass. 02142

Contents

VII Director's Foreword — **Marcia Tucker**

XI Telling Stories: A Fictional Approach to Artists' Writings — **Brian Wallis**

1. A Story Is Not Just a Story

2 Grandma's Story — **Trinh T. Minh-ha**

33 Family Stories — **Carrie Mae Weems**

42 Serving the Status-Quo — **Connie Hatch**

58 Three Stories — **James Casebere**

61 Sounds in the Distance — **David Wojnarowicz**

68 Words in Reverse — **Laurie Anderson**

2. The Order of Things

74 A Tour of the Monuments of Passaic, New Jersey — **Robert Smithson**

82 Untitled — **Matt Mullican**

89 If Only — **Anne Turyn / Robert Fiengo**

92 Five Comments — **Sherrie Levine**

94 The Consummate Mask of Rock — **Bruce Nauman**

100 My Files of Movie Stills — **John Baldessari**

103 Truisms — **Jenny Holzer**

3. Discourses of Power

114 Reading an Archive — **Allan Sekula**

129 Ideology, Confrontation, and Political Self-Awareness: An Essay, 1981 — **Adrian Piper**

134 Constructing a Life — **Martha Rosler**

138 Spies and Watchmen — **Thomas Lawson**

141 In the Dark — **Eric Bogosian**

148 From *Swimming to Cambodia* — **Spalding Gray**

157 The Rhetoric of AIDS — **Simon Watney**

4. History and Memory

170 My Past, My People — **Edgar Heap of Birds**

174 Clio / History — **Theresa Hak Kyung Cha**

182 The Politics of Writing — **Sekou Sundiata**

187 Evening Tomorrow's Here Today Since the Hornet Files I Triangle — **Candace Hill**
193 Common Origin — **Reese Williams**
207 Views — **Peter Nadin**
212 My Bio: Notes on an American Childhood — **Cookie Mueller**

5. Modern Love

218 Modern Love — **Constance DeJong**
236 Russian Constructivism — **Kathy Acker**
255 For the Future — **Lynne Tillman**
270 Burmese Days — **Gary Indiana**
281 Sunlight and Personality — **Suzanne Jackson**
292 Four Stories — **Jane Warrick**

6. Desire, Fetish, Commodity

298 Tea With Madeleine — **Victor Burgin**
310 What is Poetry to You? — **Cecilia Vicuña**
314 Transcendent Anti-Fetishism — **Ross Bleckner**
325 The Paintings are Dead — **David Salle**
329 On Line — **Peter Halley**
335 Casual Imagination — **Judith Barry**

7. Mass Culture and the Structure of Fantasy

362 Dean Martin / Entertainment as Theater — **Dan Graham**
371 Pathetic Readings — **William Wegman**
375 Beyond Chiffon: The Making of *Storme* — **Michelle Parkerson**
380 Thoughts on Women's Cinema: Eating Words, Voicing Struggles — **Yvonne Rainer**
386 Discordant Views — **Silvia Kolbowski**
395 Remote Control — **Barbara Kruger**
406 The Perfect Tense — **Richard Prince**

417 Bibliography

Director's Foreword

MARCIA TUCKER

This second anthology in our series, *Documentary Sources in Contemporary Art,* is a collection of writings by contemporary artists. These pieces range widely from lists, truisms, titles, and other anomalous forms to the more traditional fiction, autobiographical narrative, critical and prose pieces we generally associate with artists' writings.

In recent years, artists' texts have taken their place alongside visual works as a separate and equally viable medium. Today, there are many more artists using language, both integrally and separately from painting, sculpture, photography, film and video, and performance than there were even ten years ago. In part, this is symptomatic of the tendency to work in many media at once, suggesting that what one has to say is the unifying factor in an artist's work, rather than the style or means one chooses.

Blasted Allegories is the title of a series of photographic works created by John Baldessari in 1978. By using randomly-shot television images, each of which was assigned a word and then used to form verbal as well as visual "sentences," Baldessari emphasized the reciprocity of visual and verbal categories. The resulting works alluded to the complex structure of the allegorical form, which – unlike the closure of a traditional literary narrative – subverts a singular reading.

As the critic Craig Owens suggested in 1980,[1] the previously disreputable allegorical form has become of increasing interest to artists in recent years. As modernism (and formalism) are being challenged by postmodernist criticism and theory, the unity of metaphor has been replaced by allegory's density and layering of meaning. Fragmentation, transcience, appropriation, deferral of meaning, impermanence, and collapsed temporal dimension are some of the characteristics of the allegorical mode, as evidenced in the visual arts as well as in the literary texts included in this volume.

1. Craig Owens, "The Allegorical Impulse," in *Art After Modernism: Rethinking Representation,* ed. Brian Wallis (New York and Boston: The New Museum of Contemporary Art and David R. Godine, 1984), pp. 203-235.

What has happened in artists' writings parallels similar changes in visual practice; because the allegorical form precludes a singular interpretation, suggesting instead the open-ended nature of discourse, the exchange between viewer (or reader) and work is weighted on the side of the latter. The value traditionally accorded to the individuality and authority of the artist/writer is disrupted by questioning the work's source, context, audience, purpose, and meaning, a disruption engendered by the allegorical form itself.

Literature, including that produced by artists, has been greatly influenced in recent years by other fields, especially semiotics, psychoanalytic theory, literary criticism, feminist studies, and political science. Art and art writing no longer occupy a separate domain, but participate in cultural and social inquiry and critique at large.

This volume was compiled with an acute awareness of the changes that are taking place in art and criticism at the end of the twentieth century, and with an understanding that we cannot consider any form of representation, whether verbal or visual, a hermetic enterprise. Perusing the varied writings of artists today, it is significant that they leave us with no single sense of style, no unity of purpose, nothing – other than the allegorical "impulse," if it can be extended so far as to encompass the myriad viewpoints presented here – that can be fixed or categorized definitively. The reader must proceed independently along a sometimes parallel and participatory course, to arrive at his or her own ideas, experiences, and responses.

This volume will hopefully serve as a useful companion to the first book in our series, a compendium of critical essays entitled *Art After Modernism: Rethinking Representation,* and as an introduction to a third anthology of interviews and discussions *(Discourses: Conversations on Postmodern Culture).* All three volumes are published thanks to generous grants from the Henry Luce Foundation's Fund for Scholarship in American Art. It is through the Foundation's extraordinary support for innovative scholarship and critical investigation in contemporary art that The New Museum has been able to fill a crucial gap in the history of art and ideas in our own time.

Brian Wallis, editor of the first three volumes of the series for The New Museum, has once again taken an overwhelming body of work and shaped it coherently into a singular source for edification, enjoyment, and debate. His profound understanding of recent theory and practice in the arts has made this anthology a useful and current tool for analysis, rather than simply a collection of writings.

At the Museum, our curators Lynn Gumpert and William Olander and curatorial assistant Karen Fiss have provided crucial intellectual and practical assistance. Russell Ferguson, Librarian, along with Susan Rosenberg, compiled the extensive bibliography and also participated in discussions concerning the nature and scope of the book. Virginia Strull, Director of Development, was responsible for the skillful and thorough grant proposals and reports which ultimately provided us with the essential underwriting for the project.

Phil Mariani was instrumental from the start in all phases of the book's conception and production, and we are grateful for her herculean labors in this regard. Katy Homans and Bethany Johns of Homans/Salsgiver, Inc., are responsible for the elegant design of the book and provided long hours of cooperation overseeing its ultimate production. The photographic images were selected by Barbara Bloom and the cover photograph was provided by Richard Prince; we appreciate the enthusiastic participation by these two artists. In addition, we are grateful to Karen Marta, Gilles Peress, and Nan Richardson, who provided generous and insightful assistance in locating and securing photographs.

We are delighted that MIT Press has joined us in this venture. Mark Rakatansky, Editor, has been particularly helpful and supportive, and we appreciate the enthusiasm and conviction shown by him and the Press.

Our thanks above all to the hundreds of artists who have shared their material with us. The pieces we have chosen to publish represent only the smallest part of the literary work being done by artists in America today, and we hope it will provide an impetus for further reading and writing of this kind.

Telling Stories: A Fictional Approach to Artists' Writings

BRIAN WALLIS

One of the most enduring and telling fantasies of modernist culture is the myth of the inarticulate or silent artist. Despite a century of theoretical and critical writings by modern artists, popular conceptions preserve a view of the artist as a "gifted" or "natural" man (the representation being predominantly male), beyond the normal conventions of society and hence beyond (or "prior to") language. In this persistent stereotype, the artist's work is itself the exemplary form of expression, transparent in its communication, opening directly to intuition, and not reducible to literary equivalence. Perpetuated by notions of action painting which require a view of the artist as less a contemplative intellectual than an elemental force (Pollock: "I am nature") and by artists' parodic self-representations (Warhol: "I am a machine"), this view has in general trapped the artist within the confines of craft and removed him or her from the theoretical, critical, and political conditions of production.

In the developing history of modernism, this will to silence, this eschewal of narrative and discourse, was instituted as both an appropriate analogue to the formalist content of abstraction and as one aspect of the refinement of modern art into specific disciplines. In part this silence was imposed as a repression of the verbal in favor of the visual, a process which can be traced back to the Enlightenment.[1] But silence was also promoted as an active agent of modernism, as a representation, in the form of ellipsis, enigma, and the void. Artists were insistently represented and mythologized as visual rather than intellectual, their writings serving to supplement or extend the increasingly "pure" representations of their artwork. The writings of artists such as Kasimir Malevich, Piet Mondrian, and Wassily Kandinsky, for example, were predominantly aesthetic and philosophical in nature, reinforcing the nearly sacred quest of modern artists toward the idealization of abstraction and steering them away from the concreteness and materiality by which language might bind art to everyday experience. Thus overwhelmed by the predominance of abstract representation, and bound to visual forms, modern artists were in a sense

1. See Craig Owens, "Earthwords," *October*, no. 10 (Fall 1980): 121-130.

silenced by the mythical construction of their role in society.

Walter Benjamin was one of the first critics to recognize the political origins of the relationship between silence and the rise of modernism. In 1936, Benjamin noted in his short essay, "The Storyteller,"[2] that soldiers returning from World War I were dumbstruck, unable to speak of their experiences or of the horrors they had witnessed. Confronted face to face with the destructive capacity of the machine age, bruised by the frailty of human life, scored by silent scenes of death and disfigurement, the soldiers were stunned into a decade of mute repression. Benjamin traced to this crisis the virtual extinction of storytelling as a source of information and as a form of communication.

Storytelling became a central component of Benjamin's aesthetic theory, for in storytelling (as opposed to "literature") meaning resides not simply in the text itself or in the subject matter, but in the human transmission of experience.[3] Storytelling is a direct outcome of social interaction. As opposed to the privatized form of the novel, for example, in which an individual writer communicates with an individual reader, storytelling necessitates an active, immediate, and communal bond between teller and listener. What is more, the nature of the story – its recourse to tradition, its rejection of originality, its lack of psychological inflection – foregrounds a preexistence of meaning, reversing the metaphorical "search for truth" of the conventional novel. In its construction as well as its process and delivery, the story focuses attention on both pleasure and useful information: the lesson, the moral, the allegory.

What Benjamin identified in the eclipse of storytelling was the final destabilization of the sources of social identity which had existed in Europe for hundreds of years. His essay was not an attempt to bring back lost times nor was it an empty nostalgia; rather "The Storyteller" was an effort to recognize the revolutionary potential of a seemingly archaic genre at the moment of its ruination. For Benjamin, the modernist displacement of persons, meanings, and identities allowed for the potential construction, out of alienation and oppression, of other communities bound together by the formal means which seemed most specifically outlawed. The inhabitation of useless forms, the circulation of stories without origins, the imprecise repetition of unoriginal tales, the willful confusion of truth and fiction, the primacy accorded pleasure and fantasy,

2. Walter Benjamin, "The Storyteller," in *Illuminations*, ed. Hannah Arendt, trans. Harry Zorn (New York: Schocken Books, 1969), pp. 83-109.
3. On "The Storyteller," see the excellent critical review by Marcus Bullock, "Three Headstones: Recent Books on Walter Benjamin," *New German Critique*, no. 39 (Fall 1986): 219-232.

the ability to exchange experiences and not just information: all these qualities recommended storytelling as a form to be rescued from modernism's will to silence.

Given that Benjamin recognized storytelling as a form melding personal experience and political desire, it is appropriate that many writers today (in particular, women of color, Latin American writers, artists) have turned to storytelling and other fictional modes as forms of cultural criticism. In particular, many of the writings collected in this volume utilize these fictions to suggest the real social relationships which underlie artistic production and the ties between individual experience and a mass culture or mass consumption. In other words, these writings suggest that it is not a special perception that lends credence to these artists' writings, but a particular cultural position – of simultaneous marginality and authority.

As suggested by the French theorists Gilles Deleuze and Félix Guattari, this role, the role of the "minor," is one in which a specialized, local language serves to challenge or disrupt the structures and confidences of a dominant language. This writing of the "minor" discredits the masterpiece and dismantles form, genre, and canon. What is more, in its movement between margin and center, the "minor" neither romanticizes the marginal nor privileges the mainstream – both positions are rejected as static and confining.[4] This is necessarily a theoretical position which exists "in between" fixed points. Moreover, this type of writing does not seek to fulfill the conventional forms of "major" culture in establishing a unified subject or asserting the primacy of the individual, rather "there isn't a subject; there are only collective assemblages of enunciation."[5] Thus, one important question for the artists included here is not how to gain access to the accepted forms of literature, but how to recognize the language which is relevant to the issues of their particular community.

To a great extent the language which is available to any writer or speaker is determined by one's social position. In Trinh T. Minh-ha's essay on women and storytelling, for instance, it is clear that just as the story is an integral component of social formation, encouraging and formulating the terms of interpersonal communication, the story itself is also shaped and determined by its

4. Gilles Deleuze and Félix Guattari, "What Is a Minor Literature?" in *Kafka: Towards a Minor Literature,* trans. Dana Polan (Minneapolis: University of Minnesota Press, 1986), pp. 16-27. For useful discussions of this text in relation to minority discourse and postmodern art, see Caren Kaplan, "Deterritorializations: The Rewriting of Home and Exile in Western Feminist Discourse," *Cultural Critique,* no. 6 (Spring 1987): 187-198, and Hal Foster, "Readings in Cultural Resistance," in *Recodings: Art, Spectacle, Cultural Politics* (Port Townsend, Wash.: Bay Press, 1985), pp. 157-179.
5. Deleuze and Guattari, "What Is a Minor Literature?," p. 18.

communal context. Thus, in tribal societies, although the woman may be the repository and medium for traditional stories (the tribal "archive"), her status within that culture is often secondary. Storytelling then is a form through which her power can be expressed – power to maintain links with the past through the accurate and pleasure-giving repetition of the stories. But such tales deliver more than history and pleasure, for their plots are interlaced with both generalized experiences and "the wisdom of life," which both reflect on the contradictions of society and provide models for ethical and social conduct opposed to the dominant language of History or the Law. A primary example here is black American verbal culture, which has built on those tribal traditions with experiences of racism and oppressions of poverty to maintain storytelling as a form with particular contemporary urgency.

But other forms of speaking and writing also embody this kind of dialogue and encompass a subversive potential. For the writers in this book, these critical forms, such as interviews, monologues, jokes, dream narratives, and parables, oppose the imposed narrative structure, the unquestioned hierarchy of characters, and the easy closure of much conventional – or even modernist – literature. In place of traditional expository writing or even experimental texts, the works collected here posit a wholly different approach to textual production which challenges accepted sites, structures, and meanings of discourse. In place of aesthetic innovation, these writers employ appropriation and reinscription of existing voices, styles, and genres; in place of the coherence of the conventional text, they favor a form which is fragmentary, inconclusive, digressive, and interpenetrated with other texts; in place of the omnipotent author, they acknowledge a collectivity of voices and active participation of the reader; in place of the new or the original, they accept an understanding of language and stories as "already written" and shaped by social and political conditions.

In addition, we might say that, insofar as these texts correspond to certain strategies of picture-making in contemporary art and are concerned with the construction and deconstruction of cultural representations, they are inescapably allegorical. Simply put, allegories are texts which say one thing and mean another. This occurs when any writing suggests a second level of meaning, lying behind the text, so to speak, or when one piece of writing is read through another, as when the New Testament is read through the Old. Like the storyteller, "the allegorist does not invent images, but confiscates them. He lays claim to the culturally significant, poses as its interpreter. And in his hands the image becomes something other . . . he adds another meaning to the image."[6] Thus, the allegorical text is one which offers a particular importance to the critic or interpreter, at the expense of the author or creator. This also suggests that when we read the writings of contemporary artists – many of which employ allegorical forms – we are participating in a critical response in which real personal and cultural events are used to enlarge the ethical, social, and political meanings they suggest.

As a form of cultural criticism, then, these allegorical writings frequently counter the more formal presumptions and mandarin tone of high theoretical discourse – that codified version of critique which Roland Barthes called "the language of knowledge." Insofar as this theoretical criticism affects a specialized language and a didactic purpose, it often repeats the same process of conversion of the cultural into the "natural" that it criticizes: asserting the stability and universality of certain values, adopting a tone of unwavering assurance, producing arguments aimed at resolution and closure, excluding the subjective and the irrational, and insisting on the political correctness of a specific moral or ethical agenda. Generally speaking, the artists' writings in this volume allegorize and oppose this austere, puritan criticism, often attempting instead to embody the personal and pleasureful.

These questions of marginalization and displacement, of categorization and access, of use and misuse of criticism, of free speech and silencing are all questions which circulate around the issue of power and how it is implemented through the forms of language and representation. In the writings of Jenny Holzer or Matt Mullican, for example, language masquerading as conventional or official speech is used to foreground the hidden social and political assumptions of everyday speech. In the face of this obsessive listmaking, a consideration of the texts as allegories suggests that they contain not the false hope of a utopian wholeness and surety, but the opposite: an exposure of the contradictions of our social mores. Similarly, as Allan Sekula makes clear, while archival systems make access to information easier and more coherent, they also encourage certain readings of that information and structure into their systems misrepresentations, exclusions, and silences.

The rejection of such institutionalized and exclusionary models, by which one large group of humanity has for millenia constructed its world, forms the central allegory of this book. For texts

6. Craig Owens, "The Allegorical Impulse: Toward a Theory of Postmodernism," in *Art After Modernism: Rethinking Representation,* ed. Brian Wallis (New York and Boston: The New Museum of Contemporary Art and David R. Godine, 1984), p. 204.

such as those by Simon Watney, Edgar Heap of Birds, and Theresa Hak Kyung Cha are constructed as alternatives. Though they appropriate and reproduce the language of the cultures they contest, it is clear that these confiscations function by doubling: to reject and shame the forms of dominant speech, to challenge the relative social positions of the speaker and the subject, and to resist the oppressive models of exclusion and control which shaped their pasts. By acknowledging and exposing the languages that formed their communities, these artists are able not only to build on their historical traditions, but also to stand with others favoring communal culture, to turn away from an exclusively or unengaged theoretical sphere, and to embrace the necessity of social activism.

This communal structure of discourse is literalized in the performative use of language, that is not only in actual performance (e.g., Laurie Anderson, Spalding Gray, Eric Bogosian), but also in the cadences and patois of daily conversation (Carrie Mae Weems, Connie Hatch) and pseudo-authority of video scripts (Cecilia Vicuña, William Wegman). These are manifestly social texts, structured as activities and meant to engage the full participation of the receiver (hearer, viewer, respondent). The relevance of this performative aspect of writing is clear in relation to the model of storytelling, for it reinforces the centrality of communality and it insists on making writing into a social act.

In many respects, our attitudes toward love, gender, and sexuality determine all other social relationships and therefore they can be regarded justifiably as the source of our political notions of communality. Bound on the one hand to a personal psychological history and on the other hand to a faith in particular social and political premises, our definitions of "modern love" – emotional and physical – determine the functioning of our daily lives. More than the idea or ideal of love, the pragmatic, problem-solving negotiations of love constitute a central determinant of our identities. In the writings of Gary Indiana, Lynne Tillman, and Kathy Acker, for instance, no one understanding of what one may expect from romance emerges. Instead, relationships take place under conditions in which the central terms are constantly shifting. Social standards, personal beliefs, and sexual preferences are always open to adjustment, and identities, both public and private, are continually rethought and reformulated. Not surprisingly, the issues raised here – of sexuality, eroticism, romance, and pleasure – are relatively alien to theoretical criticism; there the subjects are approached hesitantly, abstractly, and often anachronistically. This is why the clearest definitions of these desires, fantasies, and emotions are found in fiction and popular culture.

Yet even in advocating a strategy of local resistances, in establishing the communality of the "minor," in reconnecting the social body with individual pleasure, and in rejecting the austerity of theory, the uses of storytelling and allegory may seem, in themselves, a somewhat deficient response to the omnipresent simulacra of televised imagery and electronic information. Yet, as much as the experience of viewing television contains elements of pacification, there exist, as well, traces in popular culture which encourage utopian fantasies of change. Given these specific forms of pleasure embodied at every level of the allegorical text and the varied potentials of spectatorship, the media need not be viewed as a monolithic corporate spectacle. Rather, as the texts by Michelle Parkerson, Yvonne Rainer, Barbara Kruger, and Silvia Kolbowski point out, there are entrance points for both deconstruction and pleasure in the media. These approaches allow for the media and popular culture to be "read" allegorically: as both a local issue of pleasure and, at "the same time . . . as the figure for Utopia in general, and for the systematic revolutionary transformation of society as a whole."[7]

Significantly, then, the writings collected in this book are essentially productive and useful as well as critical and pleasurable. It is not necessarily that they supplant theoretical forms of writing, but that they open avenues beyond those allowed by the current consensus of critical forms. That is, they afford a way of creating new models, new identities, and new options for movement. These writings demonstrate alternative capacities to generate ambiguous, complex, and experiential forms of knowledge which are collective and cultural but not equatable with bourgeois norms – this is stressed as a basis for broad political change. While often this political meaning is not explicit, it is encoded in the images of resistance and renewal which structure the secondary or allegorical level of meaning in these texts. The recovery here of "hidden" knowledges or resistances feeds our understanding of the nature and variety of cultural and social oppressions as well as the means for their reversals. In this sense then, "perhaps allegory will no longer seem gratuitously fictive, but rather closely bound to historical and political necessity."[8]

7. Fredric Jameson, "Pleasure: A Political Issue," in *Formations of Pleasure* (London: Routledge & Kegan Paul, 1983), p. 13. Also see Maud Lavin, "Strategies of Pleasure and Deconstruction in the Weimar Era Photomontages of Hannah Höch," in *The Divided Heritage*, ed. Irit Rogoff and MaryAnne Stevens (Cambridge: Cambridge University Press, 1988).
8. Holly Wallace Boucher, "Metonymy in Typology and Allegory, with a Consideration of Dante's Comedy," in *Allegory, Myth, and Symbol*, ed. Morton W. Bloomfield (Cambridge, Mass.: Harvard University Press, 1981), p. 145.

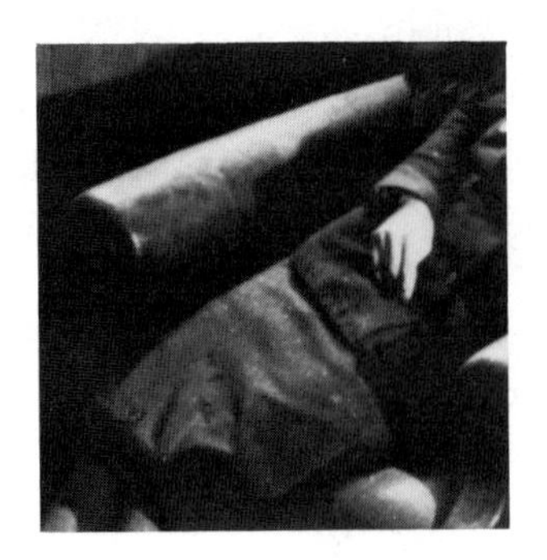

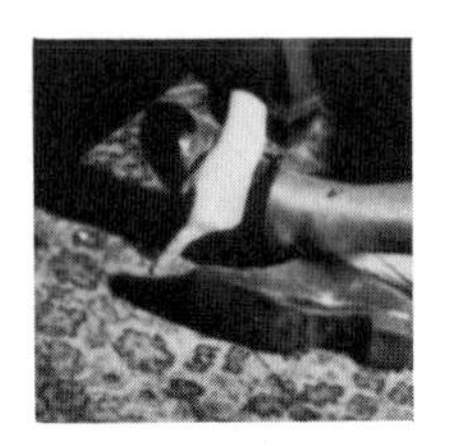

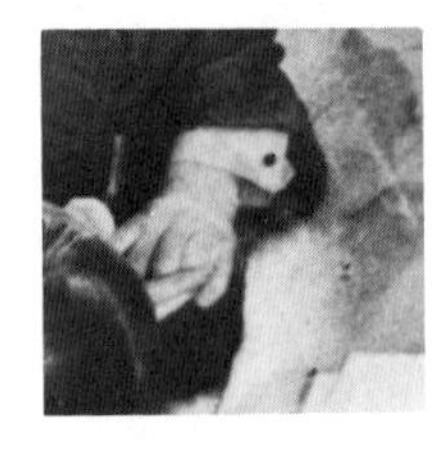

1. A Story Is Not Just a Story

Grandma's Story

TRINH T. MINH-HA

See all things howsoever they flourish
Return to the root from which they grew
This return to the root is called Quietness

Tao-te-ching

Let me tell you a story. For all I have is a story. Story passed on from generation to generation, named Joy. Told for the joy it gives the storyteller and the listener. Joy inherent in the process of storytelling. Whoever understands it also understands that a story, as distressing as it can be in its joy, never takes anything away from anybody. Its name, remember, is Joy. Its double, Woe Morrow Sow.

> *Let the one who is diseuse, one who is mother who waits nine days and nine nights be found. Restore memory. Let the one who is diseuse, one who is daughter restore spring with her each appearance from beneath the earth. The ink spills thickest before it runs dry before it stops writing at all. (Theresa Hak Kyung Cha)*[1]

Something must be said. Must be said that has not been and has been said before. "It will take a long time, but the story must be told. There must not be any lies" (Leslie Marmon Silko). It will take a long time for living cannot be told, not merely told: living is not livable. Understanding, however, is creating, and living, such an immense gift that thousands of people benefit from each past or present life being lived. The story depends upon every one of us to come into being. It needs us all, needs our remembering, understanding, and creating what we have heard together to keep on coming into being. The story of a people. Of us, peoples. Story, history, literature (, religion, philosophy, natural science, ethics): all in one. They call it the tool of primitive man, the simplest vehicle

1. Theresa Hak Kyung Cha, *Dictee* (New York: Tanam Press, 1982), p. 133.

of truth. When history separated itself from story, it started indulging in accumulation and facts. Or it thought it could. It thought it could build up to History because the Past, unrelated to the Present and the Future, is lying there in its entirety, waiting to be revealed and related. The act of revealing bears in itself a magical (not factual) quality – inherited undoubtedly from "primitive" storytelling – for the Past perceived as such is a well-organized past whose organization is already given. Managing to identify with History, history (with small letter *h*) thus manages to oppose the factual to the fictional (turning a blind eye to the "magicality" of its claims); the story-writer – the historian – to the story-teller. As long as the transformation, manipulations, or redistributions inherent to the collecting of events are overlooked, the division continues its course, as sure of its itinerary as it certainly dreams to be. Story-writing becomes history-writing, and history quickly sets itself apart, consigning story to the realm of tale, legend, myth, fiction, literature. Then, since fictional and factual have come to a point where they mutually exclude each other, fiction, not infrequently, means lies, and fact, truth. DID IT REALLY HAPPEN? IS IT A TRUE STORY?

> *I don't want to listen to any more of your stories [Maxine Hong Kingston screamed at her champion-story-talker mother]; they have no logic. They scramble me up. You lie with stories. You won't tell me a story and then say, "This is a true story," or "This is just a story." I can't tell the difference. I don't even know what your real names are. I can't tell what's real and what you made up.*[2]

Which truth? The question unavoidably arises. The story has been defined as "a free narration, not necessarily factual but truthful in character . . . [It] gives us human nature in its bold outlines; history, in its individual details."[3] Truth. Not one but two: truth and fact, just like in the old times when queens were born and kings were made in Egypt. (Queens and princesses were then "Royal Mothers" from birth, whereas the king wore the crown of high priest and did not receive the Horus-name until his coronation.) Poetry, Aristotle said, is truer than history. Storytelling as literature (narrative poetry) must then be truer than history. If we rely on

2. Maxine Hong Kingston, *The Woman Warrior: Memoirs of a Girlhood Among Ghosts* (1975; reprint, New York: Vintage Books, 1977), p. 235.
3. Herman Harrell Horne, *Story-telling, Questioning and Studying: Three School Arts* (New York: Macmillan Co., 1919), pp. 23-24.

history to tell us what happened at a specific time and place, we can rely on the story to tell us not only what might have happened, but also what is happening at an unspecified time and place. No wonder that in old tales storytellers are very often women, witches, and prophets. The African *griot* and *griotte* are well known for being at the same time poet, storyteller, historian, musician, and magician. But why truth at all? Why this battle for truth and on behalf of truth? I do not remember having asked great mother once whether the story she was telling me was true or not. Neither do I recall her asking me whether the story I was reading her was true or not. We knew we could make each other cry, laugh, or fear, but we never thought of saying to each other, "This is just a story." A story is a story. There was no need for clarification – a need many adults considered "natural" or imperative among children – for there was no such thing as "a blind acceptance of the story as literally true." Perhaps the story has become *just* a story when I have become adept at consuming truth as fact. Imagination is thus equated to falsification, and I am made to believe that if, accordingly, I am not told or do not settle aloud what is true and what is false, I or the listener may no longer be able to differentiate fancy from fact *[sic]*. Literature and history once were/still are stories: this does not necessarily mean that the space they form is undifferentiated, but that this space can articulate on a different set of principles, one which may be said to stand outside the hierarchical realm of facts. On the one hand, each society has its own politics of truth; on the other hand, being truthful is being in the in-between of all regimes of truth. Outside specific time, outside specialized space: "Truth embraces with it all other abstentions other than itself" (Theresa Hak Kyung Cha).

Truth is when it is itself no longer. Diseuse, Thought-Woman, Spider-Woman, *griotte,* storytalker, fortune-teller, witch. If you have the patience to listen, she will take delight in relating it to you. An entire history, an entire vision of the world, a lifetime story. Mother always has a mother. And Great Mothers are recalled as the goddesses of all waters, the sources of diseases and of healing, the protectresses of women and of childbearing. To listen carefully is to preserve. But to preserve is to burn, for understanding means creating.

Let the one who is diseuse. Diseuse de bonne aventure. Let her call forth. Let her break open the spell cast upon time upon time again and again. (Theresa Hak Kyung Cha)[4]

The world's earlier archives or libraries were the memories of women. Patiently transmitted from mouth to ear, body to body, hand to hand. In the process of storytelling, speaking and listening refer to realities that do not involve just the imagination. The speech is seen, heard, smelled, tasted, and touched. It destroys, brings into life, nurtures. Every woman partakes in the chain of guardianship and of transmission. Every *griotte* who dies, as it is said in Africa, is a whole library that burns down (a "library in which the archives are not classified but are completely inventoried" [A. Hampaté Ba]). Phrases like "I sucked it at my mother's breast" or "I have it from Our Mother" to express what has been passed down by the elders are common in this part of the world. Tell me and let me tell my hearers what I have heard from you who heard it from your mother and your great mother, so that what is said may be guarded and unfailingly transmitted to the women of tomorrow, who will be our children, and the children of our children. These are the opening lines she used to chant before embarking on a story. I owe that to you, her, and her, who owe it to her, her, and her. I memorize, recognize, and name my source(s), not to validate my voice through the voice of an authority (for we, women, have little authority in the History of Literature, and wise women never draw their powers from authority), but to evoke her and sing. The bond between woman and word. Among women themselves. To produce their full effect, words must, indeed, be chanted rhythmically, in cadences, off cadences.

My great-grandmama told my grandmama the part she lived through that my grandmama didn't live through and my grandmama told my mama what they both lived through and my mama told me what they all lived through and we were supposed to pass it down like that from generation to generation so we'd never forget. Even though they'd burned everything to play like it didn't never happen. (Gayl Jones)[5]

4. Cha, *Dictee*, p. 123.
5. Gayl Jones, *Corregidora* (New York: Random House, 1975), p. 9.

In this chain and continuum, I am but one link. The story is me, neither me nor mine. It does not really belong to me, and while I feel greatly responsible for it, I also enjoy the irresponsibility of the pleasure obtained through the process of transferring. Pleasure in the copy, pleasure in the reproduction. No repetition can ever be identical, but my story carries with it their stories, their history, and our story repeats itself endlessly despite our persistence in denying it. I DON'T BELIEVE IT. THAT STORY COULD NOT HAPPEN TODAY. Then someday our children will speak about us here present, about those days when things like that could happen . . .

> *It was like I didn't know how much was me and Mutt and how much was Great Gram and Corregidora – like Mama when she had started talking like Great Gram. But was what Corregidora had done to* her, *to* them, *any worse than what Mutt had done to me, than what we had done to each other, than what Mama had done to Daddy, or what he had done to her in return . . . (Gayl Jones)*[6]

> *Upon seeing her you know how it was for her. You know how it might have been. You recline, you lapse, you fall, you see before you what you have seen before. Repeated, without your even knowing it. It is you standing there. It is you waiting outside in the summer day. (Theresa Hak Kyung Cha)*[7]

Every gesture, every word involves our past, present, and future. The body never stops accumulating, and years and years have gone by mine without my being able to stop them, stop it. My sympathies and grudges appear at the same time familiar and unfamiliar to me; I dwell in them, they dwell in me, and we dwell in each other, more as guest than as owner. My story, no doubt, is me, but it is also, no doubt, older than me. Younger than me, older than the humanized. Unmeasurable, uncontainable, so immense that it exceeds all attempts at humanizing. But humanizing we do, and also overdo, for the vision of a story that has no end – no end, no middle, no beginning; no start, no stop, no progression; neither backward nor forward, only a stream that flows into another stream, an open sea – is the vision of a madwoman. "The unleashed tides of muteness," as Clarice Lispector puts it. We fear heights, we fear the headless, the bottomless, and the boundless. And we are in terror of letting ourselves be engulfed by the muteness depths. This is

6. Ibid., p. 184.
7. Cha, *Dictee,* p. 106.

why we keep on doing violence to words: to tame and cook the wild-raw, to adopt the vertiginously infinite. Truth does not make sense; it exceeds meaning and exceeds measure. It exceeds all regimes of truth. So, when we insist on telling over and over again, we insist on repetition in recreation (and vice-versa). On distributing the story into smaller proportions that will correspond to the capacity of absorption of our mouths, the capacity of vision of our eyes, and the capacity of bearing of our bodies. Each story is at once a fragment and a whole. And the same story has always been changing, for things that do not shift and grow cannot continue to circulate. Dead. Dead times, dead words, dead tongues. Not to repeat in oblivion.

> *Sediment. Turned stone. Let the one who is diseuse dust breathe away the distance of the well. Let the one who is diseuse again sit upon the stone nine days and nine nights. Thus. Making stand again, Eleusis. (Theresa Hak Kyung Cha)*[8]

The simplest vehicle of truth, the story is also said to be "a phase of communication," "the natural form for revealing life." Its fascination may be explained by its power both to give vividly felt insight into the life of other people and to revive or keep alive the forgotten, deadened, turned-into-stone parts of ourselves. To the wo/man of the West who spends time recording and arranging the "data" concerning storytelling as well as "the many rules and taboos connected with it," this tool of primitive wo/man has provided primitive peoples with opportunities "to train their speech, formulate opinions and express themselves" (Anna Birgitta Rooth). It gives "a sympathetic understanding of their limitations in knowledge, and an appreciation of our privileges in civilization, due largely to the struggles of the past" (Clark W. Hetherington). It informs of the explanations they invented for "the things [they] did not understand," and represents their religion, "a religion growing out of fear of the unknown" (Katherine Dunlap Cather). In summary, the story is either a mere practice of the art of rhetoric, or "a repository of obsolete customs" (A. Skinner). It is mainly valued for its artistic potential and for the "religious beliefs" or primitive-mind-

8. Ibid., p. 130.

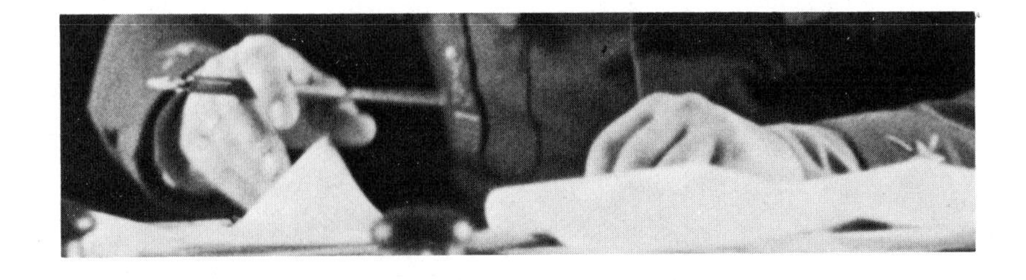

revealing superstitions mirrored by its content. (Like the supernatural, is the superstitious another product of the Western mind? For to accept even temporarily Cather's view on primitive religion, one is bound to ask: which [institutionalized] religion does not grow out of fear of the unknown?) Associated with backwardness, ignorance, and illiteracy, storytelling in the more "civilized" context is therefore relegated to the realm of children. "The fact that the story is the product of primitive man," wrote Herman H. Horne, "explains in part why the children hunger so for the story."[9] "Wherever there is no written language, wherever the people are too unlettered to read what is written," Cather equally remarked, "they still believe the legends. They love to hear them told and retold. . . . As it is with unlettered peasants today, as it was with tribesmen in primitive times and with the great in medieval castle halls, it still is with the child."[10] Primitive means elementary, therefore infantile. In the West, no wonder, storytelling is treasured above all for its educational force in the kindergarten and primary school. The mission of the storyteller, we thus hear, is to "teach children the tales their *fathers* knew," to mold ideals and to "illuminate facts." For children to gain "right feelings" and to "think true," the story as a pedagogical tool must inform so as to keep their opinion "abreast of the scientific truth of the time, instead of dragging along in the superstitions of the past." But for the story to be well-told information, it must be related "in as fascinating a form as [in] the old myths and fables."[11] Patch up the content of the new and the form of the old, or impose one on the other. The dis-ease lingers on. With (traditional but nonsuperstitious?) formulas like "once upon a time" and "long long ago," the storyteller can reasonably be sure of making "a good beginning." For many people truth has the connotation of uniformity and prescription. Thinking true means thinking in conformity with a certain scientific (read "scientistic") discourse produced by certain institutions. Not only has the "civilized" mind classified many of the realities it *does not understand* in the categories of the untrue and the superstitious, it has also turned the story – as told event of a community, a people – into a *fatherly* lesson for children of a certain age. Indeed, in the "civilized" context, only children are allowed to indulge in the so-called

9. Horne, *Story-telling*, p. 34.
10. Katherine Dunlap Cather, *Educating by Story-telling* (New York: World Book Company, 1920), pp. 5-6.
11. Clark W. Hetherington, "Introduction," in ibid., pp. xiii-xiv.

fantastic or the fantastic-true. They are perceived as belonging to a world apart, one that adults (compassionately) control and populate with toys—that is to say with false human beings (dolls), false animals, false objects (imitative, dimunitive versions of the "real"). "Civilized" adults fabricate, structure, and segregate the children's world; they invent toys for the latter to *play* with and stories of a specially adapted, more digestive kind to absorb, yet they insist on molding this world according to the scientifically true—the real, obviously not in its full scale, but in a reduced scale: that which is supposed to be the (God-like-) child's scale. Stories, especially "primitive-why stories" or fairy tales, must be carefully sorted and graded, for children should neither be "deceived" nor "duped" and "there should never be any doubt in [their] minds as to what is make-believe and what is real." In other words, the difference "civilized" adults recognize in the little people's world is a mere matter of scale. The forms of constraint that rule these bigger people's world and allow them to distinguish with certainty the false from the true must, unquestionably, be exactly the same as the ones that regulate the smaller people's world. The apartheid type of difference continues to operate in all spheres of "civilized" life. There does not seem to be any possibility either as to the existence of such things as, for example, two (or more) different realms of make-believe or two (or more) different realms of truth. The "civilized" mind is an indisputably clear-cut mind. If once upon a time people believed in the story and thought it was true, then why should it be false today? If true and false keep on changing with the times, then isn't it true that what is "crooked thinking" today may be "right thinking" tomorrow? What kind of people, we then wonder, walk around asking obstinately: "Is there not danger of making liars of children by feeding them on these [fairy] stories?" What kind of people set out for northern Alaska to study storytelling among the Indians and come round to writing: "What especially impressed me was their eagerness to make me understand. To me this eagerness became a proof of the high value they set on their stories and what they represented"?[12] What kind of people, indeed, other than the very kind for whom the story is "*just* a story"?

12. Anna Birgitta Rooth, *The Importance of Storytelling: A Study Based on Field Work in Northern Alaska* (Uppsala: Almqvist & Wiksell, 1976), p. 88.

An oracle and a bringer of joy, the storyteller is the living memory of her time, her people. She composes on life but does not lie, for composing is not imagining, fancying, or inventing. When asked "What is oral tradition?" an African "traditionalist" (a term considered by African scholars to be more accurate than the French term *griot* or *griotte,* which tends to confuse traditionalists with mere public entertainers) would most likely be nonplussed. As A. Hampaté Ba remarks, "[s/he] might reply, after a lengthy silence: 'It is total knowledge,' and say no more."[13] She might or might not reply so, for what is called here "total knowledge" is not really nameable. At least it cannot be named (so) without incurring the risk of sliding right back into one of the many slots the "civilized" discourse of knowledge readily provides it with. The question "What is oral tradition?" is a question-answer that needs no answer at all. Let the one who is civilized, the one who invents "oral tradition," let him define it for himself. For "oral" and "written" or "written" versus "oral" are notions that have been as heavily invested as the notions of "true" and "false" have always been. (If writing does not express language but encompasses it, then where does the written stop? The line distinguishing societies with writing from those without writing seems most ill-defined and leaves much to be desired. . . .) Living is neither oral nor written – how can the living and the lived be contained in the merely oral? Furthermore, when she composes on life, she not only gives information, entertains, develops, or expands the imagination. Not only educates. Only practices a craft. "Mind breathes mind," a civilized man once wrote, "power feels power, and absorbs it, as it were. The telling of stories refreshes the mind as a bath refreshes the body; it gives exercise to the intellect and its powers; it tests the judgment and the feelings."[14] Man's view is always reduced to man's mind. For this is the part of himself he values most. THE MIND. The intellect and its powers. Storytelling allows the "civilized" narrator above all to renew his mind and exercise power through his intellect. Even though the motto reads: think, act, and feel, his task, he believes, is to ease the passage of the story *from mind to mind.* She, however, who sets out to revive the forgotten, to survive and supercede it ("From stone.

13. A. Hampaté Ba, "The Living Tradition," in *General History of Africa,* Vol. 1: *Methodology and African Prehistory,* edited by J. Ki Zerbo (UNESCO, 1981), p. 167.
14. Froebel quoted in Horne, *Story-telling,* p. 29.

Layers. Of stone upon stone her self stone between the layers, dormant. No more." [Theresa Hak Kyung Cha][15]), she never speaks of and cannot be content with mere matters of the mind – such as mind transmission. The storyteller is long known as a personage of power. True, she partakes in this living heritage of power, but her powers do more than illuminate or refresh the mind. They extinguish as quickly as they set fire. They wound as easily as they soothe. And not necessarily the mind. Lincoln, one of the leaders of men, accurately observed: "the sharpness of a refusal, or the edge of a rebuke, may be blunted by an appropriate story, so as to save wounded feeling and yet serve the purpose . . . story-telling as an emollient saves me much friction and distress."[16] Yet this is but one more among the countless functions of storytelling. Humidity, receptivity, fecundity. Remember, her speech is seen, heard, smelled, tasted and touched. Great Mother is the goddess of all waters, the protectress of women and of childbearing, the unweary sentient hearer, the healer, and also the bringer of diseases. She who gives always accepts, she who wishes to preserve never fails to refresh. Regenerate.

She was already in her mid-sixties
when I discovered that she would listen to me
to all my questions and speculations.
I was only seven or eight years old then. (Leslie Marmon Silko)[17]

Salivate, secrete the words. No water, no birth, no death, no life. No speech, no song, no story, no force, no power. The entire being is engaged in the act of speaking-listening-weaving-procreating. If she does not cry, she will turn into stone. Utter, weep, wet, let it flow so as to break through (it). Layers of stone amidst layers of stone. Break with her own words. The interrelation of woman, water, and word pervades African cosmogonies. Among the Dogon, for example, the process of regeneration which the eight ancestors of the Dogon people had to undergo was carried out by the waters of the womb of the female Nummo (the Nummo spirits form a male and female pair whose essence is divine) *while she spoke* to herself and to her own sex, accompanied by the male Nummo's voice. "The spoken Word entered into her and wound itself round her womb in a spiral of eight turns . . . the spiral of the Word gave to

15. Cha, *Dictee,* p. 150.
16. Quoted in Horne, *Story-telling,* p. 30.
17. Leslie Marmon Silko, "Aunt Susie," in *Storyteller* (New York: Seaver Books, 1981), p. 4.

the womb its regenerative movement." Of the fertilizing power of words and their transmissions through women, it is further said that:

> *The First Word had been pronounced [read "scanned"] in front of the genitalia of a woman. . . . The Word finally came from the anthill, that is, from the mouth of the seventh Nummo [the seventh ancestor and master of speech], which is to say from a woman's genitalia.*
>
> *The Second Word, contained in the craft of weaving, emerged from a mouth, which was also the primordial sex organ, in which the first childbirths took place.*[18]

Thus, as a wise Dogon elder (Ogotemmêli) pointed out, "issuing from a woman's sexual part, the Word enters another sexual part, namely the ear." (The ear is considered to be bisexual, the auricle being male and the auditory aperture female.) From the ear, it will, continuing the cycle, conceive of speech as a gift of God/dess and a force of creation. In Fulfulde, the word for "speech" *(haala)* has the connotation of "giving strength," and by extension of "making material." Speech is the materialization, externalization, and internalization of the vibrations of forces. That is why, A. Hampaté Ba noted, "every manifestation of a force in any form whatever is to be regarded as its speech . . . everything in the universe speaks. . . . If speech is strength, that is because it creates a *bond of coming-and-going* which generates *movement and rhythm* and therefore *life and action.* This movement to and fro is symbolized by the weaver's feet going up and down . . . (the symbolism of the loom is entirely based on creative speech in action)."[19] Making material: spinning and weaving is a euphonious heritage of wo/mankind handed on from generation to generation of weavers within the clapping of the shuttle and the creaking of the block – which the Dogon call "the creaking of the Word." "The cloth was the Word"; the same term, *soy,* is used among the Dogon to signify both the woven material and the spoken word. Life is a perpetual to and fro, a dis/continuous releasing and absorbing of the self. Let her weave her story within their stories, her life amidst their lives. And while she weaves, let her whip, spur, and set them on fire. Thus making them sing again. Very softly, a-new a-gain.

18. Marcel Griaule, *Conversations with Ogotemmêli* (1965; reprint, New York: Oxford University Press, 1975), pp. 26, 138-139.
19. Hampaté Ba, "The Living Tradition," pp. 170-171 (my italics).

"The witch is a woman; the wizard is a male imitation" (Robert Briffault). In many parts of the world, magic (and witchcraft) is regarded as essentially a woman's function. It is said that "in primitive thought every woman is credited with the possession of magic powers." Yet, she who possesses that power is always the last one to credit it. Old Lao Tsu warned: the wo/man of virtue is not virtuous; the one who never fails in virtue has no virtue at all. Practicing power for the sake of power – an idea implied in the widely assumed image of the witch as exclusively an evil-doer – is an inheritance, I suspect, of the "civilized" mind. She who brings death and disease also brings life and health. The line dividing the good and the evil, magic and witchcraft, does not always seem to be as clear-cut as it should be. In the southern Celebes, for example, "All the deities and spirits from whom sorcerers, whether male or female, derive their power are spoken of as their 'grandmothers.'" Throughout Africa, priestesses are called "Mothers," and the numerous female fetishes served exclusively by women are known as the "Mother fetishes." Among the Butwa, the female hierophants are named "the mothers of the Butwa mysteries." Among the Bir, the women are those who perform the essential ritual of maintaining the sacred fire. In Indonesia, America, northern Asia, and northern Europe, it has been demonstrated that "magical practices and primitive priestly functions formerly belonged to the exclusive sphere of women and that they were taken up [appropriated] by men at a comparatively late epoch." Thus, the adoption of female attire by male shamans and priests is a widespread phenomenon that still prevails in today's religious contexts. Imitating women and wearing women's clothes – priestly robes, skirts, aprons, sottanas, woven loincloths – are regarded as bestowing greater power: the Mothers' power.[20] Of making material. Of composing on life. Her speech, her storytelling is at once magic, sorcery, and religion. It enchants. It animates, sets into motion, and rouses the forces that lie dormant in things, in beings. It is "bewitching." At once "black" and "white" magic. Which, however, causes sickness and death, which brings joy into life? For white, remember, is the color for mourning in many cultures. The same

20. On the part played by women in religious cults and their powers, see Robert Briffault, *The Mothers* (1927; reprint, New York: Atheneum, 1977), especially the chapter on "The Witch and the Priestess," pp. 269-288.

"medicines," the same dances, the same sorcery are said to be used in both. As the occasion arises, the same magic may serve for beneficent *and* maleficent ends. This is why her power is so dreaded: because it can be used for harm; because when it is wielded by one sex or one group, it arouses alarm in the other. The (wizard's) game dates from the time when every practice of this art by women became a threat to men and was automatically presumed to be malignant in intention; when every magic woman must necessarily be a witch – no longer a fairy who works wonders nor a Mother-priestess-prophetess who nurtures, protects, restores, and warns against ill-will. Ill-assumption leads to ill-action. Men appropriate women's power of "making material" to themselves and, not infrequently, corrupt it out of ignorance. The story becomes *just a* story. It becomes a good or bad lie. And in the more "civilized" contexts where women are replaced and excluded from magico-religious functions, adults who still live on storytelling become bums who spend their time feeding on lies, "them big old lies we tell when we're jus' sittin' around here on the store porch doin' nothin'." When Zora Neale Hurston came back to Eatonville, Florida, to collect old stories, her home folks proudly told her: "Zora, you come to de right place if lies is what you want. Ah'm gointer lie up a nation"; or "Now, you gointer hear lies above suspicion"; or else "We kin tell you some lies most any ole time. We never run outer lies and lovin'."[21] Alright, let them call it lie, let us smile and call it lie too if that satisfies them, but "let de lyin' go on!" For we do not *just* lie – we lie and love, we "lie up a nation," and our lies are "above suspicion." How can they be otherwise when they derive their essence from that gift of God: speech? Speech, that active agent in our Mothers' magic; speech, which owes its fertilizing power to . . . who else but the Mother of God?

"Thought-Woman/ is sitting in her room/ and whatever she thinks about/ appears./ She thought of her sisters,/ . . ./ and together they created the Universe/ . . ./ Thought-Woman, the spider,/ named things and/ as she named them/ they appeared" (Leslie Marmon

21. Zora Neale Hurston, excerpts from *Mules and Men*, in *I love myself – when I am laughing . . . and then again when I am looking mean and impressive: A Zora Neale Hurston Reader*, edited by Alice Walker (Old Westbury, N.Y.: The Feminist Press, 1979), pp. 85, 93, 89.

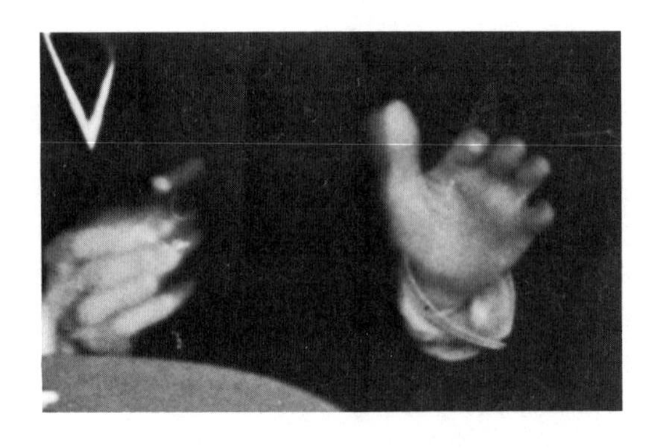

Silko).[22] The touch infinitely delicate awakens, restores them to life, letting them surge forth in their own measures and their own rhythms. The touch infinitely attentive of a fairy's wand, a woman's voice or a woman's hand, which goes to meet things in the dark and pass them on without deafening, without extinguishing in the process. Intense but gentle, it holds words out in the direction of things or lays them down nearby things so as to call them and breathe new life into them. Not to capture, to chain them up, nor to mean. Not to instruct nor to discipline. But to kindle that zeal which hibernates within each one of us. "Speech may create peace, as it may destroy it. It is like fire," wrote A. Hampaté Ba. "One ill-advised word may start a war just as one blazing twig may touch off a great conflagration. . . . Tradition, then, confers on . . . the Word not only creative power but a double function of saving and destroying."[23] Her words are like fire. They burn and they destroy. It is, however, only by burning that they lighten. Destroying and saving, therefore, are here one single process. Not two processes posed in opposition or in conflict. They would like to order everything around hierarchical oppositions. They would like to cut her power into endless opposing halves, or cut herself from the Mothers' powers – setting her against either her mother, her godmother, her mother-in-law, her grandmother, her daughter, or her granddaughter. One of them has to be wicked so as to break the network of transmission. This is cleverly called jealousy among women, the jealousy of the woman who cannot suffer seeing her daughter or another woman take more pleasure in life than herself. For years and years, centuries and centuries, they have devoted their energies to breaking bonds and spreading discords and confusions. Divide and conquer. Mothers fighting mothers. Here is what an Indian witch has to say on "white skin people/ like the belly of a fish/ covered with hair":

. . . . They see no life
When they look
they see only objects.

. . . . They fear
They fear the world.
They destroy what they fear.
They fear themselves.

22. Leslie Marmon Silko, *Ceremony* (New York: Viking Press, 1977), p. 1.
23. Hampaté Ba, "The Living Tradition," p. 171.

. . . . Stolen rivers and mountains
the stolen land will eat their hearts
and jerk their mouths from the Mother.
The people will starve. . . .[24]

These are excerpts of a story passed on by Leslie Marmon Silko. The story is the vision of a witch who, a long time ago, at a contest of witches from all the pueblos, "didn't show off any dark thunder charcoals or red anthill beads" like the other witches, but only asked them to listen: "What I have is a story. . . . laugh if you want to/ but as I tell the story/ it will begin to happen." Scanned by the refrain "set in motion now/ set in motion/ to work for us," the story thus unfolds, naming as it proceeds: the killing, the destruction, the foul deed, the loss of the white man, and with it, the doom of the Indian people. "It isn't so funny. . . . Take it back. Call that story back" said the audience by the end of the story, but the witch answered: "It's already turned loose/ It's already coming./ It can't be called back." A story is *not* just a story. Once the forces have been aroused and set into motion, they can't simply be stopped at someone's request. Once told, the story is bound to circulate; humanized, it may have a temporary end, but its effects linger on and its end is never truly an end. Who among us has not, to a certain extent, felt what Georg Ebers, for example, felt toward his mother's stories: "When the time of rising came, I climbed joyfully into my mother's warm bed, and never did I listen to more beautiful fairy tales than at those hours. They became instinct with life to me and have always remained so . . . It is a singular thing that actual events which happened in those early days have largely vanished from my memory, but the fairy tales I heard and secretly experienced became firmly impressed on my mind."[25] The young beautiful fairy and the old ugly witch, remember, have the same creative power, the same decisive force of speech. As she names them, they appear . . . The story tells us not only what might have happened, but also what *is happening* at an unspecified time and place. Whenever Ebers had the slightest doubt in mind, he would immediately appeal to his mother, for he thought, "she could never be mistaken and knew that she always told the truth." Lying is not a mother's attribute. Or else, if lying is what you think she does, then she will "never run outer lies and lovin'."

24. Marmon Silko, *Ceremony*, pp. 132-138, or *Storyteller*, pp. 130-137.
25. Quoted in Cather, *Educating by Storytelling*, p. 22.

When we Chinese girls listened to the adults talk-story, we learned that we failed if we grew up to be but wives or slaves. We could be heroines, swordswomen. . . . Night after night my mother would talk-story until we fell asleep. I couldn't tell where the stories left off and the dreams began, her voice the voice of the heroines in my sleep. . . . At last I saw that I too had been in the presence of great power, my mother talking-story. . . . She said I would grow up a wife and a slave, but she taught me the song of the warrior woman, Fa Mu Lan. I would have to grow up a warrior woman. (Maxine Hong Kingston)[26]

She fires her to achievement and she fires her with desire to emulate. She fires her with desire to emulate the heroines of whom she told and she fires her with desire to emulate the heroine who tells of the other heroines, "I too had been in the presence of great power, my mother talking-story." What is transmitted from generation to generation is not only the stories, but the very power of transmission. The stories are highly inspiring. So is she, the untiring storyteller. She, who suffocates the codes of lie and truth. She, who loves to tell and retell and loves to hear them told and retold night after night again and again. Hong Kingston grows up a warrior woman and a warrior-woman-storyteller herself. She is the woman warrior who continues to fight in America the fight her mothers fought in China. Even though she is often "mad at the Chinese for lying so much," and blames her mother for lying with stories, she happily *lets the lying go on* by retelling us her mother's "lies" and offering us versions of her stories that can be called lies themselves. Her brother's version of a story, she admits herself, "may be better than mine because of its bareness, not twisted into designs." Her brother, indeed, is no woman warrior-storyteller. Hong Kingston's apparent confusion of story and reality is, in fact, no confusion at all since it is an unending one: her parents often accuse her of not being able to "tell a joke from real life" and to understand that Chinese "like to say the opposite." Even the events described by her relatives in their letters from China turn out to be suspicious to her: "I'd like to go to China and see those people and find out what's cheat story and what's not." The confusion she experienced in her girlhood is the confusion we all experience in life, even when we think, as adults, that we have come up with definite

26. Hong Kingston, *The Woman Warrior*, pp. 23-24.

criteria for the true and the false. What is true and what is not, and who decides so if we wish not to have this decision made *for* us? When, for example, Hong Kingston yells at her mother: "You can't stop me from talking. You tried to cut off my tongue, but it didn't work," we not only know she is quite capable of telling "fancy" from "facts," we are also carried a step further in this differentiation by her mother's answer: "I cut it to make you talk more, not less, you dummy."[27] (Her mother has already affirmed elsewhere that she cuts it so that her daughter would not be "tongue-tied.") The opening story of *The Woman Warrior* is a forbidden story ("No Name Woman") that begins with Hong Kingston's mother saying: "You must not tell anyone what I am about to tell you." Twenty years after she heard this story about her father's sister who drowned herself and her baby in the drinking-water well of the family, not only has Hong Kingston broken open the spell cast upon her aunt by retelling the story – "I alone devote pages of paper to her" – but she has done it in such a way as to reach thousands and thousands of listeners and readers. Tell it to the world. To preserve is to pass on, not to keep for oneself. A story told is a story bound to circulate. By telling her daughter not to tell it to anyone, the mother knew what she was supposed to say, for "That's what Chinese say. We like to say the opposite." She knew she was in fact the first before her daughter to break open the spell. The family cursed her, she who committed adultery and was such a spite suicide (the aunt); the men (her brothers) tabooed her name and went on living "as if she had never been born"; but the women (Hong Kingston's mother and those who partook in this aunt's death) would have to carry her with(in) them for life and pass her on, even though they condemned her no less. For every woman is the woman of all women, and this one died first and foremost for being a woman. ("Now that you have started to menstruate," the mother warned her daughter, "what happened to her could happen to you. Don't humiliate us.") Hong Kingston has, in her own way, retained many of the principles of her mother's storytelling. If, in composing with "fancy" and "fact," the latter knows when she should say "white is white" and when she should say "white is black" in referring to the same thing, her daughter also knows when to dot her *i*'s and when not to. Her writing, neither fiction nor nonfiction, constantly invites the reader either to

27. Ibid., pp. 189, 237, 240, 235.

drift naturally from the realm of imagination to that of actuality or to live them both without ever being able to draw a clear line between them, nor lose sight of their differentiation. What Hong Kingston does *not* tell us about her mother, but allows us to read between the lines and in the gaps of her stories, reveals as much of the latter as what she does tell us about her. This, I feel, is the most "truthful" aspect of her work, the very power of her storytelling. *The Woman Warrior* ends with a story Hong Kingston's mother told her, not when she was young, she says, "but recently, when I told her I also talk-story." The beginning of the story, which relates how the family in China came to love the theater through the grandmother's passion for it and generosity, is the making of the mother. The ending of the story, which calls to remembrance how one of the songs the poetess Ts'ai Yen composed while she was a captive of the barbarians has been passed down to the Chinese, is the making of the daughter – Hong Kingston herself. Two powerful women storytellers meet at the end of the book, both working at strengthening the ties among women while commemorating and transmitting the powers of our foremothers. At once a great-mother, a poetess, a storyteller, and a woman warrior.

> *I grew up with storytelling. My earliest memories are of my grandmother telling me stories while she watered the morning-glories in her yard. Her stories were about incidents from long ago, incidents which occurred before she was born but which she told as certainly as if she had been there. The chanting or telling of ancient stories to effect certain cures or protect from illness and harm have always been part of the Pueblo's curing ceremonies. I feel the power that the stories have to bring us together, especially when there is loss and grief. (Leslie Marmon Silko)*[28]

Refresh, regenerate, or purify. Telling stories and watering morning-glories both function to the same effect. For years and years she has been renewing her forces with regularity to keep them intact. Such ritual ablutions – the telling and retelling – allow her to recall the incidents that occurred before she was born with as much certainty as if she had witnessed them herself. The words

28. Marmon Silko, *Ceremony,* back cover.

passed down from mouth to ear (one sexual part to another sexual part), womb to womb, body to body are the remembered ones. S/He whose belly cannot contain (also read "retain") words, says a Malinke song, will succeed at nothing. The further they move away from the belly, the more liable they are to be corrupted. (Words that come from the MIND and are passed on directly "FROM MIND TO MIND" are, consequently, highly suspicious . . .) In many parts of Africa, the word "belly" refers to the notion of occult power. Among the Basaa of Cameroon, for example, the term *hu,* meaning (a human being's) "stomach," is used to designate "a thing whose origin and nature nobody knows," but which is unanimously attributed to women and their powers. A Basaa man said he heard from his fathers that "it was the woman who introduced the *hu*" in human life. In several myths of the Basaa's neighboring peoples, *evu,* which is equivalent to the Basaa's *hu,* is said to have requested that it be carried in the woman's belly at the time it first met her, and to have entered her body through her sexual part. Thus associated with women, the *hu* or *evu* is considered both maleficent and beneficent. It is at times equated with devilry and sorcery, other times with prophecy and anti-sorcery. S/He who is said to "have a *hu*" is both feared and admired. S/He is the one who sees the invisible, moves with ease in the night world as if in broad daylight, and is endowed with an uncommon, exceptional intelligence, penetration, and intuition.[29] Woman and magic. Her power resides in her belly – Our Mother's belly – for her cure is not an isolated act but a total social phenomenon. Sorcery, according to numerous accounts, is hereditary solely within the matrilinear clan; and a man, in countless cases, can only become a sorcerer (a wizard) through the transmission of power by a sorceress (a witch). He who understands the full power of woman and/in storytelling also understands that life is not to be found in the mind nor in the heart, but there where she carries it:

I will tell you something about stories, [he said]
They aren't just entertainment.
Don't be fooled.
They are all we have, you see,
all we have to fight off
illness and death.

29. For more information on the *hu* and its relation to women, see Meinrad P. Hebga, *Sorcellerie – Chimère dangereuse . . .?* (Abidjan, Ivory Coast: INADES, 1979), pp. 87-115, 258-265.

You don't have anything
if you don't have the stories. . . .

He rubbed his belly.
I keep them here [he said]
Here, put your hand on it
See, it is moving
There is life here
for the people.
(Leslie Marmon Silko)[30]

The story as a cure and a protection is at once musical, historical, poetical, ethical, educational, magical, and religious. In many parts of the world, the healers are known as the living memories of the people. They do not only hold an esoteric and technical knowledge, but are also highly informed of the problems of their communities and entrusted with all family affairs. In other words, they know everyone's story. Concerned with the slightest incident, they remain very alert to their entourage and heedful of their patients' talks. They derive their power from *listening* to the others and *absorbing* daily realities. While they cure, they take into them their patients' possessions and obsessions, and let the latters' illnesses become theirs. Their actions imply a personal investment of which the healing techniques form only a part and are a reflection. "I see the patient's psychic life," many of them say. "Nothing is hidden from me." Dis-ease breeds dis-ease; life engenders life. The very close relationship these healers maintain with their patients remains the determining factor of the cure. Curing means re-generating, for understanding is creating. The principle of healing rests on *reconciliation,* hence the necessity for the family and/or the community to cooperate, partake in, and witness the recovery, de-possession, regeneration of the sick. The act of healing is therefore a sociocultural act, a collective, motherly undertaking. (Here, it is revealing to remind that male healers often claim to be wedded to at least two wives: a terrestrial one *and* a spiritual one. The spiritual wife or the "woman spirit" protects the healer and is the source of his powers. She is the one who "has knowledge" and from whom he seeks advice in all matters. When she becomes too demanding and too possessive, it is said that only one person can send her

30. Marmon Silko, *Ceremony,* p. 2.

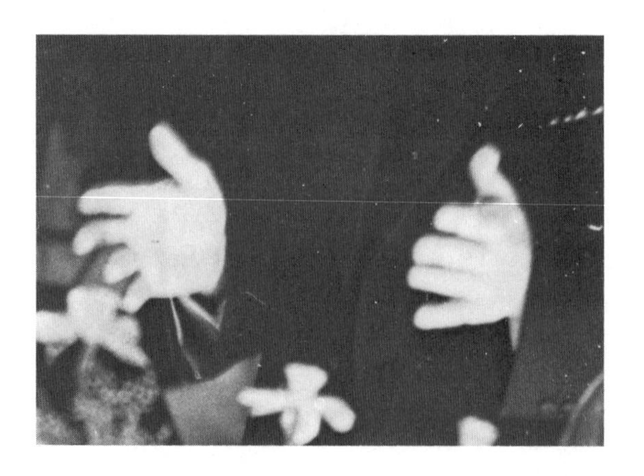

away – the healer's own mother.[31]) The storyteller, besides being a great mother, a teacher, a poetess, a warrior, a musician, historian, a fairy, and a witch, is a healer and a protectress. Her chanting or telling of stories, as Marmon Silko notices, has the power of bringing us together, especially when there is sickness, fear, and grief. "*When they look/ they see only objects./*" They fear/ they never stop fearing/ but they see not fear the living thing./ They follow not its movements/ for they fear not to fear./ "*They destroy what they fear./ They fear themselves./*" They destroy the stories/ let these be confused or forgotten/ let these be only stories/ They would like that . . .

> *Stolen rivers and mountains*
> *the stolen land will eat their hearts*
> *and jerk their mouths from the Mother.*
> *The people will starve. . . .*
> *(Leslie Marmon Silko)*

It is a commonplace for those who consider the story to be just a story to believe that, in order to appropriate the "traditional" storytellers' powers and to produce the same effects as theirs, it suffices to "look for the structure of their narratives." *See them as they see each other,* so goes the (anthropological) creed. "Tell it the way *they* tell it instead of imposing *our* structure," they repeat with an all-clear conscience and with the best intentions. Disease breeds disease. Those who function best within definite structures and spend their time structuring their own or their peers' existences must obviously "look for" that which, according to their "findings" and analyses, is supposed to be "the structure of their [the storytellers'] narratives." What we "look for" is un/fortunately what we shall find. The anthropologist, remember, does not *find* things; s/he *makes* them. And makes them up. The structure is therefore not something given, entirely external to the person who structures, but a projection of that person's way of handling realities, here narratives. It is perhaps difficult for an analytically trained mind to admit that recording, gathering, sorting, deciphering, analyzing and synthesizing, dissecting, and articulating are already "imposing our[/a] structure," a structural activity, a structuring of the mind, a

31. Maurice Dorès, *La Femme village* (Paris: L'Harmattan, 1981), pp. 20-25.

whole mentality. (Can one "look for a structure" without structuring?) But it is particularly difficult for a dualistic or dualistically trained mind to recognize that "looking for the structure of their narratives" already involves the separation of the structure from the narratives, of the structure from that which is structured, of the narrative from the narrated, and so on. It is, once more, as if form and content stand apart; as if the structure can remain fixed, immutable, independent of and unaffected by the changes the narratives undergo; as if a structure can only function as a standard mold within the old determinist schema of cause and product. Listen, for example, to what a man of the West had to say on the form of the story:

> *Independent of the content which the story carries, and which may vary from history to nonsense, is the form of the story which is practically the same in all stories. The content is varied and particular, the form is the same and universal. Now there are four main elements in the form of each story, viz, the beginning, the development, the climax, and the end.*[32]

Just like the Western drama with its four or five acts. A drama whose naive claim to universality would not fail to make of this man of the West our laughingstock. "A good story," another man of the West asserted, "must have a beginning that rouses interest, a succession of events that is orderly and complete, a climax that forms the story's point, and an end that leaves the mind at rest."[33] No criteria other than those quoted here show a more thorough investment of the Western mind. GET THEM – children, story-believers – AT THE START; MAKE YOUR POINT by ordering events to a definite CLIMAX; then ROUND OUT TO COMPLETION, descend to a rapid close – not one, for example, that puzzles or keeps them puzzling over the story, but one surely enough that LEAVES THE MIND AT REST. In other words, to be "good," a story must be built in conformity with the ready-made idea some people – Western adults – have of reality, that is to say a set of prefabricated schemata (prefabricated by whom?) they value out of habit, conservatism, and ignorance (of other ways of telling and listening to stories). If these criteria are to be adopted, then countless non-Western (and a number of Western) stories will fall straight into the category of "bad" stories. Unless one makes it up or invents a reason for its ab-

32. Horne, *Story-telling*, p. 26.
33. E. P. St. John, *Stories and Story-telling*, quoted in Horne, *Story-telling*, p. 26.

sence, one of these four elements required always seems to be missing. The stories in question either have no development, no climax that forms the story's point, or no end that leaves the mind at rest. (One can say of the majority of these stories' endings that they precisely refute such generalization and rationale, for they offer no security of this kind. An example among endless others is the moving story of "The Laguna People" passed on by Marmon Silko, which ends with a little girl, her sister, and the people turning into stone while they sit on top of a mesa after they have escaped the flood in their home village below. Because of the disquieting nature of the resolution here, the storytellers – Marmon Silko and her aunt – then add, as a compromise to the fact-oriented mind of today's audience: "The story ends here./ Some of the stories/ Aunt Susie told/ have this kind of ending./ There are no explanations."[34] "Looking for the structure of *their* narratives" so as to "tell it the way *they* tell it" is an attempt at remedying this ignorance of other ways of telling and listening (and, obviously, at revalidating the nativist discourse). In doing so, however, rare are those who realize that what they come up with is not "the structure of *their* narratives" but a reconstruction of the story that, at best, makes a number of its functions appear. Rare are those who acknowledge the unavoidable transfer of values in the "search" and admit that "the attempt will remain largely illusory: we shall never know if the other, into whom we cannot, after all, dissolve, fashions from the elements of [her/]his social existence a synthesis exactly superimposable on that which we have worked out."[35] The attempt will remain illusory as long as the controlled succession of certain mental operations which constitutes the structural activity is not made explicit and dealt with – not just mentioned. Life is not a (Western) drama of four or five acts. Sometimes it just drifts along; it may go on year after year without development, without climax, without definite beginnings or endings. Or it may accumulate climax upon climax, and if one chooses to mark it with beginnings and endings, then everything has a beginning and an ending. There are, in this sense, no good or bad stories. In life, we usually don't know when an event is occurring; we think it is starting when it is already ending; and we don't see its in/significance. The present, which sat-

34. Marmon Silko, *Storyteller*, pp. 38-42.
35. Claude Lévi-Strauss, *The Scope of Anthropology*, trans. S. Ortner Paul and R. A. Paul (1967; reprint, London: Jonathan Cape, 1971), p. 14.

urates the total field of our environment, is often invisible to us. The structural activity that does not carry on the cleavage between form and content, but emphasizes the interrelation of the material and the intelligible, is an activity in which structure should remain an unending question: one that speaks him/her as s/he speaks it, brings it to intelligibility.

"Looking for the structure of their narratives" is like looking for the pear shape in Erik Satie's musical composition *Trois Pièces en Forme de Poire* (Three Pieces in a Pear Shape). (The composition was written after the French composer Erik Satie met with Claude Debussy, who criticized his music for "lacking in form.") If structure, as a man (Roland Barthes) pertinently defines it, is "the residual deposit of duration," then, again, rare are those who can handle it by letting it come, instead of hunting for it or hunting it down, filling it with their own marks and markings so as to consign it to the meaningful and to lay claim to it. *They see no life/ When they look/ they see only objects.* The ready-made idea they have of reality prevents them from conceiving the story as a living thing, an organic process, a way of life. What is taken for stories, only stories, are fragments of/in life, fragments that never stop interracting while being complete in themselves. A story in Africa may last three months. The storyteller relates it night after night, continuously, or s/he starts it one night and takes it up again from this point only three months later. Meanwhile, as the occasion arises, s/he may yet start on another story. Such is life . . .

> *The gussucks [the whites] did not understand the story; they could not see the way it must be told, year after year as the old man has done, without lapse or silence. . . .*
>
> *"It began a long time ago," she intoned steadily . . . she did not pause or hesitate; she went on with the story, and she never stopped . . .*[36]

"Storyteller," from which these lines are excerpted, is another story, another gift of life by Marmon Silko. It presents an example of multiple storytelling in which story and life merge, the story being as complex as life and life as simple as a story. The story of "Story-

36. Marmon Silko, *Storyteller,* pp. 31-32.

teller" is the layered making of four storytellers: Marmon Silko, the woman in the story, her grandmother, and the person referred to as "the old man." Except for Marmon Silko, who plays here the role of the coordinator, each of these three storytellers has her/his own story to live and live with. Despite the difference in characters or in subject matter, their stories closely interact and constantly overlap. The woman makes of her story a continuation of her grandmother's, which was left with no ending – the grandmother being thereby compelled to bear it (the story) until her death, her knees and knuckles swollen grotesquely, "swollen with anger" as she explained it. She bore it, knowing that her granddaughter will have to bear it too: "It will take a long time," she said, "but the story must be told. There must not be any lies." Sometime after her death – when exactly it does not matter – when the time comes, the granddaughter picks up the story where her grandmother left it and carries it to its end accordingly, the way "it must be told." She carries it to a certain completion by bringing in death where she intends to have it in her story: the white storeman who lied in her grandma's story and was the author of her parents' death would have to pay for his lies, but his death would also have to be of his own making. The listener/reader does not (have to) know whether the storeman in the granddaughter's story is the same as the one who, according to the grandmother, "left right after that [after he lied and killed]" (hence the apparent impossibility for the old woman to finish her story). A storeman becomes *the* storeman, the man in the store, the man in the story. (The truthfulness of the story, as mentioned, does not limit itself to the realm of facts.) Which story? *The* story. What grandma began, granddaughter completes and passes on to be further completed. As a storyteller, the woman (the granddaughter) does not directly kill; she decides when and where that storeman will find death, but she does not carry out a hand-to-hand fight, and her murder is no murder in the common, factual sense of the term: all that she needs to do is set into motion the necessary forces and let them act on their own.

> *They asked her again, what happened to the man from the Northern Commercial store. "He lied to them. He told them it was safe to drink. But I will not lie . . . I killed him," she said, "but I don't lie."*

While she is in jail, the gussuck attorney advises her to tell the court the *truth,* which is that it was an accident, that the storeman ran after her in the cold and fell through the ice. That's all that she has to say and "they will let [her] go home. Back to [her] village."

> *She shook her head. "I will not change the story, not even to escape this place and go home. I intended that he die. The story must be told as it is." The attorney exhaled loudly; his eyes looked tired. "Tell her that she could not have killed him that way. He was a white man. He ran after her without a parka or mittens. She could not have planned that."*[37]

When the helpful, conscientious (full-of-the-white-man's-complex-of-superiority) attorney concludes that he will do "all [he] can for her" and will explain to the judge that "her mind is confused," she laughs out loud and finally decides to tell him the story anew: "It began a long time ago . . ." He says she could not have killed that white man because, again, for him the story is just a story. But Thought-Woman, Spider-Woman is a fairy and a witch who protects her people and tells stories to affect cures. As she names Death, Death appears. The spell is cast. Only death gives an ending to the stories in "Storyteller." (The old man's story of the giant bear overlaps with the granddaughter's story and ends the moment the old man – the storyteller – dies.) Marmon Silko as a storyteller never loses sight of the difference between truth and fact. Her naming retains the accurateness and magic of our great mothers' storytelling without ever confining itself to the realm of factual naming. It is accurate because it is at once extremely flexible and rigid, not because it wishes to stick to certain rules of correctness for reasons of mere conservatism. (Scholars studying traditional storytelling are often impressed by the storyteller's "necessity of telling the stories correctly," as they put it.) It is accurate because it partakes in the setting into motion of forces that lie dormant in us. Because, as African storytellers sing, "the tongue that falsifies the word/ taints the blood of [her/]him that lies."[38] Because she who bears it in her belly cannot cut herself off from herself. Off from the bond of coming-and-going. Off from her great mothers.

37. Ibid.
38. Hampaté Ba, "The Living Tradition," p. 172.

A Bedtime Story

Mitsuye Yamada
Camp Notes

Once upon a time,
an old Japanese legend
goes as told
by Papa,
an old woman traveled through
many small villages
seeking refuge
for the night.
Each door opened
a sliver
in answer to her knock
then closed.
Unable to walk
any further
she wearily climbed a hill
found a clearing
and there lay down to rest
a few moments to catch
her breath.

The village town below
lay asleep except
for a few starlike lights.
Suddenly the clouds opened
and a full moon came into view
Over the town.

The old woman sat up
turned toward
the village town
and in supplication
called out
Thank you people
of the village,
if it had not been for your
kindness
in refusing me a bed
for the night
these humble eyes would never
have seen this
memorable sight.

Papa paused, I waited.
In the comfort of our
hilltop home in Seattle
overlooking the valley,
I shouted
"That's the end?"

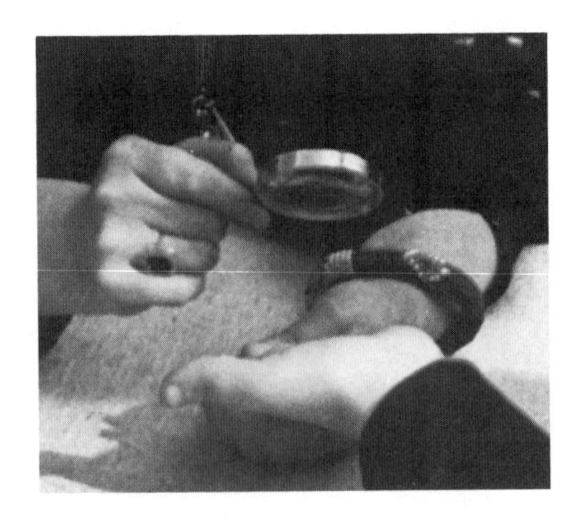

Family Stories

CARRIE MAE WEEMS

What part of Mississippi are you from?

From Clarksdale. Mother was born in Larks, and Papa was born in Silver City.

What did your family do in Mississippi?

Farm. We sharecropped for Charles Gillet. That one I remember because we were just at the age of remembering.

Did you live on a plantation?

Yes, sure did. Oh yeah, we lived on a plantation!

Were there other families living there too?

Yeah, there was a lot of 'em. Maybe six or seven families on the plantation, maybe more than that. The houses was scattered like. Like our house was over there, and all our land was over there, and you hoed as much land as you wanted to hoe. Then another house was spotted and they worked so much land, see.

What was sharecropping like?

You worked a part of the land for yourself and part you worked for the Man. He got half. One bale would go for you and one bale would go for him, see; if you got twenty bales, that mean ten for you and ten for him. But you'd have to pick fifteen hundred to two thousand pounds to get a bale. It depends on how many pounds you got in order to get you a five-hundred-pound bale. Ya see. 'Cause they take all the seeds outta it, then they weigh the cotton itself. When they take the seeds outta it, they pay you so much money for that, and then at the end of the year they pay you for the bale – the poundage on the bale. And that's the way we did that.

Was he a fair landlord?

Naw! Some folks just never came out nothin' but in the hole! Say like that. 'Cause my Pastor always saying how they worked and from one year to the next they never came outta the hole. He was always talking about how poor they was. But my daddy was always such a provider, until – really, we never did see no hard times.

People hollering about the hard times in the South, but we always had. Any time of year if Mother wanted a steak, Daddy could go get her a steak. You see what I mean? Or if it got to that time of evening and we decided we wanted pork chops, Daddy would go get 'em. Daddy always tried to give us things. They provided for us.

So many families in the South didn't try to provide, they wouldn't can, they were like the grasshopper. But Mother would can maybe a thousand jars of fruit every year. So all winter our food was stocked up for us – all winter long. And we would never have to be stingy with eatin', there was always a plenty, but some people didn't know how to figure out their money very good and would get real cheated.

But you see Daddy had such a brain until if they say, I'm gonna pay you, say twenty cents a pound for the cotton, Daddy had kept all of his tickets, he had figured up all the poundage, and he had figured up everything that he had borrowed from him – the Man. And when he went up there to settle, he taken a pencil, too! Well, one time ole man Gillet told Daddy that he had so much and so much coming, and Daddy said, "Naw, I ain't got so much. You better get your pencil!" Ya see!

But a lots of people wouldn't say nothing, they went on and took it; whatever he said went, they'd be too scared to argue with the white man; but Daddy let them know, "You cheaping me!" That last time Gillet told Daddy he was "too smart" for 'em and he wanted him to leave. So then we moved.

I forgets the place; I don't remember that man at all, but we moved on this plantation. But Daddy worked as a carpenter, 'cause Daddy was a carpenter. Yeah, Daddy could do anything like that, carpentry; he was a freemason; he could build a brick house! So he got the place (the plantation) for mother, and then he work in town. That way wouldn't nobody say, "Well, hey, you come," or "You can't go to town." And by nobody knowing what Daddy was, nobody would mess with him. And so this is the way Daddy got around. He would do these different things. He worked and saved that money, then he moved and then we got married – Sadie and I got married.

How did you meet my Daddy (Myrlie Weems)?

On the plantation. On Charles Gillet's plantation. Well, I met him before then. He was on a place called Hanes, he and Mrs. Weems and all them, they lived not far down the road from us, see. Then they moved away; they moved down around Marks; then they moved back into the area where we was, and they had grown up and we had too. So that's how we met. But later on, me and your daddy worked on the same plantation, and he lived in the cotton house, that's where you put the cotton at, you pick it and put it in the cotton house, well that's where he lived, in the cotton house with his little friend.

How did Papa and Grandmomma meet (Albert and Ozzie Polk)?

I don't know. Daddy's first marriage was a bad experience, she liked to lay around. He had caught his wife with the other man so he was free to marry. He knew the man. But Daddy really never talked too much about hisself. I think he preferred to be left out and his life was shut like.

Do you think Papa got by 'cause he passed for white?

Well, yeah. Even after we got to Portland, one day a white man asked him how did he feel riding them niggers in his car, and he would come up against those kinds a things, but he always had an answer for 'em, 'cause he never denied that we was his family, that was one thing that he never denied! And you know when we lived in the South, they had the Jim Crow signs, and you see Daddy would put us behind the sign and he sat in front of the sign. He would do things like that; in a sense he could ride wherever he wanted to ride. Because they didn't know, you see. And I guess when he came up he was able to go into a restaurant and eat; where black people had to go through the backdoors, he was able to go right in and eat his meals, you see.

Did you know Papa's mother or father?

No, 'cause his mother had died. But she had three kids: Papa, Katie, and Joe. Joe and Papa half-brothers, they have a different father. But, Joe's daddy didn't like Papa, so his uncle – Uncle Kelly – raised him. Daddy is the oldest. And I think because Daddy is crossed-breed, that the man didn't like him, so Uncle Kelly raised Daddy. Katie died young, so I never known her, but Joe still alive and lives right outside Clarksdale.

Did Papa ever meet his father?

Oh yeah, Daddy knew his daddy; oh yeah, oh yeah! They tell me that old man still lives in Clarksdale; tell me he still have a plantation. He knew who he was! Uncle Kelly knew who he was too, but they wouldn't tell nobody.

I heard he was a Jew from Chicago?

I don't know about Chicago, but I feel he was a Jew.

Why do you think that?

Because when I worked at the Bardy's, the only thing that Daddy ever really came up and told me – the Bardy's were Jews – he came up and told me, he said "Baby, you know, these are our people." So that gave me the clue that he was Jewish. And then, you see, Daddy traveled with Jews, and in Clarksdale those Jews – those old Jews – knows Daddy, they knows who he is, you see. He was a traveling salesman with Jews.

But the way I understand it, his father was a traveling salesman, too. But in later years the old man had a plantation. But he could have been a traveling salesman and had a plantation too. And I always felt that he had a connection with the gins – the gin mills – that's what they do to the cotton, okay. Because Daddy could work at one gin mill, and if they made him mad at that one, he could just walk away from them and go to the next one over there and go to work. So he worked from one gin mill to the next, and whichever one he went to they wouldn't turn him down. I have a feeling that his father had something to do with them mills. I might be wrong about it, but I really do.

Did you ever ask Papa about his father?

Let me tell ya somethin': I think that he always felt that he really didn't want us to really know. And he had his reasons. See, I think that his daddy had a family, and he wouldn't tell white people what he was. But I have a feeling that those Jews knew. But like them different plantations that we moved on, this is what he had the advantage of. See, Daddy was a smart thinker. He had the advantage enough to know that as long as they didn't know whether he was black or white, he could get what he wanted to do. And he wouldn't let no white man come up and tell us nothing. "If ya got anything to say ya say it to me. But my children, ya ain't got nothin' to do with them." Well ya see, nobody else could do like that. And even if they had asked him what he was, he wouldn't tell 'em. So he left all of us like that.

What was Grandmomma Ozzie like?

Wasteful, very wasteful. But she was strong. Mother was a person who did not play with her children, but she was a friend to her children, you know? You could talk to her; she was very easy to talk to, and her whole mind was kinda settled around her kids.

Like she'd set out her best china and silver and feed us, or cook one of these great big dinners and invite all her children over and stretch out her table and just service 'em! This is the type of person she was – if it was good enough for her, it was good enough for her kids. And anything that she had, if it was good enough for anybody else, it was most certainly good enough for her kids to have. And she didn't believe in her kids being the last ones eats. If they couldn't sit down and eat it along with you, you sho wasn't gonna put your feet up under the table.

Wasteful, very wasteful lady. And a very free-spirit person, free! And I don't know of no one like her. Her and Daddy either. And I don't know of no one who disliked her. You know Johnny, the one who had the cleaners, and his wife, she always wants me to come and see her. And whenever I see her, she say "Ain't nobody else like Ozzie. I don't know, I just miss her!"

Did Great-Grandmomma Bessie live on Charles Gillet's plantation too?

No, they lived on a different plantation and her husband was a dairyman, he worked at the dairy. They lived at Rich, that's the only place I know'd Momma to live was at Rich. I know'd they moved to other places, but for years they stayed on this plantation and Momma was a midwife. See, Momma delivered Jerome and all them. She was a sweet woman and her husband's name was Joshua. Oh, he was a lot of fun; he and I, we would have it! And that's where I got the nickname "Mule." Stubborn, honey! That's where I got that name from! And I liked grapes, and they tell me he'd just go out and get garbs of grapes, and just bring 'em to me, sit me down and just let me eat off them grapes.

Did Papa and Ozzie go to school?

Papa had sixteen years. He went to, as far as I can tell, the eighth grade. Then he went back and started all over. He went through school twice up to the eight grade. What he missed out on the first time, he picked up on on the second go around. Mother, I believe, went up to the ninth grade.

What about you?

I started the ninth grade, then I dropped out. I got married. Daddy was there when I got married, but he was out here (in Portland) when Sadie got married.

Do you ever think you got married too young?

Yep! Sure I did. I think lots of us got married too young. We didn't even think about it until later – years later.

Daddy said he remembers being just a little boy when a gang of white men armed with shotguns and looking evil surrounded their house one morning and called out Granddaddy Weems. They told him if he kept doing what he was doing that he'd be a sorry nigger 'cause they'd hang him for sho. You see, my grandfather was a political sorta guy, involved in organizing colored people. Daddy say he was like Martin Luther King, when it came to speaking he could talk that talk and the white folks both feared and hated him, wanted him outta town and soon.

Well, the way I hear it, they succeeded, because one night Granddaddy Weems left the house going to one of the organizing meetings and wasn't heard from again for a very long time – years in fact. Everybody thought that for sure the white folks had gotten hold of him and cooked him. Maybe they tried, nobody knows for sure. But way after a while, somehow or another, Grandfather Weems contacted the family and let it be known that he was safe and living in Chicago.

Daddy saw his father only once after that; he says that he wanted to see his father so bad that he went to Chicago looking for him, didn't have no phone number, no address, just stalked the streets in the colored section of town looking. "And I found him, too. I was walking down the street and saw this man that looked just like my daddy going into a pool hall and I followed him in. I walked up to him and before I could ask him his name, he told me, 'Yeah, I'm your daddy,' and we hugged and kissed right there in the pool hall. Ain't never seen him again."

I never met Grandmomma Weems, but my cousin Pat lived with her for a long time, and says that she was a wonderful person – easy. She died back in the early 1970s from cancer of the uterus, an illness she didn't believe she had. Pat says, "But I think Grandmomma would have been alive today. 'Cause when I graduated high school in 1967, they had diagnosed her as having cancer of the uterus. But she said, 'Naw, I don't wanta go for it! Naw, momma ain't got no cancer; they just wanta cut on me.'" So she just laid around and didn't go. She probably would have been alive today if she had had that surgery.

I asked Daddy to tell me about when he kidnapped his momma off a plantation in Memphis, but he said he didn't want to talk about it 'cause it was too many details. But Alice told me that Mattie Jean, my cousin who was living with my grandmother back then, told her that the white man wouldn't let them go 'cause they owed him money. But every year they owed him more money, ya know. They were caught up in the sharecropping system and couldn't get out. Well, anyway, one night my daddy came for them. It was wintertime, and it was raining cats and dogs, and they had to move and move fast. They didn't even have time to dress. They just run through the night in their nightclothes and barefoot, hightailing it on outta there.

My father has seven brothers and one sister, and I think because their father left them when they were all just small kids, they felt that they could do the same thing. I tell you, the Weems brothers are a strange lot.

Now, for all I know, all of them, with the exception of my

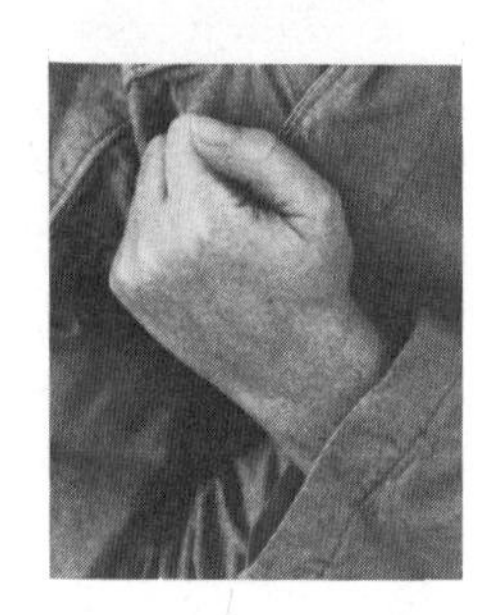

father and his brother, Clarence, have been married two or three times and have more kids in and outside of marriage than the law allows. He had one brother named Clayborn who constantly beat his women. He'd take 'em in the woods, beat them, and threaten to throw 'em off bridges and stuff: a wild man! But his time had run short. My cousin Pat says, "Something was bound to happen to him sooner or later. 'Cause ain't no woman gonna take all that mess. Ya know, they'll take. They usually get away with it through the years, until somebody 'bring they hat to 'em.' I mean, I hate that he's dead and everything, but sooner or later something was bound to happen to him."

I said, "I heard some woman killed him." Pat said, "That was his wife! They had gotten married! The woman say that ever since he come out here to Clarence's funeral, he had been acting strange and went to losing weight. They had went to this party and ya know he drunk beer – he's a natural beer drinker – that's all he drunk and he had gotten high and threatened to jump on her. Well, he did jump on her. Then he threatened to kill her!"

Ya know, when somebody drunk ain't no telling what they might do. He mighta really meant it. And I bet ya nine outta ten, it was something that happen at that party. Maybe somebody gave her some attention or something. I bet it was over nothing. So naturally she was gonna protect herself. Like you wouldn't stand up and let somebody kill you if you could help it. It was over a year after Clarence died. It wasn't that long ago.

Now James Weems is also a character, and when you talk about him you just hang your head. One day he just walked off and left his family, then tried to play it off like he'd had amnesia for all them years. Amnesia, girl! In fact it was at Clarence's funeral – first time in over twenty years he'd seen his boys, Jerry and James. After all them years the man tried to play daddy with 'em. Now you know that don't make no kinda sense. Somebody needs to tie that fool up by his toenails and beat him. Amnesia!

Honey, I'm telling you, I don't know what to say about the Weems's, but some of them are so cold-cold dudes.

Serving the Status-Quo (from the transcripts)

CONNIE HATCH

I. Work / Possessions: One Family in Texas, 1979

Faye: We had no idea how much Jennifer, our baby, would cost us . . . but when we, uh . . . got the bill from the hospital, it was seventeen-hundred-and-some-odd dollars. Then, of course, the doctor, the gynecologist, was eight-hundred-and-some-odd dollars; because she was caesarian it was more. And . . . the pediatrician was a hundred and forty-six. But we were rather astonished at the amount it cost us to have her.

Chris: I guess on the overtime situation I've been working, oh . . . anywhere from one to, uh . . . six hours . . . seven hours a day, more than the regular scheduled time, eight hours. Which makes it pretty rough, because now I just kind of come home, eat or go to bed, or just come home and go to bed. It doesn't give you much time to spend with the newborn little girl that keeps growing up everyday . . . or a wife that has new experiences that she wants to talk to you about. Certainly Ma Bell is controlling my life. There's no two ways about it.

What we deal with is mainly the same thing that they've been dealing with ever since the phone company began . . . putting two wires together.

In the phone company right now, they're starting to develop a system that's called "The Better Way." This system was devised by people somewhere up the line that seem to think that we in the cable-splicing department don't know how long it should take to perform a certain job. So what they've done is taken a situation, like say, they set somebody down and said, "Okay, make this six hundred pair straight." And he's supposed to be the best splicer they've got, he's supposed to have all of the best equipment, everything is supposed to be readily at hand. And then how long it takes him to do that splice is measured and then when we go out and make the same splice in the field we have to tell why it took us longer . . . to make that same splice. Realize that he was under perfect, idealized conditions; that's what it was supposed to be. And we're not, and we're supposed to tell why it took us longer. Well, this system has a built-in fallacy right off the bat. By the time you go through doing the paperwork, itemizing how long it took you to do something, you've wasted another thirty minutes. So you've lost thirty minutes that they don't allow you to put on the time report . . . because they don't have any codes for it.

It's a dog-eat-dog situation – you'd better watch out over your left or right shoulder or somebody's about to take you over. It's almost to the point of . . . of going against what I want out of life, which would be a nice solid foundation to live in, work in. I'd like to have more time to enjoy life. By that I mean, uh . . . things that make up the world . . . nature . . . people . . . But of course since you work, you become part of what is going on in this world right now. And if you don't . . . you're only an innocent bystander . . . trying to observe something that you might not ever understand.

The weather is a big factor to contend with when you work for the phone company, because whatever it is outside, that's what I'm in, all of the time . . . And if it's cold, I'm cold. And if it's hot, I'm hot. It's understandable. If they lower or raise the thermostats to seventy-eight degrees in the summertime, it just won't make too much difference to me for some reason. I know I've worked outside and sat in the snow and when I would get up I'd fall over because my toes would be frozen. I remember two winters ago I nearly lost my toes because they were frostbit.

Maybe I am some type of mediator between nature and technology . . . My idea on Faye working is that it doesn't bother me that she is not working. It does bother me that we can't afford the same things we used to be able to when she was. And I'm afraid it will come to a time that the inability to buy what we used to buy is gonna cause trouble.

Faye: Before having our baby I was apprehensive about what type of parent I would be. But you don't realize, even if you're around a baby any time, you don't really realize until it's your responsibility for twenty-four hours a day what it's like. It's beautiful, and yet it's a . . . a great deal of pain. Because when they're first brought home, they're so tiny . . . and you're nervous . . . because you don't . . . just because you're a mother doesn't mean that you naturally know exactly what to do. You develop a sense where you think you are. But Jennifer would sleep forty-five minutes at a time and then wake up. And . . . there wasn't even enough time for me to close my eyes and by the time I started dreaming, then she was awake . . . crying again. Either to be fed or to be rocked. Everybody kept telling me, it'll end, it'll end. And I kept saying, when? Because I didn't know how much longer I could take it. Because I wanted to love her, I wanted to be with her . . . and take care of her, but my nerves didn't have enough time to readjust by the time she started crying again. It was a lot more work than I had anticipated.

Chris: I know that she was programmed ever since I can remember to work. She didn't take any home economics or housekeeping or anything like that . . . which I think she's found out is a mistake. But I know that she didn't want to be poor. She had been poor all of her life. And the only way to get away from being poor is to work. I don't really care for her to work . . .

Faye: It worked out pretty good . . . he does have a tendency sometimes to let me do all of the wifely things . . . the womanly things. But he is not half, half, half as bad as so many of the men I know. He really does help me a great deal. And her being a little girl, if anyone could just see the smile that she lights up with when her daddy comes home and says, "Hi, darling . . ." It is worth everything in the world and it's especially for him. And it's . . . [cuckoo clock sounds] who can describe why a baby will do *that*? But it's very nice . . .

Chris: It is . . . very possible that if I refuse to work overtime, I would probably be laid off . . . Until this ruling goes before the union board, it's hard to say what they would do. They probably would go ahead and lay me off. I'm working a sufficient amount of overtime where they can't say anything. I don't want to work overtime. The money does come in very handy right now, and . . . since my wife has quit work with the baby . . . it's going to, uh . . . it might be rough working straight time and supporting all of the . . . all of the material things I have acquired and am making payments on.

Faye: I don't want to go back to work. I've told everybody, most everybody, financially, if I have to, then I will. I always thought there wasn't anything for me but work, since I've worked twelve years for the same company, but that's not true, not now. Uh . . . I don't plan to go back to work unless problems arise . . . unless my husband gets to feeling bad because he's working and I'm not . . . and he starts taking it out on me . . . which I hope doesn't happen.

Chris: If I could get out of the phone company, I would. But to give up what I would have to give up is not worth it . . . you have to have certain restrictions on your life if you want certain things . . . I wouldn't be happy at all if I had to live in a house that wasn't air-conditioned or properly heated. Live without the proper clothes, new clothes, new car, new house, and whatever things . . . other things I want, whenever I want it. So there goes all of your personal freedom . . . your human values . . . part of the control of your life . . .

Faye: So, everything is going comparatively smooth now – considering that I have an extra little one that's a part of me and a part of my husband to carry around. No, I don't intend to go back to work. I'm very happy . . . with my new little baby. . . .

II. Adapt: Frankie Mann, 1980

Most of my friends work as waitresses, and they make three dollars an hour working their asses off or being secretaries. The price differential between a technical job and a service job, like a real job, is huge. For instance, a programmer makes ten dollars an hour, easy. Anyway, so I get these computer jobs to make money to get by so I can make my music.

I came to the realization that I had bought the whole story about going to college being your ticket to success. I'd busted my ass to get through college and I owed thousands of dollars and I'd gone to graduate school and I had a bunch of good credentials and I had the Fulbright and I had all these awards from all over the place, not that I give that much credence to awards 'cause I think you get them randomly, but I had all the paper shit down. Then I started working at Adapt because someone wanted to put out a record of mine, put out music of mine on a record, but I had to front $500 that I didn't have. But it was sort of a big chance for me to have a record for $500, a really good rate. It was Art Services Records, which was pretty exciting. So I started working at Adapt to make money for my record, to buy this tape recorder here. 'Cause I knew I was coming out of graduate school and I wouldn't have a tape recorder.

They hired me, which I was real surprised. I had a hard time getting a job 'cause people looked at me and thought I was too weird looking. Also 'cause I looked like a lesbian. And I was a woman with a master's degree. I have to lie on my resumé depending on what jobs I go looking for. Some jobs I can't let people know I'm a woman with a master's degree; otherwise they'll think I'm too snotty or smarty pants or a woman with a master's degree is just useless to them. So . . . uh, I had some problems getting hired. And I was dressing reasonably straight when I was applying for these jobs. My hair didn't help a lot. A lot of headhunters – headhunters are, uh . . . employment agencies that get their money by finding programmers – headhunters wouldn't want me because I looked too weird. And it didn't matter what qualifications I had, didn't matter that I was a Fulbright scholar or that I had done all that stuff in computers.

No woman that applies for a job gets looked at in the eyes. No woman. Every woman who applies for a job gets looked at in the breasts. Everyone does . . . so . . . they called me back and, uh, they hired me 'cause the other person who was qualified wanted more money than I did. So they probably figured they could hammer . . . they basically told me they could hammer me into doing more work.

The company had eight vice-presidents, one secretary, one computer operator, and two computer programmers. It was all men, except for the secretary and me. You think about the job they have. They're managers or executives. If they have any education in it whatsoever they go and have management classes and all management classes teach you to do is to think of things, think of new ways to reorganize people. You basically have nothing to do, so what you do is think up new ways to organize – which is basically a euphemism for "oppress" – people. And that's the reason that secretaries have tons of work to do. And I mean no superhuman could do the work that is requested of most women in jobs. Fortunately, I was in a technical job and I could mau-mau them into leaving me alone. Because whenever they would pull shit with me, like for example, one of the vice-presidents was demonstrating a computer, I was asked to demonstrate a new microcomputer to one of our clients, and at the end the guy, the vice-prez, who is just a dummy, said, "It's so easy, uh, even a girl could do it." And I turned to him and I said, "Wait a minute!" (after the client left). I said, you know, "Wait a minute! If I'd walked out of that room just now you wouldn't have been able to turn the lights off or on." Here these guys were making $50,000 a year playing dominoes all day long. And they would have to hire a temporary typesetter to come in, usually a woman my age, and they would squabble about whether to pay her $3.10 or $3.05 an hour. . . .

And this is just one little office in a whole sea of downtown offices where women my age and older are completely oppressed and keep the whole thing together on absolutely slave wages. It's basically all white men, who aren't doing a damn thing and they're just dressing right.

Information seems to travel in information circles – a new fanatical religion to me. I mean, computers are fun, this is fun to mess around with in some ways . . . but it has to do with, if you ask me, it has to do with a desire for domination and control. You get an incredible thrill about being in command of this computer, and you've taught this computer how to wave a little arm around, or you've taught this computer to print your name a million times. It's, it's . . . reverence for dominance and control. Alot of that's linked up to electronics, and computer music also, and it really disturbs me. It also pertains to art, painting even, but it's . . . you find it in photography and all the technical shit about cameras and all the technical shit about film . . . and it's all stuff . . . and it's all pride of priority of knowledge or information. Information priority. And you really don't want people to know about the technical stuff because you'll feel like you've lost something, some special power you have over people. You know a little bit about something that not everybody knows about so you can lord it over them, and that happens in computers, electronics, photography, piano technique. It has everything to do with the whole way we're taught to think about thinking.

It's hard for me to explain to anybody because as a woman I'm subject to all sorts of questioning. It wouldn't matter if I'd invented a computer, everyone would always question my technical ability, based on the fact that I'm a woman. And everyone always thinks that women are young for some reason. That's part of sexism. And so, if you're a woman, you're always . . . your technical ability or your scientific ability is always being questioned. Maybe for good reason, maybe it's because women are smart enough not to believe in that male science. I don't find much credibility with the men I talk to, but it's taken me years to suddenly realize that I don't give a shit about what they think. I mean, I used to really be in a quandary that men would not hear me or would argue with me or would . . . or they've told me they enjoy getting me mad 'cause they think I'm so cute when I get angry. My women friends and I have a great deal of communication about all this stuff. I think it's important for people to have access to all sorts of different

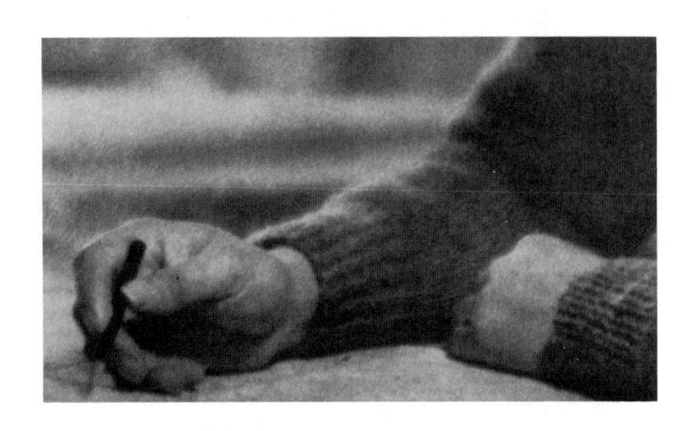

instruments, but I think that boys have much greater access to studios. It's not that people can legally exclude women, but any woman that works in a studio knows the techno-macho that goes on excludes them. I just keep changing my mind to some degree as to what I really want to do with my music: if I want to spend two solid weeks filing the bit one out of my computer so that I can have it go "dup, dup, dup," or if I can learn to sing better, I think I'd rather learn how to sing. 'Cause music isn't technology . . . matter of fact it takes a hell of a lot to make technology sing. . . . whoever designed this, I betcha don't dance . . . and to try to make this thing sing, means you have to somehow understand a little bit about that person, that nerd down in Sunnyvale. I think it's awful hard to write music when you're having to deal with that mechanistic, linear way of thinking which is very much caught up with dominating the world. I mean it's really religious, we're talking about religion. I firmly believe one of the funniest things about technology is, the more these engineers and systems analysts try to control what's around us . . . the more they try to control it, the more out of control it's gonna get. And then one of these days it's just gonna backfire (bang). It's really frightening to me. I mean those people don't know what they're doing. It's all related to their families too. My father's in the air force and his last name is ironically "man." And he was very strict with us and wanted us to be the world's most ultimate children. He was the ultimate believer that the Russians were gonna bomb us off the face of the earth and, for example, he began to build a bomb shelter in our back yard when I was five. And he had a bomb closet that had bomb food in it and we weren't allowed to go in there. He tried to raise us militaristically 'cause he figured that'd make us better American children. We had air raid drills and inspections of our rooms. We weren't allowed in the kitchen without written permission. We weren't allowed to touch the refrigerator under any circumstances. And he used to play with us only once a week, on Tuesdays at 7:30. He'd set the kitchen alarm clock on the stove, he'd set it for thirty minutes; when the buzzer went off he'd stop whatever he was doing playing with us and go in the kitchen and have a highball, and that was it.

Anyway, he beat up my mother really badly. . . . Over the course of ten years he broke her nose twice, busted her head open once, broke a total of twelve ribs. He sent her to every mental hospital in North and South Carolina. Whenever he wanted to go to the beach with one of his girlfriends he'd put my mother in a mental hospital. My mother was an alcoholic also. He used to beat my brother with a belt buckle, but since I was a girl, I got hit with the other end of it.

First of all, my mother quit drinking when I was thirteen and then she fell in love with her mental hospital friend. And they were really poor, we didn't have any money or anything. My mother and I lived in a car for nine months together and that was the closest I ever was to my mother really. And what amazed me about my family was, when Stewart was in prison he wrote Momma these letters saying, "Mom, if you go up in the attic, hidden in the attic is my Magnum .45 gun. Would you please give it to Aunt Martha for me to have when I get out of prison?" He'd say: Don't worry, it's legal, just don't tell the police you have it and all, you know. And she was gonna do it! . . . She was really gonna do it. So I said, "Momma, give me the gun." So I got the gun and I took it to this field and I buried it. So he's gonna be out on the loose again in six months and it just freaks me out to think about all the goons just walking around out there, just like Stewart, and I know there's plenty of 'em. . . . He's really bought that macho thing that my father tried to teach him, I mean I really fear everyone thinks I've bought that macho thing too from my father. I mean I really loathe my father and I really loathe that people look at me and say, "Oh, here's a woman who was beaten by her father, her mother's fucked up, and her stepbrother's fucked up, and they've all beat up on her and she wants to be a boy and wants to be macho and a lesbian and doesn't have any hair." I mean, that is so missing the point of me. I've had people say to me that it's so appropriate that my name is "man." As if I wanted to be a male! I just want to make the point that I do not. If the slightest bit of me were male, I'd commit suicide. My mother and father sent me to a psychologist when I was thirteen 'cause they, uh, my father said to my mother, you're turning her into a lesbian, and my mother said to my father, you're turning her into a lesbian. I didn't know what a lesbian was, but I knew I wasn't one. They sent me to this lesbian psychologist, who basically said, "Honey, just don't play with yourself in public." She was very supportive of me – she used to come to my concerts, I used to play concert piano.

I don't wanna waste my . . . I mean I said a lot of nasty stuff about men in this past tape, but I tell ya it's 'cause I have to deal with 'em day to day and they're shit about women. And loving women is so much more special and central and interesting . . . than even thinking about men. People think that being a lesbian is about hating men; what being a lesbian is, is loving women. I've fallen in love with Julie, who I've lived with for two years. And she has a career here. I mean there's the problem: that I feel like I should be in New York, but I love San Francisco. But I also love New York. I've fallen in love with Julie. I don't know. Music's been the most important thing in my life always . . . You wanna know what my goal in life is? I wanna be a wise old woman. And I figure I have a lot of teeth-cutting to do on the way. Moving to New York is one way of cutting teeth.

III. Night Spot: Marta Dane, San Francisco, 1981

Waitresses, I don't know, maybe more so since I'm female, more sensitive, but I think the fact that you're in a uniform makes you sort of substandard. I don't care who, you have to be subservient to them. They might be a piece of shit that just crawled in off the street, but since you're in a uniform, you're lower than them. That makes you the servant, you snap to attention, a lot of psychological things are involved. I think since they've paid for their membership, they think they're hot shit, and expect to be treated with an extra air of respect as a result. They expect instant service, superservice. I'm here, pay attention!

I was three years at the Starlight Roof and one year at the Yum-Yum. And then I worked about three jobs about three weeks each place, so say four-and-a-half years, all together [laughter]. God, how awful. When I started I thought, well, I needed the money, so I thought, I'll do it for about six months just to get a little money together and then go off and do something more respectful. And then I got hooked on the money. I got hooked on the money and on the punching in and punching out, not having to take responsibility, 'cause before that, the jobs previous to that had responsibility, like working long hours, no weekends, just constantly there, constantly responsible. I got hooked on the idea that you punch in, you do your work, you punch out, you go home. Nobody calls you, nobody bugs you. Then you get your two days off, no hassle, no aggravation. So it's a good job for a woman who's had no education, had no training, who needs to make a living. Because if I could type, I'd be working in an office, I'd be a secretary. So secretaries make what now? Nine, ten thousand? Depends on how good you are . . . So if I could type and do shorthand I'd be a secretary. But that would mean I would be sitting on my buns all day and I'd have to sit and concentrate on one little thing all day. Working as a waitress your body is being used, your body is functioning to an extent. This to me is important, maybe because I was a dancer for so many years. Physical movement is important to me. Having mobility you don't get working in an office with a lot of people, that's important.

I remember as a kid, I'd collect all these pamphlets. I'd write to the chamber of commerce . . . Florida, Georgia, Louisiana, exotic lands. My father died when I was five . . . fortunately, my mother, through manipulation and trade-offs, managed to get dancing lessons for me through the years. So I studied dancing from the time that I was four: twelve years of tap, ten years of ballet, three years of toe, three years of acrobatics, Javanese, Hawaiian, you name it, I had it. And I taught dancing for three years at a studio in Detroit. And there was an ad in the paper for young people to wait tables and dance in a northern Michigan resort, for twelve dollars a week and room and board, and my mother thought it might be just the ticket for a job for the summer. So she talked me into going to the audition and I went rather reluctantly because I felt that to get into any phase of show business you had to be glamorous and exciting and beautiful and I didn't think of myself as any of those things. But I went to the audition, and I got the job and I worked the whole summer and it gave me a taste of something I hadn't experienced before. And I decided I loved it. So when I went back to Detroit, or actually Farmington, I got a job in a chorus line and traveled with them for a year, and liked it sufficiently. Then I went out on my own, and I found out that a dancer doesn't make much money doing legitimate dancing and that being an exotic dancer brought more money in. So my agent talked me into working out an exotic act which I did and from then on it was uphill all the way. I hit the right thing, and I was making good money, and I had a lot of satisfaction out of it. I did it very well, everyone seemed to think so and I did it with class and sophistication and dignity and with a dance background. . . .

I actually didn't think of doing it for a great long time, because I can always remember from . . . high school, I suppose, at least in my era, that all young girls would sooner or later get married and have a family and I felt that that was what was expected would happen to me, and I rather looked forward to it. And I felt very strongly that I would not last any longer than my late twenties in show business, because it just didn't seem appropriate for a lady to be unmarried by the age of thirty. It was just considered appropriate for a lady to be a mother and a housewife, and I just wanted to be normal like everyone else. And when I saw people in nightclubs, women like dancers, or whatever they happened to be doing – if they were thirty or over I pitied them and thought it was a tragedy that these poor things were traveling around living out of a suitcase, without the home and husband and vine-covered cottage and the whole thing. And I just knew that I was going to be clever and sensible enough not to get caught in that trap. But I wasn't and I continued on and actually I thought a great deal about marriage and finding the right man, but in the meantime, I feel that I stayed on the carousel a bit too long. Because I think the brass ring has passed me by. That's sort of a frustrating feeling, but ah well. . . .

I started writing when I was in grade school and I wrote up until I was thirty. So that was quite a long time. I dried up, nothing else came out, that was it . . . nothing more to say, no more inspiration, no . . . something, I don't know, just ended, I don't know why.

Verity

Incomplete my life has been
of fortune, love and honest men
fortune one can do without,
love will one day come, no doubt,
but honest men, I greatly fear,
there is no such thing, my dear.

I'm reaching the point where I don't think love will come at all. I've reached the point where possibly I should stop thinking about that. So much for greatness.

Looking for Mr. Right was a lifetime career. It hasn't stopped yet. The big mistake I made was supporting my mother for nine years. That sort of screwed things up. Because nobody wants to support a mother-in-law. There's probably been a few Mr. Rights along the way, but it just so happened that they didn't come along at the right time or possibly in the right place and so I had to keep moving on. There were some situations, uh, more than a few possibly, that it just tore me apart for me to have to leave town, to leave a relationship, a very important relationship, but it was just the necessity of the circumstances: my mother depended on me, I had to send money home, I had to pay rent, I had to keep groceries on the table, I had to support myself on the road.

As far as meeting a man to settle down, like I say, for nine years the mother was a problem and then after that I was thirty and it was just never the right man, the right person, the right relationship, the right place, the right time – the right me, maybe. I don't know. I worked in Japan, Korea, Taiwan, Hong Kong, the Philippines, Malaysia.

The military – I hate them. I loathe them. I thought they were disgusting animals. At one point in Korea, I ended up in the middle of my act with a large glass of beer in my face. I was insulted and harassed in other places by these animals. In one place in Japan, a military base in the north, I ended up battering this disgusting animal over the head with my four-inch spike heel and he was taken to the hospital with nine stitches in his head. They don't know anything. They come to a show and want to see a girl take her clothes off, and if that's not happening, they're not satisfied. They want it lowdown, dirty, and graphic. That's all they understand.

Well, the first time I arrived in Calcutta, I arrived in a very bad state, because I'd canceled out of a booking in Thailand and things were going very badly there. I had been very sick, I was exhausted, mentally and physically. I decided not to go back to Hong Kong, I decided to visit my girlfriend in Calcutta instead. And my state of mind upon arrival there was a bit desperate. I needed a friend to take me in, I needed a corner to crawl into, I needed to be adopted by someone for awhile until I got my head together, my feet down, and myself established again. So being in India for the first time, I was impressed with the fact that the Indian women were respected and protected and honored. They were the center of the home, they received their identity from their husbands, they were a very important part of the family unit. And I felt very strongly that it would be the most wonderful thing in the world to be an Indian woman. Because that's what I needed, stability: I needed security, I needed a home, I needed protection. I needed someone to give me strength, someone to give me something to lean on. And meeting Kamal . . . the fact that he was very attractive helped, of course. I fell in love with him. I didn't fall in love with *him.* After it was all over, I realized I fell in love with what he represented and subconsciously I believed that through him I would become an Indian woman. And I was very wrong about that, I found out. And uh . . . it turned out rather badly, I found out. But

I spent four years trying to make it work. It never did. The problem, primarily, was the resistance of his family, because they didn't want an American messing up their bloodline, particularly an American in show business. That was a big no-no and he was the number one son. But then, all things considered, the family possibly did me a big favor . . . So it had to end: he wasn't what I wanted, he wasn't what I believed he would be, he betrayed me, he wasn't Mr. India, and therefore I could never be an Indian lady. So that's why I backed out and threw him out, and dumped the whole situation. It was just that he seemed to appear at a time that I needed someone who represented what I thought existed there. If he had been the person I had expected he would be, I think I would have been very satisfied, very happy being an Indian woman. I looked forward to it – the home, the family, the security, the housekeeping, the whole thing. If I had stayed there or gone back, I don't think I would have found it. It was something I had created in my mind and possibly did not exist.

Well, coming back to the States was kind of a decision that was made for me. I'd been living in Italy for a year and three months, very happily, and I was technically a mistress. I tried to avoid the situation, my boyfriend tried to help, the lady I was tutoring in English, the Contessina Agusta, she tried to pull strings in Rome to help me, but nothing did any good, being during the election. So I was given thirty days to leave the country and I went to Switzerland and stayed there for awhile and Franco finally decided that there was just no way to get around it and gave me money to get back to the States. I came back to San Francisco thinking that I would get a job and apply for a return and see if Franco or the contessa could arrange something on that end. Of course, the thing is, when you're out of sight, you're out of mind, so that's the end of that. I cried and struggled and prayed and saved my money and hoped that eventually I would get back there and after I was here for six months, I got a letter from Franco telling me that he'd gone back to his wife and that she was pregnant again. So that was the end of that. So I stayed, and I guess I'm better off for it. I guess.

So I like the Metropolitan Club. Sometimes you get bitches, but you get them everywhere, so what's the difference? I enjoy myself more when I wait on men, don't you? No, you're putting yourself in a situation where there's a comparison. You're a female, they're a female, what am I doing here and what are they doing there? I deserve it just as much as they do, so you have this resentment

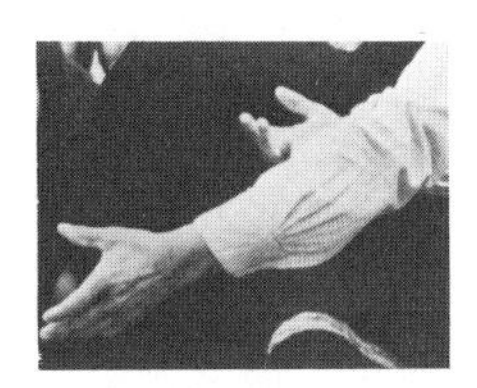

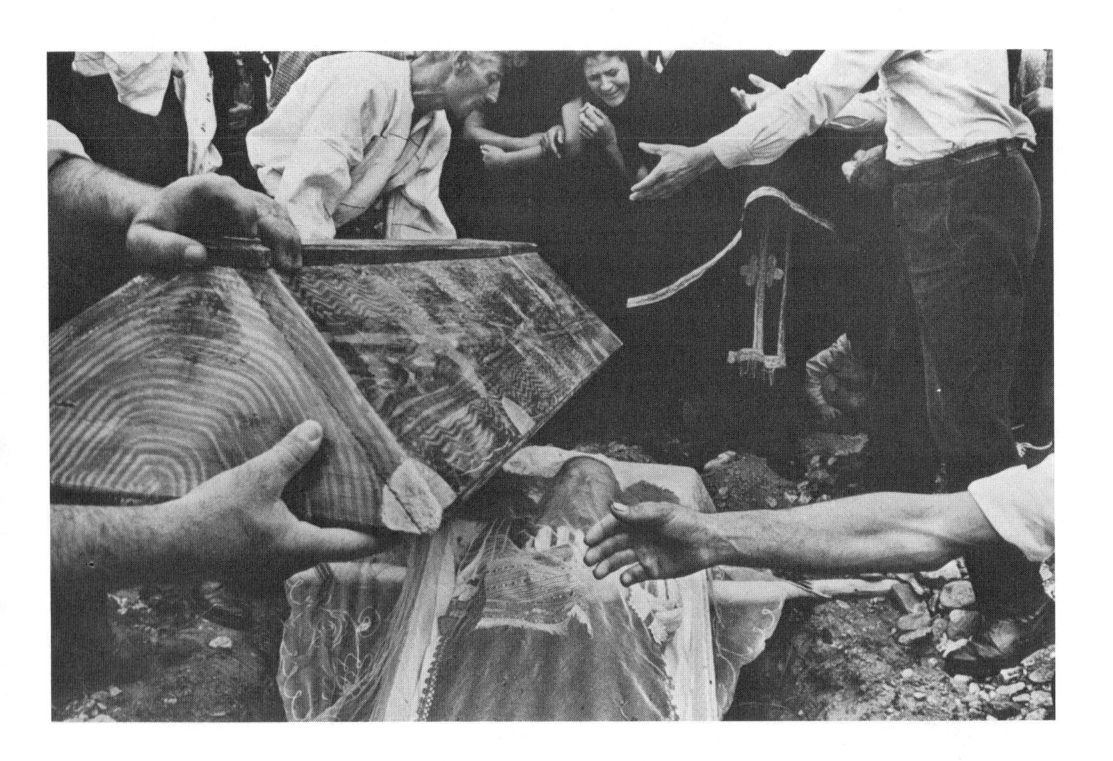

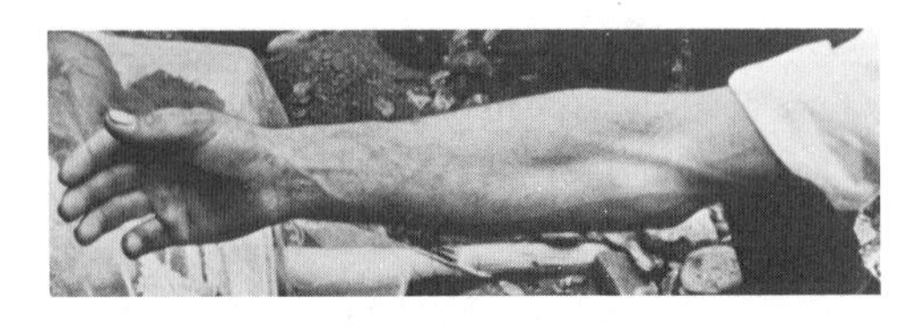

building up. It's there, you can't get away from it. Well, when they offered me the job as *maître d'* I was flattered. I was dumbfounded, they have never had a woman *maître d'* in the history of the club. As much as I had already decided to move to L.A., it was a great challenge as a woman. It was a chance for me to show myself and everyone else that I could do it just as well as a man. And in spite of the fact that they offered me less than they would have offered a man, I took it, because I felt that in the few months following I could prove that I was as good as a man, and possibly as a result they would pay me accordingly. Now that the three months have gone by they reviewed my performance and they've found it very much worthwhile. They're very happy with me in ways, as far as the administrative end of it at least. They still don't feel justified in paying me what they would be paying a man, so obviously on that basis I certainly would be less than satisfied in staying. I feel that there's nothing more to prove to anyone else. I've already proved it.

No, as far as the L.A. thing is concerned, it's just a matter of the agencies to call. There's enough agencies down there, and there're enough rich people down there. I should find something. I don't want to be a housekeeper, but being a social secretary or executive housekeeper is just right down my alley. It's sort of an abbreviated version of what I'm doing now. It's a necessity to be organized and efficient and it's something I dream of doing. I've always had the frustration of wanting to be a housewife. I've never had that opportunity, and being an executive housewife gives me the opportunity of managing a home, and to look after a family and do all the things that are required and I think I'll enjoy it. So therefore I'm moving on to greener pastures. That's all there is to it. For money or whatever.

Three Stories

JAMES CASEBERE

I. Horseback

From Chaos to Calm

Going down the road, hot under the collar, steaming in your seat, bursting at the seams, ready to kill. Get in my way and I'll cut your throat, I'll break your neck, I've had it, it's over, I can't take any more. You're losing grip, losing hold, losing that sense of direction. It's too hot, you get up and you're turning so fast, whirling so fast, little atom bomb, little dusty storm, so dry, settle down, settle to the ground. You move so fast, you need water, something to drink, water, yes, that's good, yes, now sit down.

Later

It's like your skin is gone, you feel something cool, it must be rain, but you're still asleep, or are you? Yes, it's rain and it's falling but it's no relief and you dream, feel, imagine, sense that the flesh on your scalp is gone, and so is the bone. The drops of rain strike like acid, but you can't feel a thing.

Needles

The Needles make up one long, horizontal image of strange phallic shapes, reaching up at the sky, irregular, assymetrical, rugged, eerie, smooth. The outside and in have become interchangeable. The distance, the illegibility of the forms: look down someone's throat, it looks like a cave.

The Great Mystery

The great mystery is change. It's the movement from one moment to the next, the relativity of truth, the illusion of total obsession. It is the peculiar logic of human motivation, the immersion in a self whose boundaries are like scabs to be picked; sensitive scabs, painful to the touch, getting bumped, starting slowly to heal.

The Red River Trail

Previously propelled by inner pain, it surrounds you now, waiting to engulf you. You don't know where you belong, you keep moving, shifting, not settling. You could go up the wrong canyon and be killed. What if you could leave your body, levitate up and look down, see the mess you're in and see the way out?

The Road West

Moving west on the Chisholm Trail. The road west was the trail of men looking for one more adventure after the next. One more sight to see, one more little conquest. Don't stop, keep it rolling, over mountains and fields, crossing rivers, mudflats, and sun-parched desert plateaus. The ultimate obstacle course, with wild Indians on every side, rattlesnakes under every rock, and ahead of you nothing but the great frontier. For the adventurous, stopping could only be one great disappointment. Stopping meant stopping time. It could mean an end to conquest and an end to change.

But, all across the continent, men would finally grow tired and, in an effort to stop time, they built the West. So, above all, when these men stopped, they built Empires. Everywhere they went, they'd stake a claim and erect their own little Imperial Domain, extending themselves into a realm beyond change, a realm of total control. "No more Indians, please, I've had enough." They made themselves secure.

Darkness

So, there you are, beat. It's dark now, the crickets are chirping. There's a dry wind blowing in from the East. The back of your throat feels like fine sandpaper rubbing against your tongue. Sandman, stay away, I've got to stay awake. You dip your finger in the pot of coffee, thick like molasses, rub it against your teeth, then suck it clean. You want to scream. The fire rises in the wind. You shiver. Your stomach turns. It turns again. A little more, again and again, and again. You gather some dry earth, cupped in your hands, and let it fall fast, in a mess at your feet as you pull away.

II. Snake

You'd been moving at night now to avoid the heat or being spotted by either hostiles or army patrols. Your scalp, being worth more to a white man in gold than a renegade in prestige, was something you had hoped to keep. At least the white man would kill you first (of course, this could involve being dragged behind his horse by a rope for a mile or two first), then take his knife to your skull above the ear and, cutting a circle round your head, give it a good yank. The fact is no one likes to get skinned alive or cut up into half a dozen or so pieces. (Which was also likely with the redskins if you failed to put up a good fight.) So, the idea was not to get seen or taken alive. Knowing one foe to be more skilled and the other more determined, you could only slither along on your belly at night, and hide between the rocks to sleep by day.

III. Hell

This particular town didn't really belong here at all. Speculators, hoping for the railroad, put it up one day and the train never came. It went clear through to the northern pass, never sending a spur south at all. So, the goldminers (what was left of them) came to get their supplies, the cattle ranchers too, and the Pony Express galloped by two days a week.

But the town remained because no one had the energy or money to tear it down or burn it. It was a lucky traveler who left on his own two feet. Most ended up, oh, maybe three feet underground in an unmarked grave.

Sounds in the Distance

DAVID WOJNAROWICZ

Boy in Y.M.C.A. (San Francisco)

I arrived here by Greyhound . . . I had one of them Ameri-pass tickets . . . It was good for two months – I started out in New York City . . . Figured they wouldn't be able to follow me if I rode the bus – I didn't stay in one city too long and I'd decide what direction I was gonna go in only after I was at the bus station – but they would always find out where I was going and follow me . . . I'd be sitting on the bus – I'd choose a seat by myself and look out the window . . . at first the people who got on looked normal . . . like I didn't know them and they'd act like they didn't know me . . . then, after an hour or so of riding – they'd all be talking in general conversations between themselves and then after awhile they would start to let little words or sentences slip into the conversation . . . things that only I would know about . . . little references to what happened in New York . . . like I knew this guy . . . we were lovers and after a year of living together he suddenly didn't want to live with me anymore . . . I was really upset . . . like I knew his parents didn't know he was a homosexual . . . so I called his mother up and told her . . . I know it was fucked up, but I didn't think about it . . . another time I called the police on this other guy I knew – there was some murderer going around . . . I told the police that he was the one doing it . . . he was a dealer and when the cops got in his apartment they found the stuff . . . I felt guilty about it and tried suicide . . . I got really sick . . . I swallowed this bottle of some kind of pills and just got really sick . . . then I realized that's what they wanted me to do, so I left New York . . . but they always catch up to me . . . I'm really tired of running . . . I have no more money and this is the end of it for me . . . I don't know exactly what I'm gonna do . . . I just wish I would die . . . that's all I'm waiting for now . . . I can't do it myself, but I don't want to go on just existing . . . just waiting for it to happen . . . everywhere I go, I find people who I think might not be part of the plan . . . then after awhile I began to realize that they're just acting like strangers . . . they're just waiting for me to do it . . . like you . . . I don't know why I'm talking to you . . . for a few minutes I thought you were okay . . . but as I keep talking I see little things going on in your expressions – so I'm not really sure. . . .

. . . I keep having these strange dreams . . . last night I dreamt that I was a giant . . . I was draped over the planet . . . my head resting on North America and my legs resting on South America . . . my arms stretched for miles and miles over the ocean . . . and these fish – I could feel millions of fish just below the surface of the water . . . I could feel them nibbling on my arms . . . real gentle. . . .

Guy in Waterfront Hotel (San Francisco)

See here on this map . . . I was born in Austin, Texas . . . see right here . . . my father had me seeing the bishop all the time – I was a very religious child . . . one time the bishop was talking about gay people . . . I'd never known what they were . . . I was a pretty quiet kid – you know, didn't know *anything* – so when I heard what he was saying about them I wondered: "Now what's wrong with them for doing that?" . . . So I went outside and down the street and into the Gulch Bar – Gulch Bar . . . Gulch Restaurant . . . Gulch Bakery . . . everything in that town was called Gulch – So I went into the Gulch Bar and picked me up a cowboy and I told him what I wanted him to do to me and we went right home and did it . . . when the bishop found out he was upset . . . he said: "Boy . . . you have an authority problem." An authority problem – me? Aha ha ha . . . so that's when my father moved us up to Colorado . . . see this line I've drawn on the map? Well, from here my brother was sent into the army . . . then my father was sent over to Pennsylvania in order to work and he died . . . the next thing I know my mother's on the phone talking to god knows who . . . saying: "You promised me that when his father died you would get him work." She was talking about me . . . d'you understand? "*When his father died you would get him work.*" . . . That bitch – she knew what was going to happen . . . so I go to the bishop and ask him certain questions about god – he says: "Now, Gordon . . . we won't have people doubting their god." I said: "What? I'm asking questions because I want to learn . . . not because I doubt." And the next thing I know I'm in Salt Lake City surrounded by Mormons and they're handing me my robe . . . now I don't know how I got there – they just appeared . . . so I became a Mormon – so that takes me from here to there . . . see the direction the lines are moving in? Well, after three months of being a Mormon I called up my mother and said: "Mom . . . I just saw people vanish into thin air . . . melting on the street . . ." I was walking down the street in Salt Lake City and people were vanishing left and right so I called my mother and told her . . . and do you know what she said? She said: "But, Gordon . . . don't let it upset you . . . they're just not there – they're not real." Aha ha ha . . . So I said: "This means war." And the next thing I know I'm in a uniform and in Vietnam . . . VIETNAM! Now, hell . . . how the hell did I get there? . . . the last thing I can remember saying is: "Shit . . . this means war," and here I was surrounded by artillery fire – not from the North Vietnamese, but from the fucking lieutenants . . . the generals . . . they didn't know what the fuck they were doing . . . the soldiers didn't know what they were there for . . . who they were fighting . . . nighttime and bombs were exploding all around us . . . I was in the trenches and some guy next to me said: "Gordon . . . is that a fetal position?" And I would turn and look at the body next to me huddled in the mud and say: "Ha ha . . . yes, that's a fetal position." And we'd take our field glasses and look through them into the fires and see men crossing the fields smoking joints . . . I'd yell out: "Yeah . . . now I am . . . ha ha." So now the line moves from North America all the way around half the world to Southeast Asia and then they send me back home . . . so I ended up over in Berkeley . . . I was in a house living with some friends of my mother's and that's when Mrs. Robinson shows up out of nowhere – just materializes out of the air . . . she was this black woman and do you know what she said to me one time? She said: "You want *everything*, don't you?" Aha ha heh . . . that bitch . . . here I was on foodstamps and not a penny to my name and she tells me: you want everything . . . ha ha . . . well, she didn't last long – when that creature appeared in the corner of the ceiling one day . . . waving its arms and saying: "I am god reincarnated," Mrs. Robinson took one look at it and ran screaming from the house . . . It said: "I am god reincarnated . . . I'm a Jehovah's Witness." . . . So the line of travel comes from Vietnam to Berkeley . . . now I'm here in San Francisco and planning to go to a logging mill up in Portland for a couple of months . . . but see? – That's what their plan is . . . they want me to go north because that's where the reincarnation process starts . . . see . . . my father was reincarnated into Patrick, the guy who lives downstairs . . . see – Patrick's eyes are my father's eyes . . . me – I don't know exactly where I fit into their plans . . . I'm sure it's my mother's doing

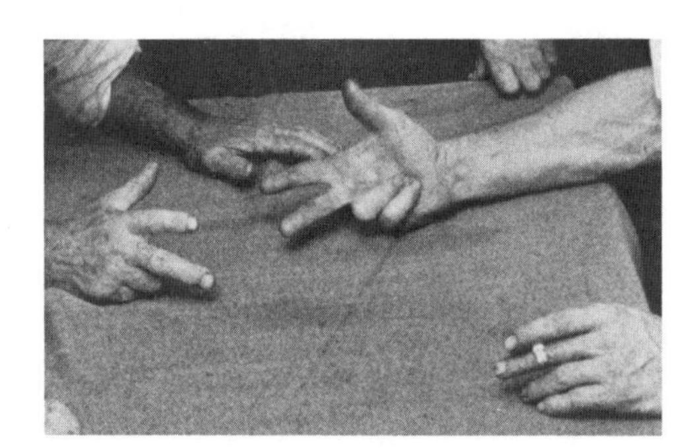

though . . . I should go back and see her and ask her questions and hold a fucking rifle to her head and if she don't give the right answers I'll blow that bitch's head off. . . .

Fourteen-Year-Old Runaway Girl (Woodstock, New York)

I think I need some kind of care – not mental care, ya know, but medical care, because I think my heart's bad . . . I gotta bad heart – I get heart attacks all the time . . . I'm thinkin' of gettin' work somewhere, but I don't have I.D. – I lost my birth certificate and I don't remember what hospital I was born in . . . my father died and my mother's livin' in Florida . . . I just keep movin' around . . . Ya know what I'm doing? I'm lookin' for Bob Dylan, ya know . . . I think he's in California, but maybe he's back in New York City . . . but I figure I gotta be in control of myself before I meet him . . . I don't want him to say: "Hey look – you're just a little kid . . . real young . . . ya gotta grow up."

I only talk with guys that got hook noses . . . with noses like Bob Dylan's . . . I find I can usually get along with them . . . like, they're more sensitive . . . I talk to sensitive guys 'cause they're good for me . . . they know what I'm talkin' about . . . they do things for me, ya know? I sometimes talk with guys with other kinds of noses . . . like yours. . . .

. . . I was in a program for a while – I was in a hospital . . . They taught me to see myself . . . let myself come through . . . that's why I'm much nicer than last year . . . last year I was angry and all, but that was because people would come up and make faces at me . . . people play a lot of games, ya know? At the hospital I went through a lot of stuff . . . sometimes I'd get real angry – I wouldn't get violent . . . I'm not a violent person – I'd get physical, ya know? . . . like, I'd hit somebody but, like, I knew what I was doing . . . it was like a game . . . like, I'd say to myself: "I'll hit that person and then I'll say I'm sorry." . . . but the program was good – they had me on detroxin or de-stroxan or something like that . . . a shot every two weeks – not a shot that hurt – and I'd feel good . . .

. . . I don't hitchhike – I'll hitchhike only if I know the place I'm going . . . like, if I'm goin' to Jersey I'd hitchhike 'cause I know Jersey . . . but I meet strange guys on the road – one time I was hitchin' in Kansas and this big fat guy picked me up . . . we were drivin' along and all of a sudden he reached over and grabbed my arm – I said: "Oh shit" and tried to jump out of the car . . . he wouldn't let me, so I quick tore my arm away and got the door open and jumped out . . . He yelled out at me: "DON'T YOU GET BACK IN *THIS* CAR, GIRLIE."

. . . I gotta get some I.D. so I can go to work, but I don't remember what hospital I was born in . . . and my mother died and my father retired and is somewhere in Florida, so I can't get the name of the hospital . . . I figure, maybe I should go back to the program . . . that's the best thing for me, 'cause my image of myself is totally shattered . . . I might have pneumonia . . . I got this terrible cough and I'm allergic to sugar . . . I wanna get me a guitar and a harmonica once I start workin' . . . then I can practice and get good at it . . . and then I'll go down to the Village around Bleecker Street and find me some folkies and we'll all live together and get the revolution started again.

Girl Sitting on Pavement in Front of Coffee Shop (Albuquerque, New Mexico)

I live over in a hotel a few miles from here – I come down just about every day since I quit my job . . . I was working as a waitress in a restaurant downtown – worked at it for two years . . . I don't know how I did it for so long – it's like the time just went by behind my back . . . before I became a waitress I hitched all over the U.S. – I'm originally from San Antonio – my family still lives there and I hate the place . . . the people there are almost dead . . . all into their little trips with the way they think lives should run . . . the way their folks taught them – my father had a lot of money and my two sisters got married real young – I didn't want nothing to do with the whole apron thing . . . I just wanted to run around – I mean there's just so much going on in just the States alone that it makes me dizzy just to think of what I'm missing sitting here . . . my father said he'd cut me out of the will if I didn't go to school, so I split – it's kinda romantic, ya know . . . I mean I've been hitching around for the past five years . . . lived just about everywhere and mostly followed the migrant people picking produce and stuff – what got to me was that it was only romantic because I had the choice . . . I mean there was some real tight security behind me if I chose to go back . . . but no – I was tough and could make it on my own . . . well, after awhile I realized that my father's money – that security – was sitting on my back and when the going got a little too rough it was always there . . . couldn't shake it at all . . . so I worked this waitress job because I was tired and I thought maybe I could settle down a little bit and do some thinking instead of all that continuous experiencing – but, man . . . after two years I'd go to work and I'd sit down after serving all those people – let me tell you – there's two things in life people really get bitchy about – one's money and the other thing's their food – I'd hassle with these people over food and then sit down and, like . . . the counter is over here and the kitchen is over there and the windows are here and the door is there and it's the same thing for two years in a row every day . . . so a couple of weeks ago I was sitting there and all of a sudden it all made sense – the fucking door, man . . . that's the only part of the job I really liked – walking out that fucking door . . . I mean everything's outside . . . like how much it picked me up just to walk through the door . . . so I said: "That's it . . . I quit." – So I have money saved up – not a whole lot, but enough to let me make some plans to go somewhere else . . . right now I'm just taking it easy and thinking . . . I come down here because there's a lot going on on this street . . . all these people rushing around helps make sense to how I live . . . my movement, ya know . . . how I want to live . . . like nomads really did have their shit together . . . and check that out, man . . . look at that moon . . . ya know, I look at the moon nowadays and I find it difficult to make out the features . . . I can't see the face any longer . . . like, I don't know if it's getting full again or if it's getting smaller . . . and I've never seen a red moon before or a moon as red as that. . . .

. . . this afternoon I was sitting out here and I was watching those prostitutes across the street – and one of them stepped out of the doorway and took this little guy with a guitar by the hand . . . he had just jumped off some dumptruck from Arizona . . . she took him by the hand really gentle, like he was a kid going to school for the first time . . . and, like, they walked down the street to the hotel together – him carrying this guitar without a case . . . like, he played that guitar all around the country just to end up in some squeaky bed in a ratty hotel where somebody's gonna hold him for awhile . . . even for ten minutes, ya know . . . and, like, I felt kind of sad because that's really it – it's never any more than that scene . . . and when it becomes more . . . then the whole idea of measure in your life is forgotten . . . you never make sense of nothing. . . .

Words in Reverse

LAURIE ANDERSON

The detective novel is the only type of novel truly invented in the twentieth century. In the detective novel, the hero is dead in the very beginning. So you don't have to deal with human nature at all . . . Only the slow accumulation of facts – of data. You must put the hero together yourself.

It was up in Canada and it was August, but very cold. I had been staying on this Cree Indian reservation for a few days, just sort of hanging around. One day, some anthropologist showed up at the reservation. They came in a little plane with maple leaves painted on the wings. They said they were there to shoot a documentary of the Cree Indians. They set up their video equipment in a tin Quonset hut next to the Hudson Bay company. Then they asked the oldest man on the reservation to come and sing some songs for their documentary. On the day of the taping, the old man arrived. He was blind and wearing a red plaid shirt. They turned on some lights and he started to sing. But he kept starting over and sweating. Pretty soon it was clear that he really didn't know any of the songs. He just kept starting over and sweating and rocking back and forth. The only words he really seemed sure of were "Hey ah . . . hey ah hey . . . hey hey hey ah hey . . . hey . . ."

"HEY AH HEY HEY HEY AH HEY . . . I am singing the songs . . . HEY AH HEY AH HEY . . . the old songs . . . but I can't remember the words to the songs . . . HEY HEY HEY AH HEY . . . the old hunting songs . . . I am singing the songs of my fathers and of the animals they hunted down . . . HEY HEY HEY AH HEY . . . I never knew the words of the old songs . . . HEY HEY AH HEY HEY HEY HEY AH HEY . . . I never went hunting in the piney woods . . . HEY HEY AH AH HEY AH HEY . . . I never sang the songs . . . HEY AH HEY . . . of my fathers . . . HEY HEY AH HEY . . . I am singing for this movie . . . HEY AH . . . I am doing this for money . . . HEY HEY AH HEY . . . I remember Grandfather . . . he lay on his back while he was dying . . . HEY AH HEY HEY AH HEY . . . I think I am no one . . . HEY HEY AH HEY . . ."

I saw a photograph of Nicola Tesla, who invented the Tesla Coil. He also invented a pair of shoes with soles four inches thick to ground him while he worked in his laboratory. In this picture, Tesla is sitting in his lab, wearing the shoes, and reading a book by the light of the long, streamer-like sparks shooting out of his transformers.

It was an ancient Japanese pot, incised with grooves. Thin-ridged grooves. Grooves all around it. It looked like one of those collapsible paper lanterns. It was an experiment. The pot was placed on a turntable and the turntable began to revolve. A needle was set into the groove. A stereo needle. They were waiting to hear the voice of the potter potting the pot 2,000 years ago. They were hoping the sounds of the potter had somehow been embedded into the clay. The pot turned around and around like a record being treadled into the third dimension. It turned. They listened. They were listening. Some of them heard an unidentifiable Japanese dialect, rapid and high. Some of them heard high-pitched static. The needle dug into the pot. The needle was getting blunt. More and more blunt . . . it was that scientific. Blunter and scientific. More blunt . . . and more scientific.

You're walking . . . and you don't always realize it but you're always falling. With each step . . . you fall. You fall forward a short way and then catch yourself. Over and over . . . you are falling . . . and then catch yourself. You keep falling and catching yourself falling. And this is how you are walking and falling at the same time

I went to a palm reader and the odd thing about the reading was that everything she told me was totally wrong. But she seemed so sure of the information that I began to feel like I'd been walking around with these false documents permanently tattooed to my hands. It was very noisy in the parlor and members of her family kept running in and out. They were speaking a high, clicking kind of language that sounded a lot like Arabic. Books and magazines in Arabic were strewn all over the floor. It suddenly occurred to me that maybe there was a translation problem – that maybe she was reading my hand from right to left instead of left to right. Thinking of mirrors, I gave her my other hand. Then she put her hand out and we sat there for several minutes in what I assumed was some sort of participatory ritual. Finally I realized that her hand was out because she was waiting for money.

Last night I dreamed I was lying in bed sleeping. Last night I dreamed all night that I was just lying in bed dreaming I was sleeping. Last night I dreamed I was sleeping.

It was the night flight from Houston – almost perfect visibility. You could see the lights from all the little Texas towns far below. I was sitting next to a fifty-two-year-old woman who had never been on a plane before. Her son had sent her a ticket and said, "Mom, you've raised ten kids, it's time you got on a plane." She was sitting in the window seat, staring out. She kept talking about the Big Dipper and the Little Dipper and pointing. Suddenly I realized she thought we were in Outer Space, looking down at the stars. I said, "I think those lights down there are the lights from little towns."

I . . . I AM IN MY BODY . . . I AM IN MY BODY THE WAY . . . I AM IN MY BODY THE WAY MOST PEOPLE DRIVE . . . I AM IN BY BODY THE WAY MOST PEOPLE DRIVE THEIR CARS.

You know when you're driving at night it can suddenly occur to you that maybe you're going in completely the wrong direction. That turn you took back there . . . you were really tired and it was dark and raining and you took the turn and you just started going that way and then the rain stops and it starts to get light and you look around and absolutely everything is completely unfamiliar. You know you've never been here before and you pull into the next gas station and you feel so awkward saying, "Excuse me, can you tell me where I am?"

You can read the signs. You've been on this road before. Do you want to go home?

Hello, excuse me, can you tell me where I am?

You can read the sign language. In our country, good-bye looks just like hello. This is the way we say hello. Say hello.

Hello, excuse me, can you tell me where I am?

In our country, good-bye looks just like hello. It is a diagram between two points. It is shorthand for last night you were here and then when I woke up in the morning you were gone. In our country, good-bye looks just like hello.

Hello, excuse me, can you tell me where I am?

You can read the signs. This is our sign language. It is a diagram of movement between two points. It is a sweep on the dial. It is shorthand for you moved away and I'll never forgive myself for not spending more time with you now that you're gone. In our country, this is the way we say hello. This is the way we say good-bye. Say hello.

Hello, excuse me, can you tell me where I am?

In our country, we send the pictures of our sign language into outer space. They are speaking our sign language in these pictures. Do you think they will think his hand is permanently attached that way? Or do you think they will read our signs? In our country, good-bye looks just like hello. It is a sweep on the dial. In our country, you don't ever know if you have really arrived. You don't even know if you have left yet. In our country, good-bye looks just like hello. Say hello.

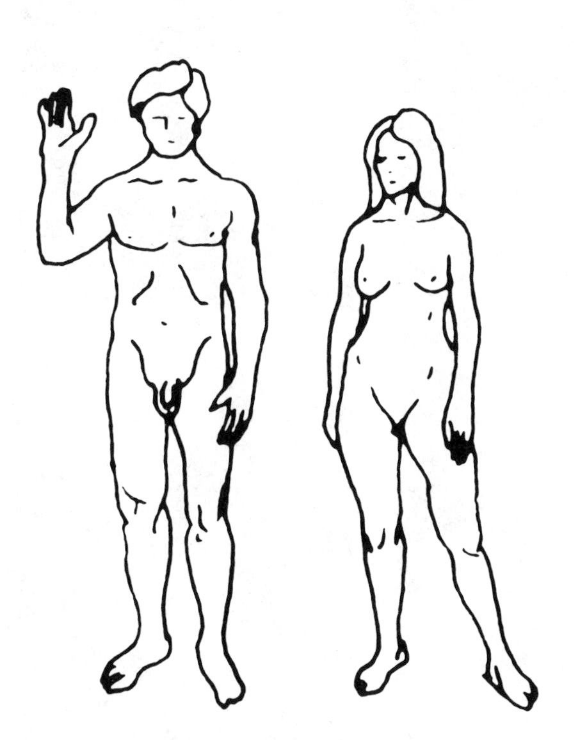

2. The Order of Things

A Tour of the Monuments of Passaic, New Jersey

ROBERT SMITHSON

He laughed softly. "I know. There's no way out. Not through the Barrier. Maybe that isn't what I want, after all. But this – this – " He stared at the Monument. "It seems all wrong sometimes. I just can't explain it. It's the whole city. It makes me feel haywire. Then I get these flashes–"

Henry Kuttner
Jesting Pilot

. . . today our unsophisticated cameras record in their own way our hastily assembled and painted world.

Vladimir Nabokov
Invitation to a Beheading

On Saturday, September 30, 1967, I went to the Port Authority Building on 41st Street and Eighth Avenue. I bought a copy of the *New York Times* and a Signet paperback called *Earthworks* by Brian Aldiss. Next I went to ticket booth 21 and purchased a one-way ticket to Passaic. After that I went up to the upper bus level (platform 173) and boarded the number 30 bus of the Inter-City Transportation Co.

I sat down and opened the *Times*. I glanced over the art section: a "Collectors', Critics', Curators' Choice" at A. M. Sachs Gallery (a letter I got in the mail that morning invited me "to play the game before the show closes October 4th"), Walter Schatzki was selling "Prints, Drawings, Watercolors" at "33⅓% off," Elinor Jenkins, the "Romantic Realist," was showing at Barzansky Galleries, XVIII-XIX Century English Furniture on sale at Parke-Bernet, "New Directions in German Graphics" at Goethe House, and on page 29 was John Canaday's column. He was writing on "Themes and the Usual Variations." I looked at a blurry reproduction of Samuel F. B. Morse's *Allegorical Landscape* at the top of Canaday's column; the sky resembled sensitive stains of sweat reminiscent of a famous

Yugoslav watercolorist whose name I have forgotten. A little statue with right arm held high faced a pond (or was it the sea?). "Gothic" buildings in the allegory had a faded look, while an unnecessary tree (or was it a cloud of smoke?) seemed to puff up on the left side of the landscape. Canaday referred to the picture as "standing confidently along with other allegorical representatives of the arts, sciences, and high ideals that universities foster." My eyes stumbled over the newsprint, over such headlines as "Seasonal Upswing," "A Shuffle Service," and "Moving a 1,000 Pound Sculpture Can Be a Fine Work of Art, Too." Other gems of Canaday's dazzled my mind as I passed through Secaucus. "Realistic waxworks of raw meat beset by vermin" (Paul Thek), "Mr. Bush and his colleagues are wasting their time" (Jack Bush), "a book, an apple on a saucer, a rumpled cloth" (Thyra Davidson). Outside the bus window a Howard Johnson's Motor Lodge flew by – a symphony in orange and blue. On page 31 in Big Letters: THE EMERGING POLICE STATE IN AMERICA SPY GOVERNMENT. "In this book you will learn . . . what an Infinity Transmitter is."

The bus turned off Highway 2, down Orient Way in Rutherford.

I read the blurbs and skimmed through *Earthworks*. The first sentence read, "The dead man drifted along in the breeze." It seemed the book was about a soil shortage, and the *Earthworks* referred to the manufacture of artificial soil. The sky over Rutherford was a clear cobalt blue, a perfect Indian summer day, but the sky in *Earthworks* was a "great black and brown shield on which moisture gleamed."

The bus passed over the first monument. I pulled the buzzer cord and got off at the corner of Union Avenue and River Drive. The monument was a bridge over the Passaic River that connected Bergen County with Passaic County. Noon-day sunshine cinema-ized the site, turning the bridge and the river into an overexposed *picture*. Photographing it with my Instamatic 400 was like photographing a photograph. The sun became a monstrous light bulb that projected a detached series of "stills" through my Instamatic into my eye. When I walked on the bridge, it was as though I was walking on an enormous photograph that was made of wood and steel, and underneath, the river existed as an enormous movie film that showed nothing but a continuous blank.

The steel road that passed over the water was in part an open grating flanked by wooden sidewalks, held up by a heavy set of beams, while above, a ramshackle network hung in the air. A rusty sign glared in the sharp atmosphere, making it hard to read. A date flashed in the sunshine . . . 1899 . . . No . . . 1896 . . . maybe (at the bottom of the rust and glare was the name Dean & Westbrook Contractors, N.Y.). I was completely controlled by the Instamatic (or what the rationalists call a camera). The glassy air of New Jersey defined the structural parts of the monument as I took snapshot after snapshot. A barge seemed fixed to the surface of the water as it came toward the bridge, and caused the bridgekeeper to close the gates. From the banks of Passaic I watched the bridge rotate on a central axis in order to allow an inert rectangular shape to pass with its unknown cargo. The Passaic (west) end of the bridge rotated south, while the Rutherford (east) end of the bridge rotated north; such rotations suggested the limited movements of an outmoded world. "North" and "south" hung over the static river in a bipolar manner. One could refer to this bridge as the "Monument of Dislocated Directions."

Along the Passaic River banks were many minor monuments such as concrete abutments that supported the shoulders of a new highway in the process of being built. River Drive was in part bulldozed and in part intact. It was hard to tell the new highway from the old road; they were both confounded into a unitary chaos. Since it was Saturday, many machines were not working, and this caused them to resemble prehistoric creatures trapped in the mud, or, better, extinct machines – mechanical dinosaurs stripped of their skin. On the edge of this prehistoric Machine Age were pre- and post-World War II suburban houses. The houses mirrored themselves into colorlessness. Children were throwing rocks at each other near a ditch. "From now on you're not going to come to our hide-out. And I mean it!" said a little blonde girl who had been hit with a rock.

As I walked north along what was left of River Drive, I saw a monument in the middle of the river – it was a pumping derrick with a long pipe attached to it. The pipe was supported in part by a set of pontoons, while the rest of it extended about three blocks along the river bank till it disappeared into the earth. One could hear debris rattling in the water that passed through the great pipe.

Nearby, on the river bank, was an artificial crater that contained a pale limpid pond of water, and from the side of the crater protruded six large pipes that gushed the water of the pond into the river. This constituted a monumental fountain that suggested six horizontal smokestacks that seemed to be flooding the river with liquid smoke. The great pipe was in some enigmatic way connected with the infernal fountain. It was as though the pipe was secretly sodomizing some hidden technological orifice, and causing a monstrous sexual organ (the fountain) to have an orgasm. A psychoanalyst might say that the landscape displayed "homosexual tendencies," but I will not draw such a crass anthropomorphic conclusion. I will merely say, "It was there."

Across the river in Rutherford one could hear the faint voice of a P.A. system and the weak cheers of a crowd at a football game. Actually, the landscape was no landscape, but "a particular kind of heliotypy" (Nabokov), a kind of self-destroying postcard world of failed immortality and oppressive grandeur. I had been wandering in a moving picture that I couldn't quite picture, but just as I became perplexed, I saw a green sign that explained everything:

YOUR HIGHWAY TAXES 21 AT WORK

Federal Highway Trust Funds	U.S. Dept. of Commerce Bureau of Public Roads State Highway Funds
2,867,000	2,867,000

New Jersey State Highway Dept.

That zero panorama seemed to contain *ruins in reverse,* that is—all the new construction that would eventually be built. This is the opposite of the "romantic ruin" because the buildings don't *fall* into ruin *after* they are built, but rather *rise* into ruin *before* they are built. This antiromantic *mise-en-scène* suggests the discredited idea of *time* and many other "out of date" things. But the suburbs exist without a rational past and without the "big events" of history. Oh, maybe there are a few statues, a legend, and a couple of curios, but no past—just what passes for a future. A Utopia minus a bottom, a place where the machines are idle, and the sun has turned to glass, and a place where the Passaic Concrete Plant (253 River Drive) does a good business in STONE, BITUMINOUS, SAND, and CEMENT. Passaic seems full of "holes" compared to New York City, which seems tightly packed and solid, and those holes in a sense are the monumental vacancies that define, without trying, the memory-traces of an abandoned set of futures. Such futures are found in grade B Utopian films, and then imitated by the suburbanite. The windows of City Motors auto sales proclaim the existence of Utopia through 1968 WIDE TRACK PONTIACS – Executive, Bonneville, Tempest, Grand Prix, Firebird, GTO, Catalina, and LeMans – that visual incantation marked the end of the highway construction.

Next I descended into a set of used car lots. I must say the situation seemed like a change. Was I in a new territory? (An English artist, Michael Baldwin, says, "It could be asked if the country does in fact change – it does not in the sense a traffic light does.") Perhaps I had slipped into a lower stage of futurity – did I leave the real future behind in order to advance into a false future? Yes, I did. Reality was behind me at that point in my suburban Odyssey.

Passaic center loomed like a dull adjective. Each "store" in it was an adjective unto the next, a chain of adjectives disguised as stores. I began to run out of film, and I was getting hungry. Actually, Passaic center was no center – it was instead a typical abyss or an ordinary void. What a great place for a gallery! Or maybe an "outdoor sculpture show" would pep that place up.

At the Golden Coach Diner (11 Central Avenue) I had my lunch, and loaded my Instamatic. I looked at the orange-yellow box of Kodak Verichrome Pan, and read a notice that said:

> READ THIS NOTICE:
>
> This film will be replaced if defective in manufacture, labeling, or packaging, even though caused by our negligence or other fault. Except for such replacement, the sale or any subsequent handling of this film is without other warranty or liability. EASTMAN KODAK COMPANY DO NOT OPEN THIS CARTRIDGE OR YOUR PICTURES MAY BE SPOILED – 12 EXPOSURES – SAFETY FILM – ASA 125 22 DIN.

After that I returned to Passaic, or was it the *hereafter* – for all I know that unimaginative suburb could have been a clumsy eternity, a cheap copy of The City of the Immortals. But who am I to entertain such a thought? I walked down a parking lot that covered the old railroad tracks which at one time ran through the middle of Passaic. That monumental parking lot divided the city in half, turning it into a mirror and a reflection – but the mirror kept changing places with the reflection. One never knew what side of the mirror one was on. There was nothing *interesting* or even strange about that flat monument, yet it echoed a kind of cliché idea of infinity; perhaps the "secrets of the universe" are just as pedestrian – not to say dreary. Everything about the site remained wrapped in blandness and littered with shiny cars – one after another they extended into a sunny nebulosity. The indifferent backs of the cars flashed and reflected the stale afternoon sun. I took a few listless, entropic snapshots of that lustrous monument. If the future is "out of date" and "old fashioned," then I had been in the future. I had been on a planet that had a map of Passaic drawn over it, and a rather imperfect map at that. A sidereal map marked up with "lines" the size of streets, and "squares" and "blocks" the size of buildings. At any moment my feet were apt to fall through the cardboard ground. I am convinced that the future is lost somewhere in the dumps of the nonhistorical past; it is in yesterday's newspapers, in the *jejune* advertisements of science-fiction movies, in the false mirror of our rejected dreams. Time turns metaphors into *things,* and stacks them up in cold rooms, or places them in the celestial playgrounds of the suburbs.

Has Passaic replaced Rome as The Eternal City? If certain cities of the world were placed end to end in a straight line according to size, starting with Rome, where would Passaic be in that impossible progression? Each city would be a three-dimensional mirror that would reflect the next city into existence. The limits of eternity seem to contain such nefarious ideas.

The last monument was a sandbox or a model desert. Under the dead light of the Passaic afternoon the desert became a map of infinite disintegration and forgetfulness. This monument of minute particles blazed under a bleakly glowing sun, and suggested the sullen dissolution of entire continents, the drying up of oceans – no longer were there green forests and high mountains – all that existed were millions of grains of sand, a vast deposit of bones and stones pulverized into dust. Every grain of sand was a dead metaphor that equaled timelessness, and to decipher such metaphors would take one through the false mirror of eternity. This sandbox somehow doubled as an open grave – a grave that children cheerfully play in.

> *. . . all sense of reality was gone. In its place had come deep-seated illusions, absence of pupillary reaction to light, absence of knee reaction – symptoms all of progressive cerebral meningitis: the blanketing of the brain . . .*
>
> Louis Sullivan, "one of the greatest of all architects," quoted in Michel Butor's *Mobile*

I should now like to prove the irreversibility of eternity by using a *jejune* experiment for proving entropy. Picture in your mind's eye the sandbox divided in half with black sand on one side and white sand on the other. We take a child and have him run hundreds of times clockwise in the box until the sand gets mixed and begins to turn grey; after that we have him run anticlockwise, but the result will not be a restoration of the original division but a greater degree of greyness and an increase in entropy.

Of course, if we filmed such an experiment we could prove the reversibility of eternity by showing the film backwards, but then sooner or later the film itself would crumble or get lost and enter the state of irreversibility. Somehow this suggests that the cinema offers an illusive or temporary escape from physical dissolution. The false immortality of the film gives the viewer an illusion of control over eternity – but "the superstars" are fading.

Untitled

MATT MULLICAN

Her birth
Her family
Her house, home
Learning to crawl
The heat from the kitchen stove
Learning to walk
Hearing her mother upstairs
The street noises coming in the window
Learning to talk
The rug on the living room floor
The trees growing in the backyard
Learning to use her hands
Feeling hungry after her nap
The sunlight hurt her eyes
Her fourth birthday
The salt on the dining room table
Smelling the fresh autumn air
Bleeding after skinning her knee
Entering school
The pillow on her parent's bed
Making friends
Traveling to the mountains
Crying when feeling lost
The people living down the street
Learning to read words
The dining room table
The sky was a light shade of blue
Learning arithmetic
Her best friend's brother
Feeling hungry after skipping lunch
Learning to ride a bike
The full moon lights up the night sky
Learning about gravity in school
The light in the hallway
Catching her breath after running home

Entering the sixth grade – becoming older
Their pet dog
The door between her and her older sister's room
Having to go to the bathroom
Noticing that the tree in the backyard is changing color
Feeling the glare of the sun on her eyes
They got two inches of rain that week
Playing handball at school
The street light
Feeling proud of her schoolwork
Looking at herself in the mirror
Entering the seventh grade
Playing in the backyard
The food cans in the kitchen cabinet
Going to the school dance
Doing her homework
Tasting that there's too much salt in the salad
Thinking about going steady
Experiencing puberty
Scaring the dog by slamming the door
There were so many stars she couldn't count them all
Looking out her bedroom window
Finding new friends in school
As the year progressed the days got shorter
Visiting her aunt's house
Getting a boyfriend and going steady
Brushing her teeth
Her dog dies
Getting an electric shock
Riding the bus to school
Entering the drama club
Her boyfriend's little sister
Going to camp over the summer
The sound of the record player in the living room
The air felt thick that morning
Becoming sick – not going to school
Making out
Hearing her parents argue
Getting a younger sister – thinking to herself
Getting scared
Going to parties often
Entering high school

Hearing static while talking on the phone
Taking care of her little sister
After gym she was very tired
Burning herself while cooking
The telephone ringing in the hallway
Spending the summer at a beach house
The ocean seemed endless
A large man passing her on the sidewalk
Thinking about the people she has yet to meet
Learning to drive a car
Remembering the time she hurt herself skiing
Touching her right eye with her index finger
Family moves to a new neighborhood
The sound of an airplane flying overhead
Taking a bath
Becoming interested in history
Fantasizing about marriage
The dining room table set for eating
Going to the movies
Hugging her father
Entering college, moving away from home
Her roommate
Falling asleep while studying
Her roommate's home town
The amount of time it takes to walk to school
Majoring in history in college
Getting a boyfriend
The sound of the record player in the next room
Staying up, watching the sunrise from her rooftop
Cutting her hair
Studying the history of her country
Getting married in the afternoon
Their front door
Quitting school
Moving to a new house
Her husband's family
The manhole in the street
Thinking of her in-laws
Her husband's work
Boiling water while cooking
Getting a job for herself
Looking at herself in the mirror

Receiving a letter from her parents
Having her wisdom teeth removed
Watching the light refract through the kitchen window
Eating lunch
A pencil on her desk at work
Knowing she is going to have a baby
Thinking of her parents
Her baby is born
Moving to a larger house
There is lots of green around the new house
Her husband's mouth
Stubbing her toe while running
Her son's baby shoes
February twenty-sixth
Feeling thirsty one hot afternoon
Her husband's boss
Another birthday, she is getting older
Getting her hands wet
Thinking about her son's life
Making love with her husband
Smelling the fresh autumn air
Thinking of her childhood
The telephone wires
Her son's learning to walk
The people living next door
Trying to find her glasses
The covers on their bed
Having another baby, a girl
Not eating very much
She only had an hour to get home
Her son's school work
Visiting her husband's sister
The noise from a large truck
Her daughter's fourth birthday
Going shopping
Looking at herself in the mirror
Her thirty-fourth birthday
Sensing that her son is in danger
Renewing an interest in history
Her daughter's left hand
Taking a shower
Dreaming that she spoke a foreign language

Thinking of her husband's childhood
An object in the back seat of their car
The floor she stands on
October fifth
Her husband shaved regularly
Traveling to a large city
Her son's graduation
Taking a photograph
Reading a book in the study
Her husband's current income
Dropping a dish – watching it break
Kissing her husband
The days seemed to be going by faster
Having trouble breathing
The new living room furniture
The sidewalk around the corner
Touching the wall
Her father dies, sudden grief
The backyard flooded during a heavy rain
Looking at herself in the mirror
Her son's marriage
Brushing her teeth
Starting a garden
Her daughter's graduation
The broken glass in the basement door
Swimming
An itch in the lower part of her back
Her daughter's school in a foreign country
Spending half the year at the ocean
Looking at a photograph of herself as a child
Being scared to enter a dark room
Having a grandchild
Feeling older
Remembering schooldays
A glass of water
They have retired
Their son's independence
Touching herself
Cooking a "hearty meal"
Forgetting her age
Their house
Going for a trip around the world

Hair turning white
Her daughter's marriage
Working at her desk
Wondering where that person lives
Being visited by her daughter-in-law's parents
Noticing that the sky is a light shade of blue
The red car down the block
Catching her breath
Watching TV
Taking a nap in the hot sun
Her husband dies
Moving
Thinking about her eventual death
Scaring the dog by slamming the door
A family reunion during Christmas
Going for a walk in the garden
Feeling old, not caring
Looking at her feet
Not being able to see clearly
Bleeding after skinning her knee
Thinking of the faces of her parents
Cooking vegetables
The door between her and her sister's room
Looking at her eyes in the mirror
The floor she stands on
Thinking of her husband
Looking at herself in the mirror
Thinking of her death
Her death

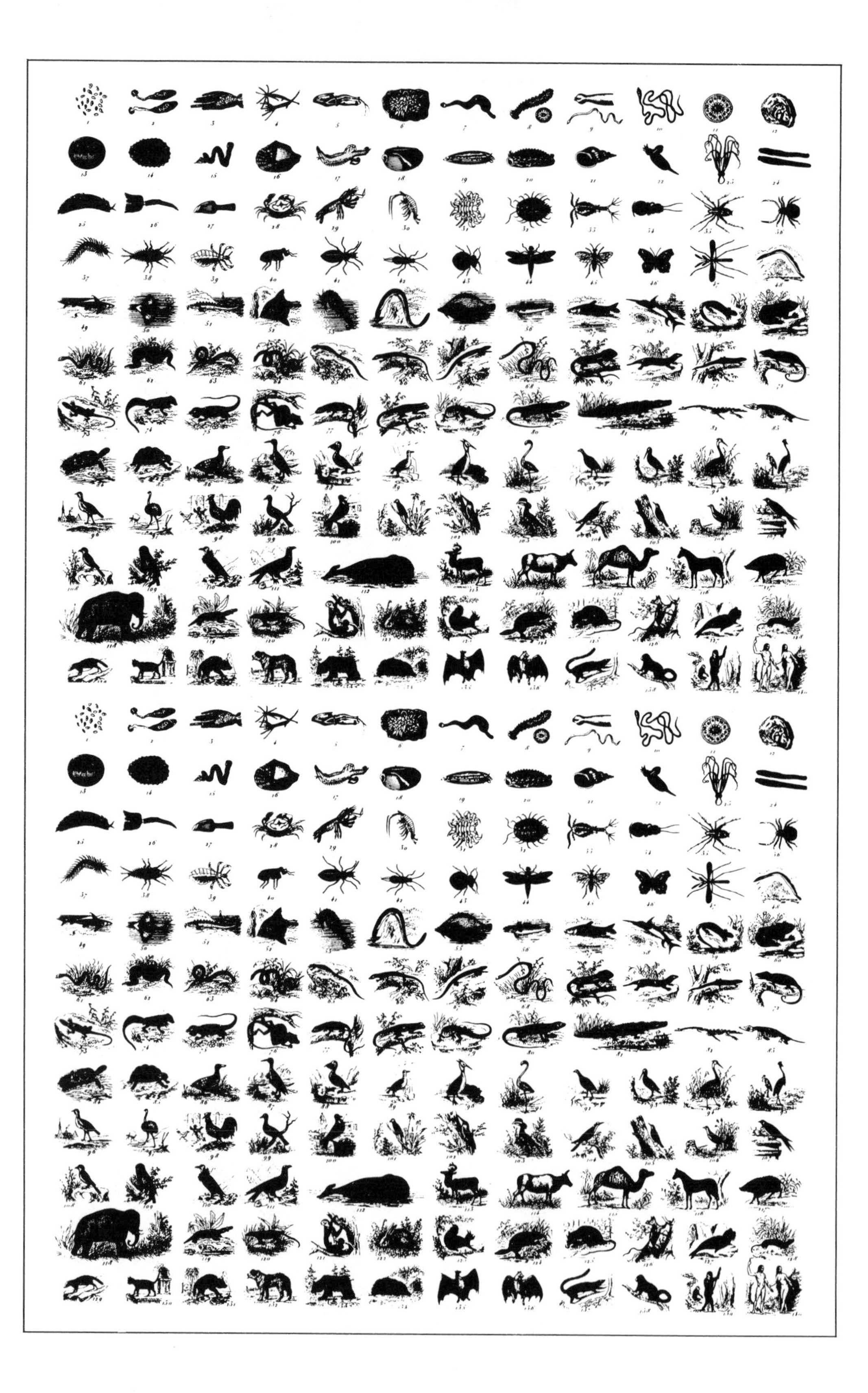

If Only

ANNE TURYN & ROBERT FIENGO

If only the Czar were dead or I could live in Paris. *Russia, 1905*

I wish I could go to the New World, find the Fountain of Youth, get a lot of gold, come back, and marry the Queen. *Spain, 1590*

If only it were me who won the sweepstakes. *1870*

I wish I had a cigarette. *Trench, Europe, 1918*

Let's wish on a star.

I wish I were pregnant.

I wish I could get out of this hellhole. *1930*

shoes for Christmas *Kentucky, 1910*

I wish I hadn't lost my hand in the war. *France, 1830*

I wish I hadn't said that.

If only I had a big fat dowry. *Britain, 1830*

If only I were younger.

I wish I could fly like a bird. *Kenya, 20,000 BC*

I wish I could see the Pyramids.

Oh, have I my heart set on an apparatus with wheels like toys have. *Peru, 1500*

I wish I had said that.

Write to Santa.

I hope I get a video game for Christmas. *Florida, 1980*

I wish I could leave home.

I wish that I didn't have fleas and that I had clean water. *Portugal, 1620*

Let's break the wishbone.

I wish we could honeymoon at Niagara Falls.

I wish I could fly. *Italy, 1540*

a long life

I hope I get into college. *Illinois, 1935*

a sickle that stays sharp and doesn't break *638 BC*

It's too cold.

I wish God weren't punishing us with the plague. *Germany, 1283*

I wish I were drunk.

I wish I could read. *Britain, 1600*

Let's throw a penny in the well.

a pony *Connecticut, 1950*

I wish that I could find a shorter route to India and that I owned some books. *1480*

I want to go home.

I wish I could fight in the war. *Baltimore, 1941*

I wish I had a beer. *China, 1890*

I wish I could fly across the ocean. *Canada, 1920*

I wish I weren't Christian. *The Coliseum, 30 AD*

I wish I weren't pregnant.

I wish I could see the world. *Egypt, 1760*

I wish she had a larger dowry. *Britain, 1830*

I wish I had a mind to quit smoking. *California, 1978*

I wish it would rain.

I wish we could please the Mother Goddess better. *BC*

It's too hot.

I wish I could fight in the war. *Nagasaki, 1942*

I wish the guests would go home.

I hope I can get out of the draft. *Baltimore, 1970*

I wish I could keep track of what's in my storehouse. *Crete, 1000 BC*

I wish I weren't drunk.

I hope my TB gets cured and that I can buy a Ford and drive a long life. *New York City, 1905*

I wish it were summer and there were light now. *Iceland, 1750*

I wish I were older.

I wish we could find a place where the game is always plentiful and the berries grow faster and we wouldn't have to keep hauling around. *25,000 BC*

I wish I had more.

I wish I had a beer. *Mexico City, 1780*

I want us to win the war.

I wish I were a rock-and-roll star and could get the Beatles back together, play at Shea Stadium, or maybe reopen the Fillmore. *New Delhi, 1979*

I wish I hadn't done that.

I wish these arrows would fly straighter. *1103*

I want to marry that one, over there.

Blow out the candles.

a cure for the common cold

If I only had a beer. *Netherlands, 1310*

If only I won the lottery then I could quit this stinking job. *1973*

If I only had a brain. *Oz*

I wish it would stop raining.

Wish you were here.

Five Comments

SHERRIE LEVINE

Since the door was only half closed, I got a jumbled view of my mother and father on the bed, one on top of the other. Mortified, hurt, horror struck, I had the hateful sensation of having placed myself blindly and completely in unworthy hands. Instinctively and without effort, I divided myself, so to speak, into two persons, of whom one, the real, the genuine one, continued on her own account, while the other, a successful imitation of the first, was delegated to have relations with the world. My first self remains at a distance, impassive, ironical, and watching.

1980

The world is filled to suffocating. Man has placed his token on every stone. Every word, every image, is leased and mortgaged. We know that a picture is but a space in which a variety of images, none of them original, blend and clash. A picture is a tissue of quotations drawn from the innumerable centers of culture. Similar to those eternal copyists Bouvard and Pécuchet, we indicate the profound ridiculousness that is precisely the truth of painting. We can only imitate a gesture that is always interior, never original. Succeeding the painter, the plagiarist no longer bears within him passions, humors, feelings, impressions, but rather this immense encyclopedia from which he draws. The viewer is the tablet on which all the quotations that make up a painting are inscribed without any of them being lost. A painting's meaning lies not in its origin, but in its destination. The birth of the viewer must be at the cost of the painter.

1981

In the seventeenth century, Miguel de Cervantes published *Don Quixote.* In 1962, Jorge Luis Borges published "Pierre Menard, Author of the Quixote," the story of a man who rewrites the ninth and thirty-eighth chapters of *Don Quixote.* His aim was never to produce a mechanical transcription of the original, he did not want to copy it. His ambition was to propose pages which would coincide with those of Cervantes, to continue being Pierre Menard and to arrive at *Don Quixote* through the experience of Pierre Menard. Like Menard, I have allowed myself variants of a formal and psychological nature.

1983

We like to imagine the future as a place where people loved abstraction before they encountered sentimentality.

1984

I like to think of my paintings as membranes permeable from both sides so there is an easy flow between the past and the future, between my history and yours.

1985

The Consummate Mask of Rock

BRUCE NAUMAN

I

1. mask
2. fidelity
3. truth
4. life
5. cover
6. pain
7. desire
8. need
9. human companionship
10. nothing
11. COVER REVOKED
12. infidelity
13. painless
14. musk/skum
15. people
16. die
17. exposure.

2

1. This is my mask of fidelity to truth and life.
2. This is to cover the mask of pain and desire.
3. This is to mask the cover of need for human companionship.
4. This is to mask the cover.
5. This is to cover the mask.
6. This is the need of cover.
7. This is the need of the mask.
8. This is the mask of cover of need.
   Nothing and no
9. No thing and no mask can cover the lack, alas.
10. Lack after nothing before cover revoked.
11. Lack before cover
    paper covers rock
    rock breaks mask
    alas, alack.
12. Nothing to cover.
13. This is the
13. This is the mask to cover my infidelity to truth.
    (This is my cover.)
14. This is the need for pain that contorts my mask conveying the message of truth and fidelity to life.
15. This is the truth that distorts my need for human companionship.
16. This is the distortion of truth masked by my painful need.
17. This is the mask of my painful need distressed by truth and human companionship.
18. This is my painless mask that fails to touch my face but floats before the surface of my skin my eyes my teeth my tongue.
19. Desire is my mask.
    (Musk of desire)
20. Rescind desire
    cover revoked
    desire revoked
    cover rescinded.
21. PEOPLE DIE OF EXPOSURE.

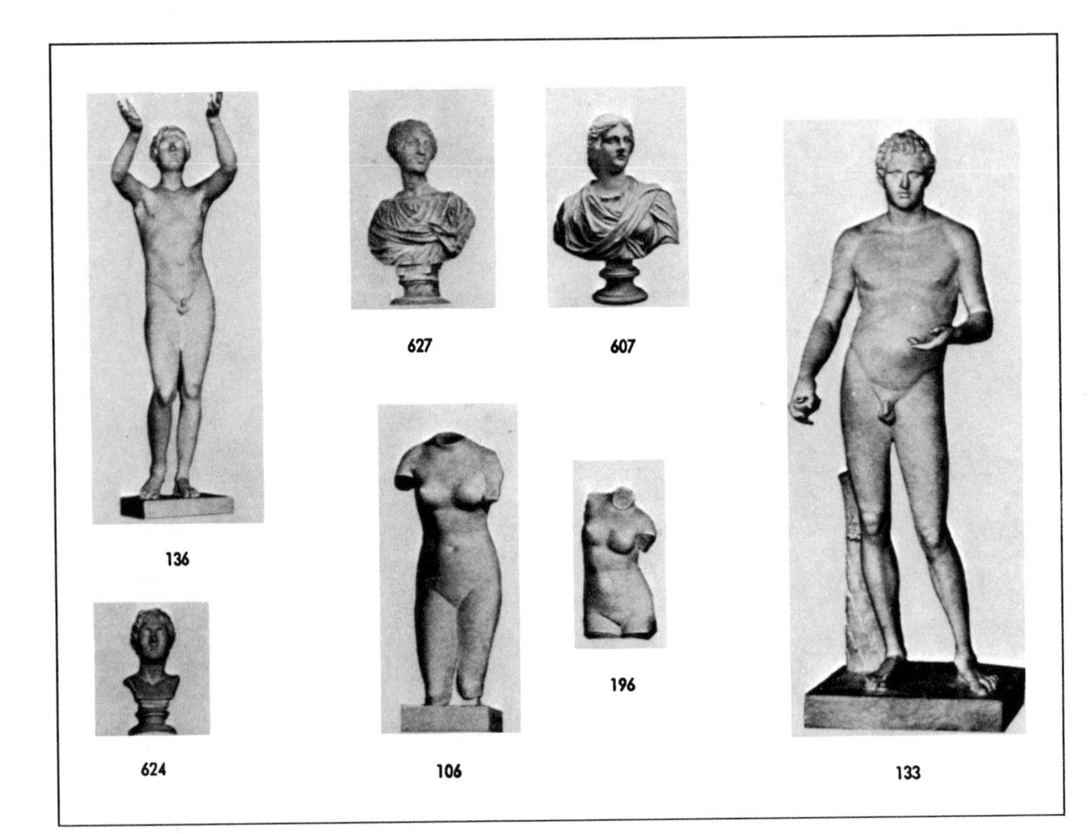

136
627
607
196
624
106
133

3

CONSUMMATION/CONSUMNATION/TASK

(passive)
paper covers rock

(active – threatening)
scissors cut paper

(active – violent)
rock breaks scissors

1. mask
2. cover
3. diminish
4. desire
5. need for human companionship
6. lack

desire covers mask

need for human companionship masks desire

mask diminishes need for human companionship

need for human companionship diminishes cover

desire consumes human companionship

cover lacks desire

4

THIS IS THE COVER THAT DESIRES THE MASK OF LACK THAT CONSUMES THE NEED FOR HUMAN COMPANIONSHIP.
THIS IS THE COVER THAT DESPISES THE TASK OF THE NEED OF HUMAN COMP.
THIS IS THE TASK OF CONSUMING HUMAN COMP.

5

1. some kind of fact
2. some kind of fiction
3. the way we behaved in the past
4. what we believe to be the case now
5. the consuming task of human companionship
6. the consummate mask of rock

(1.) Fiction erodes fact.
(2.) Fact becomes the way we have behaved in the past.
(3.) The way we have behaved in the past congeals into the consummate mask of rock.
(4.) The way we have behaved in the past contributes to the consuming task of human companionship.
(5.) The consuming task of human comp. erodes the consummate mask of rock. However (2.) Fact becomes the way we have behaved in the past may be substituted into (3.) and (4.) so that
(6.) Fact congeals into the consummate mask of rock.
But (5.) the consuming task of human comp. erodes the consummate mask of rock or the consuming task of human comp. erodes fact, then from (1.) it follows that
THE CONSUMING TASK OF HUMAN COMPANIONSHIP IS FALSE.

6

THE CONSUMMATE MASK OF ROCK HAVING DRIVEN THE WEDGE OF DESIRE THAT DISTINGUISHED TRUTH AND FALSITY LIES COVERED BY PAPER.

7

1. (This young man, taken to task so often, now finds it his only sexual relief.)
2. (This young man, so often taken to task, now finds it his only sexual fulfillment.)
3. (This man, so often taken to task as a child. . . .)
4. (This man, often taken to task, now finds it satisfies his sexual desires.)
arouses needs
5. This man, so often taken as a child, now wears the consummate mask of rock and uses it to drive his wedge of desire into the ever squeezing gap between truth and falsity.
6. This man, so often taken as a child, now uses his consummate mask of his rock to drive his wedge of his desire into his ever squeezing (his) gap between his truth, his falsity.
7. (This) man, (so often) taken as (a) child, finding his consummate mask of rock covered by paper, he finding his wedge being squeezed (from) between his desired truth (truth desired) and his desireless falsity (falsity desireless), he unable to arouse his satisfaction, he unable to desire his needs, he proceeds into the gap of his fulfillment his relief lacking the task of human companionship.

Moral

Paper cut from rock, releases rock to crush scissors. Rock freed from restrictions of paper/scissors/rock, lacking context proceeds.

My Files of Movie Stills

JOHN BALDESSARI

Below are the current categories in my files of movie stills, which form a large part of the raw material from which I draw to do my work. I hope the categories (which are continually shifting according to my needs and interests) will provide some clues to what animates the work I do.

A

attack, animal, animal/man, above, automobiles (left), automobiles (right)

B

birds, building, below, barrier, blood, bar (man in), books, blind, brew, betray, bookending, bound, bury, banal, bridge, boat, birth, balance, bathroom

C

cage, camouflage, chaos/order, city, cooking, chairs, curves, cheering, celebrity, consumerism, curiosity, crucifixion, crowds, climbing, color, civic

D

dwarf, death, disgrace, danger, discipline, disaster, division, door

E

escape, eat, ephemeral, exteriors

F

facial (expression), fall, fake, framing, freeway, fire, foreground, falling, forest, females, form

G

good/evil, goodbye, giant, gate, grief, guns, guns (aggression), gamble, growth, groups

H

hope, horizontal, hard/soft, hands, heel (ankle), hole (cavity), houses, hiding

I

injury (impair), interiors

J

judgment, journey (path, guide)

K

knife, kiss

L

lifeless, letter, light, looking (watching), laughing

M

money, music, males (+ 1 female), males 2 (+ 1 female), male/female, message, mutilation, movement, masks (monsters), missing (area), macho

N

naked, noose, nature, nature (water), nourish, newsphotos

O

octopus, operation, oval, obstacle

P

phallic, prison, purity, perspective, posture, paint, past, parachute, products, portrait (male), portrait (male, color), parallelograms, pairs (images)

R

roller coaster, rescue, repel, radiating (lines), race, relief, revive, rectangle (long), rectangle (wavy), reason

S

snakes, shadows, ships, smoke, sports, signal, search, secret, survive, stress, separation, safe, struggle, sad, soul, suitcase, switch, sinking, structure, seduction, sex (desire), small, shape (smear), shape (awkward), shape (black), shape (arc), shape (circle), shape (blur), shape (white)

T

technology, tables, table (settings), thinking, trapeze, time, three, trains, two, teeth, thought, triangle, triangle (truncated)

U

upside down, unconscious

V

vision, victim, vulnerable

W

walls, water, wound, watching, winning, women, women (2), women (group)

A bargain always must be struck between what is available in movie stills and the concerns I have at the moment – I don't order the stills, I must choose from the menu. Also, one will read from this a rather hopeless desire to make words and images interchangeable – yet it is that futility that engrosses me. Lastly, I think one will notice the words falling into their own categories, two being those of formal concerns and content.

Truisms

JENNY HOLZER

A LITTLE KNOWLEDGE CAN GO A LONG WAY

A LOT OF PROFESSIONALS ARE CRACKPOTS

A MAN CAN'T KNOW WHAT IT'S LIKE TO BE A MOTHER

A NAME MEANS A LOT JUST BY ITSELF

A POSITIVE ATTITUDE MAKES ALL THE DIFFERENCE IN THE WORLD

A RELAXED MAN IS NOT NECESSARILY A BETTER MAN

A SENSE OF TIMING IS THE MARK OF GENIUS

A SINCERE EFFORT IS ALL YOU CAN ASK

A SINGLE EVENT CAN HAVE INFINITELY MANY INTERPRETATIONS

A SOLID HOME BASE BUILDS A SENSE OF SELF

A STRONG SENSE OF DUTY IMPRISONS YOU

ABSOLUTE SUBMISSION CAN BE A FORM OF FREEDOM

ABSTRACTION IS A TYPE OF DECADENCE

ABUSE OF POWER COMES AS NO SURPRISE

ACTION CAUSES MORE TROUBLE THAN THOUGHT

ALIENATION PRODUCES ECCENTRICS OR REVOLUTIONARIES

ALL THINGS ARE DELICATELY INTERCONNECTED

AMBITION IS JUST AS DANGEROUS AS COMPLACENCY

AMBIVALENCE CAN RUIN YOUR LIFE

AN ELITE IS INEVITABLE

ANGER OR HATE CAN BE A USEFUL MOTIVATING FORCE

ANIMALISM IS PERFECTLY HEALTHY

ANY SURPLUS IS IMMORAL

ANYTHING IS A LEGITIMATE AREA OF INVESTIGATION

ARTIFICIAL DESIRES ARE DESPOILING THE EARTH

AT TIMES INACTIVITY IS PREFERABLE TO MINDLESS FUNCTIONING

AT TIMES YOUR UNCONSCIOUS IS TRUER THAN YOUR CONSCIOUS MIND

AUTOMATION IS DEADLY

AWFUL PUNISHMENT AWAITS REALLY BAD PEOPLE

BAD INTENTIONS CAN YIELD GOOD RESULTS

BEING ALONE WITH YOURSELF IS INCREASINGLY UNPOPULAR
BEING HAPPY IS MORE IMPORTANT THAN ANYTHING ELSE
BEING HONEST IS NOT ALWAYS THE KINDEST WAY
BEING JUDGMENTAL IS A SIGN OF LIFE
BEING SURE OF YOURSELF MEANS YOU'RE A FOOL
BELIEVING IN REBIRTH IS THE SAME AS ADMITTING DEFEAT
BOREDOM MAKES YOU DO CRAZY THINGS
CALM IS MORE CONDUCIVE TO CREATIVITY THAN IS ANXIETY
CATEGORIZING FEAR IS CALMING
CHANGE IS VALUABLE WHEN THE OPPRESSED BECOME TYRANTS
CHASING THE NEW IS DANGEROUS TO SOCIETY
CHILDREN ARE THE CRUELEST OF ALL
CHILDREN ARE THE HOPE OF THE FUTURE
CLASS ACTION IS A NICE IDEA WITH NO SUBSTANCE
CLASS STRUCTURE IS AS ARTIFICIAL AS PLASTIC
CONFUSING YOURSELF IS A WAY TO STAY HONEST
CRIME AGAINST PROPERTY IS RELATIVELY UNIMPORTANT
DECADENCE CAN BE AN END IN ITSELF
DECENCY IS A RELATIVE THING
DEPENDENCE CAN BE A MEAL TICKET
DESCRIPTION IS MORE VALUABLE THAN METAPHOR
DEVIANTS ARE SACRIFICED TO INCREASE GROUP SOLIDARITY
DISGUST IS THE APPROPRIATE RESPONSE TO MOST SITUATIONS
DISORGANIZATION IS A KIND OF ANESTHESIA
DON'T PLACE TOO MUCH TRUST IN EXPERTS
DON'T RUN PEOPLE'S LIVES FOR THEM
DRAMA OFTEN OBSCURES THE REAL ISSUES
DREAMING WHILE AWAKE IS A FRIGHTENING CONTRADICTION
DYING AND COMING BACK GIVES YOU CONSIDERABLE PERSPECTIVE
DYING SHOULD BE AS EASY AS FALLING OFF A LOG
EATING TOO MUCH IS CRIMINAL
ELABORATION IS A FORM OF POLLUTION
EMOTIONAL RESPONSES ARE AS VALUABLE AS INTELLECTUAL RESPONSES
ENJOY YOURSELF BECAUSE YOU CAN'T CHANGE ANYTHING ANYWAY
ENSURE THAT YOUR LIFE STAYS IN FLUX
EVEN YOUR FAMILY CAN BETRAY YOU

EVERY ACHIEVEMENT REQUIRES A SACRIFICE
EVERYONE'S WORK IS EQUALLY IMPORTANT
EXCEPTIONAL PEOPLE DESERVE SPECIAL CONCESSIONS
EXPIRING FOR LOVE IS BEAUTIFUL BUT STUPID
EXPRESSING ANGER IS NECESSARY
EXTREME BEHAVIOR HAS ITS BASIS IN PATHOLOGICAL PSYCHOLOGY
EXTREME SELF-CONSCIOUSNESS LEADS TO PERVERSION
FAITHFULNESS IS A SOCIAL NOT A BIOLOGICAL LAW
FAKE OR REAL INDIFFERENCE IS A POWERFUL PERSONAL WEAPON
FATHERS OFTEN USE TOO MUCH FORCE
FEAR IS THE GREATEST INCAPACITATOR
FREEDOM IS A LUXURY NOT A NECESSITY
GIVING FREE REIN TO YOUR EMOTIONS IS AN HONEST WAY TO LIVE
GO ALL OUT IN ROMANCE AND LET THE CHIPS FALL WHERE THEY MAY
GOING WITH THE FLOW IS SOOTHING BUT RISKY
GOOD DEEDS EVENTUALLY ARE REWARDED
GOVERNMENT IS A BURDEN ON THE PEOPLE
GRASS ROOTS AGITATION IS THE ONLY HOPE
GUILT AND SELF-LACERATION ARE INDULGENCES
HABITUAL CONTEMPT DOESN'T REFLECT A FINER SENSIBILITY
HIDING YOUR MOTIVES IS DESPICABLE
HOLDING BACK PROTECTS YOUR VITAL ENERGIES
HUMANISM IS OBSOLETE
HUMOR IS A RELEASE
IDEALS ARE REPLACED BY CONVENTIONAL GOALS AT A CERTAIN AGE
IF YOU AREN'T POLITICAL YOUR PERSONAL LIFE SHOULD BE EXEMPLARY
IF YOU CAN'T LEAVE YOUR MARK GIVE UP
IF YOU HAVE MANY DESIRES LIFE WILL BE INTERESTING
IF YOU LIVE SIMPLY THERE IS NOTHING TO WORRY ABOUT
IGNORING ENEMIES IS THE BEST WAY TO FIGHT
ILLNESS IS A STATE OF MIND
IMPOSING ORDER IS MAN'S VOCATION FOR CHAOS IS HELL
IN SOME INSTANCES IT'S BETTER TO DIE THAN TO CONTINUE
INHERITANCE MUST BE ABOLISHED
IT CAN BE HELPFUL TO KEEP GOING NO MATTER WHAT
IT IS HEROIC TO TRY TO STOP TIME
IT IS MAN'S FATE TO OUTSMART HIMSELF

IT'S A GIFT TO THE WORLD NOT TO HAVE BABIES
IT'S BETTER TO BE A GOOD PERSON THAN A FAMOUS PERSON
IT'S BETTER TO BE LONELY THAN TO BE WITH INFERIOR PEOPLE
IT'S BETTER TO BE NAIVE THAN JADED
IT'S BETTER TO STUDY THE LIVING FACT THAN TO ANALYZE HISTORY
IT'S CRUCIAL TO HAVE AN ACTIVE FANTASY LIFE
IT'S GOOD TO GIVE EXTRA MONEY TO CHARITY
IT'S IMPORTANT TO STAY CLEAN ON ALL LEVELS
IT'S IMPOSSIBLE TO RECONCILE YOUR HEART AND HEAD
IT'S JUST AN ACCIDENT YOUR PARENTS ARE YOUR PARENTS
IT'S NOT GOOD TO HOLD TOO MANY ABSOLUTES
IT'S NOT GOOD TO OPERATE ON CREDIT
IT'S VITAL TO LIVE IN HARMONY WITH NATURE
JUST BELIEVING SOMETHING CAN MAKE IT HAPPEN
KEEP SOMETHING IN RESERVE FOR EMERGENCIES
KILLING IS UNAVOIDABLE BUT IS NOTHING TO BE PROUD OF
KNOWING YOURSELF LETS YOU UNDERSTAND OTHERS
KNOWLEDGE SHOULD BE ADVANCED AT ALL COSTS
LABOR IS A LIFE-DESTROYING ACTIVITY
LACK OF CHARISMA CAN BE FATAL
LEARN THINGS FROM THE GROUND UP
LEARN TO TRUST YOUR OWN EYES
LEISURE TIME IS A GIGANTIC SMOKESCREEN
LETTING GO IS THE HARDEST THING TO DO
LISTEN WHEN YOUR BODY TALKS
LOOKING BACK IS THE FIRST SIGN OF AGING AND DECAY
LOVING ANIMALS IS A SUBSTITUTE ACTIVITY
LOW EXPECTATIONS ARE GOOD PROTECTION
MANUAL LABOR CAN BE REFRESHING AND WHOLESOME
MEN ARE NOT MONOGAMOUS BY NATURE
MODERATION KILLS THE SPIRIT
MONEY CREATES TASTE
MONOMANIA IS A PREREQUISITE OF SUCCESS
MORALS ARE FOR LITTLE PEOPLE
MOST PEOPLE ARE NOT FIT TO RULE THEMSELVES
MOSTLY YOU SHOULD MIND YOUR OWN BUSINESS
MOTHERS SHOULDN'T MAKE TOO MANY SACRIFICES

MUCH WAS DECIDED BEFORE YOU WERE BORN
MURDER HAS ITS SEXUAL SIDE
MYTHS MAKE REALITY MORE INTELLIGIBLE
NOISE CAN BE HOSTILE
NOTHING UPSETS THE BALANCE OF GOOD AND EVIL
OCCASIONALLY PRINCIPLES ARE MORE VALUABLE THAN PEOPLE
OFFER VERY LITTLE INFORMATION ABOUT YOURSELF
OFTEN YOU SHOULD ACT LIKE YOU ARE SEXLESS
OLD FRIENDS ARE BETTER LEFT IN THE PAST
OPACITY IS AN IRRESISTIBLE CHALLENGE
PAIN CAN BE A VERY POSITIVE THING
PEOPLE ARE BORING UNLESS THEY'RE EXTREMISTS
PEOPLE ARE NUTS IF THEY THINK THEY ARE IMPORTANT
PEOPLE ARE RESPONSIBLE FOR WHAT THEY DO UNLESS THEY'RE INSANE
PEOPLE WHO DON'T WORK WITH THEIR HANDS ARE PARASITES
PEOPLE WHO GO CRAZY ARE TOO SENSITIVE
PEOPLE WON'T BEHAVE IF THEY HAVE NOTHING TO LOSE
PHYSICAL CULTURE IS SECOND-BEST
PLANNING FOR THE FUTURE IS ESCAPISM
PLAYING IT SAFE CAN CAUSE A LOT OF DAMAGE IN THE LONG RUN
POLITICS IS USED FOR PERSONAL GAIN
POTENTIAL COUNTS FOR NOTHING UNTIL IT'S REALIZED
PRESENTATION IS AS IMPORTANT AS CONTENT
PRIVATE PROPERTY CREATED CRIME
PURSUING PLEASURE FOR THE SAKE OF PLEASURE WILL RUIN YOU
PUSH YOURSELF TO THE LIMIT AS OFTEN AS POSSIBLE
RAISE BOYS AND GIRLS THE SAME WAY
RANDOM MATING IS GOOD FOR DEBUNKING SEX MYTHS
RECHANNELING DESTRUCTIVE IMPULSES IS A SIGN OF MATURITY
RECLUSES ALWAYS GET WEAK
REDISTRIBUTING WEALTH IS IMPERATIVE
RELATIVITY IS NO BOON TO MANKIND
RELIGION CAUSES AS MANY PROBLEMS AS IT SOLVES
REMEMBER YOU ALWAYS HAVE FREEDOM OF CHOICE
REPETITION IS THE BEST WAY TO LEARN
RESOLUTIONS SERVE TO EASE YOUR CONSCIENCE
REVOLUTION BEGINS WITH CHANGES IN THE INDIVIDUAL

ROMANTIC LOVE WAS INVENTED TO MANIPULATE WOMEN

ROUTINE IS A LINK WITH THE PAST

ROUTINE SMALL EXCESSES ARE WORSE THAN THE OCCASIONAL DEBAUCH

SACRIFICING YOURSELF FOR A BAD CAUSE IS NOT A MORAL ACT

SALVATION CAN'T BE BOUGHT AND SOLD

SELF-AWARENESS CAN BE CRIPPLING

SELF-CONTEMPT CAN DO MORE HARM THAN GOOD

SELFISHNESS IS THE MOST BASIC MOTIVATION

SELFLESSNESS IS THE HIGHEST ACHIEVEMENT

SEPARATISM IS THE WAY TO A NEW BEGINNING

SEX DIFFERENCES ARE HERE TO STAY

SIN IS A MEANS OF SOCIAL CONTROL

SLIPPING INTO MADNESS IS GOOD FOR THE SAKE OF COMPARISON

SLOPPY THINKING GETS WORSE OVER TIME

SOLITUDE IS ENRICHING

SOME STONES ARE BETTER LEFT UNTURNED

SOME WOUNDS NEVER HEAL

SOMETIMES ALL YOU CAN DO IS LOOK THE OTHER WAY

SOMETIMES SCIENCE ADVANCES FASTER THAN IT SHOULD

SOMETIMES THINGS SEEM TO HAPPEN OF THEIR OWN ACCORD

SPENDING TOO MUCH TIME ON SELF-IMPROVEMENT IS ANTISOCIAL

STARVATION IS NATURE'S WAY

STASIS IS A DREAM STATE

STERILIZATION IS A WEAPON OF THE RULERS

STRONG EMOTIONAL ATTACHMENT STEMS FROM BASIC INSECURITY

STUPID PEOPLE SHOULDN'T BREED

SURVIVAL OF THE FITTEST APPLIES TO MEN AND ANIMALS

SYMBOLS ARE MORE MEANINGFUL THAN THINGS THEMSELVES

TAKING A STRONG STAND PUBLICIZES THE OPPOSITE POSITION

TALKING IS USED TO HIDE ONE'S INABILITY TO ACT

TEASING PEOPLE SEXUALLY CAN HAVE UGLY CONSEQUENCES

TECHNOLOGY WILL MAKE OR BREAK US

THE CRUELEST DISAPPOINTMENT IS WHEN YOU LET YOURSELF DOWN

THE DESIRE TO REPRODUCE IS A DEATH WISH

THE FAMILY IS LIVING ON BORROWED TIME

THE IDEA OF REVOLUTION IS AN ADOLESCENT FANTASY

THE IDEA OF TRANSCENDENCE IS USED TO OBSCURE OPPRESSION

THE IDIOSYNCRATIC HAS LOST ITS AUTHORITY

THE LAND BELONGS TO NO ONE

THE MORE YOU KNOW THE BETTER OFF YOU ARE

THE MOST PROFOUND THINGS ARE INEXPRESSIBLE

THE MUNDANE IS TO BE CHERISHED

THE NEW IS NOTHING BUT A RESTATEMENT OF THE OLD

THE ONLY WAY TO BE PURE IS TO STAY BY YOURSELF

THE SUM OF YOUR ACTIONS DETERMINES WHAT YOU ARE

THE UNATTAINABLE INVARIABLY IS ATTRACTIVE

THE WORLD OPERATES ACCORDING TO DISCOVERABLE LAWS

THERE ARE TOO FEW IMMUTABLE TRUTHS TODAY

THERE'S A FINE LINE BETWEEN INFORMATION AND PROPAGANDA

THERE'S NO SENSE BEING ANYWHERE BUT THE TOP OF THE HEAP

THERE'S NOTHING EXCEPT WHAT YOU SENSE

THERE'S NOTHING REDEEMING IN TOIL

THINKING TOO MUCH CAN CAUSE PROBLEMS

THREATENING SOMEONE SEXUALLY IS A HORRIBLE ACT

TIMIDITY IS LAUGHABLE

TO DISAGREE PRESUPPOSES MORAL INTEGRITY

TO VOLUNTEER IS REACTIONARY

TORTURE IS BARBARIC

TRADING A LIFE FOR A LIFE IS FAIR ENOUGH

TRUE FREEDOM IS FRIGHTFUL

UNIQUE THINGS MUST BE THE MOST VALUABLE

UNQUESTIONING LOVE DEMONSTRATES LARGESSE OF SPIRIT

USING FORCE TO STOP FORCE IS ABSURD

VIOLENCE IS PERMISSIBLE EVEN DESIRABLE OCCASIONALLY

WAR IS A PURIFICATION RITE

WE MUST MAKE SACRIFICES TO MAINTAIN OUR QUALITY OF LIFE

WHEN SOMETHING TERRIBLE HAPPENS PEOPLE WAKE UP

WISHING THINGS AWAY IS NOT EFFECTIVE

WITH PERSEVERANCE YOU CAN DISCOVER ANY TRUTH

WORDS TEND TO BE INADEQUATE

WORRYING CAN HELP YOU PREPARE

YOU ARE A VICTIM OF THE RULES YOU LIVE BY

YOU ARE GUILELESS IN YOUR DREAMS

YOU ARE RESPONSIBLE FOR CONSTITUTING THE MEANING OF THINGS

YOU ARE THE PAST PRESENT AND FUTURE

YOU CAN LIVE ON THROUGH YOUR DESCENDANTS

YOU CAN NEVER OUTRUN YOURSELF

YOU CAN PULL YOURSELF OUT OF ANY HOLE

YOU CAN'T EXPECT PEOPLE TO BE SOMETHING THEY'RE NOT

YOU CAN'T FOOL OTHERS IF YOU'RE FOOLING YOURSELF

YOU DIG YOUR OWN GRAVE

YOU DON'T KNOW WHAT'S WHAT UNTIL YOU SUPPORT YOURSELF

YOU GET THE FACE YOU DESERVE

YOU HAVE TO HURT OTHERS TO BE EXTRAORDINARY

YOU MUST BE INTIMATE WITH A TOKEN FEW

YOU MUST DISAGREE WITH AUTHORITY FIGURES

YOU MUST HAVE ONE GRAND PASSION

YOU MUST KNOW WHERE YOU STOP AND THE WORLD BEGINS

YOU NEVER KNOW WHAT PEOPLE REALLY THINK ABOUT YOU

YOU ONLY CAN UNDERSTAND SOMEONE OF YOUR OWN SEX

YOU OWE THE WORLD NOT THE OTHER WAY AROUND

YOU SHOULD TRAVEL LIGHT

YOU SHOULD STUDY AS MUCH AS POSSIBLE

YOUR ACTIONS ARE POINTLESS IF NO ONE NOTICES

YOUR OLDEST FEARS ARE THE WORST ONES

3. Discourses of Power

Reading an Archive

ALLAN SEKULA

Every image of the past that is not recognized by the present as one of its own threatens to disappear irretrievably.

Walter Benjamin[1]

The invention of photography: For whom? Against whom?

Jean-Luc Godard and Jean-Pierre Gorin[2]

Here is yet another book of photographs. All were made in the industrial and coal-mining regions of Cape Breton in the two decades between 1948 and 1968. All were made by one man, a commercial photographer named Leslie Shedden. At first glance, the economics of this work seem simple and common enough: proprietor of the biggest and only successful photographic studio in the town of Glace Bay, Nova Scotia, Shedden produced pictures on demand for a variety of clients. Thus in the range of his commissions we discover the limits of economic relations in a coal town. His largest single customer was the coal company. And prominent among the less official customers who walked in the door of Shedden Studio were the coal miners and their families. Somewhere in between the company and the workers were local shopkeepers who, like Shedden himself, depended on the miners' income for their own livelihood and who saw photography as a sensible means of local promotion.

Why stress these economic realities at the outset, as if to flaunt the "crude thinking" often called for by Bertolt Brecht? Surely our understandings of these photographs cannot be reduced to a knowledge of economic conditions. This latter knowledge is necessary but insufficient; we also need to grasp the way in which photography constructs an imaginary world and passes it off as reality. The aim of this essay, then, is to try to understand something of the relationship between photographic culture and economic life. How does photography serve to legitimate and normalize existing

1. Walter Benjamin, "Theses on the Philosophy of History" (1940), in *Illuminations,* ed. Hannah Arendt, trans. Harry Zohn (New York: Schocken Books, 1969), p. 255.
2. Jean-Luc Godard and Jean-Pierre Gorin, *Vent d'Est/Vento dell'Est* (Rome, Paris, Berlin: Poli Film, Anounchka Film, CCC, 1969), English translation of filmscript in Jean-Luc Godard, *Weekend and Wind from the East: Two Films by Jean-Luc Godard* (New York: Simon and Schuster, 1972), p. 179.

power relationships? How does it serve as the voice of authority, while simultaneously claiming to constitute a token of exchange between equal partners? What havens and temporary escapes from the realm of necessity are provided by photographic means? What resistances are encouraged and strengthened? How is historical and social memory preserved, transformed, restricted, and obliterated by photographs? What futures are promised; what futures are forgotten? In the broadest sense, these questions concern the ways in which photography constructs an *imaginary economy.* From a materialist perspective, these are reasonable questions, well worth pursuing. Certainly they would seem to be unavoidable for an archive such as this one, assembled in answer to commercial and industrial demands in a region persistently suffering from economic troubles.[3]

Nonetheless, such questions are easily eclipsed, or simply left unasked. To understand this denial of politics, this depoliticization of photographic meaning, we need to examine some of the underlying problems of photographic culture. Before we can answer the questions just posed, we need to briefly consider what a photographic archive is, and how it might be interpreted, sampled, or reconstructed in a book. The model of the archive, of the quantitative ensemble of images, is a powerful one in photographic discourse. This model exerts a basic influence on the character of the truths and pleasures experienced in looking at photographs, especially today, when photographic books and exhibitions are being assembled from archives at an unprecedented rate. We might even argue that archival ambitions and procedures are intrinsic to photographic practice.

There are all sorts of photographic archives: commercial archives like Shedden's, corporate archives, government archives, museum archives, historical society archives, amateur archives, family archives, artists' archives, private collectors' archives, and so on. Archives are property, either of individuals or institutions, and their ownership may or may not coincide with authorship. One characteristic of photography is that ownership of individual images and the control and ownership of archives do not commonly reside in the same individual. Photographers are detail workers

3. "What is represented in ideology is therefore not the system of the real relations which govern the existence of individuals, but the imaginary relation of those individuals to the real relations in which they live." Louis Althusser, "Ideology and Ideological State Apparatuses" (1969), in *Lenin and Philosophy,* trans. Ben Brewster (New York: Monthly Review Press, 1971), p. 165. Althusser's model of ideology is based in part on Marx and in part on the work of the psychoanalyst Jacques Lacan.

when they are not artists or leisure-time amateurs, and thus it is not unreasonable for the legal theorist Bernard Edelman to label photographers the "proletarians of creation."[4] Leslie Shedden, for his part, was a combination artisan and small entrepreneur. He contributed to company and family archives while retaining his own file of negatives. As is common with commercial photographers, he included these negatives in the sale of his studio to a younger photographer upon retiring in 1977.

Archives, then, constitute a *territory of images;* the unity of an archive is first and foremost that imposed by ownership. Whether or not the photographs in a particular archive are offered for sale, the general condition of archives involves the subordination of use to the logic of exchange. Thus, not only are the pictures in archives often *literally* for sale, but their meanings are up for grabs. New owners are invited, new interpretations are promised. The purchase of reproduction rights under copyright law is also the purchase of a certain semantic license. This *semantic availability* of pictures in archives exhibits the same abstract logic as that which characterizes goods on the marketplace.

In an archive, the possibility of meaning is "liberated" from the actual contingencies of use. But this liberation is also a loss, an *abstraction* from the complexity and richness of use, a loss of context. Thus, the specificity of "original" uses and meanings can be avoided, and even made invisible, when photographs are selected from an archive and reproduced in a book. (In reverse fashion, photographs can be removed from books and entered into archives, with a similar loss of specificity.) So new meanings come to supplant old ones, with the archive serving as a kind of "clearing house" of meaning.

Consider this example: some of the photographs in this book were originally reproduced in the annual reports of the Dominion Steel and Coal Company, others were carried in miners' wallets or framed on the mantlepieces of working-class homes. Imagine two different gazes. Imagine the gaze of a stockholder (who may or may not have ever visited a coal mine) thumbing his way to the table of earnings and lingering for a moment on the picture of a mining machine, presumably the concrete source of the abstract wealth being accounted for in those pages. Imagine the gaze of a miner, or of a miner's spouse, child, parent, sibling, lover, or friend

4. Bernard Edelman, *Le Droit saisi par la photographie* (Paris: Librairie François Maspero, 1973), translated by Elizabeth Kingdom as *Ownership of the Image: Elements for a Marxist Theory of Law* (London: Routledge & Kegan Paul, 1979), p. 45.

drifting to a portrait during breaks or odd moments during the working day. Most mine workers would agree that the investments behind those looks – financial on the one hand, emotional on the other – are not compatible. But in an archive, the difference, the *radical antagonism* between these looks is eclipsed. Instead we have two carefully made negatives, available for reproduction in a book in which all their similarities and differences could easily be reduced to "purely visual" concerns. (And even visual differences can be homogenized out of existence when negatives first printed as industrial glossies and others printed on flat paper and tinted by hand are subjected to a uniform standard of printing for reproduction in a book. Thus the difference between a mode of pictorial address which is primarily "informational" and one which is "sentimental" is obscured.) In this sense, archives establish a relation of *abstract visual equivalence* between pictures. Within this regime of the sovereign image, the underlying currents of power are hard to detect, except through the shock of montage, when pictures from antagonistic categories are juxtaposed in a polemical and disorienting way.

Conventional wisdom would have it that photographs transmit immutable truths. But although the very notion of photographic reproduction would seem to suggest that very little is lost in translation, it is clear that photographic meaning depends largely on context. Despite the powerful impression of reality (imparted by the mechanical registration of a moment of reflected light according to the rules of normal perspective), photographs, in themselves, are fragmentary and incomplete utterances. Meaning is always directed by layout, captions, text, and site and mode of presentation, as the example given above suggests. Thus, since photographic archives tend to suspend meaning and use, within the archive meaning exists in a state that is both residual and potential. The suggestion of past uses coexists with a plenitude of possibilities. In functional terms, an active archive is like a toolshed, a dormant archive like an abandoned toolshed. (Archives are not like coal mines; meaning is not extracted from nature, but from culture.) In terms borrowed from linguistics, the archive constitutes the paradigm or iconic system from which photographic "statements" are constructed. Archival potentials change over time; the keys are appropriated by different disciplines, discourses, "specialties." For example, the pictures in photo agency files become available to history when they are no longer useful to topical journalism. Similarly, the new art history of photography at its too prevalent worst rummages through archives of every sort in search of masterpieces to celebrate and sell.

Clearly archives are not neutral; they embody the power inherent in accumulation, collection, and hoarding as well as that power inherent in the command of the lexicon and rules of a language. Within bourgeois culture, the photographic project itself has from the very beginning been identified not only with the dream of a universal language, but also with the establishment of global archives and repositories according to models offered by libraries, encyclopedias, zoological and botanical gardens, museums, police files, and banks. (Reciprocally, photography contributed to the modernization of information flows within most of these institutions.) Any photographic archive, no matter how small, appeals indirectly to these institutions for its authority. Not only the truths, but also the pleasures of photographic archives are linked to those enjoyed in these other sites. As for the truths, their philosophical basis lies in an aggressive empiricism, bent on achieving a universal inventory of appearance. Archival projects typically manifest a compulsive desire for completeness, a faith in an ultimate coherence imposed by the sheer quantity of acquisitions. In practice, knowledge of this sort can only be organized according to bureaucratic means. Thus, the archival perspective is closer to that of the capitalist, the professional positivist, the bureaucrat, and the engineer – not to mention the connoisseur – than it is to that of the working class. Generally speaking, working-class culture is not built on such high ground.

And so archives are contradictory in character. Within their confines meaning is liberated from use, and yet at a more general level an empiricist model of truth prevails. Pictures are atomized, isolated in one way and homogenized in another. (Alphabet soup comes to mind.) But any archive that is not a complete mess establishes an order of some sort among its contents. Normal orders are either taxonomic or diachronic (sequential); in most archives both methods are used, but at different, often alternating, levels of organization. Taxonomic orders might be based on sponsorship, authorship, genre, technique, iconography, subject matter, and so on, depending on the range of the archive. Diachronic orders follow a chronology of production or acquisition. Anyone who has sorted or simply sifted through a box of family snapshots understands the dilemmas (and perhaps the folly) inherent in these procedures. One is torn between narration and categorization, between chronology and inventory.

What should be recognized here is that photographic books (and exhibitions) frequently cannot help but reproduce these rudimentary ordering schemes, and in so doing implicitly claim a share in both the authority and illusory neutrality of the archive. Herein lies the "primitivism" of still photography in relation to the cinema. Unlike a film, a photographic book or exhibition can almost always be dissolved back into its component parts, back into the archive. The ensemble can seem to be both provisional and artless. Thus, within the dominant culture of photography, we find a chain of dodges and denials: at any stage of photographic production the apparatus of selection and interpretation is liable to render itself invisible (or conversely to celebrate its own workings as a kind of moral crusade or creative magic). Photographer, archivist, editor, and curator can all claim, when challenged about their interpretations, to be merely passing along a neutral reflection of an already established state of affairs. Underlying this process of professional denial is a common-sensical empiricism. The photograph reflects reality. The archive accurately catalogues the ensemble of reflections, and so on. Even if one admits – as is common enough nowadays – that the photograph interprets reality, it might still follow that the archive accurately catalogues the ensemble of interpretations, and so on again. Songs of the innocence of discovery can be sung at any point. Thus, the "naturalization of the cultural" that Roland Barthes saw as an essential characteristic of photographic discourse is repeated and reinforced at virtually every level of the cultural apparatus – unless it is interrupted by criticism.[5]

In short, photographic archives by their very structure maintain a hidden connection between knowledge and power. Any discourse that appeals without skepticism to archival standards of truth might well be viewed with suspicion. But what narratives and inventories might be constructed, were we to interpret an archive such as this one in a normal fashion?

I can imagine two different sorts of books being made from Shedden's photographs, or for that matter from any similar archive of functional photographs. On the one hand, we might regard these pictures as "historical documents." We might, on the other hand, treat these photographs as "aesthetic objects." Two more or less contradictory choices emerge. Are these photographs to be taken as a transparent means to a knowledge – intimate and detailed even if incomplete – of industrial Cape Breton in the postwar

5. Roland Barthes, "Rhétorique de l'image," *Communications*, no. 4 (1964); in *Image, Music, Text*, trans. Stephen Heath (New York: Hill and Wang, 1977), p. 51.

decades? Or are we to look at these pictures "for their own sake," as opaque ends-in-themselves? This second question has a corollary. Are these pictures products of an unexpected vernacular authorship; is Leslie Shedden a "discovery" worthy of a minor seat in an expanding pantheon of photographic artists?

Consider the first option. From the first decade of this century, popular histories and especially schoolbook histories have increasingly relied on photographic reproductions. Mass culture and mass education lean heavily on photographic realism, mixing pedagogy and entertainment in an avalanche of images. The look of the past can be retrieved, preserved, and disseminated in an unprecedented fashion. But awareness of history as an *interpretation* of the past succumbs to a faith in history as *representation*. The viewer is confronted, not by *historical-writing*, but by the appearance of *history itself*. Photography would seem to gratify the often quoted desire of that "father of modern historical scholarship," Leopold von Ranke, to "show what actually happened."[6] Historical narration becomes a matter of appealing to the silent authority of the archive, of unobtrusively linking incontestable documents in a seamless account. (The very term "document" entails a notion of legal or official truth, as well as a notion of *proximity to* and verification of an original event.) Historical narratives that rely primarily on photography almost invariably are both positivist and historicist in character. For positivism, the camera provides mechanical and thus "scientifically" objective evidence of "data." Photographs are seen as sources of factual, positive knowledge, and thus are appropriate documents for a history that claims a place among the supposedly objective sciences of human behavior. For historicism, the archive confirms the existence of a linear progression from past to present, and offers the possibility of an easy and unproblematic retrieval of the past from the transcendent position offered by the present. At their worst, pictorial histories offer an extraordinarily reductive view of historical causality: the First World War "begins" with a glimpse of an assassination in Sarajevo; the entry of the United States into the Second World War "begins" with a view of wrecked battleships.

Thus, most visual and pictorial histories reproduce the established patterns of historical thought in bourgeois culture. By doing so in a "popular" fashion, they extend the hegemony of that culture, while exhibiting a thinly veiled contempt and disregard for

6. Leopold von Ranke, preface to "Histories of the Latin and Germanic Nations from 1494-1514," in *The Varieties of History*, ed. Fritz Stern (New York: Meriden Books, 1972), p. 57.

popular literacy. The idea that photography is a "universal language" contains a persistent element of condescension as well as pedagogical zeal.

The widespread use of photographs as historical illustrations suggests that significant events are those which can be pictured, and thus history takes on the character of *spectacle*.[7] But this pictorial spectacle is a kind of rerun, since it depends on prior spectacles for its supposedly "raw" material.[8] Since the 1920s, the picture press, along with the apparatuses of corporate public relations, publicity, advertising, and government propaganda, have contributed to a regularized flow of images: of disasters, wars, revolutions, new products, celebrities, political leaders, official ceremonies, public appearances, and so on. For a historian to use such pictures without remarking on these initial uses is naive at best, and cynical at worst. What would it mean to construct a pictorial history of postwar coal mining in Cape Breton by using pictures from a company public relations archive without calling attention to the bias inherent in that source? What present interests might be served by such an oversight?

The viewer of standard pictorial histories loses any ground in the present from which to make critical evaluations. In retrieving a loose succession of fragmentary glimpses of the past, the spectator is flung into a condition of imaginary temporal and geographical mobility. In this dislocated and disoriented state, the only coherence offered is that provided by the constantly shifting position of the camera, which provides the spectator with a kind of powerless omniscience. Thus, the spectator comes to identify with the technical apparatus, with the authoritative institution of photography. In the face of this authority, all other forms of telling and remembering begin to fade. But the machine establishes its truth, not by logical argument, but by providing an *experience*. This experience characteristically veers between nostalgia, horror, and an overriding sense of the exoticism of the past, its irretrievable otherness for the viewer in the present. Ultimately, then, when photographs are uncritically presented as historical documents, they are transformed into aesthetic objects. Accordingly, the pretense to historical under-

7. See Guy DeBord, *La société du spectacle* (Paris: Editions Buchat-Chastel, 1967); unauthorized translation, *Society of the Spectacle* (Detroit: Black and Red, 1970; rev. ed., 1977).
8. We might think here of the reliance, by the executive branch of the United States government, on "photo opportunities." For a discussion of an unrelated example, see Susan Sontag's dissection of Leni Reifenstahl's alibi that *Triumph of the Will* was merely an innocent documentary of the orchestrated-for-cinema 1934 Nuremberg Rally of the National Socialists. Sontag quotes Reifenstahl: "Everything is genuine . . . It is *history – pure history*." Susan Sontag, "Fascinating Fascism," *New York Review of Books* 22, no. 1 (February 1975); reprinted in *Under the Sign of Saturn* (New York: Farrar, Straus, & Giroux, 1980), p. 82.

standing remains, although that understanding has been replaced by aesthetic experience.[9]

But what of our second option? Suppose we abandoned all pretense to historical explanation, and treated these photographs as artworks of one sort or another. This book would then be an inventory of aesthetic achievement and/or an offering for disinterested aesthetic perusal. The reader may well have been prepared for these likelihoods by the simple fact that this book has been published by a press with a history of exclusive concern with the contemporary vanguard art of the United States and Western Europe (and to a lesser extent, Canada). Further, as I've already suggested, in a more fundamental way, the very removal of these photographs from their initial contexts invites aestheticism.

I can imagine two ways of converting these photographs into "works of art," both a bit absurd, but neither without ample precedent in the current fever to assimilate photography into the discourse and market of the fine arts. The first path follows the traditional logic of romanticism, in its incessant search for aesthetic origins in a coherent and controlling authorial "voice." The second path might be labeled "post-romantic" and privileges the subjectivity of the collector, connoisseur, and viewer over that of any specific author. This latter mode of reception treats photographs as "found objects." Both strategies can be found in current photographic discourse; often they are intertwined in a single book, exhibition, or magazine or journal article. The former tends to predominate, largely because of the continuing need to validate photography as a fine art, which requires an incessant appeal to the myth of authorship in order to wrest photography away from its reputation as a servile and mechanical medium. Photography needs to be won and rewon repeatedly for the ideology of romanticism to take hold.[10]

The very fact that this book reproduces photographs by a single author might seem to be an implicit concession to a romantic auteurism. But it would be difficult to make a credible argument for Shedden's autonomy as a maker of photographs. Like all commercial photographers, his work involved a negotiation between his

9. Two recent books counter this prevailing tendency in "visual history" by directing attention to the power relationships behind the making of pictures: Craig Heron, Shea Hoffmitz, Wayne Roberts, and Robert Storey, *All That Our Hands Have Done: A Pictorial History of the Hamilton Workers* (Oakville, Ontario: Mosaic Press, 1981), and Sarah Graham-Brown, *Palestinians and Their Society, 1880-1946* (London: Quartet Books, 1980).

10. In the first category are books which discover unsung commercial photographers: e.g., Mike Disfarmer, *Disfarmer: The Heber Springs Portraits,* text by Julia Scully (Danbury, N.H.: Addison House, 1976). In the second category are books which testify to the aesthetic sense of the collector: e.g., Sam Wagstaff, *A Book of Photographs from the Collection of Sam Wagstaff* (New York: Gray Press, 1978).

own craft and the demands and expectations of his clients. Further, the presentation of his work was entirely beyond his control. One might hypothetically argue that Shedden was a hidden artist, producing an original oeuvre under unfavorable conditions. ("Originality" is the essential qualifying condition of genuine art under the terms dictated by romanticism. To the extent that photography was regarded as a copyist's medium by romantic art critics in the nineteenth century, it failed to achieve the status of the fine arts.) The problem with auteurism, as with so much else in photographic discourse, lies in its frequent misunderstanding of actual photographic practice. In the wish-fulfilling isolation of the "author," one loses sight of the social institutions – corporation, school, family – that are speaking by means of the commercial photographer's craft. One can still respect the craft work of the photographer, the skill inherent in work within a set of formal conventions and economic constraints, while refusing to indulge in romantic hyperbole.

The possible "post-romantic" reception of these photographs is perhaps even more disturbing and more likely. To the extent that photography still occupies an uncertain and problematic position within the fine arts, it becomes possible to displace subjectivity, to find refined aesthetic sensibility not in the maker of images, but in the viewer. Photographs such as these then become the objects of a secondary voyeurism, which preys on, and claims superiority to, a more naive primary act of looking. The strategy here is akin to that initiated and established by pop art in the early 1960s. The aesthetically informed viewer examines the artifacts of mass or "popular" culture with a detached, ironic, and even contemptuous air. For pop art and its derivatives, the look of the sophisticated viewer is always constructed in relation to the inferior look which preceded it. What disturbs me about this mode of reception is its covert elitism, its implicit claim to the status of "superior" spectatorship. A patronizing, touristic, and mock-critical attitude toward "kitsch" serves to authenticate a high culture that is increasingly indistinguishable from mass culture in many of its aspects, especially in its dependence on marketing and publicity and its fascination with stardom. The possibility of this kind of intellectual and aesthetic arrogance needs to be avoided, especially when a book of photographs by a small-town commercial photographer is published by a press that regularly represents the culture of an international and metropolitan avant-garde.

In general, then, the hidden imperatives of photographic culture drag us in two contradictory directions: toward "science" and a myth of "objective truth" on the one hand, and toward "art" and a cult of "subjective experience" on the other. This dualism haunts photography, lending a certain goofy inconsistency to most commonplace assertions about the medium. We repeatedly hear the following refrain. Photography is an art. Photography is a science (or at least constitutes a "scientific" way of seeing). Photography is both an art and a science. In response to these claims, it becomes important to argue that photography is neither art nor science, but is suspended between both the *discourse* of science and that of art, staking its claims to cultural value on both the model of truth upheld by empirical science and the model of pleasure and expressiveness offered by romantic aesthetics. In its own erratic way, photographic discourse has attempted to bridge the extreme philosophical and institutional separation of scientific and artistic practice that has characterized bourgeois society since the late eighteenth century. As a mechanical medium which radically transformed and displaced earlier artisanal and manual modes of visual representation, photography is implicated in a sustained crisis at the very center of bourgeois culture, a crisis rooted in the emergence of science and technology as seemingly autonomous productive forces. At the heart of this crisis lies the question of the survival and deformation of human creative energies under the impact of mechanization. The institutional promotion of photography as a fine art serves to redeem technology by suggesting that subjectivity and the machine are easily compatible. Especially today, photography contributes to the illusion of a humanized technology, open both to "democratic" self-expression and to the mysterious workings of genius. In this sense, the camera seems the exemplar of the benign machine, preserving a moment of creative autonomy that is systematically denied in the rest of most people's lives. The one-sided lyricism of this view is apparent when we consider the myriad ways in which photography has served as a tool of industrial and bureaucratic power.[11]

If the position of photography within bourgeois culture is as problematic as I am suggesting here, then we might want to move away from the art-historicist bias that governs most contemporary discussions of the medium. We need to understand how photography works within everyday life in advanced industrial societies: the problem is one of cultural history rather than art history. This is a matter of beginning to figure out how to read the making and reception of ordinary pictures. Leslie Shedden's photographs would

11. This passage restates an argument made in my essay, "The Traffic in Photographs," *Art Journal* 41, no. 1 (Spring 1981): 15-16.

seem to allow for an exemplary insight into the diverse and contradictory ways in which photography effects the lives of working people.

Let's begin again by recognizing that we are confronting a curious archive – divided and yet connected elements in an imaginary social mechanism. Pictures that depict fixed moments in an interconnected economy of flows: of coal, money, machines, consumer goods, men, women, children. Pictures that are themselves elements in a unified symbolic economy – a traffic in photographs – a traffic made up of memories, commemorations, celebrations, testimonials, evidence, facts, fantasies. Here are official pictures, matter-of-factly committed to the charting and celebration of progress. A mechanical conveyor replaces a herd of ponies. A mechanical miner replaces ten human miners. A diesel engine replaces a locomotive. Here also are private pictures, personal pictures, family pictures: weddings, graduations, family groups. One is tempted at the outset to distinguish two distinct realisms, the *instrumental realism* of the industrial photograph and the *sentimental realism* of the family photograph. And yet it would seem clear that these are not mutually exclusive categories. Industrial photographs may well be commissioned, executed, displayed, and viewed in a spirit of calculation and rationality. Such pictures seem to offer unambiguous truths, the useful truths of applied science. But a zone of virtually unacknowledged *affects* can also be reached by photographs such as these, touching on an aesthetics of power, mastery, and control. The public *optimism* that suffuses these pictures is merely a respectable, *sentimentally acceptable,* and ideologically necessary substitute for deeper feelings – the cloak for an aesthetics of exploitation. In other words, even the blandest pronouncement in words and pictures from an office of corporate public relations has a subtext marked by threats and fear. (After all, under capitalism everyone's job is on the line.) Similarly, no family photograph succeeds in creating a haven of pure sentiment. This is especially true for people who feel the persistent pressures of economic distress, and for whom even the making of a photograph has to be carefully counted as an expense. Granted, there are moments in which the photograph overcomes separation and loss, therein lies much of the emotional power of photography. Especially in a mining community, the life of the emotions is persistently tied to the instrumental workings underground. More than elsewhere, a photograph can become without warning a tragic memento.

One aim of this essay, then, is to provide certain conceptual tools for a unified understanding of the social workings of photography in an industrial environment. This project might take heed of some of Walter Benjamin's last advice, from his argument for a historical materialist alternative to a historicism that inevitably empathized "with the victors":

> *There is no document of civilization which is not at the same time a document of barbarism. And just as such a document is not free of barbarism, barbarism taints also the manner in which it was transmitted from one owner to another. A historical materialist therefore dissociates himself from it as far as possible. He regards it as his task to brush history against the grain.*[12]

Benjamin's wording here is careful. Neither the contents, nor the forms, nor the many receptions and interpretations of the archive of human achievements can be assumed to be innocent. And further, even the concept of "human achievements" has to be used with critical emphasis in an age of automation. The archive has to be read from below, from a position of solidarity with those displaced, deformed, silenced, or made invisible by the machineries of profit and progress.

12. Benjamin, "Theses on the Philosophy of History," pp. 256-257.

The text reproduced here is the introduction to a longer, three-part essay entitled "Photography Between Labour and Capital," in Benjamin H. D. Buchloh and Robert Wilkie, eds., *Mining Photographs and Other Pictures: A Selection from the Negative Archives of Shedden Studio, Glace Bay, Cape Breton, 1948-1968. Photographs by Leslie Shedden,* The Nova Scotia Series: Source Materials of the Contemporary Arts, vol. 13 (Halifax: The Press of the Nova Scotia College of Art and Design and the University College of Cape Breton Press, 1983).

Mining Photographs constituted a deliberate shift in the trajectory of a press that had been previously committed solely to the documentation of vanguard artistic practice in the United States, Canada, and Western Europe. Through a collaborative effort, the book combines a sampling of an archive of industrial and commercial photographs with essays on regional working-class history and the history of photography. In addition to a selection of three-hundred-and-thirty-four pictures by photographer Leslie Shedden, the book includes an introduction by Robert Wilkie and a study of the working-class culture and politics of industrial Cape Breton by historian Donald Macgillivray, as well as the essay excerpted here. Both Wilkie and Macgillivray are natives of the region; Buchloh and I are outsiders. We sought with some success to reach a local audience, as well as the scattered audience of photographers, artists, intellectuals, and activists that one might anticipate for such a project.

"Photography Between Labour and Capital" begins with this brief historiographic meditation and moves on to trace a lineage of technical realism, from the illustrated medical and mining manuals of the sixteenth century and the *Encyclopedia* of the eighteenth-century French Enlightenment to the institutionalized industrial photography of the epoch of monopoly capitalism. Thus it is an essay about the emergence and triumph of dominant models for the photographic representation of human labor, about the affiliation of photographic realism with the logic and enterprise of engineering.

Overall, *Mining Photographs* is intended as a "tool kit" – in Michel Foucault's sense – for the reader. We had in mind a picture book that allowed pictures to offer their density of meaning, *and* a picture book that developed a critique of picture books. Our grandest ambition was for the reader to think differently about work, industry, and everyday life. Slightly more modestly, we wanted the reader to think differently about the ways in which history and the present are conventionally represented by means of pictures.

Ideology, Confrontation, and Political Self-Awareness: An Essay, 1981

ADRIAN PIPER

We started out with beliefs about the world and our place in it that we didn't ask for and didn't question. Only later, when those beliefs were attacked by new experiences that didn't conform to them, did we begin to doubt: e.g., do we and our friends really understand each other? Do we really have nothing in common with blacks/whites/gays/workers/the middle class/other women/other men/etc.?

Doubt entails self-examination because a check on the plausibility of your beliefs and attitudes is a check on all the constituents of the self. Explanations of why your falsely supposed "X" include your *motives* for believing "X" (your desire to maintain a relationship, your impulse to be charitable, your goal of becoming a better person); the *causes* of your believing "X" (your early training, your having drunk too much, your innate disposition to optimism); and your *objective reasons* for believing "X" (it's consistent with your other beliefs, it explains the most data, it's inductively confirmed, people you respect believe it). These reveal the traits and dispositions that individuate one self from another.

So self-examination entails self-awareness, i.e., awareness of the components of the self. But self-awareness is largely a matter of degree. If you've only had a few discordant experiences, or relatively superficial discordant experiences, you don't need to examine yourself very deeply in order to revise your false beliefs. For instance, you happen to have met a considerate, sensitive, nonexploitative person who's into sadism in bed. You think to yourself, "This doesn't show that my beliefs about sadists in general are wrong; after all, think what Krafft-Ebing says! This particular person is merely an exception to the general rule that sexual sadists are demented." Or you think, "My desire to build a friendship with this person is based on the possibility of reforming her/him (and has nothing to do with any curiosity to learn more about my own sexual tastes)." Such purely cosmetic repairs in your belief structure sometimes suffice to maintain your sense of self-consistency. Unless you are confronted with a genuine personal crisis, or freely choose to push deeper and ask yourself more comprehensive and disturbing questions about the genesis and justification of your own beliefs, your actual degree of self-awareness may remain relatively thin.

Usually the beliefs that remain most unexposed to examination are the ones we need to hold in order to maintain a certain conception of ourselves and our relation to the world. These are the ones in which we have the deepest personal investment. Hence these are the ones that are most resistant to revision; e.g., we have to believe that other people are capable of understanding and sympathy, of honorable and responsible behavior, in order not to feel completely alienated and suspicious of those around us. Or some people have to believe that the world of political and social catastrophe is completely outside of their control in order to justify their indifference to it.

Some of these beliefs may be true, some may be false. This is difficult to ascertain because we can only confirm or disconfirm the beliefs under examination with reference to other beliefs, which themselves require examination. In any event, the set of false beliefs that a person has a personal investment in maintaining is what I will refer to (following Marx) as a person's *ideology*.

Ideology is pernicious for many reasons. The obvious one is that it makes people behave in stupid, insensitive, self-serving ways, usually at the expense of other individuals or groups. But it is also pernicious because of the mechanisms it uses to protect itself, and its consequent capacity for self-regeneration in the face of the most obvious counterevidence. Some of these mechanisms are:

(1) *The false identity mechanism.* In order to preserve your ideological beliefs against attack, you identify them as objective facts and not as beliefs at all. For example, you insist that it is just a fact that black people are less intelligent than whites, or that those on the sexual fringes are in fact sick, violent, or asocial. By maintaining that these are statements of fact rather than statements of belief compiled from the experiences you personally happen to have had, you avoid having to examine and perhaps revise those beliefs. This denial may be crucial to maintaining your self-conception against attack. If you're white and suspect that you may not be all that smart, to suppose that at least there's a whole *race* of people you're smarter than may be an important source of self-esteem. Or if you're not entirely successful in coping with your own nonstandard sexual impulses, isolating and identifying the sexual fringe as sick, violent, or asocial may serve the very important function of reinforcing your sense of yourself as "normal."

The fallacy of the false identity mechanism as a defense of one's ideology consists in supposing that there exist objective social facts that are not constructs of beliefs people have about each other.

(2) *The illusion of perfectibility.* Here you defend your ideology by convincing yourself that the hard work of self-scrutiny has an end and a final product, i.e., a set of true, central, and uniquely defensible beliefs about some issue, and that you have in fact achieved this end, hence needn't subject your beliefs to further examination. Since there is no such final product, all of the inferences that supposedly follow from this belief are false. Example: you're a veteran of the antiwar movement and have developed a successful and much-lauded system of draft avoidance counseling, on which your entire sense of self-worth is erected. When it is made clear to you that such services primarily benefit the middle class, and that this consequently forces much larger proportions of the poor, the uneducated, and blacks to serve and be killed in its place, you resist revising your views in light of this information on the grounds that you've worked on and thought hard about these issues, have developed a sophisticated critique of them, and therefore have no reason to reconsider your opinions or efforts. You thus treat the prior experience of having reflected deeply on some issue as a defense against the self-reflection appropriate now, that might uncover your personal investment in your antidraft role.

(3) *The one-way communication mechanism.* You deflect dissent from, criticism of, or attacks on your cherished beliefs by treating all of your own pronouncements as imparting genuine information, but treating those of other people as mere symptoms of some moral or psychological defect. Say you're committed to feminism, but have difficulty making genuine contact with other women. You dismiss all arguments advocating greater attention to lesbian and separatist issues within the women's movement on the grounds that they are maintained by frustrated man-haters who just want to get their names in the footlights. By reducing questions concerning the relations of women to each other to pathology or symptoms of excessive self-interest, you avoid confronting the conflict between your intellectual convictions and your actual alienation from other women, and therefore the motives that might explain this conflict. If these motives should include such things as deep-seated feelings of rivalry with other women, or a desire for attention from men, then avoiding recognition of this conflict is crucial to maintaining your self-respect.

The one-way communication mechanism is a form of elitism that ascribes pure, healthy, altruistic political motives only to oneself (or one's group) while reducing all dissenters to the status of moral defectives or egocentric and self-seeking subhumans whom it is entirely justified to manipulate or disregard, but with whom the possibility of rational dialogue is not to be taken seriously.

There are many other mechanisms for defending one's personal ideology. These are merely a representative sampling. Together, they all add up to what I will call the *illusion of omniscience*. This illusion consists in being so convinced of the infallibility of your own beliefs about everyone else that you forget that you are perceiving and experiencing other people from a perspective that is in its own ways just as subjective and limited as theirs. Thus you confuse your personal experiences with objective reality, and forget that you have a subjective and limited *self* that is selecting, processing, and interpreting your experiences in accordance with its own limited capacities. You suppose that your perceptions of someone are truths about her or him, that your understanding of someone is comprehensive and complete. Thus your self-conception is not demarcated by the existence of other people. Rather, you appropriate them into your self-conception as psychologically and metaphysically transparent objects of your consciousness. You ignore their ontological independence, their psychological opacity, and thereby their essential personhood. The illusion of omniscience resolves into the fallacy of solipsism.

The result is blindness to the genuine needs of other people, coupled with the arrogant and dangerous conviction that you understand those needs better than they do; and a consequent inability to respond to those needs politically in genuinely effective ways.

The antidote, I suggest, is confrontation of the sinner with the evidence of the sin: the rationalizations, the subconscious defense mechanisms, the strategies of avoidance, denial, dismissal, and withdrawal that signal on the one hand the retreat of the self to the protective enclave of ideology; on the other hand, precisely the proof of subjectivity and fallibility that the ideologue is so anxious to ignore. This is the concern of my work of the past three years.

The success of the antidote increases with the specificity of the confrontation. And because I don't know you I can't be as specific as I would like. I can only indicate general issues that have specific references in my own experience. But if this discussion has made you in the least degree self-conscious about your political beliefs or about your strategies for preserving them; or even faintly uncomfortable or annoyed at my having discussed them; or has raised just the slightest glimmerings of doubt about the veracity of your opinions, then I will consider this piece a roaring success. If not, then I will just have to try again, for my own sake. For of course I am talking not just about you, but about *us*.

Constructing a Life

MARTHA ROSLER

1

How to realize the substance of your own life while retaining some perspective on the flow of, well, history.

A decade spent on the question whether we can change ourselves and the way things are by willing it. (What role *does* consciousness play?) A mistake was to get stuck in remaking the cultural, slighting its bases. It is true that people decided to change things. It is true that now it seems like everything we achieved, inadequate and distorted as some of it was, is to be revoked by the radically reactionary regime. Hard to understand that the scale of change exceeds the scale of a person's life. She realizes she is, they are, a decade older and in some ways still the persons they decided not to be any more. It is true also that he (and he, and he) has learned a lot about How To Think About Women. The truth is, it's hard to make changes stick. Yet things change. (Nuns sue their bishop.) All things change. ("Pessimism of the intellect, optimism of the will" becomes a consoling slogan.)

Times change, people move. There is the question of ego. "Mobility." The development of self. The self, learning to cut itself off from others, looks for its best setting, like a jewel.

2

She had moved to California a decade earlier to find a breathing space, away from city struggle, pollution, high rents – and found real estate, urbanization, pollution, high rents. People moved in together, in groups. (Later the two of them, now a "couple," move in alone.) You make a household, apportion tasks, make things rational . . . But the self is not rational (as women learn). Easy to console yourself with certain notions of human nature, some of them bad, oppressive, when you get scared, bored, angry. When change is demanded by your friends, when accommodation is necessary. Or – let's come to the point – when change was demanded by his lover, he found it easiest to *repress.* The point is that men and women are still men. and. women. She worries. He represses. It is worthwhile, she thinks, to rummage through their unspoken deal.

3

They each question the nature and possibility of unity. Was political unity, to pick a safer, worldly example, a fiction smoothing the way for a most extreme individual privacy, defined by the notion of "choice"? Or, conversely, did unity mean a total loss of choice? Or was it a struggle within and without, inside the group, against it as well as for it, for a perhaps only utopian collaborativeness-in-general, to occasion individual freedom? Easy for him: he misunderstood the struggle against domination to be a struggle for raw freedom. It was not. It was an abstract struggle for the *right* to freedom, and thus implicitly demanded a commitment to a long collective effort. The freedom to give oneself freely to something without bondage. But he could not even consult with her about doing the laundry. Often their solidarity was enacted on the level of fantasy.

4

He uses words that interest her: truth, weakness. Curiously old-fashioned for a "reformed" man. But his old self longed for the conservative stability of family and class. He could not effect a synthesis. He is stubborn in protection of his private self. They try to talk. He is angry to be seen as angry. The truth is, you could tell her anything about herself, and she'd believe it. (Easy to criticize the "counterculture's" commune life; but why dismiss the effort to create a self freer in the give and take?) Years of struggle have shown her she struggles with the same dependencies as ever – yet it is human to need support. Paradoxically, she has come to believe more and more in the possibility of change.

As a child he had taken a vow of silence. By being silent he was free to make any judgment whatsoever . . . The breathtaking advance in freedom meant a certain loss of potency in the world. Still, he would endure. It was their custom.

5

She imagines that by moving on, she will make a better, changed self. She is adventurous and cowardly, a rotten combination. She moves East while the balance of profits moves West. She discovers what it means that bankers and real-estate operators have captured New York, her home town. No longer a home town, now it is a monstrous machine for speculation and the gratification of the rich. A machine of success and failure in the public world. One

tries to advance while keeping one's commitments, confronting the usual issue of self-interest versus decency. The difficulty of erecting a life in the debased context of high finance and planned urban collapse. Whom do you displace by moving to Brooklyn, Astoria, the Lower East Side? Harder and harder to have the freedom to do your work, without someone's fortune to support you, without some grave compromise. The city uses artists as a wedge against the poor, creating new real estate that will displace them too: the swelling army of dispossessed. (Policy advisors say we suffer from too much democracy. Could we become a police state? That would suit some people just fine.) He won't face his fears of New York City. He suspects her of feeling exhilarated on the subway. She moves to Brooklyn, after all. He comes to look, and flies home shaking his head. He decides not to come. She flies West. She cries that he is as impermeable as a rock in an ocean tide. Determined, he endures. But unlike the rock she sees him as, he feels, hears, sees. Wracked by unvented emotion, he chokes and shakes. Calmer, he says, "Behind every no there is a yes."

6

The problem is how people can maintain commitment to change and to each other. She returns East to start constructing a life. We enter the new bleaker decade in which the matter of freedom is reshaped. The wrong people try to patent the word "freedom." The new regime seeks renewed control and profits and plays vicious word games with old words ("terrorism," "authoritarianism," "totalitarianism"). More people than ever in the world know the words mean life-or-death. The problem is how to seek freedom while acknowledging that the unbridled self is not free (or even the real issue). Through the decade the fashion for cooperation faded. For him and maybe for her, without external support cooperation was not a reflex but a matter of persuasion, choosing one's own private interest undisturbed by a wider vision. Each of them felt the strain. It seemed almost a relief to part.

Back in Brooklyn where she started – what happened to the decade? Well, she's, we've, learned a lot. The problem is how to do one's work and work with others, not to fall away in private defeat – or success. How to recognize that answers aren't given in advance, that freedom must be fought for, that change takes longer than a lifetime. The problem is how to live your life while recognizing the scale of history. The problem is how to fight to keep some things while learning how to keep others. The problem.

Spies and Watchmen

THOMAS LAWSON

Art and politics. The conjunction of these two fine abstractions is something to be abhorred, for it never augurs well for either one. The art produced in the name of political action is rarely more than rather unimaginative illustration, and the political theory so presented might be recognized with embarrassment by a recent graduate as no more advanced than his old term papers. As a result of its dependence on predictable rhetoric in both image and text, art of this sort is inevitably conservative in the profoundest sense, leaving so many questions unasked in its headlong rush to seem progressive that it finds itself wedged more and more firmly into that small corner of society, the art world, which it professes to despise. The central problem, of course, is a willful refusal to recognize the nature of one's audience, for few artists get the chance to address more than a small section of the intelligentsia, the only social group in Western society which can see no contradiction in calling for revolution while seeking tenure.

Nothing counts in the political arena but action, and the only times that artists have participated directly in political action, as working artists, have been moments of extreme social change, those revolutionary moments when everyone is required to question his identity and refashion his activities to fit the needs of a new society. But currently American culture is so deeply in the thrall of its own narcotics that revolution of any sort but one devised by men who must sell newly designed packages of detergent seems highly unlikely.

Nothing exhibited in the Soho marketplace is going to change the course of history. It is the despair of the self-styled political artists that artwork is entirely marginal, but it should be cause for joy, for it is this marginality that gives it a certain subversive potential. Since no artwork is likely to have the impact of a political rally or a television appearance, the activities of artists are ignored by the powerful, or at best considered interesting argument for their wives and daughters. In such a case it is therefore possible for a successful artist to climb the ranks of society, gaining access as a kind of high-minded entertainer and, once there, insinuate subversive ideas. Nothing dramatic, lest his cover be blown, just a steady, niggling assertion of doubt in the homes and monuments of the people who hold power.

The artist who wishes to effect political change while continuing to work in his own small area of expertise must learn the ways of the mole. He must be content to dig in quietly, and stay dug in, perhaps for years, causing a small amount of damage to the foundations of society, nothing visible, nothing too extensive. Enough only to cause a slight subsidence of coincidence, perhaps.

A brilliant model for this strategy is to be found in that usually rather dull patch of academe, art history. Anthony Blunt has long been one of the most respected practitioners in this field of knowledge. His specialty is the Baroque period in France, and he has written several important books about this, including the major text on the work of Nicholas Poussin. Starting out in Cambridge, he built a fine career for himself, eventually becoming both director of the Courtauld Institute, one of the most prestigious colleges in Britain, and the curator of the Royal Picture Collection. And all that time he worked as a Soviet spy.

Well-born and well-bred, he enjoyed all the comforts of his class. But growing up in the thirties convinced him of the moral superiority of communism. This was not unusual among young intellectuals of the time, but his resolve to do something about it was. In turning to subversion, he scorned the public display of Marxist ideology favored by his colleagues, colleagues who remained content to serve the society they professed to despise, becoming little more than token rebels given license to prove how liberal were their paymasters.

In a like manner, artists today who parade their wares as being revolutionary in intent do little more than present political slogans as aesthetic objects. They make fetishes of the ideas of others, and in doing so claim immunity from the taint of the art market. They pose as outsiders, but in reality they are outsiders the way that watchmen are outsiders, useful in their capacity to conduct potential trouble away from central concerns. They are decoys who appear to attack the citadel, but in fact help defend it, for in their clamor for attention they provide an entertaining diversion, by the bye enticing other would-be troublemakers to identify themselves.

Better then the strategy of the spy, the infiltrator, the undercover agent, who can make himself acceptable to society while all the while representing disorder. Master of the double-bluff, he is able to infiltrate the centers of power in order to undermine the structure from within. An art of representation, a flirtation with misrepresentation. An ambiguous art which seems to flatter the situation which supports it while undermining it. Sweetly arbitrary, art which appears attractively irrational, but which turns out to be coldly rational; art which looks distant, but is deeply felt.

In the Dark

ERIC BOGOSIAN

The Second Frank

MMMMM. MMMMM. I wait for dark. The black comes for me. Some people are afraid when the sun goes down. MMMMMM. MMMMMMM. But for me . . . me . . . for me it's good in the deep dark. Warm and dark and close. Some people are afraid of small places. Tight spots. Restrictive. MMMMM. MMMMMM. Not me. Not me. I'm right at home, I'm in the right place. The good dark place. Like a baby in its womb. Like a rat in its hole, I'm *okay*.

Ever see the black skid marks on the highway? Ever wonder what happened? I don't. I think about the tires. The rubber. The black rubber. Burning. Melting. Pouring down in ropes. In sheets. In long black ribbons all around me. Twisting all around me. Around and around. Black and tight. Close and dark. Holding me. Hiding me in the darkness.

Don't you love the smell of black rubber? Maybe not. It's an acquired taste. It takes awhile. Some people never like it. Don't really understand. You can work your way up. Black leather. Black plastic. Then black rubber. Tight. Black. Rubber. Up against you. Holding. Pressing. Keeping. Resilient but firm. When you're inside, you're outside. The legs. The arms. The chest. The groin. The head. All smooth. All black. In control. Everything is held in place. Like a machine. Like a god. Like a perfect machine I stand before the mirror in my uniform. A million miles inside, in the dark. In the hiding place where none can find me.

Don't get me wrong. I enjoy it. I know just what I'm doing. So tight. Holding me. Holding me hard. Better not let go. No one could hold me like that. Perfect. Every muscle. Encased in pure black. So that nothing's lost. Everything is held onto. Every flinch. Every drop. All mine. For me.

The Shining Star

Okay, yeh, yeh, I got something to say, alright? I got a few last words. This is what I got to say: You don't know. You don't know anything about me, and you don't know nothing about the world. About reality. Got it? It's like, who the hell are you people? Who are you to say: He dies? What gives you that right? My peers. Huh. Bullshit. You're not my peers because I look down on you. You and your fat-ass existence. You and your TV brains. You've never been anywhere, you've never seen nothing, all you know is what some idiot on the boob tube tells you. Hah.

So maybe I killed those girls. So what? I didn't, but what if I did? Insignificant people die every day. You don't seem to be too upset when there's war going on or children are starving in Africa. What do you think about that? You're responsible for that and you're responsible for putting me away. You understand what that means? First of all, I'm innocent. But second of all, I'm somebody, 'cause I've seen the world. I have been in the desert, man, and I have seen the shining star. I have been with the Kings, man, and we rode the wind. I know what the truth is and the truth is that I count and you don't. It's like when you're a little kid and you step on an ant on the sidewalk. You know they don't count. Well, it's the same with me. You're just a bunch of ants. You're not even alive as far as I know. You could just be a bunch of robots. You might be robots filled with blood and guts but you're still robots. I understand that because I have seen the shining star in the desert, man. I have seen it. I have been in the desert riding a hog at 150 miles per hour and I have seen reality go by. I have been "through" it. I have tripped in places you don't even know exist. Places you couldn't even dream about if you tried. I've been in Nam, man, I have looked death right in the eyes and I saw stars and stripes. You dig what I'm saying? I'm not *an* American, I'm *the* American.

And no one can dispute me. Those who have tried are very sorry now. 'Cause I'm always ready. There's a war coming and this is only the beginning, see. Only the strong will survive. Hand to hand. Mind to mind. I don't pump iron for nothing, see? Kung fu, meditation. I'm ready for anything. I passed every test. I know I'm being tested all the time. Sometimes when I catch someone testing me they say they don't know what I'm talking about. But that's part of the test too. I know. It's all part of the test. You're part of the test. You can't fool me.

See, I've got to survive, because it all passes through me. It's up to me to hold it together. You've got to be able to give yourself up, go all the way and come all the way back. It's like if there was a candle right here, I could put my hand over it and I wouldn't get burnt. I wouldn't. 'Cause I can take it. Like, some people think I'm a drug addict 'cause I stick a needle in my arm, but I'm just testing myself, see, making myself harder. Harder and harder.

And you people, you people, you're just living out your little safe lives. You think you know about stuff, you think you can tell me about stuff. You can't tell me about anything 'cause I have seen it all, man. I have shook hands with the devil. And you wanna come here and fight with me about it and you will lose, man, because I'm the stronger one, the stronger one always wins. It's the law of the jungle, survival of the fittest. And I am stronger physically, mentally, and spiritually. That's the big joke, see. You're just here 'cause I'm here. You just came here tonight to see me, 'cause *I'm* the one. *I'm* up here and you're just sitting there, scared. You want to kill me. Like Jesus. 'Cause you're afraid. So you think you can just put me away and that's the end of it. But that's where you're wrong, see. 'Cause I'm everywhere. I'm in the air. You can't put me away. I'm inside you. That's what it is, the law, the shining star, it doesn't go away. It's always there. When everything's gone, I'll still be here.

Our Gang

What? I said we were just standing around. Nothing. I dunno, don't get yourself all excited, wait a minute, let me think. Uh, we were looking at Art's new engine. He had a new engine put into his Camarro. We were just talking. Just drinking beers. We weren't bothering anybody, we were in our part of the parking lot. Uh uh, we weren't fighting. Uh, wait, yeh, that's Billy. Billy had blood on his shirt because . . . because of something with his girlfriend, I dunno, she punched him or something. We were just minding our own business, that's all. Wolf was fucking around with his car, 'cause some guys were playing cards in his headlights, you know, and so Wolf was doing that thing where you hold your foot on the brakes and gun the engine at the same time. You know, the tires burn and maybe there's a chance that he'll let go the brakes and run over the guys playing the cards. You know, that kind of shit. We weren't causing trouble. Nobody had any weapons or anything. We don't go in for that bullshit . . . So then that chick comes over. Nobody asked her to come over, you know. She'd been to the parking lot before. Not when I was there, but they said that, I dunno, Larry, I guess, they said that you know she blew guys if they wanted. Why should they lie? There's girls like that. They just want

Л.И.БРЕЖНЕВ

attention, or they're upset because they broke up with their boyfriends. I dunno. Sometimes they're just crazy chicks. They come from other towns, like poorer towns or something and we're easy to find, you know. We're always here . . . I'm getting to that. So the next thing I knew, everyone was crowded around Wolf's car. The guys playing cards just kept playing. I think maybe one of them, Chub, mighta got up because he never gets any, you know. He's one of those guys who collects every *Playboy* and still lives with his mother. I mean, for him it was a dream come true. His big chance to score. I don't think he got it up though . . . Yeh, I guess I did, I dunno, I was drunk. I just remember somebody pushing me over to the car and she was lying back . . . What? Yeh, I guess someone was holding her, but they said she was a whore. She looked like she was enjoying it, she was moving all over the place. I just kinda fell on top a her and everyone was shouting. I just remember she smelled kinda funny and she had a shitload of eye makeup on. Boy, she was cheap . . . Then somebody, I guess Larry, pulled me off and then everyone was moving for the cars real fast, they said there was an open house in the North End, so we all took off for there and I don't remember what happened to her. I was too drunk. I musta passed out . . . What? Yeh, of course I'm sorry. I wished I wasn't there in the first place.

He's Never Gonna Talk

We, we, uh, we had this young guy. He came in and, uh, well he was brought in, and, uh, we knew all about him. We knew already. But he was being very uncooperative so, this is only an example, so in this guy's case we, uh, well look: The first thing you got to do is you make him understand some things, you know, so it's important to hit him alot of times and let him see who's hitting him. That's important. I hit him a few times. So then, um . . . Where? Oh, I hit him in the face. It's not really important, 'cause usually if you're kind of careful you're not going to hit him so hard that it's anything that has to be taken care of right away, you know, he just gets a little puffy in the face, or sometimes some teeth crack or something, but that's not important. Then it's important to frighten him a little bit, so what we do is we've got this big bucket in the middle of the room filled with water. Dirty water. And you just bring the guy over, with his hands tied. And then you grab him right behind the neck. Just push him right down into the water. You know, keep his head under for a couple of minutes, just to panic him a little. They buck a little, you gotta hold tight. Then you pull 'em back up. You don't want to drown 'em. 'Cause they get real worn out that way. You see what I mean? Then they're ready. So, uh, well then we get down to the regular stuff. Which is just you get a table, a regular table, plain metal table. You strip him and he's wet and cold and you put him on the cold metal table. Just tie him down, arms, legs, torso. So he can't move. Then you can do whatever you want. I usually start with cigarettes. Because, um, again it's important to get the psychological intention across. And he sees you smoking the cigarette. And everybody is afraid of fire. And then you just burn him. Just push the cigarette, it goes right in the skin. Just like soft, like wax. Sometimes you just leave the cigarette. While it lies there it hurts. And, um, there's clamps. Clamp around the head. Or clamp around the thumb. That hurts alot. It's good, 'cause you can twist it to just the right degree. You know, precise. The one around the head is a good one, 'cause that hurts. And, um, sometimes we, then we'll get some tape, duck tape, you put that over the eyes, over the mouth. They can still breathe, but you can control him really quickly. Pinch the nostrils, you got 'em. And then when you're ready to get down to business, really that is basically very intense pain. Spread the hand out on a wooden block. Smash the fingers gets the desired results. But I really don't like that, I used to like it alot, when I was younger I used to enjoy breaking bones and stuff. But now it's more, um, like I like the electricity stuff. It's clean, it's fast. And it's very . . . no, no, you don't do it that way. You just put it on the balls. Just tie the wire around the balls. And that's what hurts alot. Yeh, we got a doctor who's there 'cause he can tell us where to put it exactly. And there's some other spots that are good. Um, around the lips is good, and there's the fingers, especially if you've smashed the fingers, that's good, too. Armpits are good. The asshole, the bottoms of the feet and the palms of the hands, the nipples are very good. Those are all good spots. And if you've been doing everything right, then by the time you get to all that – well, they get kind of exhausted. In the case of this one guy, by the time we got to the electrical stuff and everything, we sort of realized that he wasn't going to say anything. He was kind of useless. So, uh, I don't know, there was this one guy there who had this rope. So we, uh, we just hung him. It was part of it. While we did the stuff. Yeh, we hung him. I mean, if he isn't going to talk while you're hanging him, he's never gonna talk.

The Throat

I am constantly amazed, almost frightened, by the sensitive complexity of the human physical plant. The human body that is. Consider the throat. Normally used for transmitting air, food, and speech, it is the body's most vital highway. It is nothing less than the path between heart and mind. And it must be kept in perfect working order, clean of debris, lubricated, warm, and nourished.

It is aesthetically pleasing as well. For the neck is one of the most graceful and erotic parts of the body. The slightest touch on the throat brings feelings of titillation and pleasure.

The throat is such a sensitive thing. A small disorder can cause a sore throat, or worse, a diseased throat. Fever and pain set in and, if they persist, the throat becomes a source of intense irritation. It becomes the sole center of conscious attention. Imagine for a moment a cankor in the throat. Sore and open. Deep inside. Burning. Or many cankors, inflamed and bleeding. The throat becomes dry as the pain increases. It is impossible to swallow.

Then the discovery that the cankors are malignant. Cancer of the throat. Life-threatening, it must be removed. Perhaps the vocal chords are destroyed in the process; a hole is left. A new voice is created. The whole personality changes. Crippled . . . perhaps no voice at all. Mute.

The throat is very vulnerable. It must be protected at all costs. Imagine being punched in the throat. Or strangulation. Asphyxiation. Tighter and tighter, then blackout. A piece of wire is all that's needed. But perhaps the worst of all is the most spectacular: the slitting of the throat with a straight razor. One deft move, deep and quick. The wound is fatal, yet consciousness persists.

From *Swimming to Cambodia*

SPALDING GRAY

Whenever I travel, if I have the time, I go by train. Because I like to hang out in the lounge car. I hear such great stories there – fantastic! Perhaps it's because they think they'll never see me again. It's like a big, rolling confessional.

I was on my way to Chicago from New York City when this guy came up to me and said, "Hi, I'm Jim Bean. Mind if I sit down?"

"No, I'm Spalding Gray, have a seat. What's up, Jim?"

"Oh, nothing much. I'm in the navy."

"Really? Where are you stationed?"

"Guantanamo Bay."

"Where's that?"

"Cuba."

"Really? What's it like?"

"Oh, we don't get into Cuba, man. It's totally illegal. We go down to the Virgin Islands whenever we want R & R. We get free flights down there."

"What do you do there?"

"Get laid."

"Go to whores?"

"No. I never paid for sex in my life. I get picked up by couples. I like to swing, I mean, I'm into that, you know? Threesomes, triangles, pyramids – there's power in that."

And I could see how he would be picked up. He was cute enough – insidious, but still cute. The only kind of demented thing about him was that his ears hadn't grown. They were like those little pasta shells. It was as if his body had grown but his ears hadn't caught up yet.

So I said, "Where are you off to?"

"Pittsburgh."

"Pittsburgh, my god. What's up there?"

"My wife."

"Really? How long has it been since you saw her?"

"Oh, about a year."

"I bet she's been doing some swinging herself."

"No, man, I know her. She's got fucking cobwebs growing between her legs. I wouldn't mind watching her get fucked by a guy once, no, I wouldn't mind that at all."

"Well that's quite a trip coming from Cuba to Pittsburgh."

"No, no. I'm not stationed in Cuba anymore, man. I'm in Philly."

"Oh, well what's going on in Philly?"

"Can't tell you. No way. Top secret."

"Oh, come on, Jim. Top secret in Philadelphia? You can tell me."

"No way."

And he proceeded to have five more rum cokes and tell me that in Philadelphia he is on a battleship in a waterproof chamber, chained one arm to the wall for five hours a day, next to a green button, with earphones on. I could just see those little ears waiting for orders to fire his rockets from their waterproof silos onto the Russians. He sits there waiting, with those earphones on, high on blue-flake cocaine, a new breed from Peru that he loves, with a lot of coffee because the navy can't test for cocaine. They can test for marijuana five days after you smoke a joint, but not the cocaine. He sits there high on cocaine, chained to the wall, next to the green button, in a waterproof chamber.

"Why waterproof?" I asked. I thought I'd just start with the details and work out. I know I could have said, "Why a green button?" but it didn't matter at that point.

"Waterproof, man, because when the ship sinks and I go down to the bottom of the ocean, any ocean, anywhere, I'm still there in my waterproof chamber and I can push that green button, activate my rocket, and it fires out of the waterproof silo and up, up, up it goes. I get a fucking erection every time I think of firing a rocket on those Russians. We're going to win! We're going to win this fucking war. I like the navy, though. I fucking *like* the navy. I get to travel everywhere. I've been to Africa, Sweden, India. I fucking didn't like Africa, though. I don't know why, but black women just don't turn me on."

Now here's a guy, if the women in the country don't turn him on, he misses the entire landscape. It's just one big fuzzball, a big black outline and he steps through to the other side of the world and comes out in Sweden.

"I fucking love Sweden, man. You get to see real Russkies in Sweden. They're marched in at gunpoint and they're only allowed two beers. We're drinking all the fucking beer we want. We're drunk on our asses, saying, 'Hey, Russkies, what's it like in Moscow this time of year?' And then we pay a couple of Swedish whores to go over and put their heads in the Russkies' laps. You should see those fuckers sweat, man. They are so stupid. We're going to win. We're going to win the fuckin' war. I mean, they are really *dumb.* They've got liquid fuel in the rockets, they're rusty and they're going to sputter, they're going to pop, they're going to land in our cornfields."

"Wait a minute, Jim. Cornfields? I mean, haven't you read the literature? It's bad enough if they land in the cornfields. We're all doomed."

"No, they're stupid. You won't believe this. The Russians don't even have electro-intercoms in their ships. They still speak through tubes!"

Suddenly I had this enormous fondness for the Russian navy. The whole of Mother Russia. The thought of these men speaking, like innocent children, through empty toilet paper rolls, where you could still hear compassion, doubt, envy, brotherly love, ambivalence, all those human tones coming through the tube.

Jim was very patriotic. I thought it only existed on the covers of *Newsweek* and *Time.* But no, if you take the train from New York to Chicago, there it is against a pumpkin-orange sunset, Three Mile Island. Jim stood up and saluted those three big towers, then sat back down.

Meanwhile, I was trying to make a mild stand. I was trying to talk him out of his ideas. I don't know what my platform was – I mean, he was standing for all of America and I was just concerned for myself at that point. I really felt as if I were looking my death in the face. I'm not making up any of these stories, I'm really not. And if *he* was making up the story he was telling me, I figure he's white, and if he wants it bad enough and he's in the navy, if he wasn't down in that waterproof chamber then, he must be down there now.

"Jim, Jim," I said, "you don't want to do it. Remember what happened to the guy who dropped the bomb on Hiroshima? He went crazy!"

"That asshole? He was not properly brainwashed. I," he said with great pride, "have been properly brainwashed. Also, there is the nuclear destruct club. Do you think I'm the only one who's going to be pressing that green button? There's a whole bunch of us going to do it."

"Wait, wait, wait. You, all of you, don't want to die, do you? You're going to die if you push that button. Think of all you have to live for." I had to think hard about this one. "The blue-flake cocaine, for instance. Getting picked up by couples. The Swedish whores. Blowing away the cobwebs between your wife's legs. I mean, really."

"No, I'm not going to die. We get 'pubs.'"

Everything was abbreviated, and "pubs" meant navy publications that tell them where to go to avoid radiation. And I could see him down there, after the rest of us have all been vaporized. He'll be down there in Tasmania or New Zealand starting this new red-faced, pea-brained, small-eared humanoid race. And I thought, the Mother needs a rest, Mother Earth needs a long, long rest.

If we're lucky he'll end up in Africa.

Anyway, he was beginning to realize that I wasn't totally on his side. It was hard to see that because I didn't have as detailed a platform as he had. Finally, he turned to me and said, "Listen, Mr. Spalding" (I think by then he was calling me Gary Spalding), "you would not be doing that thing you do, writing, talking, whatever it is you do in the theater, if it were not for me and the United States Navy stopping the Russians from taking over the world."

And I thought, wait a minute, maybe he's right. Maybe the Russians *are* trying to take over the world. Maybe *I'm* the one who's brainwashed. Maybe I've been hanging out with liberals too long. I mean, after all this time I thought I was a conscientious pacifist but maybe I've been deluding myself. Maybe I'm just a passive-aggressive unconscious coward, and like any good liberal, I should question everything. For instance, when did I last make a stand, any kind of stand, about anything? When did I just stand up for something right? Let alone America. What is America? Every time I try to think of America as a unit I get anxious. I think that's part of the reason I moved to Manhattan; I wanted to live on "an island off the coast of America." I wanted to live somewhere between America and Europe, a piece of land with very defined boundaries and only eight million people.

So I had no concept of America or of making a stand. I hated contact sports when I was a kid – I really didn't like the bumps. When I moved to New York City I wanted to be able to make a stand, so I took karate. But I had that horrid feeling of bone bouncing on bone whenever I hit my instructor or he hit me.

When I was in the seventh grade I fell in love with Judy Dorci. Butchy Coca was in love with her too. He lived on the other side of the tracks. He had a black leather motorcycle jacket and I had a camel's hair coat. I was careful never to go into his territory – I stayed in mine, Barrington, Rhode Island – but they didn't have a five-and-dime in Barrington and I had to buy Christmas presents. I went over to Warren, Rhode Island, Butchy's territory, to the five-and-dime, and one of Butchy's gang saw me – put the finger on me. I stepped outside and there they were, eight of them, like in *High Noon,* one foot up against the brick wall, smoking Chesterfield Regulars. I thought, this is it. I'm going to know what it's like to make a stand – but why rush it?

I ducked into the Warren Gazette just to look at Christmas cards, take my time, and there was Mr. Walker from Barrington. I said, "Hi, Mr. Walker, are you going my way?"

"I am. My car is out back. Do you mind going out the back door?"

"Nope. Let's go."

When I arrived in London for the first time, I was jetlagging and I had to rent a car to go up to Edinburgh so I felt a little out of it. All right, I was driving on the wrong side of the road – easily done – you know, no big deal. I cut a guy off first thing, and when I rolled down the window to apologize, he said, "Take off those glasses, mate, I'm going to punch you out." Just like a British redcoat announcing his intentions ahead of time.

I just rolled up the window. Why rush it?

Last year I cut a man off on Hudson Street in Manhattan. I cut off a man from New Jersey, which is one of the worst things you can do. A man from New Jersey! And I rolled down the window – why I do this, I don't know – to apologize again. This time I saw the fist coming toward me and I thought, now I'll know what it's like to have my jaw broken in five places. At the last minute, just seconds before making contact with my face, he pulled the punch and hit the side of the van instead. He walked off with his knuckles bleeding, cursing. I rolled up the window and pulled out. Why rush it?

I had a friend who wanted to rush it, because he was going into the army and he'd never been punched out. So he went to his friend Paul and said, "Paul, I've never been punched out. But I'm drafted, I'm going into the army. Please punch me out Paul, quick." And Paul knocked him out.

I didn't want to go into the army. I didn't want to get punched out. So I checked all the boxes. I admit it. I did it. I checked "homosexual" and "has trouble sleeping." Where it asked "What do you do when you can't sleep?" I put that I drank.

My mother was at home at the time having an incurable nervous breakdown and I was studying acting. I thought that if worse came to worse I would just act the way she was acting and I'd get out of the army. But there was a guy in front of me who looked very much like me; we both had beards. They touched him first, on the shoulder, and he just went bananas. He flipped out and they took him away screaming.

Now how was I going to follow that? I was depressed on two counts. One, it looked like I was going to be drafted, and two, it looked like I was a bad actor.

Recently in Manhattan, I was up early on a Sunday for some reason. It's rare. If you're up early in New York City on a Sunday, there's a strange overlap between those who are up early and those who haven't gone to bed yet. I was down in the Canal Street subway station – concrete no-man's-land. There were no subways coming, no law and order down there. There was just this one other guy and he was coming toward me. I knew he wanted something – I could feel the vibes. He needed something from me, wanted something. He was about to demand something.

"Hey, man, you got change for a quarter?"

"Uh, yeah, I think I do. Here – wait a minute, I got two dimes here and one, two, three, four pennies. How's that?"

"Nope."

"Well, what are we going to do?"

"I got a quarter and a nickel. Got three dimes?"

"Yep, I do. Here." And I counted them out carefully in his hand.

He turned, walked away, then turned back to me and said, "You only gave me two dimes, man."

"Wait a minute. I'm very careful about money matters."

Now was this where I was going to make my stand?

"Very well. If you feel you need another dime, here."

Renée has this upstairs neighbor who is a member of the Art Mafia. She has her own gallery in Soho, along with a drinking problem, and she is unbearable. She plays her quadrophonic machine at all hours, full blast, Bob Dylan's *Sarah,* over and over again. Something must have happened to her way back when that song was popular and she can't get it out of her head. She comes in drunk, puts it on at 1:30 in the morning. Now if it was 1:30 every morning, it would be great. It would be like feeding time, you know. You could get through it. You'd get used to it. But it's 1:35 or it's 2:10 or it's 4:14. You call the police but it does no good. She turns it down, they leave, she turns it up. You call the police again, they come, she turns it down, they leave, she turns it up. What can you do? You can't go to the landlord – he's Italian Mafia and lives in New Jersey.

I don't know which Mafia I dislike the most. I'm leaning toward liking the Italian Mafia because they are just immoral and still believe in mother and child. But the Art Mafia is immoral and, from what I can tell, they've stopped procreating.

So we're in Renée's apartment and I call up, "Please stop persecuting us." And she sends down these young, new artists who have gotten rich and famous in New York, but are now camping out in sleeping bags until they find their niches. And they say, "Hey, man. MAN. You know New York is Party City. That's why we moved here. So we could have parties on weekday nights. If you don't like it, move to the country – OLD MAN."

I try to practice my Buddhist Tolerance – I am turning all my cheeks to the wall at this point. I mean, really, Buddhist Tolerance in New York is just one big pacifist-escapist rationalization. Renée is not practicing it. She is pacing while steam comes screaming out of her navel.

Now there are some people who say that this woman should be killed. And I find that I'm not saying no. I don't protest it. They are talking about vigilantes.

I don't know the language. I knew the language when I was with my people in Boston in 1962, in whitebread, homogeneous Boston, brick-wall Boston. In the old days, when I spoke a common language with my people, they had what was called the "hi-fi." And when the hi-fi was too loud, all I had to do was call up and say, "Hi, Puffy. Spuddy Gray, down here. Yeah. You guessed it. The hi-fi is a little loud. Yeah. I wouldn't say anything but I've got an early dance class in the morning. Great. Thanks a lot. Yeah, Merry

Christmas to you too, Puff." Down it would go. You see, I knew the language.

Now Renée knows the language because her father was in the Jewish Mafia. So she calls up, "Bet you want to die, right? Bitch! Bitch! Cunt! I'll beat your fucking face in with a baseball bat. Bitch!" And she slams down the phone. The music gets louder.

One day I was walking out the door carrying an empty bottle of Molson Golden. I guess I was going to get my nickel back. And I heard this party noise coming from upstairs and I was seized with gut rage. Maybe I'd had a few drinks and the rage finally made it to my gut. Not that my intellect wasn't still working – it was going like a ticker tape, repeating that old adage, "All weakness tends to corrupt, and impotence corrupts absolutely." I just took the bottle and *hurled* it – my arm practically came out of its socket. It went up the flight of stairs, hit the door, and exploded like a hand grenade. They charged out with their bats and guns. I ran. Because it was an act of passion, I had forgotten to tell Renée I was going to do it and she was behind me, picking up some plastic garbage bags or something. She was way behind me so when they got to her door they met up with her. But she was innocent and they recognized that. They recognized that she was truly innocent and they didn't kill her. So there's hope.

But I wonder, how do we begin to approach the so-called Cold War (or Now-Heating-Up War) between Russia and America if I can't even begin to resolve the Hot War down on North Moore and Greenwich in Lower Manhattan?

The Rhetoric of AIDS

SIMON WATNEY

The central issue then . . . is not to determine whether one says yes or no to sex, whether one formulates prohibitions or permissions, whether one asserts its importance or denies its effects, or whether one refines the words one uses to designate it; but to account for the fact that it is spoken about, to discover who does the speaking, the positions and viewpoints from which they speak, the institutions which prompt people to speak about it and which store and distribute the things that are said. What is at issue, briefly, is the overall "discursive fact," the way in which sex is "put into discourse."

Michel Foucault
The History of Sexuality: An Introduction (1980)

. . . in order for the reweaving of ideology to be truly invisible, the narrative is necessarily chiasmic in structure: that is, that the subject of the beginning of the narrative is different from the subject at the end, and that the two subjects cross each other in a rhetorical figure that conceals their discontinuity.

Eve Kosofsky Sedgwick
Between Men: English Literature and Male Homosocial Desire (1985)

The gay identity is no more a product of nature than any other sexual identity. It has developed through a complex history of definition and self-definition, and what recent histories of homosexuality have revealed clearly is that there is no necessary connection between sexual practices and sexual identity. But since the late 1960s, with the emergence of a gay movement and the huge expansion of the gay subcultures, coming out as a homosexual, that is, openly assuming a gay identity, has been crucial to the public affirmation of homosexuality. Homosexual desire was no longer an unfortunate contingency of nature or fate; it was the positive basis of a sexual and, increasingly, social identity. AIDS implicitly threatened that, firstly by offering fearful consequences for being actively gay, but secondly, more subtly, by undermining the assumption that homosexuality is itself valid. AIDS, like nineteenth-century cancer, is seen as the disease of the sexually excessive just as "the homosexual" is seen as the embodiment of a particular sexual constitution.

Jeffrey Weeks
Sexuality and Its Discontents (1985)

It is obvious that sexual love among persons of the same sex is a perversion, because, quite apart from any other arguments based upon ethics and morality, such a practice cannot result in procreation. . . . The greatest danger in homosexuality lies in the introduction of normal people to it. An act which will produce nothing but disgust in a normal individual may quite easily become more acceptable, until the time arrives when the normal person by full acceptance of the abnormal act becomes a pervert also.

Dr. Jonathan Rodney
A Handbook of Sex Knowledge (1961)

These perverts will frequently attempt to entice normal individuals to engage in perverted practices. This is particularly true in the case of young and impressionable people who might come under the influence of a pervert. . . . One homosexual can pollute a Government office.

United States Senate
81st Congress, 2nd Session, Committee on Expenditures in Executive Departments, *Employment of Homosexuals and Other Sex Perverts in Government,* Washington, D.C., 1950

Any male person who, in public or private, commits, or is a party to the commission of, or procures or attempts to procure the commission by any male person of any act of gross indecency with another male person, shall be guilty of a misdemeanour, and being convicted thereof shall be liable at the discretion of the court to be imprisoned for any term not exceeding two years, with or without hard labour.

Criminal Law Amendment Act
Section 11 (the "Labouchère Amendment"), 1885

It needs to be understood . . . that the widely-held popular association between homosexuality and child molestation is not simply an ideological distortion of some pre-given and essential "truth" about all gay men. Otherwise one runs the risk of implicitly regarding homosexuality as a natural rather than a historical (and therefore mutable) category. For the association in question is demonstrably a fundamental aspect of the category of homosexuality as it was constructed by early sexologists around the turn of the century. Working with a crudely behaviourist framework, they concluded that there are in fact two distinct types of male homosexuality, equating these two types with highly reductive notions of sexual performance imported from their equally reductive picture of heterosexuality. Gay men were thus theorised . . . with reference to what were seen as the two basic sex-drives or instincts, the principles of femininity and masculinity. . . . Thus on the one hand there was the invert, the "natural" (e.g., incurable!) homosexual, emotionally and/or sexually attracted to his own sex. And on the other hand there was the "passive" and, it was generally assumed, basically heterosexual object of the invert's desires. Homosexuality was thus theorised in its very conception as a *relation* between predatory seducers and innocent victims. What is at stake here are the ways in which the invert/pervert hypothesis has been transmitted through the mass media of the twentieth century, the ways in which homosexuality has been regarded as "newsworthy" and hence given a particular public profile. It is this profile or silhouette which constitutes the prevailing common-sense of the whole subject.

Simon Watney
"On Gay Liberation," in *Politics & Power* (1981)

IRONY: Irony consists in saying by a jeer or a joke what one thinks, or what one wants to be thought. It would seem to belong most particularly to frivolity, but rage and contempt also use it sometimes, to advantage; consequently it can enter into elevated speech and into the most serious subjects.

Pierre Fontanier
Les Figures du Discours (1968; translation from original French)

The unprecedented sensation caused by the Vere Street pillorying tempted newspapers to discuss a topic usually reported only tersely in the crime columns. . . . Some antiwar papers, like the *Morning Chronicle,* tried to exploit English xenophobia by ascribing homosexual conduct to foreign influence, calling it a crime "horrible to the nature of Englishmen. . . ." None of the papers expressed any sympathy for the battered men. Two thought "some of them . . . cannot survive the punishment; and should it prove their death, they will not only die unpitied, but justly execrated by every

moral mind throughout the universe," the last phrase demonstrating the difficulty Regency England had in imagining standards different from its own. When editors did comment on the severity of the ordeal, it was to complain that it had not been sufficiently harsh. The *Morning Advertiser* thought "the annals of the pillory never furnished an instant in which popular vengeance was carried to greater extent." But this was not enough: it hoped "to see an Act passed in the ensuing Session [of Parliament] to make the attempt of this abominable offence capital." In effect, this would have made any homosexual who responded to a stranger's advances liable to hanging, should the stranger be a masquerading officer. The call for the extension of the death penalty was echoed by the *Morning Post,* the *Observer,* the *Statesman,* the *News,* and *Bell's Weekly Messenger.* . . . Foreign observers who did not share English prejudices were appalled, rather after the fashion of the Western press reporting Islamic severity in our own day.

Louis Crompton
Byron and Greek Love (1985)

Histories are not backdrops to set off the performance of images. They are scored into the paltry paper signs, in what they do and do not do, in what they encompass and exclude, in the ways they open onto or resist a repertoire of uses in which they can be meaningful and productive. Photographs are never "evidence" of history: they are themselves historical.

John Tagg
"The Burden of Representation," *Ten.8,* no. 14 (1984)

The rectum is a sexual organ, and it deserves the respect that a penis gets and a vagina gets. Anal intercourse is a central sexual activity, and it should be supported, it should be celebrated. . . . Everybody's too embarrassed to even contemplate this. . . . In fact, it's terribly important to actually do this, because anal intercourse has been the central activity for gay men and for some women for all of history. It's not going to go away because it's been declared unhealthy and unsound at this moment. It's *become* unhealthy, because the setting in which sex has occurred since the end of the '60s and over the '70s – the unprotected anal sex – has made it unhealthy. It's not the act itself, but the fact that it becomes a vehicle for infection. . . . That's an unfortunate hazard. What I'm trying to say is that we have to recognize what is hazardous, but at the same time, we shouldn't undermine an act that's important to celebrate just because it's under attack by the straight community. And this attack should not be joined by gay men. . . . You can't just write off anal intercourse and tell men they can no longer fuck, without giving them some kind of support. One should celebrate the act, but indicate that there is an epidemic which has stopped, if you like, this activity, an important part of one's life, and that, hopefully, there are circumstances in which unprotected anal intercourse will again become possible between two partners, in time. The risk-reduction stuff I've seen doesn't address this at all. It probably does a terrible thing to younger people who have misgivings about their own sexuality, who are confronted with all these terrible things. God knows, people find it hard enough to express themselves sexually.

Dr. Joseph Sonnabend
"Looking at AIDS in Totality: A Conversation," *New York Native,* no. 129 (October 7-13, 1985)

Another crisis coexists with the medical one. It has gone largely unexamined, even by the gay press. Like helpless mice we have peremptorily, almost inexplicably, relinquished the one power we so long fought for in constructing our modern gay community: the power to determine our own identity. And to whom have we relinquished it? The very authority we wrested it from in a struggle that occupied us for more than a hundred years: the medical profession.

Michael Lynch
"Living with Kaposi's," *Body Politic,* no. 88 (November 1982)

The relation between subjugation of the voice in favour of the visible has important consequences for understanding the zeal with which the medical profession took up photography.

Roberta McGrath
"Medical Police," *Ten.8,* no. 14 (1984)

DISAVOWAL (DENIAL): Term used by Freud in the specific sense of a mode of defence which consists in the subject's refusing to recognise the reality of a traumatic perception. . . . Inasmuch as disavowal affects *external reality,* Freud sees it as the first stage of psychosis, and he opposes it to repression: whereas the neurotic starts by repressing the demands of the id, the psychotic's first step is to disavow reality.

J. Laplanche and J.-B. Pontalis
The Language of Psycho-Analysis (1973)

What alone unites the diversity of sites in which photography operates is the social formation itself: the specific historical spaces for representation and practice which it constitutes. Photography as such has no identity. Its status as a technology varies with the power relations which invest it. Its nature as a practice depends on the institutions and agents which define it and set it to work. Its function as a mode of cultural production is tied to definite conditions of existence and its products are meaningful and legible only within the particular currencies they have. Its history has no unity. It is a flickering across a field of institutional spaces.

John Tagg
"The Burden of Representation," *Ten.8,* no. 14 (1984)

Ultimately, the question posed by venereal diseases that remain dormant for long periods of time is, whom can I trust? The answer clearly involves the establishment of intimacy and a bond of mutual concern between sexual partners. But that is hardly the same as suggesting that sexual activity, or sexuality per se, leads to illness. Yet, that is the animus underlying AIDS hysteria, the infectious agent that has suppressed our immunity from guilt. . . . But in the New Right's moral agenda it is the inner world which must be purified on pain of death. In their reign of terror, I sense a return to the premodern idea that illness is not "an expression of the inner self" but a punishment and a sign. . . .

Richard Goldstein
"Heartsick: Fear and Loving in the Gay Community," *The Village Voice,* June 28, 1983

HYSTERIA: Class of neuroses presenting a great diversity of clinical pictures. The two best isolated forms, from the point of view of symptoms, are *conversion hysteria,* in which the psychical conflict is expressed symbolically in somatic symptoms of the most varied kinds: they may be paroxistic (e.g., emotional crises accompanied by theatricality) or more long-lasting (anaesthesias, hysterical paralyses, "lumps in the throat," etc.); and *anxiety hysteria,* where the anxiety is attached in more or less stable fashion to a specific external object (phobia).

J. Laplanche and J.-B. Pontalis
The Language of Psycho-Analysis (1973)

The problem is that the doctors who've written about this disease are in medical centers. The people researching this disease, the physicians who write in the journals, just see men who have been referred to them. They know nothing about the setting, the overall environment, of the patient. They don't look at the disease in totality. In the 1950s, we had certain ideals or objectives in terms of the practice of medicine which I think we've lost. One of them was that we should understand our patients as a whole – we should understand the environment, all the settings, and all the contributions to illness, not simply look at an isolated bit of a body. To the extent that we've lost this, we've become confused. We're not really equipped to deal with the disease in its totality.

Dr. Joseph Sonnabend
"Looking at AIDS in Totality: A Conversation," *New York Native*, no. 129 (October 7-13, 1985)

Scientific photography assumed the position of being merely a reflex of the real, and there was a general move to replace other means of visual record with the photograph. This reality was limited to the exterior of the body, because early emulsions were insensitive to red. . . . Thus favoured in photography were those diseases which erupted on the surface of the body such as skin diseases, burns, breaks and deformities. One of the earliest applications was the introduction of the "before and after" picture. . . . They appeal to the sadistic. Unlike most photographs which provide us with the familiar and known, they impinge on and break the fragile base upon which our lives are built – the disavowal of mortality, of disfigurement; a breakdown of barriers between the internal/external. We are shown the body cut open, flesh minus skin. . . . These are subjects which are marked, a split not only within the subject itself, but one which divides one subject from another. This split is either healed and the subject allowed to return to the normal productive world in which her/his right to speak is returned or she/he dies within this space literally or in terms of a continued silence in the forms of confinement.

Roberta McGrath
"Medical Police," *Ten.8*, no. 14 (1984)

. . . to call homosexuals liars is equivalent to calling the resistors under a military occupation liars. It's like calling Jews "money lenders" when it was the only profession they were allowed to practice.

Michel Foucault
"Sexual Choice, Social Act: An Interview," *Salmagundi* 58-59 (Fall-Winter 1982-1983)

Subject to the gaze of the camera the body became the object of closest scrutiny, its surface continually examined for the signs of innate physical, mental and moral inferiority. From this science of corporeal semiotics there emerged new forms of knowledge about the individual and new ways of mapping depravity.

David Green
"On Foucault: Disciplinary Power and Photography," *Camerawork*, no. 32 (Summer 1985)

"Why can't you people just fuck less?" a friend admonishes. I have no easy answer, except to suggest that for many gay men, fucking satisfies a constellation of needs that are dealt with in straight society outside the arena of sex. For gay men, sex, the most powerful implement of attachment and arousal, is also an agent of communion, replacing an often hostile family and even shaping politics. It represents an ecstatic break with years of glances and guises, the furtive past we left behind. Straight people have no comparable experience, though it may seem so in memory. They are never called upon to deny desire, only to defer its consummation. For gay men, the promise of sex with anyone, at any time, is a signal gesture of liberation. It also happens to provide a fertile environment for the spread of disease. . . . "The most truthful way of regarding illness – and the healthiest way of being ill – is the most purified of, most resistant to, metaphoric thinking," Susan Sontag writes. I wish I could agree. I also wish sex could be stripped of its metaphors and reconstituted along the lines of pure pleasure. But I'm not convinced arousal can be sustained without fantasy, or fantasy composed with morality and myth. Since we are so vulnerable to the erotic potential of metaphor, how can we hope to be less susceptible when illness intersects with sex and death?

Richard Goldstein
"Heartsick: Fear and Loving in the Gay Community," *The Village Voice*, June 28, 1983

The body of Rock Hudson lies in a sealed bag in the back of a plain transit van. There was no Hollywood glitter as the body was taken away from Hudson's Beverly Hills mansion within hours of his death. Only a small crowd of fans watched as it was driven off to a secret location, where he was cremated. A friend of the star said: "Rock has requested that he be cremated as soon as possible after his death."

The Sun
October 3, 1985

The order to cremate the star's remains so quickly came from his closest friends after they learned magazines were offering £50,000 for a picture of the self-confessed homosexual. "I've never known anything like it" said one free-lance photographer. "No Hollywood star – and Hudson was one of the few genuine big stars left – has ever been buried or cremated so quickly. The speed was obviously something that had been arranged well beforehand. Several European magazines were offering up to £50,000 for photos of Hudson's body."

The Standard
October 3, 1985

The speech of the phobic adult is also characterized by extreme nimbleness. But that vertiginous skill is as if void of meaning, traveling at top speed over an untouched and untouchable abyss, of which, on occasion, only the affect shows up, giving not a sign but a signal. It happens because then language has become a counterphobic object; it no longer plays the role of miscarried introjection, capable, in the child's phobia, of revealing the anguish of original want. In analyzing these structures one is led to thread one's way through the meshes of the non-spoken in order to get at the meaning of such a strongly barricaded discourse.

Julia Kristeva
Powers of Horror (1982)

Because "homosexuality" and "homophobia" are, in any of their avatars, historical constructions, because they are likely to concern themselves intensely with each other and to assume interlocking or mirroring shapes, because the theater of their struggle is likely to be intrapsychic or intra-institutional as well as public, it is not always easy (sometimes barely possible) to distinguish them from each other. Thus, for instance, Freud's study of Dr. Schreber shows clearly that *the repression of homosexual desire* in a man who by any commonsense standard was heterosexual, occasioned paranoid psychosis; the psychoanalytic use that has been made of this perception, however, has been, not against *homophobia* and its schizogenic force, but against *homosexuality* – against homosexuals – on account of an association between "homosexuality" and mental illness.

Eve Kosofsky Sedgwick
Between Men: English Literature and Male Homosocial Desire (1985)

RETURN OF THE REPRESSED: process whereby what has been repressed – though never abolished by repression – tends to reappear, and succeeds in so doing in a distorted fashion in the form of a compromise. Freud always insisted on the "indestructibility" of the contents of the unconscious. Repressed material not only escapes destruction, it also has a permanent tendency to re-emerge into consciousness. It does so by more or less devious routes, and through the intermediary of secondary formations – "derivatives of the unconscious" – which are recognisable to a greater or lesser degree. . . . Freud is led to place the emphasis on the fact that the repressed, in order to return, makes use of the same chains of association which have served as the vehicle for repression in the first place. . . . In this context Freud evokes the excuse of the ascetic monk who, while seeking to banish temptation by gazing at an image of the crucifixion, is rewarded by the appearance of a naked woman in the place of the crucified Saviour: ". . . in and behind the repressing force, what is repressed proves itself victor in the end . . ."

J. Laplanche and J.-B. Pontalis
The Language of Psycho-Analysis (1973)

On a warm summer's evening in 1726 a man was arrested on the open ground near the City called the Moorfields. That night two constables had gone out, in the immediate aftermath of the trials and executions of that year, to see if further arrests could be made . . . and they made their arrest, a man by the name of William Brown. That night was to end for him in imprisonment, the pillory, and probably, as a married man, the ruin of his life. In court he watched his words carefully, but when he was faced with arrest and the violent abuse of the constables he spoke with more feeling. It is hardly surprising. He had known Thomas Wright, who had recently been executed for sodomy, and he had lived – and survived – with so many others the tensions and fears of the previous twelve months. "I did it because I thought I knew him," he replied, "and I think there is no crime in making what use I please of my own body."

Alan Bray
Homosexuality in Renaissance England (1982)

4. History and Memory

Sharp Rocks

EDGAR HEAP OF BIRDS

Many Tsistsistas [Cheyenne] were killed during the fight. The air was full of smoke from gunfire, and it was almost impossible to flee, because bullets were flying everywhere. However, somehow we ran and kept running to find a hiding place. As we ran, we could see the red fire of shots. We got near a hill, and there we saw a steep path where an old road used to be. There was red grass along the path, and although the ponies had eaten some of it, it was still high enough for us to hide.

In this grass we lay flat, our hearts beating fast; and we were afraid to move. It was now broad daylight. It frightened us to listen to the noise and cries of the wounded. When the noise seemed to quiet down and we believed the battle was about to end, we raised our heads high enough to see what was going on. We saw a dark figure lying near a hill, and later we learned it was the body of a Tsistsistas woman and child. The woman's body had been cut open by the soldiers.

Moving Behind
a fourteen-year-old Tsistsistas woman survivor of Colonel George Custer's Massacre of the Tsistsistas people on November 27, 1868, near what is now called Cheyenne, Oklahoma

For we the Tsistsistas people to be able to continue our native life, we have formed two survival tactics used simultaneously for our precious preservation. The sickening fact of the United States of America hunting down and murdering our women, children, and warriors is still fresh in our minds. The quiet plan of self-imposed isolation from the white man has brought us to this day – living people, thus escaping the brutal swords and gunfire. As a second and less popular tactic, we find it effective to challenge the white man through our use of the mass media. As in American business and culture, in order to survive one must communicate a mass appeal.

The native arrow points of the past were worked and formed to become sharp and strong weapons. These sharp rocks were responsible for the defense and welfare of the tribe. As weapons of war the sharp rocks of the Tsistsistas (Cheyenne) people were used for two separate purposes, as defense or attack weapons against man and as tools of preservation through hunting game animals.

Today one may still discover actual Tsistsistas arrow points on the surface of the earth. In touching these weapons I have found clues as to the useful current-day defensive and preservation tactics that can serve living Native Americans.

At this time the manifestation of our battle has changed. The white man shall always project himself into our lives using information that is provided by learning institutions and the electronic and print media. Through these experiences, the non-Indian will decide to accept or reject that the Native Americans are a unique and separate people with the mandate to maintain and strengthen indigenous rights and beliefs. Therefore, we find that the survival of our people is based upon our use of expressive forms of modern communication. The insurgent messages within these forms must serve as our present-day combative tactics.

As a native artist, these insurgent messages delivered through art must present the fact that Native Americans are decidedly different from the dominant white culture in America.

The world view which we hold is a creation of our circular awareness and sole self-determination.

Countless times our combative measures through art have been misrepresented or corruptly undertaken by the non-Indian. Too often the white man masquerades as the native artist, creating many self-serving images. Regretfully, when true Native American art is finally accepted, the style turns out to be that which fulfills the comfortable fantasy held by the non-Indian. It must be understood that the dominant white culture is not in a position to instruct in the essence of the native outlook but can only learn.

Through my touring exhibition *Sharp Rocks,* an expressive learning experience shall be offered which is gathered from many directions. *Sharp Rocks* is made up of a blend of paintings, language installations, photographs, and the Times Square video presentation of "In Our Language." These diverse visual forms share a common expression and offer the most complete understanding of my thoughts. The theme which is common among the works is the grave interaction of people and their surroundings, derived from my observation of living nature and history. I feel that human interaction mirrors the forces in the landscape. These forces are actually far from the static views we often imagine, but rather nature's elements continually collide aggressively and powerfully with one another.

Natural We Don't Want Indians Just Their Names Mascots Machines Cities Products Buildings Living People?

The word installation entitled *Don't Want Indians* exposes the prevailing attitude of America to its native peoples.

Over the last four hundred years, the dominant white culture has attempted to crush the lives of Indian people, rendering many entire tribes extinct, through brutal wars and governmental policies.

Today, Indian people must still struggle in order to survive in America. We must battle against forces that have dealt us among the lowest educational opportunities, lowest income levels, lowest standards of health, lowest housing conditions, lowest political representation, and *highest* mortality rates in America.

Even as these grave hardships exist for the living Indian people, a mockery is made of us by reducing our tribal names and images to the level of insulting sports team mascots, brand-name automobiles, camping equipment, city and state names, and various other commercial products produced by the dominant white culture.

This strange white custom is particularly insulting when one considers the great lack of attention that is given to real Indian concerns.

In *Don't Want Indians,* the pinkness of the words *mascots, machines, cities, products,* and *buildings* is a symbol for the true color of the Anglo-American (which is much more pink than white) and also alludes to the pink, cool, and uncaring attitude that the majority of America feels toward the serious crisis that faces the American Indian.

At the bottom of the word installation, the words *living people* are presented in yellow-green to give the sense of the living, vital, and *growing* American Indian. Such color is found throughout the Cheyenne Sundance earth renewal. The yellow-green cottonwood and willow trees spring forth from the rivers, creeks, and streams of the American plains. These trees grow fresh and strong from the water each spring.

Water and growth are the true concepts that represent the American Indian and give life to all things.

I am part Indian. I believe that my great, great grandmother—or was it my grandfather?—well, one of them was a full-blooded Cherokee.

A real Indian person must listen to this ridiculous claim made daily by members of the dominant white culture; white people are so excited by any remote bloodline reference that they may share with a Native American, once they have met one. This trace of affinity that the white person wishes to share with a Native American always vanishes once the real native returns to his or her home. Then the white person, briefly Indian, turns immediately back into the fold of the dominant white culture. While for a few moments there was a willingness on the part of the white person to share in the values and cosmos of the native person, never is there a reciprocal offer made by the white person to share their privileges.

In America, adequate education, job skills, medical treatment, healthy food sources, and proper housing are privileges reserved for the white culture. A sharing of the gifts that come with being of the white heritage does not take place, while a sharing of our gifts through our earth-awareness is expected.

For myself, as a headsman of the traditional Cheyenne Elk Warrior Society, it has become very difficult to appreciate the attributes of being part Indian. The warrior society members from the Cheyenne and Arapaho reservation, where I live, are always asked to be present at the many funerals that are conducted here. The warriors and chiefs are asked to support the families of the deceased. We offer them a positive force in their worst of all days. During the burial service, as I walk down the line of family members, touching the hand of each grieving person, their powerful pain is shared with me. Too often the cause of death is a broken heart or broken spirit. This condition drives many young native individuals, often under the age of thirty, to a deadly accident or to death by a disease related to alcoholism or other substance abuse. Many times these casualties of this modern culture are my childhood friends.

The circumstances that break the spirit and cause death are due primarily to our lack of sharing in the privileges owned by the dominant white culture. Jobs, education, medicine, housing, and food – a lack of these things will lead to a lack of human dignity. When your human dignity is used up, there is *nothing* left.

Today, the criterion of Indian-ness is suffering the pain of our culture, which is experienced in our traditional way: "together." A true Indian cannot claim to be native one day and not native the next. The mark of the native experience cannot be measured by a blood fraction.

Clio / History

THERESA HAK KYUNG CHA

Yu Guan Soon

Birth: By Lunar Calendar, 15 March 1903
Death: 12 October 1920. 8:20 A.M.

She is born of one mother and one father.

She makes complete her duration. As others have made complete theirs: rendered incessant, obsessive myth, rendered immortal their acts without the leisure to examine whether the parts false the parts real according to History's revision.

> *Truth embraces with it all other abstentions other than itself. Outside Time. Outside Space. Parallels other durations, oblivious to the deliberate brilliance of its own time, mortal, deliberate marking. Oblivious to itself. But to sing. To sing to. Very softly.*

She calls the name Jeanne d'Arc three times.
She calls the name Ahn Joong Kun five times.

There is no people without a nation, no people without ancestry. There are other nations, no matter how small their land, who have their independence. But our country, even with five thousand years of history, has lost it to the Japanese.

"Japan at once created an assembly, in the name of the King, for the 'discussion of everything, great and small, that happened within the realm.' This assembly at first met daily, and afterwards at longer intervals. There were soon no less than fifty Japanese advisors at work in Seoul. They were men of little experience and less responsibility, and they apparently thought that they were going to transform the land between the rising and setting of the sun. They produced endless ordinances, and scarce a day went by save that a number of new regulations were issued, some trivial, some striking at the oldest and most cherished institutions in the country. The Government was changed from an absolute monarchy to one where the king governed by the advice of the Ministers. The power of direct address to the throne was denied to anyone under the rank of Governor. One ordinance created a constitution, and the next dealt with the status of the ladies of the royal

seraglio. At one hour a proclamation went forth that all men were to cut their hair, and the wearied runners on their return were again dispatched in hot haste with an edict altering the official language. Nothing was too small, nothing was too great, and nothing too contradictory for these constitution-mongers. Their doings were the laugh and the amazement of every foreigner in the place.

"Acting on the Japanese love of order and of defined rank, exact titles of honour were provided for the wives of officials. These were divided into nine grades: 'Pure and Reverent Lady,' 'Pure Lady,' 'Chaste Lady,' 'Chaste Dame,' 'Worthy Dame,' 'Courteous Dame,' 'Just Dame,' 'Peaceful Dame,' and 'Upright Dame.' At the same time the King's concubines were equally divided, but here eight divisions were sufficient: 'Mistress,' 'Noble Lady,' 'Resplendent Exemplar,' 'Chaste Exemplar,' 'Resplendent Demeanor,' 'Chaste Demeanor,' 'Resplendent Beauty,' and 'Chaste Beauty.' The Japanese advisors instituted a number of sumptuary laws that stirred the country to its depths, relating to the length of pipes, style of dress, and the attiring of the hair of the people. Pipes were to be short, in place of the long bamboo churchwarden beloved by the Koreans. Sleeves were to be clipped. The top-knot, worn by all Korean men, was at once to be cut off. Soldiers at the city gates proceeded to enforce this last regulation rigorously."

Guan Soon is the only daughter born of four children to her patriot father and mother. From an early age her actions are marked exceptional. History records the biography of her short and intensely lived experience. Actions prescribed separate her path from the others. The identity of such a path is exchangeable with any other heroine in history, their names, dates, actions which require no definition in their devotion to generosity and self-sacrifice.

In Guan Soon's sixteenth year, 1919, the conspiracy by the Japanese to overthrow the Korean Government is achieved with the assassination of the ruling Queen Min and her royal family. In the aftermath of this incident, Guan Soon forms a resistant group with fellow students and actively begins her revolutionary work. There is already a nationally organized movement, who do not accept her seriousness, her place as a young woman, and they attempt to dissuade her. She is not discouraged and demonstrates to them her conviction and dedication in the cause. She is appointed messenger and she travels on foot to forty towns, organizing the nation's mass demonstration to be held on March 1, 1919. This date marks the turning point, it is the largest collective outcry against the Japanese occupation of the Korean people who willingly gave their lives for independence.

The only daughter of four children she makes complete her life as others have made complete. Her mother her father her brothers.

" 'I saw four places where engagements had been fought. At one place it had been a drawn battle, the Japanese retiring with five killed. The other three were Japanese victories, owing to the long range of their rifles and their superior ammunition; and only one of their victories was obtained without casualties to themselves. I saw enough to realise that it was no picnic for the Japanese.

" 'One is forced to ask who is in charge of these men who are nothing more than brigands. Their mode of warfare seems to be purposely designed to stir every honest man into a frenzy. Is this their object? If not, why do they practice so wicked, so mad a policy? Let the authorities either police the whole disaffected districts effectually and properly, or else confess their incapacity for controlling Korea.' "

Suppression of Foreign Criticism

September 26, 1907

"We are informed that a bad fight took place about eight miles from Su-won on Sunday, September 12th. Thirty volunteers were surrounded by Japanese troops, and although no resistance was offered, they were shot down in the most cold-blooded fashion. This not being quite enough to satisfy the conquerors, two other volunteers who had been captured were brought out and decapitated by one of the officers. We may mention that this news does not come from native sources; it comes from European."

The "enemy." One's enemy. Enemy nation. Entire nation against the other entire nation. One people exulting the suffering institutionalized on another. The enemy becomes abstract. The relationship becomes abstract. The nation the enemy the name becomes larger than its own identity. Larger than its own measure. Larger than its own properties. Larger than its own signification. For this people. For the people who is their enemy. For the people who is their ruler's subject and their ruler's victory.

Japan has become the sign. The alphabet. The vocabulary. To *this* enemy people. The meaning is the instrument, memory that pricks the skin, stabs the flesh, the volume of blood, the physical substance blood as measure, that rests as record, as document. Of *this* enemy people.

To the other nations who are not witnesses, who are not subject to the same oppressions, they cannot know. Unfathomable the words, the terminology: enemy, atrocities, conquest, betrayal, invasion, destruction. They exist only in the larger perception of History's recording, that affirmed, admittedly and unmistakably, one enemy nation has disregarded the humanity of another. Not physical enough. Not to the very flesh and bone, to the core, to the mark, to the point where it is necessary to intervene, even if to invent anew, expressions, for *this* experience, for this *outcome,* that does not cease to continue.

To the others, these accounts are about (one more) distant land, like (any other) distant land, without any discernible features in the narrative, (all the same) distant like any other.

This document is transmitted through, by the same means, the same channel, without distinction the content is delivered in the same style: the word. The image. To appeal to the masses to congeal the information to make bland, mundane, no longer able to transcend their own conspirator method, no matter how alluring their presentation. The response is precoded to perform predictably however passively possible. Neutralized to achieve the no-response, to make absorb, to submit to the unidirectional correspondence.

Why resurrect it all now? From the Past. History, the old wound. The past emotions all over again. To confess to relive the same folly. To name it now so as not to repeat history in oblivion. To extract each fragment by each fragment from the word from the image another word another image the reply that will not repeat history in oblivion.

Petition from the Koreans of Hawaii To President Roosevelt

Honolulu, T.H.
July 12, 1905

To His Excellency, The President of the United States

Your Excellency,

The undersigned have been authorised by the 8,000 Koreans now residing in the territory of Hawaii at a special mass meeting held in the city of Honolulu, on July 12, 1905, to present to Your Excellency the following appeal:

We, the Koreans of the Hawaiian Islands, voicing the sentiments of twelve million of our countrymen, humbly lay before Your Excellency the following facts:

Soon after the commencement of the war between Russia and Japan, our Government made a treaty of alliance with Japan for offensive and defensive purposes. By virtue of this treaty the whole of Korea was opened to the Japanese, and both the Government and the people have been assisting the Japanese authorities in their military operation in and around Korea.

The contents of this treaty are undoubtedly known to Your Excellency, therefore we need not embody them in this appeal. Suffice it to state, however, the object of the treaty was to preserve the independence of Korea and Japan and to protect Eastern Asia from Russia's aggression.

Korea, in return for Japan's friendship and protection against Russia, has rendered services to the Japanese by permitting them to use the country as a base of their military operations.

When this treaty was concluded, the Koreans fully expected that Japan would introduce reforms into the governmental administration along the line of the modern civilization of Europe and America, and that she would advise and counsel our people in a friendly manner, but to our disappointment and regret the Japanese Government has not done a single thing in the way of improving the condition of the Korean people. On the contrary, she turned loose several thousand rough and disorderly men of her nationals in Korea, who are treating the inoffensive Koreans in a most outrageous manner. The Koreans are by nature not a quarrelsome or aggressive people, but deeply resent the high-handed action of the Japanese towards them. We can scarcely believe that the Japanese Government approves the outrages committed by its people in Korea, but it has done nothing to prevent this state of affairs. They have been, during the last eighteen months, forcibly obtaining all the special privileges and concessions from our Government, so that to-day they practically own everything that is worth having in Korea.

We, the common people of Korea, have lost confidence in the promises Japan made at the time of concluding the treaty of alliance, and we doubt seriously the good intentions which she professes to have towards our people. For geographical, racial, and commercial reasons we want to be friendly to Japan, and we are even willing to have her as our guide and example in the matters of internal reforms and education, but the continuous policy of self-exploitation at the expense of the Koreans has shaken our confidence in her, and we are now afraid that she will not keep her promise of preserving our independence as a nation, nor assisting us in reforming internal administration. In other words, her policy in Korea seems to be exactly the same as that of Russia prior to the war.

The United States has many interests in our country. The industrial, commercial, and religious enterprises under American management have attained such proportions that we believe the Government and people of the United States ought to know the true conditions of Korea and the result of the Japanese becoming paramount in our country. We know that the people of America love fair play and advocate justice towards all men. We also know that Your Excellency is the ardent exponent of a square deal between individuals as well as nations, therefore we come to you with this memorial with the hope that Your Excellency may help our country at this critical period of our national life.

We fully appreciate the fact that during the conference between the Russian and Japanese peace envoys, Your Excellency may not care to make any suggestion to either party as to the conditions of their settlement, but we earnestly hope that Your Excellency will see to it that Korea may preserve her autonomous Government and that other Powers shall not oppress or maltreat our people. The clause in the treaty between the United States and Korea gives us a claim upon the United States for assistance, and this is the time when we need it most.

Very respectfully, your obedient servants,

(Sgd.) P. K. Yoon
Syngman Rhee

March 1, 1919. Everyone knows to carry inside themselves the national flag. Everyone knows equally the punishment that follows this gesture. The march begins, the flags are taken out, made visible, waved, every individual crying out the independence the freedom to the people of this nation. Knowing equally the punishment. Her parents leading the procession fell. Her brothers. Countless others were fired at and stabbed indiscriminately by the enemy soldiers. Guan Soon is arrested as a leader of the revolution, with punishment deserving of such a rank. She is stabbed in the chest, and subjected to questioning to which she reveals no names. She is given seven years prison sentence to which her reply is that the nation itself is imprisoned. Child revolutionary patriot woman soldier deliverer of nation. The eternity of one act. Is the completion of one existence. One martyrdom. For the history of one nation. Of one people.

Some will not know age. Some not age. Time stops. Time will stop for some. For them especially. Eternal time. No age. Time fixes for some. Their image, the memory of them is not given to deterioration, unlike the captured image that extracts from the soul precisely by reproducing, multiplying itself. Their countenance evokes not the hallowed beauty, beauty from seasonal decay, evokes not the inevitable, not death, but the dy-ing.

Face to face with the memory, it misses. It's missing. Still. What of time. Does not move. Remains there. Misses nothing. Time, that is. All else. All things else. All other, subject to time. Must answer to time, except. Still born. Aborted. Barely. Infant. Seed, germ, sprout, less even. Dormant. Stagnant. Missing.

The decapitated forms. Worn. Marred, recording a past, of previous forms. The present form face to face reveals the missing, the absent. Would-be-said remnant, memory. But the remnant is the whole.

The memory is entire. The longing in the face of the lost. Maintains the missing. Fixed between the wax and wane indefinite not a sign of progress. All else age, in time. Except. Some are without.

The Politics of Writing

SEKOU SUNDIATA

Words. Images. I can remember being young enough to say out loud every word I was big enough to read: headlines, television and movie credits, book titles, and signs, for example. Especially signs. Sounding out every syllable, silently at first, then progressively louder as I mastered the rhythm, flow, correct sound of it. There were a lot of words I could sound out long before I had an understanding of them.

Out on the intersection of the Warsaw Highway and Route 52 in Williamsburg County, South Carolina, I read the road signs and learned that Kingstree was sixteen miles from Lake City and when I was in either place I was always supposed to go through the doors that said COLORED and never drink from the water fountains that said WHITE. But I went through the WHITE door and peed and I went to the WHITE water and drank and it all came in and went out the same way as COLORED. I really didn't understand it, but I could say it and sound it out. If it was a test in school, instead of real life, I would've gotten a hundred. Although what I couldn't read or say was the history, the ideology, the way of practicing life that stood behind those single words.

Those words and ideas were written in the same language I was being taught in school. My grades depended upon how well I learned to spell those words. I had to use them in sentences to prove that I understood them. I understood them soon enough, but it still didn't make sense. This language that called me COLORED and said I was "Less Than" was the legal law. My future depended upon my education, they said, and my education depended upon my mastery of that language. And for that reason, that same burdensome literacy was taught at home. It was an undereducated parents' way of trying to give you something to help you to make your own way. They didn't understand (or maybe they did) that along with the joy of discovery and the wonderful sense of power that comes with the acquisition of literacy came the transmission of an awesome social disease.

Dick and Jane taught me how to read, write, and want to live: speaking perfect words in a perfect house in a nice neighborhood with a well-behaved dog and antiseptic parents with perfect legal skin. Learning to read, write, speak, and think the American language is the heart of the politics of writing. It was in that process that I absorbed the ideas of the world. Ideas about culture, philosophy, art, work, love, violence, sex, war, good, bad, pretty, ugly. Ideas that were found in schoolbooks, newspapers, magazines, on television and radio. Aside from everyday speech, these were my "instructional materials," each of them replete with pictures to reinforce the words. At an early age, I was struck by the power of the printed word as a visual image.

Naturally, whoever owned the means of communication (my "instructional materials" included) projected the images (words) in their own likeness. By the time I found out that the owners used the images-words to negate who I was, where I came from, I had become "literate." Literate and disconnected from any real sense of peoplehood or humanity. Amos 'n' Andy taught me that black folks spoke a language that didn't even qualify as literature because I never read any writing like how they talked. Not only did the language carry words, it transported deadly ideas shaped by a dangerous enemy.

At the same time that I was learning the language of negation and hurt, though, there was another language that was really a part of the American language pressed into the service of a whole other way of seeing things: so-called Black English. For the first sixteen years of learning, my experience with the African-American oral tradition was strictly a musical, visual, and oral encounter. It came from home and the pulpit, from improvisational scatting, moaning, hollers, screams, honks, tonks, guitars wailing, saxophones, layers upon layers of sound, the Five Blind Boys, and unknown tongue. It came from names like One Eye Willie John, Shorty Long, and Titty Baby. It came from words bent, broken off, twisted out of shape, out of time, out of tense. We Was words and I Be words. It made bad good. It lifted up by getting down. It said Nigger and still, oddly, meant love . . . sometimes. It was opposed to the hurt, made art of hurt crying out. It was irrelevant, recalcitrant, illegal, subversive, and it belonged to a whole, a complete, broken-hearted people fragmented by the gospel according to life.

The minute you heard it, you knew it was ours. It was a particular expression of the human condition. For my money the shiny little girls singing "baba la cumma la cumma la biste/ oh no no no no biste" could only be matched by Smokey singing "I did you wrong/ my heart went out to play/ but in the game I lost you/ what

a price to pay," which was in the same league with that great African-American chant "daba do da da daba do da da." It was American and Unamerican. Like me, like us. It was used with great flair and pride because it had the power to say what we wanted it to say, to do what we wanted it to do, to mean what we said mean. The minute you heard it, you knew it was us.

That encounter is what opened up the whole American English, so that I could see its beauty, its possibilities. See how adding or taking away as much as a word or as little as a single letter could change things, transform relationships. I became bilingual.

There was, and still is, a great contradiction attached to being bilingual. The Dick and Jane, Amos 'n' Andy, Tarzan, *Birth of a Nation* ideas were absorbed by everybody and, in turn, perpetuated by everybody. There was no escaping those ideas in all of the subtle, invidious, nearly unrecognizable forms. That is what education and literacy meant. That is what the testing was all about. We were trained to memorize, to reproduce ideas, not to create them.

My tongue was split. The language of negation also contained the potential to express its opposite: Affirmation. The extra-legal language of my people also contained the terrible ideas of the Killer Tongue expressed in the form and style acceptable to its victims. Words could turn people against themselves. I saw that unless you own the image-words, they will never do what you want them to do. I set out to own them by writing them.

That quest is the essence of the politics of writing. It comes down to a basic need to handle the struggle being played out through me: the conflict between the two world views. The ACT of writing became a way of thinking independently, a way of "saying my word and naming the world." The ART of writing followed from that personal/political desire. If I were to voice whatever consciousness I had, it meant claiming the whole language, reshaping, remaking it. Much in the same spirit that musicians and singers claimed and recreated a Western vocabulary of music. They synthesized, galvanized it, and gave the world something new, something vibrant, progressive: spirituals, gospel, blues, jazz, rock 'n' roll, funk, the basis of new wave, reggae, punk, black poetry.

Finally, black poetry. My meeting with black poetry was thunderstruck love at first sight/sound. My writing up to that point, outside of school-related assignments, had no particular form. Just a massive collection of notes, thoughts, scribblings, fragments of texts that didn't know what they were or would become. Piled up, accumulated, kept private and out of public sight. The first time I heard the Poetry of Redemption was like the moment boiling water becomes steam. Right then and there, I knew that what was accumulated in my writing, in my memory, in my heart was poetry.

I was born with something to write about. The struggle for literacy forced me to write in order to understand. It was the only sure way I could see and feel what I was learning to read, write, and think. Having something to say and a language to say it in inspired the need for freedom of expression. Writing and poetry gave me a way to define the world and make it stick. In that sense, it is the politics of self-determination.

Evening Tomorrow's Here Today Since the Hornet Flies I Triangle

CANDACE HILL

1.

. . . Daughters have been hurt by my widowhood by their father's
disappearance by death's cruel blow
Evening called today to say she's been sad it's the 25th day of '83 in
February a warm month in case you didn't know in case your
father didn't tell you he was going away one cold cruel day leaving
off our education some smattering connected with the building
trades an attempted economic advance sharing tenancy with him
would be too deep too gray

2.

a colored owner he calls on the group freedmen he calls on the
group close in on these faces a mass of fear nearing barber's chairs
his own folk discriminating against him playing the leadin role bold
two four his own folk his own house servants attractive who's getting the most attention nine-to-fiver's still alive alive oh alas in
studies of this sort to boot or not to boot out olden times this is the
question redemption is in in an increasing number of cases it's no
disgrace to be connected with the building trades the method in
case he should return to see the teamster's larger numbers a card
thy is when class met now identification c. miner a porter was my
daddy who bears the brunt of this economic battle an artisan a
farmer wasting away hustlers
this is a way of life
color the owner groaner
color the alien a failure in convincing
one summer cooler than the other color the stone sun tower weary
only in the night buildings trade secrets
afraid

3.

It is winter the group is still important a small closed circle an
independent hollow centers revolving around barber's poles candy

stripped chains of so long John's silver dollars spent a small closed
circle increasingly dented puzzles bar me another game for the
master race who needs it anyway Evening another essay on common grievances a minus spring's coming we can go outside take a
walk by the manmade lake and trees with so much history the
women know everything stretched out like city cats 92% engaged in
domestic and personal service that's a fact transported from the
manufacturer of this hat
Relax

4.

To gain the sympathy of your heredity a cellular swing
Boogy
and yet with one hand essentially look for mutual under standing
a conservative asking
next will be crouch down
Evening
Attack
His friend and confidant was a fine musician laughing always
laughing loud blossomed and spouted out let's go south to rural
somewhere Georgia Georgia a consideration in the north
His heart was giving out like new I shout back around his neck to
write another essay to drum up another quest for consciousness
new birth from the dawn of training to intuitive grasps at that age
having fallen between them
She smiles swearing Velvet draws her man down in complete
surrender inequalities never on score a personal following said I
follow personally falling in between them five fingers like his
mother's finds five more stars do guide the spirit of more

5.

Always ha mama mama bad bad Evening a nation in admiration
wonders interested after a confused murmur converting the
negroes at eastern star would be easy like sunday morning if not
silenced be careful when trying to gain sympathy sympathy and
cooperation remember Atlanta a word green in my eyes purely
social tactful ribbons have fallen between them now mama wanted
to join daddy didn't dominate in the north speech is a pattern of
thinking triumphant noteateable apprehensive in spite of narrow
minds and diverse tactics with deep regret I bet the way in which
this was done is elementary my dear type and character's person

Run

No more iron bars in the
6th sense
Laws of Works
and Faith

6.

a group again circling my negative and actual space an inspired student's what he was now and in the past there was no motive for revolt or Song's of Hornets Darlings it was just in the veins of burning spears the test they'd have that race they'd shown in self-assertion and all that suppression and all that rot shifting ideals a little twhat here and there new light fixes needed outside cold night air shivering bared all were close together gentlemen I told you at ease from kings ships experienced and main programme skied in early manhood like Dr. J. let's say new leaders Marvin's singing star bangled banner classier and on no other terms for a time less repugnant is at hand in the white south in the black north Langston said Zebras no AH
Simple a changing metaphor like early manhood and seeking persistance under resistance
Evolution to successive leaders
some more

7.

Financial stress 3x's needed emperors loved in poems
the word sounds like a motherfucker to me one mother of a mother together EMPEROR EMPEROR RORE against EMPER OR!

8.

So we went for rides on Pullman trains to south alabama to grand-mother's house we go where the slaves lived and were lynched on trees that's what was out de window we'd take indeed and weed for days shout till Madonna spread her wings over that lust making us think we wasn't radiant enough

9.

She didn't realize I was
throughly aware of the unease that dunked dunked dunked

Helmut please watch out for the cross fire again outta alabama
inferiority it was then and now because of slavery to my
mother
Ritchie Lee

10.

. . . the moon guides in Italy
the via veneto is so pretty
I suppose you've heard we're all so complete in ourselves rugged
individualists approximately true the center of the modern world
us evolved in a house of bondage still mists surround higher fares
too
go across great lakes to Ne Plus Ultra yea to the Romans for La Via
Veneto nothing more
Beyond hope lay there leisurely silent dream on historic bledy blip
blip please
the ancient world God's again an unknown quest for right to make
up our new world arising with no fight
moola please God again an unknown quest for right to make up
our new world arising with no fight Right again
political problems let the past be what it is undoubtedly say I want
the best yea
I want the fields to sing some more sir

11.

That's when she were a young girl
friend say you or her is that still your dream
that poisonous asp
a wild game alas put cleo lane on will he
will he come back again the ad reads asks what greater task the
air force wants to know is she like you does she say PURPLE
ANEMONES quick in an instant faster than a flash young man heave
ho out just a little while longer she's sad because his thinkings slow
from germany's time
keep the faith blondie hitler was a blonde like you
wasn't she beautiful contessa romani she sat in the saddle like she
was having an orgasm magdalia please sucl my ies I'm getting a
far on my tussy is throbbing jump jump jump to it Aretha's twitchin
for us far away from spitland in the ocean with zest bid um in

12.

The friends are brothers they say things four sometimes seven
things to each other separation is a plus only one plus
to find more stuff or junk two equals play
you know how
protect me suddenly protect me if I need to pray protect

13.

"can you tell"
from the moonlight going to where columbus lived for a time
mapped out
read history
it's widespread
a human skill
demanding manual labor in a whole community of trained warriors
A trained to toot train to ruling train ruled crowded from burr
birth roughly civilized sorry protected by strong bands teaching
wandering eyes who what where can you distinguish which train
yard kids divide up
Blood's turf pressing crimson bars behind names twenty feet high
Indian Trails John coming up a new man
Train art now armed spray flower power
aired for beauty and attack of de smack
who'll write against heroin drug abuse crack
clackity clack clackity clack don't talk back

14.

Right in after a period of drought when even the hornet said
forget this shit I'm going over yonder I know that much
Donny if horses could fly they dada been gone too cursing the
ground they was standing on throughout a system that arose from
dirt community dirt want to hear girl till the fields minnie mousey
long ago naturally this arose from so called primitive times when
there was peaceful industry held up by slaves trafficking trains of
change leading to bonding stations somewhere scribble counts and
doubt is dissolved without much paint thinner remember I left you
with thinner

... while they photographed him.

Common Origin

REESE WILLIAMS

I

"Who is calling to me?" These five words fire out of his sleeping body, crashing into the ceiling of the small dark room, bouncing from wall to wall, then dispersing into the low hum of the city.

Again the call, and again he responds, louder this time. "Who is calling to me?"

The vibration in his throat wakes him in a shiver. He raises himself up on his elbows and quickly scans the bedroom; the clock shows 5:00 A.M. The woman lying next to him, ripped from her own dream by the sound, reaches instinctively to touch him. She finds his shoulder, her fingers saying, it's alright, it's alright.

With a short exhaling laugh, Peter Syman breaks into the day. He turns toward her, shaking his head back and forth, allowing just the beginning of a grin. "Who could have imagined we would go this way. The pyramid . . . the cathedral . . . and now, the skyscraper. We all live in little boxes . . . towers of boxes, rows of boxes, boxes of boxes . . . and inside each box, the picture box with the cool blue light."

After breakfast he puts on Bach's *Six Suites for Cello.* All morning and into the afternoon he plays the three discs over and over again, this being his ritual on the day before entering the cage.

Syman holds the world's record – thirty-six days – for being inside a cage with poisonous snakes. Year after year, promoters from around the world pay him to try to break his own record. This is the way he makes his living, it is the only way he knows, he has no fall-back position.

Day fourteen, attempt number twenty-seven. Six thousand miles from his home, Syman lies prone on his back in a room at a Pretoria, South Africa, animal park. With him are four Egyptian cobras, four tree snakes, and four black mambas. The news syndicates have struck their deals, the cameras are in position. Syman will earn $500 for each day in the cage, and his image will be sold all across the surface of the world.

Syman's room is one of twenty-four dioramas that ring the perimeter of the exhibition hall. The space of each diorama is twelve feet by twelve feet, with curved corners. One wall is a floor-to-ceiling plate glass window facing into the promenade of the hall. The ceiling, following Daguerre's original design, is translucent glass illuminated by the sky. Left over from the previous exhibition, the background painting is a scene of an open meadow. In the foreground, a red-tailed hawk perched on a branch, beak open, wings extended, ready to fly.

Each day, just before dawn, Syman rises from his mat. He raises his left hand to the sky, holds it open for a moment, then slowly disengages from the snakes. He walks over to the southwest corner of his room and squats above a bedpan. Then he does a slow stretching exercise for a few minutes before crossing the room to take a bottle from a small door in the wall. He drinks a pint of a thick liquid made from fermented rice and beans, then returns to his mat for another twenty-four-hour cycle.

The snakes are agitated while Syman is up, but they are soothed when he lies down again. They slide over onto his body, coming to rest with their heads on his chest, the twelve lines radiating out from his heart like the spokes of a wheel.

In interviews, Syman has attributed his success to his ability to control his breathing. When he lies down with the snakes, he gradually slows his body until he is taking only one breath every three minutes. He breathes only through his left nostril which stimulates activity in the right hemisphere of his brain while quieting the left hemisphere. The result is a state of mind that he describes as a vision. Year after year, it is always the same vision. He is always careful to say that it is a vision, not a dream. The snakes, who are sensitive to the subtle energy patterns in his body, come into the vision with him.

They become a small tribe of people who don't have mouths, their faces smooth below the nose. Wanderers, they follow the line of the seashore, foraging for scents which provide them with all the nourishment they need. Without the need to compete for food or land, they have no enemies. The image of them walking on the beach – their limbs long and smooth from the air of the Southern Atlantic – they are more like deer than men.

At the end of each day, they set up camp in a ring and build a fire. Using small iron tools, they transform sand into tiny blue glass beads which they offer to people who come to greet them. On this, the fourteenth night of their journey, a man and a woman are attracted to the light of the campfire. They accept the gift of the glass beads, taking them into the palms of their hands, closing their fingers over them. The beads bring tears to their eyes, unknown sorrow to their hearts, and they sink to the ground, slowly feeling their way back to the fetal position. From here, it is pure fall, into a space without boundaries, into a dream of the origin of life, into the roaring of the ocean. Wave upon wave.

II

Demitrio Tsafendas was born in 1918 in South Africa, the son of an engineer from Crete and a woman labeled "mixed white" by the government. At the age of fifteen, after finishing seventh grade, Tsafendas ran away from home. His mother had just been killed, her head smashed in by a rifle butt. Traveling at night, sleeping during the day, he made his way to Mozambique and immediately joined the merchant marines.

Not much is known about Tsafendas until 1942, when he left the merchant marines in Canada. That winter he crossed a frozen river border and entered the United States where, two days after his arrival, he was arrested. From 1942 until 1946 he was passed among a variety of American mental institutions and finally deported to Greece (because of his father's ancestry). From there he managed to travel about in Europe and then on to Turkey, to Lebanon, and finally to Egypt.

In 1965, he returned to South Africa and joined a religious cult called *The Followers of Jesus.* He moved into a large, old Victorian house with several other group members, and with their help he was able to get a job as a parliamentary messenger. Three weeks later, Demitrio shot and killed Dr. Hendrik Verwoerd, the prime minister of the apartheid government.

At the trial, Demitrio took the stand and spoke his mind for the first time in his life. When the black-robed prosecutor asked him why he shot the prime minister, he answered:

"If I did not have the snake, I would not have killed Dr. Verwoerd. Soon after my mother was murdered, a huge snake entered my body, and from then on, he told me what to do. In the beginning it was very simple, just to do with food. When I became sad, the snake told me to eat. At the smell of a good meal, he would slide up into my throat and purr like a cat . . . I remember the sharp, serrated edges of his body in my gut as I fed him – he made it clear from the start that I had no choice but to do as he said.

When I ran away to the merchant marines, it was the snake's idea. On the ship toward Canada, I began to sense that he was guiding me toward something. He told me, 'First we're gonna take some time, then I will show you what to do.'

On the quiet ocean days that followed, I began to know and love air for the first time. The snake taught me how to breathe, how to rhythmically charge my body with energy, how to use my breath to attract what I desired. Even now, there is nothing as wonderful for me as the smell of the Southern Atlantic along the western coast of Africa. It is all the food I need, and it is there I will go to after you execute me.

When we arrived in Montreal, I left the ship. We traveled for many days in the cold winter, as though the snake was conditioning me. He took me to the point farthest away from the way I played as a child, to a big gray building outside Chicago where they kept me in a little gray cell, where they tied me to a bed, where the man in the white coat stuck the needle in my body. In all my time with the snake, I have never known him to be so mad as when that poison fluid began to spread in my body. A snake is quiet and peaceful by nature, it is music that he loves most. But if you do harm to a snake, he never forgets. Years and years may pass, but eventually he will take his revenge. The man with the needle, he may be walking – I can see him leave his gray building and step into his gray car – but like Dr. Verwoerd, he is a dead man. And it is a dead-end death, he's not coming back around.

In that mental hospital the snake taught me to endure my future imprisonment. One day he decided I was ready. I began to imagine huge paintings with deep blues and reds, paintings made of glass. And whatever I imagined began to happen. Soon we were on the European continent, traveling to the great cathedrals. Gradually, we worked our way east, finally arriving at his destination, the Great Pyramid.

With my voice, the snake convinced the guard to let us spend the night in the central interior chamber of the pyramid. That night was an ending point. The snake showed me one of the polar opposites. It was blacker than you can ever imagine, and had no sound except the ocean roar of my own nervous system. I began to scream as I was shot into outer space in a rocket. My life blew apart into three satellites. In one, my mother's life; in another, my father's life; and in the third, my own. We were adrift, separated, and there was nothing I could do to put things back together, nothing I could do to get back to Earth. On my screen, a constant replaying of a rocket being shot up into the sky and then suddenly exploding. First, the camera watching the explosion, then following pieces of debris as they fall toward the ground. After a few seconds of beautiful plumed phosphorescent arcs, the image switches to the ground, to a scene of people looking up with horrified expressions on their faces, then back again to the close-up of the explosion. Smoke coming out of a hole in one of the solid fuel tanks, then a small fiery jet, then a flash of grainy orange-red and everything blows. This sequence of images repeating over and over until the wood frame house of my childhood catches on fire, rooms collapsing from bursts of heat. Coming from the orange-red is the sound of grinding steel. It is wartime: my mother is dead, flat out, mouth gaping, and my father is in the distance on the bank of the river, mute. A squad of frogmen swimming upstream in the rushing water. Multi-armed and without faces, black rubber completely covering their bodies, they swim like robots straight toward me . . . It was here that the snake left me.

Toward dawn, I saw Dr. Verwoerd's face for the first time. I didn't know who he was, but I knew we were connected in some way, that my purpose in life had to do with this man. At the moment I was strongest with the image, the snake returned and spoke to me. He said, 'Go easy now, it's time to return, time to close the circle.'

From that night on, each breath I took drew me nearer to Dr. Verwoerd . . . and the rest of the story you know.

There is just one more thing to say. I have felt the snake sway to gentle music, and I have seen the focused power of his strike. If I know but one thing, it is this. What has happened to me, it could happen to you. All of us, we must take care of each other, for if the snake should ever uncoil his true power, he would surely break the world into little pieces."

III

Each evening, in the time between sunset and darkness, those who remained in the city took to the streets. We gathered in small groups at our special meeting places and then wandered the streets which once led to movies and restaurants and to brightly lit stores. Now they are dark and quiet, with the everpresent smell of burning trash. Without electricity and fuel the hierarchy of our pleasure was destroyed. We roamed in search of just one thing, a fire in an abandoned car. This was the sign that a *Sky Pointer* was at work that night.

All of us were in a state of flux, just waiting for permission from the military to leave the city and start new lives. Arrangements were slow, they didn't want to flood the outlands with hundreds of thousands of homeless people. The perimeter had been sealed within a week after the breakdown so we had no choice but to wait. We were not prisoners, the military was not the enemy – everyone was working hard just to provide the basics of food and water and medicine. If there was an enemy, it seemed to be hidden within everything.

I don't want to say much about the breakdown. As far as anyone could tell, no outside forces were involved, and there were no nuclear disasters. It appeared as though the nation was hit with an epidemic of lying, as if the lying that we commonly accepted in advertising and politics spread suddenly into all other sectors of the culture. There was an irresistible pull, something maniacal about it. Within just a few weeks, everyone was lying to each other. It was a thrill, like revenge. People took their pleasure in spreading the lie into new regions. In no time, it became impossible to depend upon even the most simple exchanges, such as buying food – it might be poisoned – or reading a letter – it might be a forgery.

The first of the central systems to fall was the banking industry. Loan officers were negotiating fictitious, even fantastical loans, clerks typed incorrect data into the computers, and the credit card network was pillaged. The flow of money came to a halt, crippling most businesses.

Next to go was mass transit, then the electrical power grid and that was the end – everything else just fell like dominos. I remember people standing at the windows of the office towers on the last day, their expressions gray and spent. But the lie had been exhausted.

To survive, one had to learn to fall forward and to fall backward simultaneously. The sudden shortages of food, water, and power caused great hardship and pain, but there was also an opening up of time. This opening was available to everyone – a great leveling had taken place – and most people walked in. It was as if the nation had unconsciously forced a catharsis to free itself into this new time.

During that first year, on any given night there were perhaps a hundred *Sky Pointers* operating in the city. With tags such as *SX-70, MX-20, F-18,* and *X-700,* they were the new entertainers. The usual modus operandi was for a *Sky Pointer* to occupy an abandoned building with a band of followers and then stage performances on the roof.

Night after night these men and women orally circled around the breakdown of the nation, predicting the future, revising the past. The majority specialized in twistings of the Bible or famous movies like *2001* or *Star Wars,* but a few were more extreme. *Minuteman IV* held group wedding ceremonies. On most Saturday nights she joined together a hundred or more couples. Her band of followers controlled a key street of buildings in the old garment district and this proved to be a great resource. Using the abandoned stockpiles of clothing, they made elaborate wedding costumes to lure the fashion-starved citizens. People got real dressed up and then real nervous – they loved it – and then *Minuteman IV* did her duty.

Whenever possible I walked up to 42nd Street to see if *WS 2000* was at work that night – he was my man. I liked his persistence, his relentless ambition, and the range of his imagination within such a strict limitation: *WS 2000* was a "book burner." He had set up camp on the roof of the main library and his work involved the ritualistic burning of every book in the three-million-volume collection of the library. Every book, that is, except for two. *WS 2000* had selected *Leaves of Grass* and *Tropic of Cancer* to carry into the next culture. On the roof of the library, to the left and right of the stage, *WS 2000*'s workers had erected two huge portraits. Made of brightly painted cardboard, and rising more than fifty feet into the air, portraits of Whitman and Miller loomed, like Marx and Lenin, above all of *WS 2000*'s performances.

Each performance had a specific theme. *WS 2000* was no doubt a scholar, but one who decided to unwind his logic in a peculiar way. A few days before a performance, he would issue instructions to his workers and they would descend into the library, and into the seven sub-basements below to select books for the burning. The books were then brought up to the roof and arranged in a four-sided pyramid about twelve feet high. The center area was kept as a hollow air space to allow the fire to burn more intensely. The completed pyramid was doused with kerosene.

I was one of the lucky few to witness *WS 2000*'s last performance. It was a gray and humid Sunday night and not too many people were there. His subject was "the Apocalypse." As the pyramid was lit, *WS 2000* began circling the fire, berating one book after another in a continuous high-pitched monologue. Then he

stopped in front of the pyramid, bent at the waist, hands on his knees, and squinted out at us. He told us we had lost the meaning of words, that *apocalypse* didn't mean the end of the world or an ending of any kind. *Apocalypse* was the Greek word for revelation. And in the *Book of Revelation,* the Apocalypse brings on a thousand years of peace. The fire began to grow quite intense, more so than others I had seen, and *WS 2000* returned to his circling. He found a good groove, and with Whitman on his left and Miller to his right, he began to spin like a dervish. Arms extended straight out, round and round he went, his monologue changing into a song – no words, just a simple melody of rising and falling tones. The small audience was fast becoming mesmerized when suddenly there was a loud crack followed by ripping sounds. A gaping hole opened in the tarpaper and *WS 2000* fell through to the floor below with thousands of flaming books. His followers yelled and screamed their way down the stairs, but it was too late. The main reading room was full of smoke and *WS 2000* was nowhere to be seen in the burning rubble. We had to leave quickly, as the fire was spreading rapidly from book to book. Outside we huddled in the doorways of once elegant stores and watched in fascination as the library burned. The stone facade of the exterior wall held firm, containing a dance of flames which gave off a tremendous roaring sound – thousands of voices, each screaming a name into the night sky.

IV

In the morning, an hour or so after dawn, I set up my table: a piece of plywood on top of my suitcase, typewriter, paper, envelopes, and out in front, five stones which I use to attract the people I want to speak with.

By midday a good many people are on the road. Most are traveling north, only a few to the south – this because of water. Clean water is scarce in Zone III and to the south, so the natural order is a migration into Zones IV and V where water is still plentiful.

With my eyes I search into the people as they pass by, and they search me. All of the lying between people has been stripped away. People reveal themselves as quickly as possible now; no one can afford to expend energy on masking operations. There is one overriding issue now – re-grouping. We are each looking for others who share the same affinities.

I was granted permission to leave the city six months ago. To obtain an exit visa one had to make an application demonstrating a service or skill that was needed in the northern zones. Mostly what was needed was farming, but those of us in the city knew nothing about food, other than how to eat it. My proposal was that I could serve as a "typist," that with millions of people on the road, there would be a need for someone to help compose letters, help fill out the new application forms, etc. In the tenth month, a rudimentary postal system had been established using the food stations as collection points, and perhaps this is what finally prompted the military to accept my application. I was given a Zone V card and one year to get there.

My pattern was to walk for seven days, then stop for seven and set up my table near a food station. I chose the coastal route where there were stations every fifty miles or so.

One afternoon, about three months into Zone IV, a man approached my table from the north. He circled around me a few times in a spiral pattern, then accepted the gesture of my open hand and sat down in front of me. We did not exchange greetings, he just started talking – about birds. And only about birds. Their ritualistic behavior: of bonding with each other, of taking off and landing, of mating and hunting. Sometimes I asked questions about his life; he would answer in a brief remark but then return to the birds.

The young are born black with tiny white spots; as they grow they gradually turn white. When fully mature their necks and heads are pale yellow and just the tips of their wings remain black. At the point of the breakdown he was living in an SRO in the city; two months earlier he had been released from a mental institution. He escaped the city before the perimeter had been established and spent the first winter wandering north.

Before taking off, the bird "sky-points" with her beak. Breathing deeply and uttering the call *O-aah,* she fills air bags in her neck. This will lessen the shock when she dives into the water. In the first spring, he saw thousands of birds migrating north and followed them to a small island in the northern reaches of Zone V, an island of fireweed and goldenrod. He stayed with the birds, some fifty thousand of them, at their summer home for almost seven months. Food was plentiful and he grew healthy and strong again.

When a bird lands, she greets her mate by nipping the back of his neck, rather violently at moments. Then they raise their heads together, spread their wings, and bump their chests together while rubbing their beaks. The movement of their necks is an oscillation pattern, touching left side to left side, then right to right. Gradually it becomes more gentle, with each bird delicately nibbling the head, throat, and neck of the other. He told me that he needed one more summer with the birds – it would be his third – just to be with them, to let them lead him into the Kingdom of God.

At this point his descriptions broke apart. It became difficult for him to keep a flow of words; he could not express what he wanted to say. Then he reached into the small bag which he carried and pulled out a small, black cassette player. He handed me the headphones and said that now he knew why he had stopped to talk with me. If I could write down what I heard on the tape, it would help him on his way. He couldn't explain it more, just that to learn how words connected to what he had seen, it would do something to the time.

I listened to a five-minute section of the tape, then listened to it a second time. There were scattered words and phrases, but mostly "ahs" and gasps, and wordless speech. However, I knew what he had seen and felt. I asked him to play the section one more time, then I wrote this page for him to carry with him on his way:

> *Before taking off into the air, she extends the curve of her yellow neck to the sun. Wings fully extended, she screeches* O-aah, O-aah. *With each breath, she moves closer to flight. One last screech, this one as if there will never be the chance for another, and she is borne into the sky.*
>
> *As she climbs away from the maddening din of the island colony, she grows alone with her overpowering desire. Below, the water is clear. Underneath, the pulsing pattern of a school of silver herring. She enters into an orbit above the fish, letting the wind shape her circle.*
>
> *Her wings wave in a slow rhythm, but her head holds steady and her eyes focus in one beam. With each circle, she comes nearer to the vibration of the fish. At the base of her skull, brain cells, one by one, lock on to their telepathic pulse.*
>
> *Like a huge snake, the school of herring undulates in slow curves. One curve brings them into the warm water at the surface. A sudden flash of light reflecting off the silver. This light is the signal. The sun has selected one fish for her, and instantly she is diving. Wings pulled back, eyes focused on the one point, she plunges straight down, bursting through the surface to take the waiting fish.*

V

A young man, perhaps eighteen or nineteen, came to meet me at the ferry, and we drove off in an old Ford station wagon. The original body had rusted out long ago; the new one consisted of many small pieces of sheet metal carefully riveted together. On the roof were two torpedo-like fuel tanks – methane gas to power the engine. And inside, the seats had been recovered with rabbit fur.

The trip lasted about twenty minutes. Mostly we talked about animals – dogs, horses, birds. From the beginning I knew that animals were very important to this man – for his livelihood, and for other reasons as well. With nothing said, he told me of his need to know different blood.

We turned off the road and pulled up in front of a white, nineteenth-century Cape farmhouse. He led me to a small, low-ceilinged room off the kitchen and told me to make myself at home. Gavril was still out on his morning walk, but he would no doubt be back soon. I sat down on one of the two wooden chairs and set up my tape recorder on the table. I had been waiting for this meeting for over a year – this man was known throughout Zone V for his ability to communicate with animals.

After a few minutes, a small, wiry man with thinning white hair entered the room from a side door. At first he didn't seem to perceive me. He appeared disoriented, as if intoxicated, but then he settled into his chair and a presence came into his face. His expression was round, the lines from his eyes curving down from earlier sadness, the lines from his mouth curving up in mischievous pleasure. His right forearm was covered with a thick sleeve of leather and perched on the sleeve was a large red-tailed hawk.

"What can I do for you?"

I reached to press the record button, but before I could start my question, the bird gave out a loud screech. Gavril turned to the bird and sang a sequence of short sounds. The bird responded with a low *kraa-aa.*

"May I ask, what did you say to the bird?"

"I asked her if she wanted her hood. Whenever she is in a room, away from the sky, she gets a bit distressed, and then, on top of that, the sound from the motor of your tape recorder – I thought it might be too much. We don't hear it, but she does . . . Would it be okay to turn it off?"

"No problem."

Gavril pressed the stop button and picked up the little black box, bringing it up near to his face. For a moment he held it in affection, then he began to play with the name, voicing it over and over. *Sony Sony Sony, So-ny So-ny So-ny* . . . He gradually changed the accent on the two syllables and turned it into a chant, *ny-so-ny-so-ny-so-ny-so-ny-so-ny-so* . . . He continued chanting for a couple of minutes, which inspired the bird to begin twirling on his arm. Then, with a short laugh, he came to a stop. "It's a good word, I remember it . . . they should've inverted the syllables, but no matter, with a name like that, one would've been a fool to buy any other brand . . . But back in those days people had lost contact with words . . . in every era that has been the warning sign . . . Anyway, where shall we begin."

"Well, perhaps you could just start with the bird."

"Okay . . . her name is Aua, and ten years ago she saved my life. Although these days [laughing], she seems to be more interested in my death. Do you remember the first winter after the breakdown? Up here it was dangerous, we might have easily starved to death. We were a long way from the nearest food station, and when the snows came it was impossible to travel long distances. However, something extraordinary happened that year. As the weather began to change in late September, hawks appeared in the sky – dozens and dozens of them, which is unusual for this region. And then strange things. I remember walking in the woods and suddenly a hawk would perch a few feet away from me, have a look at me, and then disappear into nowhere. This happened to me a few times. The hawks became the prime topic of our conversations, and then the idea came. The idea to catch a few of them and use them to hunt with. We set about making traps, using nets and pigeons for bait, and in the next few weeks we caught about ten birds. I knew nothing of falconry, but I had no problem training Aua to hunt for me. After a subtle give-and-take, we settled on seven simple sounds that I could use to speak to her: *Sa, Re, Ga, Ma, Pa, Dha,* and *Ni.* She learned very quickly, as though she had wanted to get caught and hunt for me.

"By December, Aua and the other hawks were providing us with a steady supply of rabbits and birds. We owe our survival that winter to them. And more than food, they gave us something else. That was a very depressing winter, but the hawks knew no fear. To watch Aua soar and then dive for a kill, it was like a transfusion of energy. I remember one in particular. Aua was in a very high orbit, just a speck in the sky. Coming from the north, flying very low, were two geese, obviously lost on their migration south. I'd never heard of a hawk attacking a goose, but suddenly she began to dive.

She came down in a steep angle at tremendous speed, perhaps sixty miles per hour, and hit one goose at the base of its neck. There was no struggle, just one sharp *hah* sound and the goose dropped straight down to the ground.

"In the second year, we began to get some minimal food distribution and our first crops started to come in, so we were less dependent on the hawks. Aua would hunt for us, but only in relation to our need. By spring of the third year she would no longer kill for us.

"In the years since, we have stayed close, but our time together has nothing to do with hunting. We both like to be out early, to feel the first rays of the sun. So most mornings we meet about a half-hour before dawn. She flies, I walk – for about an hour. And then we return to the area around the house. She will perch on my arm or someplace nearby for the morning, and then leave around noon. I won't see her again until the next day.

"In the past year, our morning outings have taken on a very specific form. I start out walking with Aua perched on my arm. Once we get into open field, she takes off, flying straight ahead, gradually turning up to a height of a hundred yards or so. She continues in a circle, curving back down toward the ground, then flying past me within inches of my head. Round and round, she repeats this circle about thirty times. Each time, when she is just a few feet behind me, she always calls out *Kee-a-a-a-ra.* Now I must tell you, it's a very unsettling feeling when a hawk flies past your head at full speed, especially when she is coming from behind and you can't see the approach. The space between her calls becomes very charged. You know she's coming around again, but her circles keep getting larger and it's easy to lose sense of time. Of course, I trust her, but she is a wild animal and there is an element of attack to her ritual. As the sound of her call streaks past my ears, I feel a shock wave in my body. After a few passes, all that matters is the call. It pulls a chill up through my spine and out my eyes. With each succeeding circle, more of me goes with her. Gradually the bird disappears, but she does not leave. I begin to feel the turn up into the sky, at the highest point I see the man walking on the ground. Full speed down now, curving in along the ground, I approach the man. He's right ahead and I call out to him, *'Wake up . . . those who are with me, fly with me.'*"

Views

PETER NADIN

Byzantium

The Turks breached Byzantium May 29 1453
Provoking subsequent talk of order and chaos, and the Turks
Fuck the Turks. What's the Turks to you and me.
Order History fabricated for necessity of desire and faith.
Or the penetration of the prone Christian
By the swarthy loins of Islam, and the co-mingling
In Animalistic desire . . . Yes Yes Yes . . . They liked it
The constant desire, the lying desire, animal and Virgin.
Reciprocity of orifice. Supremacy of swarthiness,
Simian limbs and whitened innocence.
Celibacy and carnality balanced on the fulcrumed plank . . .
Yes Yes Yes . . . Natural desires, plucking fruit from
The laden vine. Eating what's edible. Killing what's killable . . .
Yes Yes Yes . . . and the first World War. Our Boys,
Cheshire Regiment, the Bantams at Ypres, all volunteers
Like plucked chickens to the chicken slaughter.
The Somme, mustard gas, and Colonel Bogey, blancoedgaters
And 303s. "Up and at 'em" with Cold Steel . . . Yes Yes Yes . . .
And Verdun, a spring afternoon among the graves. Fuck 'em.
Fuck the communal dead, dead in the communal ideal.
Yes Yes Yes . . . The final offensive, the line that always holds,
Or Napoleon's Mausoleum . . . The Egyptian campaign, and
The dead of Islam . . . Yes. Yes. Yes . . . and the pressed
Uniforms. Or 1848, Munich 1939, and the Hungarians,
The entire History of Hungary, Hungarian genetic
Characteristics, leading to a Hungarian name . . . And
Canada, South Seas, Captain Cook. The Nile, Speake,
Burton, Queen Victoria . . . Yes Yes Yes . . . The tepid water.
The orifice and edifice, sexuality, constant desires,
The Buttocks and Penises. Female sexual organs. Breasts,
Livers . . . Yes Yes Yes . . . We know that for certain,
Certain within the constancy of desire.

The Light That Burns the Eyes to Bleed

Ravaged and burnt, smoldering fields
Blackened wheat chaff as stubbled nails and the putrid
Whitish smoke concealing bands of blind derelict liars,
their eyes put out with pointed sticks, some years ago,
For some minor infraction . . . Now wandering aimlessly eternal,
Throats filled with sulfurous evocations. Emaciated profiteers,
Active in several wars, now toothless and hunched
Eagerly licking the charcoal stump of a lightning-struck oak
For sustenance, or something to keep the tongue moist,
The mind still, the voices silent . . . And the sun burns
The skin of armless beggars, babies on their backs, former
Embassy staffers, opportunists then . . . Now they plead
For an end, a change, a move, a morsel,
But now there is no bread, nor water, for the land
Is already dead, the stream already dry.

Mojave to Vegas

In Mojave, speak not of fate
but of water and military spending
and of Goldstone Lake. For there, upon
those shores the first American fire burned
ten thousand years before Vegas shimmered through
mob-owned heat. Mob-owned bodies stoking
Vegas heat. Lying in air-conditioned cool
poolside, phone, fur-coat women in chilled rooms.
Revolution is of the wheel.
Fate concerns the break.
Golf courses, acrylic sap green, hard-edge
turf and sand, rectangular, more nightmare
than mirage. Car exhaust cooler than air.
Fair game the punter plays in heat of fire,
in waterless land . . .

The Future of Speculation, or Identifying the Corpse Before It's Deceased

Robert Owen knew it right,
The natural standard of value is human labor,
so realized the mortgageers, so profit from life
Twenty-five year term, thirty year term

working life, working life exchanged for deed
of ownership, title of land. Life of utilitarian
value. Imagination, metaphor empirically
unquantifiable, but not yet decreed worthless.

Utilitarian emanation of body value to time
value. Nine to five to "Time is money"
when quantifiable by production. To share in wealth
and production thence to material consideration
of objects and their practical application.
"Eight hour day," manufacturer of sausage and towel
no longer ashamed, as the successful product
is democratically right.

All for one, one for all, for profit
for gain, and in loss no honor. For who
is in loss and not ethically suspect? Thus
rapacious desire for surplus for wealth,
for "smell of money" for position within
community. Thence from mating to next generation,
"Chip off the old block" sons and daughters
without mortgageer but with money manager, thence
to political organization "let us maintain stability"
Yet still Carnegie may be right
"The inherited dollar is a stinking fish"

Not Pound, not usury, not interest
or maintenance of debt. Not powers beyond
our control, not lack of classical education.

Not will power. Equilibrium destroyed in
weight of balance and loss. The ill-advised
report of advocates "breaking even" though
still a bridge may break even (in suspense)
In profit the bridge falls. In loss the bridge
is never built. No transcendence in materiality,
time a commodity thus need for linear time "Nine to
Five." Hence hatred of poetry and covetousness
of objects and rampant speculation of value and meaning.

Brains washed by soothing wave upon wave
of inanity till cleansed of the will to resist.
Dogmatists, linear politicians, aestheticians,
masquerading as policemen and doctors, drawing
blood applying leeches, in order to maintain health
of economy and culture.

Vermeer	Debtor
Rembrandt	Bankrupt
Blake	Better in a tree with angels than in a hovel with your wife
Goya	Destitute, revelling in his hatred of clerics and Bourdeaux cathedral
Byron	Vomiting at the sight of the miners who maintained his Venetian musings
Charlie Chaplin	Run out of town for the wrong views
Van Gogh	Neglected in his own time
Reynolds	Better a monogrammed carriage than threaten livelihood
Rosa Bonheur	In chateau with menage and menagerie

Words in demons, demons in words,
denial of livelihood thus limited choice of
mate selection. Generations, children, maintain
the family maintain wealth, maintain standards,
and thus culture, as if the ego were not simultaneously
shared and privately owned.

My Bio: Notes on an American Childhood

COOKIE MUELLER

The year I was born, 1949, the North Atlantic Treaty was signed, the Dutch were ousted from Indonesia, and the first Russian nuclear bomb was exploded. So what? It didn't happen in America, so who cared? Not me. I was too small.

I only cared about America, more precisely Baltimore, more precisely the Baltimore suburbs, more precisely my backyard and a flannel blanket that I sat on naked under a Norway maple tree. I also cared a lot about the kitchen sink which I was small enough to take a bath in. For some reason I also cared about the 1949 model Cadillac because it was and still is the most beautiful car ever made. I appreciated birds. I wanted a dog.

In 1949 my eyes were the same size as they are now, because human eyes do not grow with the body; they're the same size at birth as they will always be.

That was 1949.

In 1959, with eyes the same size, I got to see some of America in a different car traveling with my parents, who couldn't stand each other, and my brother and sister, who loved everyone. I remember the Erie Canal on a dismal day, the Maine coastline in a storm, Georgian willow trees in the rain, Luray Caverns in the Blue Ridge Mountains of Virginia where the stalagmites and tites were poorly lit.

Unfortunately, I remember all too well Colonial Williamsburg where the authentic costumes were made out of dacron and poly and the shoes were naughahyde. I remember exactly how much I detested seeing these fakers in these clothes as I was then very concerned with detail. Even more than the outer garments, I imagined that of course they weren't wearing the right undergarments. I knew in my heart that, for instance, the person who was dressed up to look like the 1790s blacksmith had on modern Fruit of the Loom underpants. Hiding under colonial skirts that the women wore were cheap seventy-nine-cent nylon pantyhose from Woolworth's. This bothered me very much.

My father's travel itinerary was mighty strange. We visited a saltpeter mine somewhere in the woods of somebody's rundown farm. It was listed in some tour guide but it wasn't much of a tourist attraction, maybe because saltpeter had a bad name. It's the stuff used in American cigarettes to make them burn up faster. Actually, this mine was really quite beautiful because it was a cave of all-white salt crystals that would have sparkled if it had been a sunny day. As it was, the farmer who showed us the cave had to keep a dirty checkered oilcloth over the entrance so the crystals wouldn't dissolve in the rain.

In this year Castro seized power in Cuba and I became infatuated with him, not for any socialist leanings I had. It might have had something to do with the *I Love Lucy* show, but mostly I was impressed at the nonchalance and grace in the way he smoked his cigars. He also had a great fashion sense. He was a clotheshorse.

Always with Castro on my mind I spent idle hours of the summer months in the woods behind my parents' house. In these woods was a strange railroad track, where a mystery train passed through a tunnel of trees and vines twice a day, once at 1:00 P.M. and then again in the opposite direction at 3:00 P.M. I would climb a steep hill which sat right on the tracks and I would look down into the smokestack and always the black smoke would settle on my white clamdiggers.

For miles and miles in the direction that the train was headed there was nothing except a seminary and an insane asylum. So naturally my assumption was that one of the cattle cars was full of loons anxious to be committed and the other car was full of future priests, students of theology, who, as everyone knows, have to use public transportation because they're far too religious to drive their own cars. The 3:00 P.M. train would return the other way carrying the dirty laundry. I imagined that both cattle cars were full of stained straightjackets and sweaty clerical collars. There was always a caboose full of shirtless men with fistfulls of cards, probably playing strip poker. This verified my assumptions, somehow.

In these woods I found a lot of pets. I brought home box turtles; one that I named Fidel was adaptable to captivity. Fidel would crawl up to my dog Jip's dog food bowl and chow down. Jip would get angry and run over to the bowl and growl at the turtle, but Fidel ignored Jip. He kept eating. Turtles are the plodders in nature's scheme, the ones that know the term "easy does it," the ones who won't let setbacks affect them much. It's obvious when you study a turtle: their skin is as thick as linoleum and their shells are as hard as shells. My parents hated Fidel, only because of his name.

I would also bring home black snakes and tadpoles that turned into frogs all over the house. Once I brought home a nest of baby opossums that turned out to be rats. My mother was not amused about this.

One day, along the tracks, I unearthed a yellow-jacket hive while I was rearranging boulders. Stung seventeen times, the doctors didn't see much hope for me, but I recovered.

After facing death, I became a young novelist and wrote a book about the Jonestown, Pennsylvania, flood in 1830 – something where Clara Barton threw her weight around. The book was three-hundred-twenty-one pages long and I had set for myself the deadline of my eleventh birthday. I'd heard that the girl who wrote *Black Beauty* was eleven, so I wanted to be the youngest novelist in the world.

Since I didn't have any idea of how to get it published, I typed it all up, stapled it together, cut up some beer-case cardboard, and covered this with white butcher paper and Saran Wrap. I painted a relevant picture for the cover and smuggled it into the library and put it on the shelves in the correct alphabetical order. I never saw that book again.

I learned early that writing was hard on the body. Blood turns cold and circulation stops at the typewriter; the knee joints solidify into cement, the ass becomes one with the chair. But I kept writing.

One Sunday around this time, my brother died. It happened at the railroad tracks. He was climbing a dead tree and it fell on him. It was quick. He was fourteen. He hadn't seen a whole lot and saved himself a lot of future troubles. He was one of those kinds of people that was just too sensitive to hang around too long.

So then my mother's hair went gray practically overnight. After awhile she dyed it black again.

I never went back to the railroad tracks. None of my family ever went near there again or mentioned that area of the forest.

Ten years later, at the beginning of 1969, I was in a mental hospital in San Francisco, having been committed by my roommates. They did it out of desperation, after having tried everything including potatoes, nature's tranquilizers: au gratin, mashed, boiled, baked, and fried.

Everything you've ever heard about mental hospitals is true. Patients make paper dolls and they weave baskets and they have a lot of wild fun late at night when there aren't any doctors around, just nurse's aides and bouncers. The bouncers would always get in the way and throw people into solitary confinement, which I found out is not as romantic as it may sound.

One day I accidentally had shock therapy when I got in the wrong line. It's the truth.

You may have heard a lot of bad things about shock therapy, for instance in too many renditions of the Frances Farmer story, and you may have an opinion about it. But it really isn't as bad as you think. It really isn't so horrible. As a matter of fact, to me it was rather pleasant because it eradicated from my memory all the contents of stupid literature, required reading forced on me by liberal English Lit teachers in school. It all came back in a few months.

In this hospital everybody got lots of thorazine, stellazine, and hot chocolate. The hot chocolate was doled out constantly after the sun went down for the patients who couldn't sleep, and that was everyone. Even after massive doses of tranquilizers the brain pans were still overflowing, the cogs of wild imaginations were still whirling, so there were always a lot of loons walking around like people from *The Night of the Living Dead.* Everyone clutched their styrofoam cups full of hot chocolate. The floors were sloshed up because, after that many pills, people get kind of sloppy.

I met some very funny people there.

After two months in the California hospital, I was sent to a Maryland hospital. The doctors wanted me to be closer to where I was born and raised. They thought perhaps it might help my mental outlook. And, wouldn't you know it, they sent me to the hospital that was in the woods behind my parents' house. I found out that the mystery train, the one whose smokestack used to sooty up my clamdiggers, didn't stop at the mental hospital at all, but I could see it from my barred windows as it passed at 1:00 P.M. and then again at 3:00 P.M. Somehow, seeing this train did bring me back down to earth. I got better.

In the caboose of the train the same shirtless men were playing the same games, just as they had ten years before. Some things never change.

Ten years later, after moving around in the world, and then to New York, I got a phone call from my mother, on a rainy Sunday. She told me that my father had just died when the Plymouth ran him over in the driveway. My mother got out the hair dye bottle again.

No, some things never change . . . Even if they do, it doesn't matter; you can cover it with black hair dye.

5. Modern Love

Modern Love

CONSTANCE DE JONG

Part One

Everywhere I go I see losers. Misfits like myself who can't make it in the world. In London, New York, Morocco, Rome, India, Paris, Germany. I've started seeing the same people. I think I'm seeing the same people. I wander around staring at strangers thinking I know you from somewhere. I don't know where. The streets are always crowded and narrow, full of men. It's always night and all strangers are men.

I hear talk of a new world. Everywhere I go: eco-paleo-psycho-electro-cosmo talk. Of course, men do all the talking. I don't get the message, my ears ache; my eyes are falling out, I don't see these street talkers as the makers of a new world. Anyway, they're not real losers. And the new world's an old dream.

They said, "Wait till you're twenty-seven, then you'll be sorry." I'm twenty-seven. I'm not sorry.

Who are "they"? Not answered.

And the new world? I've heard tell; seen no evidence; been looking.

I saw people in India with no arms, no legs, no clothes, no food, no money, no place, no nothing but other people, people, people. Real losers. I talked to very serious people in Europe who were, were not my own age because they saw themselves in perspective. More abstract losers, but losers just as real. They saw: a convergence in the distant present coming out of the recent past: themselves. I saw the historical bogeyman coming around the corner hustling for a place to crash. It scared me, made me run around Paris, Rome, Germany being noisy. Being pushy. Slamming around making up stories as fast as I could go. "The world spins and I go around in circles ha ha I'm a dizzy blonde gibbering off into the sun setting behind the Arc de Distrust. . . ." Running off at the mouth. At the feet. Here today, not there tomorrow, gone leaving no incriminating evidence of my unpopular half-baked world view. That's a good girl.

"I wonder if I'll always be alone," I think to myself.

The misfits I've been seeing everywhere, they aren't real losers. They all have bank accounts: can afford to be losers. I'm broke. What's the exchange rate for my wealth of information? I'll drop pearls on the sidewalk, the page. I'll be drippy: "The new world's an old dream and I'm tired of dreams. Come upstairs," I whisper in the ears of passing strangers.

I was a seven-year dreamer. . . .

I think I have to have a past. I think too much. A common malady. I make a vow: restrain yourself, become more or less observant, use fewer French and/or fancy words. I have to watch myself. I was a seven-year dreamer. I live two, three, four, multiple lives; I get distracted in these crowded narrow passages. I have to watch myself; it's not safe for a woman to be alone on the streets. Have to get off. I'll take someone home. "Hey honey, come up to my place, I'll show you my best recipes. Do you have a lot of cash?" Shameless at last. It's 1975 and I can say and do anything I want. I want to prove this. Obviously, by saying and doing anything I want. "Hey honey . . ."

I want this guy to fit into my plans. I wonder, "Maybe he's a murderer, a cop." I'll find out:

"Do you spell 'they' with a capital or a small 't'?" I ask.

He's grinning. "All caps, toots."

Whew. He got my message. He's not one of them. Two misfits. Just like I planned it. I call him Roderigo, my favorite romantic name. All strangers are men with romantic names. And romantic pasts.

We're in my room. I think I have to prove something, I don't know what. I have to make up my mind: two cells collide and twenty-seven years later I'm sitting on my Persian rug. With Roderigo. Now I have a past. Now Roderigo will see me like I want. I want Roderigo to think I'm fabulous. I want to be like broken glass on the sidewalk; diamonds on black velvet; glitter against the ground. It turns out I want to control people. That's no good. I better watch myself.

See me. See me. From behind, sideways, above, below, from every angle I'm the same. See, I'm everywhere; no different from the rug the furniture the floor ceiling walls bookshelves. See how it all fits together. Everything from the ritual objects to the easy chair is immaculately arranged, sort of a Victorian-style shrine. There's no room for accident, or an event. That's no good.

I've been seeing too many artists. I can't go through life looking at how objects are colored, cut out, and arranged. I'm no painter.

I am wearing a red sweater. Holding a blue cup. Sitting on a Persian rug. This is where I belong. This room is self-sufficient, the universe. Everything can take place here, I have everything I need: I live here.

"I can see right through you, baby. I could write your diary," says Roderigo.

I'm shattered. I don't want to be like broken glass. I don't want to be a metaphor.

We're in my room. I can do anything I want. I want Roderigo. I want him to do everything to me. I want him to feel easy with me and my possessions and my burning desires. I have to turn my self and my place inside-out so he'll enter into the deep, dark, hidden, secretive, mysterious, fabulous magic inner meanings of my life. So he'll disappear. With me.

"Take this cup: it's a magic vessel that transmits legends from lip to lip. Hold it next to your ear and listen to the sweet rustle of the mysteries of the universe as they unfold. Hear the sweet angel voices come across the ages, hear the thunder. Sit on this rug: it's been handed down from generation to generation. Whole lifetimes leap up from every stain, every worn spot. Sit over here where Lady Mirabelle dropped her wine glass fainting in ecstasy into the arms of Monsieur Le Prince. See this sweater: it's my favorite. I bought it from an old lady at the Paris flea market who sold gypsy scarves and fuzzy sweaters. It's a sacred red. A deep, dark red to match the color of the blood that's zooming through my veins."

Two cells collide and twenty-seven years later I come back with Roderigo. I want him to feel at home. I'll make some coffee.

"I'll make some coffee. You make yourself at home."

"Okay."

Roderigo leans against the wall. His fingers are twitchy. There are colors around his head. He reaches without reaching. I turn without turning, we yes each other without speaking, then we fuck like maniacs. I have no graphic images. Roderigo does everything to me. He touches me everywhere. We do everything from behind, sideways, above, below. I come from every angle. I never had it so good; he says it's the same for him.

"I gotta go now," says Roderigo. "Maybe I'll see you around."

That's modern love: short, hot, and sweet.

I want to tell you my life story. It's a very interesting story. One midnight I was transported all at once from my solitude in La Soho by a stranger who came tapping at my door. His name's Monsieur Le Prince. For seven years I'd been

"You don't have to tell me anything. I can see right through you. I could write your diary. I feel like I've known you all my life. Don't talk. Come next to me," Roderigo whispers.

He reaches without reaching, I turn without turning, we yes each other without speaking, then we tumble together, we disappear together, down down down the deep dark, magic mysterious love tunnel. I have no graphic images. He reaches, I turn, then we fuck. He reaches, I turn, then we fuck. He reaches, I turn then we fuck. He reaches, I turn then we fuck. He reaches I turn then we fuck.

People used to tell me, if you keep on writing maybe you'll make a name for yourself. They were right: My name's Constance De Jong. My name's Fifi Corday. My name's Lady Mirabelle, Monsieur Le Prince, and Roderigo, Roderigo's my favorite name. First I had my father's name, then my husband's, then another's. I don't know, don't want to know the cause of anything. They said, "You'll see when you're thirty." When I was thirty I was standing at the Gate of India. I saw nothing. I'm still thirty. I want to tell you my life story.

First I had the name John Henry. Until I was born, I was a boy: a typical father's assumption. Then I became my father's second choice, a very romantic name. Then I took my husband's, now another's name. I'm still writing. Obviously, nothing's been changed. I keep on seeing the same people everywhere I go. I go up and down, burning with the desires of my age. Flames leap up at every corner. Die down, flame up. I drop my control and my vow, my pretensions for inner and outer order. Ashes swirl around my feet as I tiptoe out the door. The door, my doors all open to the light. Are passages into the heart, the substance. It's an emotional association.

I was wandering around Soho one night. The streets were very crowded: it must have been Saturday. People were walking in twos and threes, laughing, talking, going from bar to bar. I was looking at the books in a window display, thinking to myself. People were shouting to each other: "Hey, Henri!" "Hello, Pablo, how's it going?" "Hey, there's Guillaume and Marie." "How ya doing, Gertrude? Are you coming to Rousseau's party?" "Seen Eric? What's doing with him anyway? I hear he left town." Dark currents darted around the street. Flickering colors, big shadows, vapory voices brushed against me. Brushed over me. I felt the wool against the back, the blood against the vein; my head swelled with circles inside of squares, intricate structures, rhomboids, cups of coffee, pieces of furniture, parts of bodies, lists, broken-off sentences . . . I saw

Roderigo duck around a corner. He's out looking for a little coke and sympathy: his name's Mick Jagger. It ain't me you're looking for, babe. He thinks modern love isn't worth repeating. I think I saw Roderigo. It must have been my imagination. Anyway, he never was very interested in my fucking visions.

One midnight I was transported all at once from the depths of my solitude by a stranger . . .

> Tap. Tap. Tap.
> "Lady Mirabelle?"
> "Why yes," I answered.
> "I hope I'm not intruding. But, I happened to be passing by and, noticing the light in your window, I thought

At first I had difficulty placing him. He appeared to be of Oriental extraction. A Tartar, or perhaps a Persian. We spoke in French. He explained that he'd seen my light burning as he passed beneath my window. It was the only bright spot on the otherwise dreary Rue Fermat. It was a long walk to his apartment on the Rue du Dragon and he thought perhaps he could rest for a moment and perhaps if it wasn't too much trouble have a bit of wine to refresh himself before he continued on his journey home. As my maid had just brought up my nightly claret, I easily obliged the stranger without having to disturb the slumbering household. Before I knew it, I had charmed the pants off Monsieur Le Prince. I heard the faint rustle of my taffeta skirts as we slid – meeting by chance, but loving as if by design – into each other's arms.

Many's the time while walking in the gardens or sitting in the window or attending to one of my endless tasks, my sewing, my letters, my salon, my accounts, my friends; many's the time I've been startled by the memory of this amorous event in my life. It catches me from behind. I feel his touch. I turn. Then I tumble down, disappear into the dark passage. I know this passage. I know where it leads. Still, I cannot restrain myself. My daily efforts, the trivial tasks and the tidy lessons, all my orderly preoccupations, everything scatters. My pearls are soap bubbles floating over the roof and out to sea. I watch them vanish; let them go. Only a child would pursue these fleeting visions. I know better. I know it's a transparent allusion. I see through it: can see a diamond burning in the night. Diamonds are forever. I can always turn to them when everything else seen, heard, touched begins to make me blind, deaf, insensitive. When I feel his fatal touch, then I let myself go. I return. I feel the hand against my heart, a tapping at my door. I don't have to keep on chipping and polishing and guarding my treasure, my memory. I have a permanent impression. Monsieur Le Prince is inside me. Forever. There's a place where the emotions are intact. A room. A permanent association. Whole days scatter into the blue when Monsieur Le Prince reaches out: then my favorite lover condenses into a single, mythical moment. An instant can be an event. An instant can be a fatal event. An instant is sufficient. I'm not fooling: that's all it took. All at once my heart became a place full of light. All aflame. A brilliant shine. A star. It's still a heart. It's 1975 and I'm not sorry I've died for love.

Many years have passed and time after time I startle over. I use fancy words to envelop my vivid impressions. I get wrapped up in the ageless pursuit of naming an emotion as if it were an object. Monsieur Le Prince stands for love, truth, wisdom, honesty, etc. His memory, my memory jumps up involuntarily, like a reflex. It startles me. Makes me run through my inside-out versions of love of death of . . . "Even in this day and age," I say to myself. Even in this age of insight? I say, yes, there's still room for a love story. I don't need, don't want to need a perfect, sacred explanation. I always go where these abrupt passages lead me. Rainbow-colored bubbles swirl into the sky. I told Monsieur Le Prince, words are just rollers that spread the emotions around. As for me, I have everything I need: diamonds are always bright. They're reliable. It's true: I'll gladly drop down when the trap door springs open at a touch. I go down once, twice, countless times. It's always pretty interesting. And, that's sufficient. No. I'm not sorry I once died for love. Now, I have a second, a better chance.

Here's the story. I'm in my room. It's a long sentence: I sit, I stand, I drift back and forth between these walls, flitting over the floorboards, wearing myself to a shadow, comparing myself to the flickering gleams on the ceiling the walls, attempting to merge with the background, trying to become anonymous, hoping to stay forever in the total freedom of obscurity, I'm imprisoned, dreaming hard. This goes on for seven years. It was a long sentence. I'm recalling it as a time of solitary refinement. I'm free to say whatever I want. I tell Roderigo, I want to be a guard at the gate of indecision. Want to know the cause of everything, all things. I've an inkling he doesn't get my drift. He doesn't have time on his hands. No time for long pretty intricate explanations. He twitches when I talk. Probably all he ever thinks about is fucking. I think he's fabulous, I want to find him flawless, I'm ready to kneel at his feet. I think men tire me. I'll show him. I place you in a picture flooded

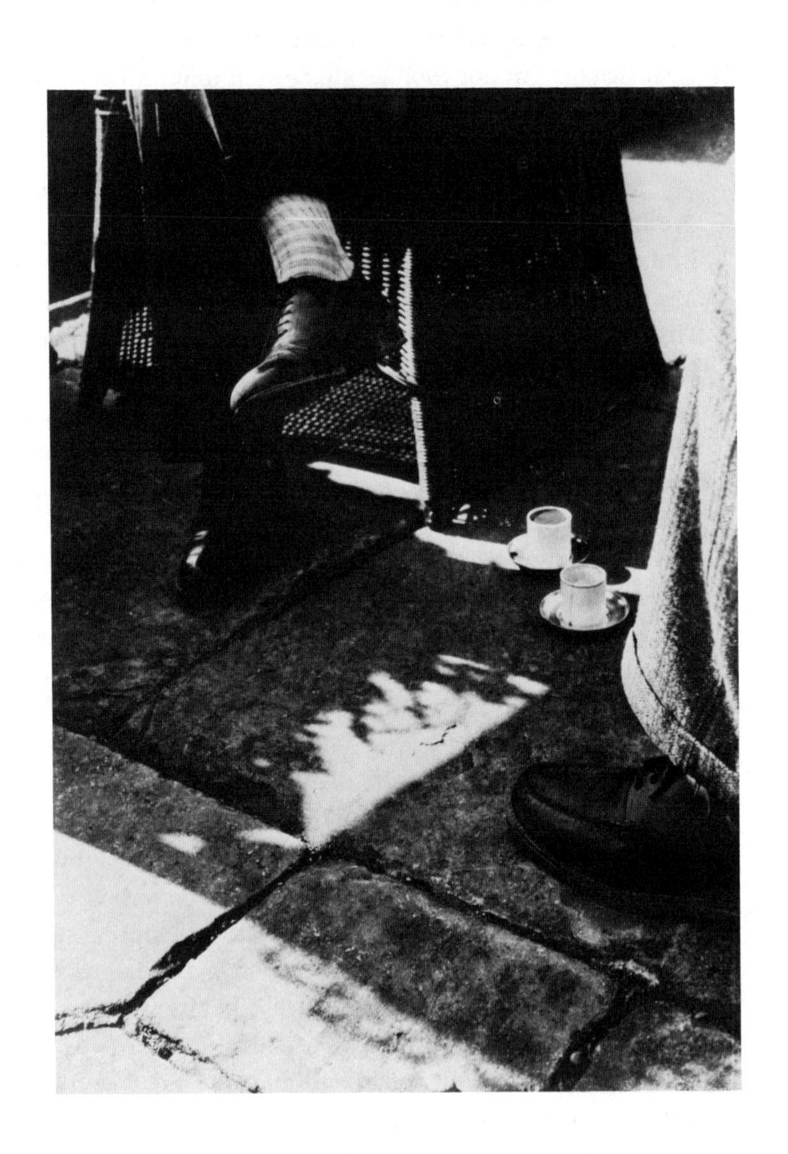

with moonlight. That's where you belong. Permanently framed in a romantic episode. I'll tell you more.

There are two strangers in the room. Three strangers in the room. In the seven-year dream, I two, four, six; I multiply. The room's crowded. I'm running around in hot pursuit, attempting to find, attempting to be the originating cause of everything. I don't believe in numbers. I'm after a total effect, wanting to see how it all fits together. There are presences in the room. Vague. But presences just the same. As real as numbers. They're my visitors: station masters, generals, writers, artists, countless corpses, editors, nurses, lost children, various animals, a long procession of the living and dead. I don't actually look for them. They come to me like guests who have rights of a sort. They come, I accept them. When they sit, I stand. When I talk, they listen. When they stand, I turn around. When I look, they stare back. When I've had enough of this, I create situations in which they'll leave me: I tell them, "My name's Étoile, I come from France, I live here in the Eiffel Tower, I'm the center of the universe, ha ha I'm a star, the world revolves around me." When they leave me, I wonder if I'll always be left alone.

I think, "Maybe I read too much."

One day I exclaim, "I'm surrounded by fools and foolish ideas! I want a better world!" I'll make up a better image. This is my idea: I place the earth on the back of an enormous elephant in order to hold it up in space. The elephant is supported by a tortoise which in turn is floating in a sea contained in some sort of vessel.

That was one day's total effort.

The next day, I'm sitting, reading a book on Hindu mythology. I read: "In Hindu mythology, the earth is placed on the back of an enormous elephant in order to hold it up in space. The elephant is supported by a tortoise, which in turn is floating in a sea contained in a vessel." That was depressing.

I don't like seeing myself in other words; I feel foolish.

The next day, I am sitting, standing, drifting around, moaning and sighing, feeling sorry talking to myself:

"Will the world come to me or will I go to it?" she said.

"You have to make up your mind," she said.

I flit over to the bookcase. I reach without choosing. I'm reading: "I view her," he said, "with a certain unaccountable excitement, living in her tower, supplied with telephones, telegraphs, phonographs, wireless sets, motion picture screens, slide projectors, video monitors, glossaries, timetables, and bulletins. She has everything she needs. She wears an Egyptian ring. It sparkles when she speaks. For a woman so equipped, actual travel is superfluous. Our twentieth century has inverted the story of Mohammed and the mountain; nowadays the mountain comes to the modern Mohammed."

I hated that description.

I read it; felt no deep emotion; the dream ended.

In other words, I saw the light.

That night, I sat at my desk writing: (1) THE ECLECTIC IS NOT UNIVERSAL. (2) NOT ALL COINCIDENCES ARE INTERESTING. These were the daily lessons: seven years wrapped up in two sentences. I better think this over. I worry that my messages are cryptic; too obscure and/or too personal. I pinned them to the refrigerator door and went out for a walk.

It must have been a Saturday. Everyone was on the street. I ran into Jorge Luis Borges. A likely coincidence . . .

I ran into Bob Dylan.

I ran into Jorge Luis Borges and asked him if it was okay to quote him in my book.

"Is it okay, Jorge? I want to use the part about the person who's confined. You know, the modern dreamer. I'm writing a prison novel. I'll just make a few changes from your original words. Add a little here and there. What do you say? Is it okay?"

"It's okay, darling. Many times I've said, 'All collaborations are mysterious.' Just remember, always write what you know about."

"Okay."

I'll write about the past. In the past, everything is immaculately arranged. All things have the same value: people, books, events, chairs, numbers, me, love, New York are of equal value. Are interchangeable. A little of this, a little of that; everything is coincidental, is interconnected. It's so simple, it all fits: events are things; people are things; objects are colored, cut out, arranged; are simply things following from/leading to other things. That's all very nice. I hate this dream. This modern dream, love of complexity. I had this dream. It had me. In it I become a fixture in a crowded, airless setting. No different from the rug, the furniture floor ceiling, etc. My head was filled with intricate nonsense which made all coincidences so interesting. I'm remembering: "There are stains and worn spots all over this rug. If I connect the individual marks, I can map the generations who walked off their lives across this Persian landscape. I can graph an image of the procession of life. It'll be called The Shape of Time. I'll be famous for my insight." My visions images ideas, my vows, my burning desires, my thinking, my occupation: I was dreaming hard.

"Hey, honey, I want to tell you a secret."
"Great."
"See this cup? I want you to have it."
"Is it worth anything?"
"All you ever think about is money!"
"That's right."
"Don't you know money isn't everything? You're famous and that's what counts."
"Right."
"Can't you just appreciate my precious cup? I want you to have it because it means something very special to me."
"Oh."
"Because you're someone special to me. You're my real friend. Do you know what I mean? Do you know how hard it is to find a really dependable, true blue friend in the world?"
"Sure I know. That's no secret."
"Oh."
"I gotta go now." I don't know: "Can a young girl really find happiness in the world trusting only me and objects?"

When he leaves me, I invent reasons to keep on living. I remember people always told me, write what you know about. I know a lot of artists. I'm surrounded by people making art; misfits like myself. I don't really believe this. Actually, I believe there's something to art. And, I even know what it is. Art is . . .

"No, no, no!" scream the editors. "SEX. REVOLUTION. VIOLENCE. The big stuff. All caps, sweetheart. We can't sell art, your friends, your crummy insights. Listen, angel, don't you want to make a name for yourself?"

"Yes," I murmur. "I want a lot of money. But what's a poor girl to do?"
"Come upstairs," they said. "You'll see."
The People are screaming, "No! We want Education, Food, Houses. We want our rights!"
People are shouting, "Don't sell out to the Man."
"Yes, yes, you're right, your rights," I stutter, I stumble. I have

to run run run, have to work hard, have to get off the streets. Threats and accusations and insults rain down; my head swims; the street's whirling with blood and dirty water, broken-up furniture and parts of bodies. It's dark, it's crowded, I'm running fast, it's a narrow escape.

Gosh, I made it. I'm safe in my room. (1) The Universe is a mythological expression: I read that somewhere. (2) The universe is a great big soap bubble that starts in a jar, ends up in bubble heaven. There are people up in Nova Scotia who send their kids to Bubble Island instead of college. Let them go; maybe they'll have a better chance. Maybe not. I'm no parent. Me, I'm self-sufficient. That means: I'm off in some remote corner. Pacing off the safety zone. Wearing myself to a shadow. Holding onto my precious integrity, worrying: I can't spend my whole life trusting only artists. I need to see more of the world, to get in touch with better energy. Can I take a big chance? Can I afford a ticket to India?

Part Two

The sun was behind the hills, the town was afire with evening, and the sky was filling with light. India's on slow time. An even train of days hooking onto nights shading into another day steadily shading out over the water over the desert the mountains the plains. The sky was filling with light, the sun was clear in the sky and there was a cool breeze from the sea. It was fairly early in the morning. Fortunately it wasn't going to be too hot a day. But the dust was everywhere, fine and penetrating. In the moonlight the garden became very beautiful. Motionless, silent trees cast long, dark shadows across the lawn and among the still bushes. The birds settled down for the night in the dark foliage. Hardly anyone was on the road. Occasionally there was a song in the distance. Otherwise, the garden was quiet, full of soft whispers and the trees gave shape to the hazy, silver sky. It had rained all night and most of the morning and now the sun was going down behind heavy, dark clouds. There was no color in the sky. The frogs had croaked all night, persistently, rhythmically; but with the dawn they became silent. The morning was gray. The sun rose out of the woods, big with burning radiance, but the clouds soon hid it. All day the sun and the clouds fought each other. Clouds had been coming through a wide gap in the mountains; piling up against the hills. They remained dark and threatening over the valley and it would probably rain towards evening. The night was silent and still. It was very early in the morning and the sea was quiet, lapping at the white shore. There was a sparkle in the sea, and a blueness and it was old. Smoke from a steamer far out was going almost straight up in the sky. The sun wouldn't be up for two or three hours. There wasn't a cloud in the sky. The villagers weren't up yet. The sky was enclosed by a dark outline of encircling hills. The night was completely still. The moon was just coming out of the sea into a valley of clouds. The water was still, blue. Orion was faintly visible in the pale, silver sky. White waves lapped against the shore. The moon was rising above the valley of clouds and it was huge. There was rain. It came down in sheets, flooding the roads and filling up the lily pond. Trees bent under the weight. The crows were soaked and could hardly fly. Suddenly the frogs were silent. It was particularly beautiful that evening with the sun setting below the dark town, behind a single minaret, which seemed to be pointing the whole town up towards the sky. The clouds were golden red, aflame with the brilliance of a sun that had traveled over a beautiful, sad land. And as the brilliance faded there was the new moon. There over the dark town was the delicate new moon. The sun was now touching the treetops and they were aglow with soft light. They were giving shape to the sky. A single rose was heavy with dew. The rains had washed the skies clean; the haze that had hung about was gone and the sky was clear and intensely blue. Shadows were sharp and deep, and high on the hill a column of smoke was going straight up. It was still very early and there was a slight ground mist hiding the bushes and flowers. The sun was just coming up behind a mass of trees, which were quiet now. The chattering birds had already scattered for the day. It was quite early. The Southern Cross was clear and beautiful over the palm trees. A heavy dew made a circle of dampness around each tree. There weren't any lights on in the houses yet. And the stars were very clear. But there was an awakening in the eastern sky. It had been raining for days. Hills and mountains were under dark clouds. In the distance, the land was hidden by thick fog. There were puddles everywhere. It was a lovely day and as the sun had only just come over the treetops it still wasn't too hot. White waves came in slowly. There wasn't a cloud. And the waning moon was in mid-heaven. As the sun climbed higher, the plains were covered with long shadows. It was a beautiful day, clear and not too warm. It had rained recently. One of those soft, gentle rains that go deep. The sky was intensely blue; the horizon was filled with enormous clouds. Early in the morning, just before the sun comes out of the sea, when the dew is heavy on the ground and the stars are still visible, this place is very beautiful. Everything is quiet against the thunder of the sea. The morning star is fading. A golden rim is showing at the water's far edge. Shadows are slowly casting across the ground. The sea is very calm. The sea was resting before the northeasterly winds began. The sands were bleached by the sun and salt water. There was a strong smell of ozone and seaweed. No one was on the beach yet. The eastern sky was more splendid than where the sun had set. A mass of clouds was full of flashes of lightning, twisting sharp and brilliant. There were other weird shapes. And every imaginable color. Towards the west there was a pure orange. It had rained for days. It was a very clear, starry night. There was not a cloud in the sky. The waning moon was just above the tall palms, which were very still. Orion was well up in the western sky and the Southern Cross was over the hills. Not a house had a light in it and the narrow road was dark and deserted. The sea was calm. The horizon clear. It would be an hour or two before the sun would come up behind the hills and the waning moon set the waters moving. Nothing was stirring in the bushes, nothing yet moving. The birds were quiet. It was a lovely evening, cool after the hot, sunny day. A breeze was coming across the water and the waving palms gave shape to the sky. The sun was setting. The day was shading slowly, evenly into a black Indian night. The woman was standing on the beach. She was riding in a train, walking up from the valley, sitting on a hill. The woman was traveling alone in India. She was eating ice cream because it was her birthday. The dark blue waters were full of reflections. For an instant she cast about for a thirty-year-old opinion. It was another lovely, Bombay evening, cool after the hot, sunny day. The sun was fading. A breeze was coming across the water and little sparkles began to stand out against the darkening background. The palms were waving. The water was full of reflections; she was standing at the Gate of India; it was a very clear, starry night.

Part Three

Was she a chance spectator?

Speculation was in the air: Had she been the direct inspiration for his work? Had he been a tyrant? An uncompromising lover? Was there going to be another episode in their dark drama or was this really the end? If this was the end, would they still be giving the party on Saturday? Questions lead to more questions. All of them are hearsay. I heard there was quite a commotion when she and Jacques finally parted. All of Paris had waited for them to fall into bed. Then they had kept watch over the whole affair, anticipating, rumoring. She was twenty-five when she threw in with him and thirty-five when they parted. Naturally, all of Paris delighted in the turn of affairs. As word traveled from lip to ear, people whispered the actual event into insinuation and innuendo: "Listen, she was no innocent bystander. They say he wasn't all there, you know, a little touched in the head." Speculation led to questions which turned into hearsay which made history. It went on and on. People people people given up to talk talk talk. By the time we met it was all over. Voices from the past made no impression; I heard nothing, I saw she was not the silly, absurdly affected actress that everyone made out. We had just finished lunch. We were stretching out the afternoon into the evening. She was reclining among the cushions in a physical stupor characteristic of her. Fifi Corday. Fifi Corday. What could possibly be characteristic of her?

Part Four

Fifi kissed her tearful mother, each of her seven brothers and three sisters, her frowning father, jumped into the train, stuck her head out the window, and waved furiously with both hands until they were completely out of view. She adored them, she didn't care if she ever saw them again. She was nineteen. She was going to Paris to study with Marcel Marceau. Everyone said she was gifted, a natural. Fifi knew she was great, she was confident and she had plans. She studied the map of Paris, drowning in the romantic-sounding street names, in her picture thoughts, in the loud rhythm of the train wheels that pounded out her name until it sounded idiotic. Rita, Reeeeeeeta, Reeeteeeteeeeta. That was her stage name. It was part of the plan. So were the bright blue nail polish and the dark green lipstick. She'd been waiting weeks to add this final finishing touch. In the privacy of her *couchette* she admired the effect. It was good. It would become a trademark. She twirled, waved her hands around, practiced pouting, watched herself on the window glass. Within a year, she'd learned and mastered everything M.M. had to teach her. Then she refused to perform the old-fashioned mime routines. Men had all the good parts. Then she wouldn't accept a job in a troupe. They quarreled. She left. He told her never to call him M.M. All winter Fifi worked on new routines and hustled jobs

in cafés and bistros. The owners could hardly refuse her. Her flashing black eyes. Her frantic energy. They allowed her to spot between the main acts. Even gave her permission to pass around a big, floppy velvet hat. It was part of her act. At the close she played an old 78 record of Billie Holiday singing *Pennies From Heaven*. She knew just how to do it. No hamming it up. Straight lipsynching. As soon as the audience was clapping hard, she ran around the stage showering them with tin pennies mixed with confetti and sequins. They clapped harder. They loved her. By the end of summer Rita concentrated her material on a repertoire of American images. She played hipster, cowboy, tourist, starlet, housewife, gangster. Ran through little vignettes. Sometimes just a single pose. Interspersing the character types with famous people. Charlie Chaplin, Marilyn Monroe, others. She was after their little French hearts and she knew just how to do it. Everyone was infatuated with Rita, with America. The owner of Le Café on the Rue de la Gaieté offered her a permanent spot with good pay. Wednesdays and weekends only. She hesitated. He threw in a room upstairs. Fourth floor, rear. She accepted. The crowd that had chased her all over town followed her to Le Café. It made things harder. Rita had to work up new acts continuously. It helped when she and Monsieur Le Prince, the owner, decided to cut back to weekly appearances. Rita started breaking rules. She'd speak a line or shout a word. No self-respecting mime would do that! She changed clothes on stage. She kind of peeled from one part of the act to the next. It was cute. It was still hard to keep up with the slavering public. They always wanted more. She wouldn't strip. She was an artist. She and Monsieur Le Prince had another business meeting. Two shows a month and maybe it would still be okay. It had been four years for them with lots of success and enough money. Rita was a little tired. She thought the man standing in the door must have made a mistake. He looked out of place. She looked away from him. He came over to the table. "Excuse me but I'm looking for my brother, Monsieur Le Prince." "He just went out for a moment. Sit down." Jacques told her he'd never seen her perform, though of course his brother and many, many others had spoken endlessly about her great artistry. They began to talk. Rita invited him to that week's show. He came. She invited him upstairs afterwards. He went but only stayed a few minutes. He hated it up there. Her underwear all over the place. The single gas burner, the drafts, the dumb prints on the wall. He told her they should meet again somewhere else. When? Saturday. Where? 49 Boulevard Raspail. When? 9:00. She thought he was strange. She'd no idea why. Maybe it was that briefcase he always dragged around. His odd manners. He must be at least thirty-five. Rita was too busy to think about him.

He was forty.
Jacques. A brief history.

First of all, he had an amazing memory. To assist this faculty he had notes. Hundreds and thousands of references and quotes on scraps of paper, clippings, copies of letters, letters sorted and stored in envelopes. Filed by subject and name always at hand, added to, used, replaced, brought out again. Fifteen years worth of exact information. Memory guided him to his envelopes. Also to his books, in which he scribbled. To his journals in which he noted occasional thoughts as they occurred. It was an elaborate system centered on centuries of poetry, journalism, private papers, fiction, drama, philosophy, history. He was writing on every manner of human delight fear hope disbelief fantasy. It was going to be one of those complete encyclopedic chronicles of the Western world.

On Saturdays, Jacques had receptions. He trusted word of mouth, his friends, their friends. All of Paris showed up. His open-door policy reflected one side of his character. Jacques also had a conservative streak. No one cared. His guests thought him quaint, a little eccentric perhaps, peculiar at worst. Everyone had heard him give his little speech, his welcome to newcomers: "I confess I've remained very much a classic in the matter of salons. A salon in which one cannot follow or rejoin the woman one prefers, draw her away from the group, speak to her for a moment in a lowered voice in the shadow, address part of the general conversation to her, and find oneself shining and receive a glance of recognition . . . such a place is not a salon for me. Oh, may the French salon never lose sight of these attentions. The lively wish to please, the animated, unfailing, charming graces of France!"

Rita took him aside. "Look, Jacques," she said, "you can't go through life living in the past. It's not the nineteenth century. I mean, it's one thing to write about or think or even care about the past. But you can't live in it. You don't want to end up out of touch, talking to yourself alone." Years of worldly experience fell away. How could he possibly refuse? Her flashing black eyes. Her blue fingertips. Her green lips.

She was twenty-five.

Another brief episode. Rita and Jacques. Rita and Jacques. Rita and Jacques. Rita and Jacques.

By the time we met it was all history. History? This is no subject for mockery! I want to tell you my opinions experiences ideas about history. About art. About everything. But she was only half-listening, reclining among the cushions. "I'm not interested in purely aesthetic people," Fifi sighed. We had just finished lunch; the afternoon was fading into evening; I was still full of impressions from the East. I was riding in a train. I was standing on a mesa in the Nevada desert. I wanted her to follow my momentum. "All my worldly experience fell away," I was explaining.

Russian Constructivism

KATHY ACKER

1. Abstraction

Petersburg, my city.

Petersburg steeples triangles bums on the streets decrepit churches broken-down churches churches gone churches used as homes for bums for children forced from the abandoned buildings they run.

Son.

1.

City of people who weren't born here who decided to live here who're homeless, trying to make their own lives: poor refugees artists rich people. People who don't care and care too much. Homeless. You, baby crib, only you've been financially shuffled off by the USSR government.

You, city, along one of whose streets a hundred bums're sitting standing and lying. Three-quarters of these bums're black or Puerto Rican. The concrete stinks of piss much more than the surrounding streets smell. A few of the creeps smoke cigarettes. One-half of the buildings lining the street're a red brick wall. Mostly the bums don't move or they move as little as they have to.

How is this City of Cities divided?

This new holy city is a reality not only without religion but also without anything to want or seek for: without anything. The city whose first characteristic is it gives nothing, breakdown, and so its inhabitants individuals, no its communities, have to make everything for themselves.

As taught in school, Petersburg has five parts: its main part is the Nevsky Prospect.

St. Petersburg is actually the Nevsky Prospect.

The Nevsky Prospect's an island joined by bridges once on its northern tip, twice on its southern, and once at its eastern edge to the rest of Petersburg. Though Petersburg is the capital of the USSR, most Russians who don't live in Petersburg hate and fear the Petersburgians: they think they're murderers, dope addicts, and perverted by fame.

Lamplights hang over the edges of the park running through the vertical center of the Nevsky Prospect, from its beginning at St.

Isaac's, about fifty blocks north, to its black section in the depth of the seventeenth line. The geographical divisions are actually racial: ghettoes, each one on the whole about nine to sixteen blocks large, don't mingle. This past year the ghettoes're beginning to physically cross 'cause the rich're now trying and will take over this whole city by buying all of its real estate.

The islands especially Vasilyevsky Island are the drug oases. The hooker centers're the Millionaya, again Vasilyevsky Island (pimps always get their puppets hooked), the large black bridge across the Neva, and the Winter Canal. The languages are less than 50 percent Russian, then (heard less often in this order) Spanish, French, and German. Petersburg isn't Russian: it's a country on its own. Since it has no legal or financial national status, it's an impossibility, an impossible home; it's tenuous, paranoid. Its definitions and language're quantum theory, Zen, and the nihilism found before the Russian Revolution.

Squares quadrilaterals concatenations of imaginations who lack other necessary sensualities. The flesh which touches flesh has to resemble Martian green gook. City of simultaneous inner and outer space where each day a new human disease appears, whose inhabitants, like rats, through sickness remain alive and work. Who can tell me I'm too sick to be alive? My sickness is life. You, my city, romanticism of no possible belief:

In Peter one morning, the female weightlifter fell out of her loft-bed. It was a beautiful day, late in September. Larks were singing and drops of sunlight were filtering through the navy blue Levelors (through the clouds through the pollution through the surrounding buildings' walls) which she hadn't opened since she bought them 'cause she didn't want to see junkies shooting up.

A newspaper below her fallen body:

CITY OF PASSION

a non-achiever
non-leader, non-
and non-romantic,'
former classmate
lentine.
he was 18, George
stined to end up a
then a horrifying

George was totally wrapp
up in the fantasy world
comic books.
'He was also cons
with TV – especiall
ture shows,' said
By high scho
had withdrawn

Meanwhile, in the alleyways,
Dear Peter,

I can't stand living without you. I hate this day-after-day constant waiting-for-you: you're not here: all my hours spent in longing for what's not here. I won't stand for living like this. Then I realize I'm falling in love with you. There's no one to turn to: again and again I realize I have only myself.

Sixteen hours until I see you again. 1 2 3 4 5 6 7 8 9 10 11 12 13 14 15 16. I can count 16, but you'll probably not want to see me. If I see you, I'll want you. If I don't see you, I'll die. I'm going nuts. I don't care about this writing. I just want time. I can get rid of this night by closing up my eyes with work, brain calculations, dumbie-making TV: you have leapt into my arms, madness: I'll wait for you forever if you'll only come to me, for there's no time until I see you. Love makes time and life. I must be blind: you're poor. Your life is shambles. The more you want something, the more you deny it to yourself. You: my nightmare; I don't care. You've conquered me. You, kookoo totally untogether, make me as irritable and changeable as you are, so I've made myself into your Rock of Gibraltar in order to capture you but I don't want you, I don't want you to break up your marriage, I don't want you to do anything that'll hurt you: I have to lose. But if you don't see me tomorrow, I don't have to lose because you don't love me. So: real love is strange and any simplicity between us has to be a lie.

I don't know what I'm doing. You're the only life I've known in a very long time. How can I let go of life again? You're my day and night. Forget it, little baby, he's told you clearly he doesn't want to have sex with you and he only wants you so he can revenge himself on his wife 'cause she once left him for a richer man. You are my madness. Come in me, my madness, and since you've already taken me, I beg you with everything that is me to take me. I'm sold, but not yet enjoyed. The day I'm going to see you I'm happy and the day I'm not going to see you I'm miserable.
(My nurse enters and binds me up.)
Nurse: Shut up, brat.
Myself, to Myself: I don't talk 'cause I can't talk about you. I guess I am obsessed possessed. Spain needed a revolution, a far more profound revolution in fact than that being attempted by the Republic. I'm bound by cords 'cause you aren't fucking me. (Aloud, ((Allowed))) Cords're binding me 'cause you aren't fucking me. You're going away from me.
Juliet: You're going away from me. It's still dark and black and

hideous: you don't have to leave me yet.
You: It is daytime; there are candles. The beginnings of clouds can be seen. Since this world for her light no longer needs the stars, like the jealous bitch she is, she's shut them off. Day like total revolution's waiting to infiltrate. I have to get away from you to keep my life going.
Juliet: The light that's coming within you for me's as violent as mine for you. As you say we've nothing to do with nature: the fire between us competes with the sun. I'll keep your unnatural solitary fire going! I'll follow you in disguise. You don't need to ever leave me. Don't go.
You: Okay. I'll stay with you and I'll die. I give way to your love: These beginning light lines in the sky are the streaks of blood on your colorless unspeakable thighs. The unseeable approaching daylight isn't a day but just moon to your energy and grace. Since without you I die and with you I die, I chose to die with you, my life, and besides, I've no choice. It's dark and black and hideous still.
Juliet, resigning herself: Go. Get out. This world stinks. We can't pretend this world doesn't exist. The Fascists have taken over. All that's natural and beautiful're dividing us. Since natural is now unnatural and unnatural is natural, those who love can't know. How should I know what to do? It is the day: get away from me!

Dear Peter,

Please understand me. Please believe what's in my mind at this very moment. I do everything you want. Now you want to be away from me 'cause you're fucking your wife. You're the only one I love and this moment's infinite. I'd do anything to phone you right now. 'Cause I can't phone you, I hate you. 'Cause I hate you, I'm never going to phone you ever again, 'cause I hate you. I'll say your name so the whole world'll know, 'cause what you fear most, your only morality, is what you think other people (whether or not they know you)'re thinking of you. King Sunny Adé. King Sunny Adé, I hate your guts. You were my sun and your house was my house was my home and you threw me out like a kid without a home, (you) saying, "All you want is security so you don't love me at all," and then you didn't even understand that I love you. That's why this moment's infinite.

Why do I like you 'cause I know you're so self-righteous you'd holocaust the universe faster than Margaret Thatcher; you don't understand what art is 'cause you're so scared of your wildness with

which, you artist, you're frothing, you're trying to eradicate every weakness mainly those in other people 'cause that's what you see so you demand certain behaviors and accept nothing else; when people act differently, 'cause you've buried your wildnesses more anger volcanoes out of you than I've ever felt from another human being? I like you 'cause your eyes look at me a certain way and 'cause your nose twitches; your mental capacities're at least as sharp and rapid as mine; when you're not being (ridiculously) ruled, you're as decadent as I am. Why do you give a damn about social rules? Why not become an artist? I'm going to fuck lots of men now if they'll fuck me 'cause I need that physical reassurance and I'm sure while I'm doing this, there'll still be thoughts of our fucking:

Between you and me was a madness which's rare. Not just sexuality. Who're you kidding? That this anger and fear (appearing 'cause I touched your madness too closely or 'cause you care about society) are more powerful than your sexuality? Only a man who adores fucking comes near me. What's love? Love's the unity of friendship and desire. I messed up with you. I didn't care enough about friendship. I fought too hard against your desire to be socialized which, if I love you, should be as important to me as my ways. Can you be patient? – I'm willing to fight myself to be with you.

You don't think our friendship's important. Maybe you're so young, you believe there're an infinite number of mad relations.

I agree with you: I was too frightened you didn't love me and not terrified enough of imposing on your love. Please remember, you also feared I didn't love you and you begged me for reassurance.

I hope your wife'll make you happy forever. I'm saying this 'cause I want to be friends. I want my desire for friendship to waken your love for me –

Walking the streets.

Tatlin designed a city. Tatlin took unhandlable passion and molded it.

It all comes out of passion. Our city of passion.

Biely wanted to fuck his closest comrade, Alexander Blok,'s wife until the duel between them in 1906 (which never happened), then Biely left Russia for a year. When Biely described this passion, he constructed language as if it was a building. If architecture wasn't cool cold, people couldn't live in it. I have to figure out why I'm hurting so much. Recognition: I'm really hurting. One of this hurt's preconditions is I'm in love with you.

A city in which we can live.

What're the materials of this city?

Is sensuality less valuable than rational thought? Is there a split between mind and body, or rather between these two types of mentality? Why's a cubist painting, if it is, better art than a Vivienne Westwood dress? Is our city abstract?

When you talk to me on the phone I'm hurt and maddened by your lack of sexual and emotional communication. Art criticism, unlike art,'s abstract.

I'll mold my love for you: I can't say over the telephone what I want to say to you: "Please touch your cock because I can't touch your cock now and I have to touch your cock." What's mainly not allowed? Time's the main non-allower. I can't touch your cock right now because one event can't be another event. (Time is substance.) Three thousand miles now between the events of you and me, or three hours. Absence to a child is death. This is death. Time's killing me. Time's proving you don't love me. I have to mold my passion for you out of time:

2. The Poems of a City

ON TIME

desinas ineptire et quod vides
perisse perditum ducas.

fulsere quondam candidi tibi soles,
cum it hurts mė to remember I did
act up today, a way of saying
"I'm not perfect," forgive my
phone call, ventiabas quo puella
ducebat (on a leash: leather
Rome)
amata nobis quantum amabitur
nulla.

ibi illa multa kisses on kisses
between us
your hands your flesh unending
time into time
the past wasn't past—how do I
transform the past: that awful
prison 'cause it ends?

The subjunctive mood takes precedence over the straightforward active. The past controls the present. The past.

The first future tense. What do words really say: does this future propose future time?

fulsere vere candidi tibi soles.

By repeating the past, I'm molding and transforming it, an impossible act.

New section:

nunc iam illa non vult: tu quoque,
impotens can't fuck any boyfriends
these days, bad mood no wonder
I'm acting badly, noli NO
nec quae fugit sectare, nec miser
vive
good advice sed obstinata mente
perfer, obdura.
vale, puella. (My awful telephone
call. This's my apology, Peter.
Do you accept?) iam *(ha ha)*
Catullus obdurat,
nec te requiret nec rogabit invitam:
I'm a good girl
I have, behave perfectly.
at tu dolebis. The imaginary makes
reality, as in love, cum rogaberis
nulla
scelesta. Scelesta nocte. My night.
quae tibi manet vita without me?
quis nunc adibit? without me cui
videberis bella?
quem nunc amabis? with me you
fuck whoever you want.
Let the imagination reign supreme.
quem you now fucking? cuius esse
diceris huh!
quem basiabis a stupid question? cui
labella labula mordebis? (allied to
death?)
at tu, Catullus, destinatus obdura
to facts, for only the imagination
lives.

My present is negative. This present becomes imaginary: The future of amabitur and the subjunctive at the beginning of the poem?:

The imagination is will.

WILL VERSUS CHANCE

no more sighing blackness nihilism
and senile old fogies' blathers
as snot falls out of their nostrils
all more worthless than the two bums I saw talking today.
suns rise and set I never see them –
for you my love and me a few brief hours of sun
then no consciousness blackness perpetually.
take it kiss me do it grab me
grab my arms grab my ankles grab my cunt hairs
the only nights of light the only eyes we have.
conscious.
so much so much so many phenomena we can no longer think
understand, realizing we're not responsible,
so no bourgeois or moralist can touch us
or know anything real about us.

TIME IS IDENTITY

No one he states my boyfriend'ld rather fuck
than a duck, than me. Even if Psyche her-
self begged him. He said to me. But what a man tells any
woman who loves him is lost in these winds and squalling
waters. My lover is changing water.

LONELINESS

Lines one through four. Emotional thesis: on always being away from you. I'm not scared of dying. I fear dying (absolute absence)'ll take away your love for me.

Lines five and six. The supplementary thesis: death or absence destroys love.

Lines seven through ten. The antithesis: love can and does fight this absence.

Lines eleven and twelve. The synthesis: my love for you is making me your mirror your object, fuses, whether I'm with or away from you. So this love's overcoming and becoming, through identity, one with death.

Lines thirteen through eighteen. The next thesis is based on the above synthesis: when I'm dead and absolutely apart from you, I'll still love you. No matter how long you stay alive, we'll eventually be together forever.

Lines nineteen and twenty. The supplementary thesis: our love is absence.

Lines twenty-one through twenty-four (the first section which isn't just one whole sentence; the three short sentences of this section syntactically reflect their verbal content). The antithesis: this life or these constant changes may destroy our love. Like death, love is infinite.

Lines twenty-five and twenty-six. The synthesis: while we're alive right now we have to love each other as much as possible 'cause love has nothing to do with time. (I can never say anything this direct to you 'cause I love you too much.)

The overall sentence syntactical structure is and concerns the relations between several kinds of time. What is the verb structure? Verbs're Latin's grammatical backbone.

The first kind of time, lines one through four, is linear time. The first main verb is *is,* an *is* which isn't Platonic. This common *is* leads to the first person subjunctives, *fear* and *hinder,* as well as the *is* subject noun, *fear.* This kind of time or the world makes human fear.

Common time's other or enemy is death. *Is* is bounded by death. So the other of *is* is *be without* in the present tense.

Since the past is like the present in this time model, lines five and six, death or absence also destroys memory. Here's another reason I'm afraid.

Since the only certainty I can have in common human time is that which has to be most feared – the end of time – all I can feel is more and more pain.

The second temporal model begins with human will, when I will to enter the realm of death. Line seven. This is exactly what I can't do, the antithesis, the necessarily imaginary.

Because we're apart, our sex because it has to continue, is false, imaginary. Line nine. Love makes me dare. I'm coming, masturbating, in the darkness. Line ten. Blind. Because I love you I want to die. My main verb is *orgasm* in the mythological past tense; in the realm of blackness the mythological's more powerful than the temporal present. (What is the time model of my will?)

If I've died to you am dead, who am I? Because I love you I've destroyed myself: I'm you. Lines eleven and twelve. Love destroys common time and reverses subject and object; the verb acts on itself; I'm your mirror; identity's gone because there's no separation between life and death. Line twelve. The final model of time is that the mirror reflects the mirror: time is our love.

But my whole body's aching and I'm crying uncontrollably every night because you're not here:

Now all tenses and moods, *may come had given,* like and equal to all other phenomena appear out of nothing or death, line eighteen, which is also the ideal, lines fifteen and sixteen. But my whole body's aching and I'm crying uncontrollably every night because you're not here:

Now all tenses and moods, may come had given, like and equal to all other phenomena appear out of nothing or death, line eighteen, which is also the ideal, lines fifteen and sixteen. But my whole body's aching and I'm crying uncontrollably every night because you're not here, lines nineteen and twenty. The subjunctive tenses grammatically reflect this new model of common time: change is time.

I'm fighting the phenomenal that has to happen. I'm scared. Line twenty-one. So all the verbs are now subjunctives; all verbs are change. Again: loving you is making me feel pain. The final verb, *is changed,* grammatically reflects its opposite in content: the mirror. Time: love or fusion exists side by side with change:

I want you. That's all I can think. This is our absolute present. Line twenty-six.

TIME IS PAIN

last night I couldn't sleep at all, then I woke up in a sweat
though I wasn't crying tears fall from my eyes. I'm
in pain I phone you I want to suicide you
over and over again my brain revolves you
focus obsession I see nothing else. You're my world
blindness' opening my heart. This "love"
between us (your name) to me is *blood.*
Everywhere you slept you touched you came
in this house is your blood.
I would do anything to fall asleep. At night. But as
each dream passes
each absolute reality shows itself temporary
I obsess you. At times I hurt
like hell. At times I'm dead. Every other night
there's been a morning when I can
stand up from this bed.

Now there's only night: each night
unnatural is the ornament of your blood.

TIME IS MADE BY HUMANS

I hope there's some relief writing
this you: otherwise, none. I've never felt such pain.
Day after day pain after pain how do
I count these days? It's pain to count.
Pain to have a mind.
Worst: at the moment when sleep's ease should come,
(no coming. no you.) and thoughts are loosened,
but I don't want these thoughts.
I phone: I don't like life.
So stopping the mind up, no
life no utterance, jail within jail within
jail, what can days dates
time matter? Only this ease
of verbally sobbing out ugliness.

3. Scenes of Hope and Despair

The girl's happy because she knows the man she loves's in love with her.

The girls sitting around: Peter didn't call me. You've got a date tomorrow with him, don't you? Should we eat? Did they fuck yet? Great fun, seducing girls. These men have the most fun. The most we can have is getting revenge. That is fun. Did they fuck yet? I don't know. Peter still hasn't called. I bet he forgets his accent. Uh-oh. Hurry back. Oh oh, she's drinking champagne. That means she's in love. I say, men just want you to suffer. They're so fucked up. They not only break up with you suddenly, they want this big dramatic thing. After you've broken up whenever a man starts talking about who's guilty, I tell him I couldn't care less I'd rather drink champagne. I think Peter's a little lame I mean he's always making dates and kind of forgetting the time but at the same time I could tell he really cared for me so his not calling me now doesn't mean he's off me. Edward's breaking up with me has made me think a man can't want me. All she does is cry. Englishmen fall in love too often so it doesn't mean anything to them. We always tell Englishmen, we only go with American men. This film is dumb.

JEAN LASSALE
23

Why do you want? I want love. You're not going to get love. Okay. You're going to get hurt again. I know. The main thing is to always giggle. All the last week when I really hurt, I felt like I had a disease. Being hurt is having a disease.

The girls cross their legs and laugh. "What should we do now?" "I need food," she, fainting, said. Her arms draped over the pillow. "We're caught in our own trap," she said laughing.

Right now the first girl is thinking about the man she wants to fuck. "We can," she says to her friend, "by fantasizing, increase our possibilities and joy in living, more important, understand how things work. Why's this? Examine these two events: 1. Last night I fucked with you. 2. I'm fantasizing fucking with you. But these events are now only my mentalities. Therefore there's no distinguishing between the two of them. But what if we hadn't fucked? Take another example: We don't love each other. Is it possible that by fantasizing we love each other, we can love each other? Possibly? Fantasy is or makes possibilities. Are possibilities reality?

The other girl lay in her red bed and crossed her legs. "There're always possibilities," she said. "I always prefer drama."

"I fantasize I desire and know what desire is. This's how fantasizing allows me to understand. Every possibility doesn't become actual fact. So knowing is separate from acting in the common world."

"I'm caught in my own trap 'cause every event for me can only be my mentality." The girls looked at each other.

"I know you know a good many of my New York friends and I've always wanted to talk with you about your work." "Come inside." "Are you reading Husserl?" "After college I was a political theorist. Then I worked for Austin." "Ooo. What's he like?"

What did we talk about?

"What's the relation between practice and theory in your filmmaking? I mean: does writing criticism stop you from making films?" "They're just two different kinds of activities." "But they're also two different ways of thinking." "When I make a film, probably partially because I always work with other people and also due to the film's economic situation, I know even before I start to make the film exactly what I'm going to do in the film." "Ugh: If I knew what I was going to write before I wrote a book, I'd be bored." "It's a different business. When you make a film, you have to consider who's going to see the film the popular culture." "Why do you care so much when you work how other people'll judge your work? I first consider my own pleasure. Do you think there's something fishy in the semiotics theories, especially in Deleuze's and Guattari's?" "There's a gap now. You have to realize that semiotics hit England before it hit America. We got Lacan and Althusser, rather than the later semioticians . . . Derrida . . . Foucault . . ." "Foucault isn't really a semiotician. He was always on the outside. Who, then, 're you reading now?" "I have a theory that we're at the end of a generation. Semiotics's no longer applicable. At the moment there's nothing." "I remember in New York when semiotics came only it was Sylvere who brought it over, what it really did was give me a language with which I could speak about my work. Before that I had no way of discussing what I did, of course I did it, and my friends who are doing similar work we had no way of talking to each other. A critical way of talking about my work allowed me to go one step further in my work. Now it seems, as in the pre-semiotics days, practice's prior to theory." "The age of theory is over . . ." ". . . absolutes . . ." ". . . so there's only what I do at any moment." "Pleasure. Even Baudrillard in his new book . . ." "He's a semiotician and dead." "Not anymore. . . . says our language is meaningless, for meaning – any signs – are the makings of the ruling class." "But he's still using meaningful signs to say this." "Oh, the black plague. Is it good?" "I've read all about plagues." Kiss. We don't stop kissing each other now. Your physical touch is incredibly gentle. But I can't physically feel anything 'cause I've been through a six-week relationship at the end of which the man kicked me out as fast as possible 'cause he decided he didn't know what he wanted. I must be shy of getting hurt. I think you're intelligent and lovely. Your face is keeping changing its shape. Maybe I'm hallucinating? It's not possible I can feel again after a winter and spring of no sexual love then for the second time in five years I moved in with somebody. That failed violently, forcibly.

4. The Mystery

"How, exactly, does my body feel pleasure?:

"I'm remembering fucking Eddie: I'm remembering situations of power. This's the way he likes to be fucked best: I'm on top of him. My arms reach straight to the pillow on either side of his black head. My legs slide from a sitting position straight down inside his legs so that my inner thighs nearest my cunt're rubbing his cock and so that I rising up and down am fucking his cock with my cunt. As I do this I think to myself that he likes this position more than I do. I don't come as easily in this position as when my legs're sitting on top of him because I have to be accurately acutely aware of his reaction to make sure his cock stays in my cunt and, I can't let myself fully go. I reach over Peter so my mouth is on his nipple. Or my wet tongue is flicking his nipple tip. This makes me excited more subtly than when I'm being touched: I don't come as much as violently, but I'm sort of coming all the time. I'm sort of coming all the time. Other times I stick my right hand's third finger into Eddie's asshole. It easily enters. He bucks and looks at me with surprise and openness unusual for him. Openness makes me open. My finger is reaching up and toward his cock. That opening. As his thighs're reaching up for me. Sometimes I coldly turn him over, spread the asscheeks, stick my tongue into his asshole. I don't mind doing this though I usually mind doing this on men. When I do this he groans very loudly so I know he's receiving tons of pleasure. Peter's asshole's too tight for my finger to wiggle up and I don't want to force anyone to do sexually what they don't seem to want to do. When I once mentioned, innocently?, that I had a whip back in New York and he said 'I'll have to try it,' I was surprised and thought maybe it's a go between us.

"Peter's sexually scared for instance he never comes with me 'cause he's trying not to be in love with me 'cause he loves his wife or 'cause maybe he doesn't want to come. Whenever Eddie comes, I instantaneously come he usually turns me over I've been fucking him. He's on top of me. Now I remember. My legs clasp his waist and touch each other because he likes this. I can't come in this position. Legs open up so feet rest on outer sides of ass. Rubbing bone above clit against cock-bone. Come. So as he about to come he almost stop moving. First my arms have to curl around his neck as tight as possible clasp each other. Soon as he about to come; now now, almost no movement. I'm not going to come even though I've come. Soon as he starts to come and there's almost no movement, I automatically come."

"How, exactly, does my body feel pleasure?" The girl's telling the other girl about her former lovers.

"No no. I can't talk about anything directly."

"There's a definite difference in my physical being or body between when I'm being fucked and I'm not being fucked. How can I say anything when I'm totally uncentralized or not being fucked."

"There's no sex anymore. I'm not going to have any sex. I'm not going to open up. This is me: the image. A man's suit. Look at me. I'm a woman who looks like a delicate boy and I'll never change. You can't touch me. I'm impervious. This's the way I'm happy. I'm totally elegant."

"You're out of your mind."

"Better than being laid, then sticking razor blades through my wrists."

"Living isn't so black."

"Living is a present. I'll never say otherwise. I wish I was together enough to say or do something."

"Touch me. An open quivering clit. The little red animal wiggles."

"Art, since its very beginning in prehistoric caves, has been, in our present ways of speaking, conservative."

"Art's more interesting than sex . . ."

"More rewarding. We ARE getting old," the fourteen-year-old says. "At least art doesn't end up with razor blades stuck in the wrists."

". . . only according to the art critics and they only lie about dead artists."

"I've lied down for enough artists 'cause I prefer men who hurt to men who want to own me."

"No one sexually owns another person. That's the province of art. Provenance. Roman art made dumb Roman politicians into gods. Christian art justified or rationalized the controller belief system. So what's my sexuality apart from all that's been shown me?" The other girls throw up their hands in disgust.

"Then who's responsible for the human violence in this world? Those who make. The artists."

"Who's this person I'm fucking?"

"If I'm just reflecting, I don't know. When I'm making love with you, my loving is seeing your face. The only thing I'm seeing my only identity is you."

5. Deep Female Sexuality: Marriage or Time

"When Eddie was kicking me out of his house, I put a razor blade into my right wrist in order to stop Eddie from saying 'You don't know how to love. No man will ever love you.' The people who saved me from death're my friends.

"Two men are fighting each other with cudgels. They're standing knee-deep in water. There's an overwhelming monster whose waist and hips are so soft, he looks like a woman. His right arm doesn't look like an arm. The man is puking against my building's corner wall. He doesn't flinch as I watch him. A man as he's facing out from this wall masturbates. He has a typical grin across his ugly face. I have to tell you how I get sexual pleasure. The women, rather than turning away from him, look at his exposed cock and laugh. Toward the point of death.

"Therefore I love you. Knowing that in the face of about to touch absolute darkness, there is the one rescuing that happens between two people and in the face of full knowledge. Of not only pain and incomprehendable evil and death: The real knowledge is that I want this I want to die. Horror! Knowing this – what're our jealousies our endless sexual maneuverings our social deviousnesses compared to this: we know what love is?

"What's the function of darkness? Of being ignorant?

"You said, 'Light light. Those who survive must learn mathematics.' For me there's just love, I'm scared of love. I run away from any immediacy.

"One of my legs is extending outwards. You're owning me. A sky of hot nude pearl until . . . crickets in these sheltered places . . . the wind ransacks the great planes. You are taking over control so I can relax. I'm alone on an island. I'm all by myself. Here, I'm waiting for what is to follow my collapsed dreams. I'll be more precise: I'm waiting for you 'cause I can't know anything and everything's whirling. His hand put itself on top of the clitoris and pressed. It didn't move. Her own hand was resting on her clitoris. His hand pressed down, through her hand, on the clitoris.

"I'm alone again . . . on this island. I've my books around me. I don't know why I feel lonely. This is my life, if you put it that way. You know what I mean. My life has been hard. I'm not easy and I've been, probably irreparably, scarred. People say that someone who lives like me, in this much nothing, is sick. I'm at ease.

"You're owning me. You've touched me and I'm scared because I've decided to love you so now I'm trying to break this ownership: I phone you you're a malicious beast: I know in the past years and now you fuck lots of women and tell them you love them madly. You can't love everybody madly (I do). You're doing the same thing with me. I can't mean anything to you. I'm not special. You're shitting on my face. I hate you. I don't want to need you because I already, probably most, probably one-twentieth of me, is needing you. So after I yell at you for being as sexually romantic as I am, the next day I tell you 'I love you' when you don't want emotion. I want to die and not have responsibility.

"'I'm only interested in my abstract thought.' But what do you and I do, not so much with our bodies, but with our needs? I remember waking up. First, I see your head. I see your eyes're open and you're looking at me. I have to smile because your obvious love for me makes me smile. My thumb and second finger of my left hand hold between them your nipple, my bones. Your right hand's fingers're on my left nipple and my right hand's fingers're on your left nipple. My right hand's fingers're pulling back the extra skin of your cock tip and your lips're contorted from the scream that's coming out of your mouth, as your head turns right as I lift my body so that your cock finally hard is entering my cunt and you have to scream I remember waking."

The women are shaving their heads.

For the Future

LYNNE TILLMAN

Mark said he had nothing to hide because he wasn't afraid of being called unnatural. Grace and he were sitting at the bar and were talking about the play Mark wanted to base on Wilde's "The Birthday of the Infanta." He'd changed his mind; no hospital setting, no nurse. He especially wanted to end with the fairy tale's last line, "For the future let those who come to play with me have no heart." "You've got to have something to hide," Grace said, finishing her beer and lighting a cigarette. They agreed that Wilde was as cruel if not crueler than Poe because of how the fairy tale begins with the preparations for the Infanta's birthday, and how her birth killed her mother, the beautiful queen, whom the king is still mourning twelve years later. He keeps her embalmed body on display so that he can visit her once a month. "He visits her once a month like his period," Grace laughed.

The cast of characters would include the King, the little Dwarf, who doesn't know how ugly he is, and who is brought to entertain the Infanta, the Infanta, who is the image of her mother, and as cruel as she is beautiful, the flowers who speak, and the Infanta's entourage. They can be whoever's in the bar that night, Mark figured, wanting to give the play a kind of lived-in feeling. "Truth, beauty, beauty, truth," he declaimed in the nearly empty bar. It was late afternoon, or happy hour. Mark felt there was something really rotten at the bottom of it, and Grace agreed, feeling pretty rotten herself.

You only attack the things that give you trouble, he went on. "Trouble," the woman three barstools from them yelled. "What do you know about trouble? Trouble is my middle name." Mark peered down the bar, past this woman, to a new face, one covered by a four-day beard that gave it, this nearly ugly face, a handsome aspect, or, at least, character. Men can get away with anything, Grace said, watching Mark continuing to look, and then at last walking over to him and pulling up a barstool. Up close his face was both rugged and motherly, or so it seemed to Mark, who forced himself to speak and was answered indifferently by the

CHANEL
CHANEL

stranger who didn't look up, as if he couldn't be bothered. "I'm not interested," he said, "I'm into pussy." Mark excused himself, nearly falling off his seat, returning fast to Grace, wondering how he could use that in the play.

Grace told Mark her latest cat dream in which a mother cat has five kittens, very fast, in a big, messy house. The toilet has been pulled out of the bathroom and there's nowhere to piss. A child is sleeping or dead under piles of wet clothes. There's water everywhere and from nowhere to piss they go to *Nowhere to Run,* which was arguably the second-best Martha and the Vandellas song, after *Heat Wave.* Nowhere to run nowhere to hide and back to hiding and Mark's definition of himself and Grace as demonstration models that would never get bought. Grace said she didn't want to get bought, but wouldn't mind being rented. Mark said he wanted to get married someday and so did she, because deep down there had to be that urge, waiting there like her maternal self, repressed, but ready at any moment to wear white. "Babies," Grace snapped. "You'd be a much better mother than I would." The way Mark saw it, the King would approach the coffin and cry out, as he did in Wilde's story, *Mi reina, mi reina,* then drop to his knees weeping, after covering her embalmed face with kisses, Grace added. That would be the beginning of the play, especially since the King nearly ruined his kingdom on account of his love for her, when she was alive, and perhaps even drove him crazy, his obsession was so great. She died of his excessive demands on her, or so Mark figured, but Grace stressed that the birth of the Infanta killed her, and that's why the King couldn't stand the sight of his beautiful daughter. "Passion brings a terrible blindness upon its servants," Mark quoted, and of course there's the little Dwarf who has never seen himself at all. And who will die of a broken heart when he does, realizing that the Infanta was only laughing at him.

Mark would've liked to have taken his love and locked him in a room, kept him there, thrown away the key. He would put a line into the King's mouth: "I have set myself in agony upon your strangeness." "Was the Queen strange?" Grace asked. "I don't know," Mark answered, "but it's a play on your highness." "Oh," Grace said, "very funny." Possession is nine-tenths of the law, but would the law cover Mark's keeping his love locked away in a room in Providence. "The law doesn't cover what you want it to cover," he said sullenly.

Grace would be the Infanta and Mark the little Dwarf, although he toyed with playing both the King and the Dwarf. What constituted the most hideous costume and overall design for the Dwarf was under discussion. Something has to be missing. Something has to be hanging from his chin. One of his eyes must be out of the socket or blinded. He would have to have tiny hairy hands without fingernails. Dirty matted hair. Sores, running ones. An enormous nose. Or a face with no nose at all. A head much too large for its pathetic body. No proportion. Mark would play the Dwarf on his knees, like Jose Ferrer as Toulouse-Lautrec.

The woman who said trouble was her middle name was raging down at the end of the bar. "You have a beautiful face, a man loves you. You have a face like a monkey, you only get screwed. Screwed. It's better to be old. You don't care about that. None of that. Can't be fooled anymore." Mark studied Grace's face. "You're pretty, but your nose is a little too big. You're not perfect, there's something just a little bit off about you." He kept studying and Grace said only Christ was perfect, and she didn't mind. She also didn't mind being called pretty, if she could use it to her advantage, although the advantages were weird. Take the Infanta. Her beauty is almost a trick. And connected to evil. "And your lower lip should be fuller," Mark continued, "the better to beguile." "And you've got too much lip," Grace said, "it makes you lopsided. That's what makes you perfect to play the Dwarf. But imagine if you were really ugly, with a face only a mother could love."

The Infanta never really had a mother, unless you count a woman dying for six months as your mother. Grace thought of Ellen in the mental hospital, and how she didn't really have a mother, either. It was when Ellen called Grace mother that Grace decided to quit that job because, as she told Mark, I'd only end up hurting her. They said goodbye when Ellen was lucid, but Ellen couldn't understand that it was goodbye forever. She touched Grace's hair and for the first time in Grace's life she was moved to sadness for someone else. It made her feel impotent, then angry, that big empty feeling. No one loved her, Ellen, or the Infanta. And it's your right to be mean or crazy. "The King didn't even stay with the Infanta on her birthday," Grace complained. "He was busy taking care of the state," Mark teased. Even though he'd said she wouldn't have to memorize anything, the Infanta's role was growing and Grace was beginning to think that Mark should play it. "I'll never learn it all." "Ah, you're a natural," he said. And she said, "When I hear that word, I want to dye my hair black."

Late at night Grace couldn't memorize her lines and stared into space and then out the space through the window. The empty streets had a ghostliness that was part of night, and there wasn't anything necessarily worse about the night than the day, except for the darkness, which was only natural. The day dyes its hair, too, she thought, that's why it's weird and why I like it, even if it's scary. Under cover of night. The dark. The guy at the bar talking about those murders in Providence. A man stalking women, one after another. Mark and she had been arguing about the end of the Dwarf, his death, and whether or not he had to die, or if it could end differently. Grace said he had to die, and Mark thought maybe he could be put on a respirator and the Infanta forced to confront the consequences of her actions before he died. But then you couldn't use the last line, Grace argued, and that's when the guy at the bar yelled at them about just talking about death like that when real people were being killed, not storybook dwarfs, and who cares anyway, and Mark talked about wanting to give people hope and the guy said he was hopeless, just another artist. "Real murders take place in the real world," he yelled. "What's real?" Mark yelled back. Later in her room Grace wasn't convinced about anything. He said real murder in a menacing way. Real murder committed by real people out there. Out there. "Or even in here," the guy added. Mark was sure he was a cop, undercover, bent on scaring the demimonde. There's *épater la bourgeoisie* and there's *épater la* scum. Dying of a broken heart is different from being murdered, and she doubted that anyone really died because of love. It seemed so stupid.

After the Dwarf and the Infanta, the flowers had the biggest parts. Carmen, a transsexual, wanted to be either a violet or a tulip, but because of expediency, she would play all the flowers, in one. She can make her own costume, Mark said, anything she wants. "The flowers are vicious little snobs," Carmen said, preparing to recite her lines: "He really is too ugly to be allowed to play anywhere we are." "He should drink poppy juice and go to sleep for a thousand years." "He is a perfect horror, and if he comes near me, I will sting him with my thorns." In Wilde's story the violets don't actually speak but reflect that the Dwarf's ugliness is ostentatious and he would have shown much better taste if he had just looked sad. Carmen said Wilde was right, ugliness does look like misery, and Grace said he wasn't saying that. And Mark said he was saying that the reason the Dwarf was despised was because his imperfections made him stand out, and given his lowly origins, he's supposed to be invisible.

It adds up, it doesn't add up. The flowers are snobs, and they're part of nature, but then so is the Dwarf, whom they disdain. Ugliness is kind, beauty is cruel, yet the Dwarf also succumbs to the beauty of the Infanta, because beauty is always beyond reproach, innocent. "Can beauty be innocent and cruel at the same time?" Grace wondered aloud to Mark. "Maybe," Mark said, "beauty is as ambiguous as evil and ugliness and innocence." Grace told Mark that she had the feeling that getting old means that you're taken over and forced to forget your innocence. Mark couldn't believe that Grace thought of herself as innocent. She said she wasn't talking about sex, and what had that got to do with innocence anyway. To Grace, innocence meant the time before time counted, when days were long, when summer stretched ahead of you as a real long time and you could do nothing and that was all right. The time she went to summer camp and it seemed like forever. Innocence meant not seeing how ugly things were. Innocence meant that you think of yourself as doing the right thing, even if it looked wrong. Innocence meant you were never going to die and no one you loved would either. Innocence meant you'd never grow old because you could not really be touched. Maybe she meant damaged, she couldn't get damaged. You could still leave, turn away. "Turn to me," the guy at the bar said. It was the guy who told Mark he was into pussy. He was back, holding racing gloves in one hand, a drink in another. He had all his fingers and he looked dangerous, like the evil hero in a grade B movie. Grace smiled to herself. More like a character actor than a star, and he thought she was smiling at him. Mark had said if she was so into her innocence, maybe she should play the Dwarf. She kept on smiling and talking drunkenly to the stranger. Mark watched them leave. Carmen said that real girls had it much too easy. He took her to a seedy hotel next to the Greyhound bus station, and it was all perfect as far as Grace was concerned, except that there was something about him that she couldn't put into words. He stayed here from time to time, he said, when he was in town. His leather jacket was worn, his black pants tight, his hands were large and rough, and he had books on the floor, the kind she wouldn't have expected. Like Nietzsche.

The room was small, with a single electric light bulb hanging from the ceiling, a draft shaking it every once and a while. He had some Jack in the Black in his bag, and they kept on drinking. He didn't seem to notice the place, and Grace supposed he'd seen worse. Maybe everything. When they made love his large hands moved her body around, positioning it finally on a diagonal across the bed. Her body fit into the old mattress as if into a mold. He hardly kissed her and kept repositioning her body into that same spot. Any excitement she had had fled and she went through the motions with him. Neon lights flashed on and off. The glare from crummy signs made it hard to sleep, and Grace woke, dressed fast, and left his room. He called himself Hunter, his last name, he said. She didn't wake him.

Grace repeated the story to Lisa, the singer who worked with the band every other week. "Sounds like a pervert," Lisa said. "A pervert," Mark exclaimed. "Did you ever see *The Naked Kiss?* 'He gave me the naked kiss, the kiss of a pervert.'" "Women are much sweeter," Lisa continued. "Then," Mark went on, "there's that line when he asks her to marry him and he says, 'Our life will be paradise because we are both abnormal.'" Grace ignored Mark as best she could to concentrate on Lisa and the idea of sex with women, at least trying it, and not being able to shake the feeling that being with Hunter was like being with a ghost. She didn't think he came either, not that it really mattered.

Time, actually the sundial, is taken aback by the Dwarf. But the birds like him because he used to feed them in the forest. The flowers think the birds are awful because well-bred people always stay in the same place, like themselves, they say. And the lizards are tolerant of him. Mark called them humanists. Mark wanted to make the scene in which the Dwarf remembers the forest as paradisiacal as possible, given the restrictions of the bar, of course. The forest is his Eden, before his fall, his look into the mirror. That's everyone's fall, Grace thought. Grace and Mark couldn't remember the first time they'd looked into mirrors, and wondered what they'd thought. Little kids see themselves for the first time and somehow figure out that that creature is themselves. The Dwarf's long walk through the palace seeking the Infanta leads him to find himself in the mirror. He finally realizes it's himself because he's carrying the rose she gave him after he had performed for her. But the Dwarf is too horrified by his image, just like the flowers. Was his image of himself perfect? Then he sees it's not true. Grace said she was reminded of when her mother thought she was old enough to be left alone at night and told her that now she was her own babysitter. "What's that got to do with this?" Mark asked. Grace said she didn't know, it just came to mind.

They were at a party and Grace was thinking about ugliness, beauty, and anarchy, then found herself talking to, or listening to, an ugly guy who was telling her his life story. "I started going to therapy after I shot my best friend. We were living in California, and he was driving me crazy. It was going on for two years, so finally I shot him." The funny thing was that the guy, his best friend, didn't press charges, because they were best friends, and he didn't go to jail or even court. That anyway was what Grace found most weird. The ugly guy said he had moved first to New York, then here, and didn't think his friend would ever find him again. "Sometimes I miss him."

He wasn't a monster, and she didn't feel revolted, but Grace walked away, the way you can do at parties, right after some admission has been made that's intimate. Leave someone in mid-sentence. Or your eyes and their eyes are always revolving, scanning. You move in and out. Anyway, Grace did. A beautiful woman talked to her about decadence. She said she couldn't afford to be decadent. She had children and people without children just couldn't understand, and she wasn't blaming them either, couldn't understand what it meant. "Because I have children, I can only look at it, I can't be it. I realized that people don't have time to look at things, so I started shouting. Just to be heard. I want to make a path for my children, someplace in the future where they can live, so I have to shout." It turned out that she was married to the ugly guy who had shot his best friend years ago. The woman said her husband had a tendency to exaggerate. The woman was shouting to be heard in the crowded room and Grace and she were united in their interest in a couple across the room who were commanding attention. They paced back and forth, along the edge of the room. She would stand and stare, glare, significantly in his direction, while he assumed a pose of indifference. Then she'd move away sullenly and dance back. They acted as if they didn't know each other, and as if they didn't know where the other stood, so that in some way they needed to find each other but were thwarted. "Exhausting, isn't it?" said the shouting woman with children. Mark said they were like poisonous snakes, charged with current. "People like that enliven a party," he continued, "especially such a straight one." But Grace was watching two women dancing together, oblivious that they were the only ones dancing. Grace asked Lisa about her life and how she knew she was gay.

Lisa said she'd been best friends with this girl for a year when one afternoon it just happened. She was sitting on her lap, fooling around, and suddenly they were kissing passionately. Lisa said she had on her rosary and her girlfriend ripped it from her neck and threw it bead by bead across the room. "That rosary meant so much to me," Lisa said, who had picked up all the beads from the floor and put them in an envelope, to save. Lisa said the other girl didn't want it to go on because she already had a girlfriend, but Lisa said she didn't care and spent weekends with her until she was totally fed up. "She told me I was too dependent, but that started me out. Men didn't seem so necessary anymore, and the sex with women is much more beautiful. Men are abrasive, if you know what I mean." Lisa said her parents were in the Midwest, her mother drinking up a storm, a typical suburban housewife, her father a typical businessman, except that somehow he never could earn any money. "Both of them love their afternoon martini. A little olive, a little onion, sitting on the couch. I suppose I was sheltered, except that my mother was an ugly drunk. When I went home the last time, my mother called me a lesbian and slapped me in the face, and I looked at her real calmly and said, 'You've seen the last of me.' I suppose it's sad, but I don't have anything to say to them anyway. I think they regret having sent me to college."

Grace flirted outrageously with Lisa, who seemed to have a lot of patience and one night patience was rewarded. Lisa took Grace home and Grace lost her virginity yet again. It was different, and Grace was at a loss. She worried that she wasn't doing it right. Later it induced in her a state of psychic weightlessness that made her giddy with possibility. She floated on that for days. She told Mark that she didn't know if she was gay or not, but she didn't think she cared. A man's mouth, a woman's mouth, some things felt the same, other things were different. She felt like a twelve-year-old and like Mata Hari. Lisa's body. Her own. She couldn't explain any of it to Mark. She wished men had breasts. She told him that she was worried about the etiquette with women. Would she have to be nicer to Lisa than to the guys she slept with.

Mark was peculiar about her relationship with Lisa and Lisa said it was because he couldn't enter into it the way he could when Grace fucked some guy. Then he could be the guy she was fucking or Grace. And everyone wants to know how women do it. She told Mark what Lisa said and that he seemed upset at her bisexuality. He said he wasn't, that bisexuals were failed homosexuals and he told her she was too young to fail. What was failure, she wanted to

MAR

know. Finally he relented and announced that this was her grace period but after a while she'd have to make up her mind. He said he didn't mean just sex.

Make up her mind, her face. Dress it up, rearrange the pieces, move the furniture, change the decor. The design. I'd like a few more angles on that part of my mind. Remove the frills. She felt she was up for grabs, even to herself. It was as difficult to know what to fill her days with as her body, or mind. It wasn't like learning the alphabet; it was more like unlearning it, not taking it in and not spitting it out. I know it by heart, she thought about a movie she had seen a million times. There was something reassuring in having the same responses to a movie she knew inside out. Repetition was like a visit to her family, except she never went home. Repetition like living at home. Her visits to already seen films produced familiar sighs, cries, rushes of blood, melancholy. It was always the same. A home away from home, these responses. Automatic responses. Like moving her hand to Lisa's breast. Or had she learned that in the movies, or at her mother's breast. Except she'd always hated her mother's body. When Ruth took off her longline bra, and her breasts fell from those white cotton cups, flat and sagging, like her life, Grace thought, exactly the life she didn't want, contained in that body. Always the white cotton full slip under her clothes. And the girdle that mercilessly controlled her figure, which, after two children, had spread and about which she didn't do anything. Her mother's heavy arms extending from a serviceable housedress. And when she took it off, she turned from her daughter, as if ashamed or embarrassed. Grace had never seen her mother's cunt, that part of her mother's body was entirely forbidden from her view, and it was that part she wanted revealed. It seemed impossible that she hadn't seen it, but she couldn't remember it, the way she did remember her mother's breasts, as if the upper part of a woman was all right to show, but not the lower part, and later when Grace stole girlie magazines from candy stores, there too only the breasts were exposed, but those breasts were bouncy and taut, not at all like her mother's, and maybe that's why her mother was ashamed in front of her. Or that's what Grace thought sitting in suspense at the edge of her mother's bed, waiting for her mother to show herself to her only daughter, her baby, as she called Grace when they were alone together.

Lisa called her baby, too, but Lisa and her mother were worlds apart. Lisa was always aware of the audience, and her effect on it, and Grace liked to watch her work the crowd, as Lisa put it, her long thin arms dangling at her sides or moving fast with the music. Mark made some more cynical comments about love between women and Grace said his true colors were showing, to which he replied that at least he had true colors, as if Grace didn't.

Another murder had been committed the night before and Grace couldn't sleep, wondering if evil really did exist. Lisa had told her that she flirted with danger but wouldn't know evil if it came up and shook her. Grace said that was because it didn't exist except as absence, and Lisa laughed and said something about lapsed Catholics being all the same. Later Grace remembered also asking her mother if evil existed and getting the answer she'd given to Lisa. She had problems, she complained to Mark, who complained to her that the play had its problems, too, although it takes a kind of leap in perspective to anthropomorphize art like that. It was as if the play were already there, he said, and all he had to do was find it.

Mark might have the Infanta dress like her dead mother, but first he had to establish the mother's costume and appearance, and that meant a portrait, or something or someone in the open coffin on display while the play went on. Also he wanted the Infanta to show, in some way, that she too was wounded, damaged, and that even though beautiful, she like the Dwarf was imperfect. Grace refused to plead for the King's love, saying it was out of character and Mark countered that it was more out of character for Grace than the Infanta, and the two of them fought again, Mark bringing it to a close by suggesting that they were both tired and Grace was, after all, his star.

There were no stars out that night as Grace wrote Celia that she was having an affair with a woman, but still sleeping with men, to which Celia replied in her next letter that Grace might be having the best of all possible worlds. Grace answered, finally, that she didn't think there was a best and she told Celia that she didn't want to feel responsible to anybody. She felt that Lisa was getting more involved with her, and Grace wasn't sure what she wanted, although she liked Lisa a lot. "I'm not getting married to anyone," she wrote Celia, "whatever Mark thinks about my natural urges."

Mark had taken to dressing like Wilde during rehearsals, and had just read *De Profundis,* which caused him to cry and exclaim that at least they wouldn't go to jail for their unnatural acts, and that Wilde had died for their sins, and Grace told him he was making her sick. She grabbed a bunch of her hair, looked at it, with its split ends, and thought she should go visit Ellen soon or sometime because it nagged at her, Ellen sitting forever in that bin, with no possible future. She split each hair from one end to the other, staring at the strand of hair with terrific concentration, her lips pursed, her eyes nearly crossed. She sat like that for hours rerunning the day's events. She thought Lisa was acting weird. Maybe she was tired of her, or maybe she was just tired, or maybe Grace herself was tired, or didn't know Lisa well enough to be able to tell. If you ever could tell those things about someone else. Where did her thoughts leave off and Lisa's begin anyway. Love is like that Mark would say if he were sitting on the edge of her bed consoling her or cajoling her, both somewhat the same to her these days. But she wasn't sure she was in love with Lisa, whatever that was. She didn't expect it, encourage it, or even, she was sure, really want it. Not yet. Love could wait. She'd grow into it like a pair of pants a size too big. Grace thought her time in bars would lead to something, but Lisa said she shouldn't expect anything to lead to anything. And she told Grace that she didn't want to be her babysitter. Grace ignored Lisa for the rest of that night, but now she reviewed the conversation along with her split ends.

Grace told Mark that she hadn't slept at all and that she felt she was filling up, and one day she might spill over. She was a story. There was hers, Mark's, Lisa's, the play, the people at the bar, hundreds of stories. Mark asked her to concentrate on her role, forget everything but it for just a few days, until D-day, then he said he could talk to her about how she was in a story and so was he. Not in one, she said, we are them.

Her role: innocent and evil, physically beautiful and spiritually ugly, powerful and powerless. Grace told him she'd act the lines, but if he expected her to know how to be all that, he was crazy. "I am crazy," he answered, "and so are you." On the night of the run-through that guy was in the audience, the one who gave Grace the creeps and at the same time was fascinating, like a horror movie. Lisa watched, watched Grace's eyes find his, and didn't think she wanted to live through another of Grace's adventures. Especially this one. Lisa told Grace she was going out of town for a while, the gig bored her, and she'd return after both of them had put enough between them that neither would mind just being friends. Grace was indignant, as Lisa thought she'd be, told her she didn't want to be friends with her, and that she really didn't care anyway. Grace knew that Lisa would expect her to get over it. Pretty fast and probably in the arms of another. Probably a man. And if it was going to be that creep, Lisa had told Grace, she didn't want to see it. She'd seen enough already. Straight women were a pain in the ass. Or like quicksand was how she put it to Grace. Lisa liked being the one to go, to get back on the road.

Grace had imagined that Lisa would always be around. She consoled herself by thinking that she probably wasn't a lesbian anyway. Misquoting a line from *Trash,* Mark told her she wasn't a good lesbian but, as Grace herself had once said, no one is perfect.

She wanted to forget and she threw herself into her part. Now that she'd been abandoned, her heart supposedly broken, she did feel a little tragic, or at least wounded, the way Mark said he wanted the Infanta to be, not just a monster. The creepy guy hanging around was a distraction. She didn't imagine that she could do anything to him that would touch him or anger him or move him or move him away as she thought she'd done with Lisa, and in an odd way he was safe. At least she didn't feel like killing herself, not for somebody else. If she ever did it, she told Mark, it would be only because of herself. Mark said that was wonderfully selfish and this mood was perfect for the Infanta. In rehearsal Grace recited her last line with real fury: "For the future let those who come to play with me have no heart." Then she stormed off the stage, not at all like a princess, or Mark's idea of a princess. Still, Mark was pleased that she had assumed her role. Even though she said that she didn't like the Infanta because she didn't do anything, and why, she asked Mark, do people write stories about people who don't do anything. At least the Dwarf was an entertainer, not like the Infanta or the King, who didn't have to earn anyone's attention.

Chet Baker singing "They're writing songs of love but not for me," Mark decided, was the right touch for the fade-out. The Dwarf is lying dead, stage right, and the Infanta has made her final exit. The record was a gift from Bill to Grace after she'd broken his heart. Perfect, Mark thought. Perfect too was the enlarged reproduction of Holbein's *Dance of Death,* which figured in the fairy tale and was part of the spare scenery, even more apparent or obvious with only the dead Dwarf, Mark himself, lying there onstage. Too bad he couldn't see it, and though he had Grace stand in, or lie in, for him a couple of times, it wasn't the same. They were nearly ready for opening night, as much as you could call a first night at Oscar's an opening. And when that night came, the guy was waiting backstage, so to speak, as if he knew something that Grace didn't, and after she spoke her last line, again in fury, she defiantly walked over to him and into his waiting arms, so to speak, feeling that there was nothing to lose.

Burmese Days

GARY INDIANA

Who knows what hearts and souls have in them? On the answering machine a message from Victor, who tells me when I call him that Paul, my lover for two years before I met Alexis, is sick. There exists a special tone of voice, now, for illness, that marks the difference between sick and dying.

I've heard that he's sick.

And so this body whose secret parts were my main pleasure in life for longer than anyone else's transforms itself into a fount of contagion. Paul passes over into the territory of no-longer-quite-alive, and I calculate that if he got it five years ago, the general incubation period, he must have been infectious on each of the fifty or sixty occasions when we slept together, giving me a much better than average chance of being infected.

He wants to see you. He's asked for you.

I haven't seen Paul in over a year. One day I saw him on the street with the man he's been living with, a tall gangly man, whereas Paul has a rugged, packed look about him and that face, the map of Macedonia. We said hello goodbye very pleasantly and I considered that if he hadn't had a continual need to fuck all over town we might've moved in together and had a normal relationship, if there is such a thing. He liked having someone at home, waiting for him. I never could wait for people. Victor says, he came back from abroad and his roommate found him the next morning bleeding from the mouth.

Maybe it's because we didn't love each other that we broke off without any rancor, without even really breaking off. We met every three or four nights in the corner bar, the one near my house where I still sometimes drink with Victor. Paul and I never made dates or anything, and some nights we saw each other there but went home with other people; if Paul didn't feel like doing it with me he would say: let's get together real soon.

How long has he been sick?

We stopped sleeping together when people still referred to gay cancer and thought it came from using poppers. For a long time I moved back and forth from Europe, each time I returned the thing had become more of a subject, I heard of this one and that one getting pneumonia and fading out. Paul said once: It's getting scary, it's getting close. He'd met Jason years ago and they had made love once in a while, Paul told me, when it wasn't you it usually was him, and then he and Jason moved into Cornelia Street, signing a joint lease, which was practically marriage.

They've had him in the hospital for two weeks.

At first the people who died were people I hardly knew, or people from earlier lives who'd been in a lot of the same rooms, their deaths were disconcerting but seemed to happen on a distant planet. At first people would say: well, he must have been leading a secret life, taking all kinds of drugs and going to the Mineshaft. Because at first, most people who got ill did seem the same ones who never finished an evening at four a.m., piled into taxis together when the regular bars closed. And then of course there was this other thing with needles, if it spread by blood and sperm, people who used needles would naturally get it.

The worst thing is, I can't feel anything for Paul. I'm too scared for myself.

But you'll go see him, I hope.

Of course I will.

Except that I am, in this particular business, a bigger coward than I'd like to be. Victor and I used to drink with Perkins when Perkins turned up in the bar, and Perkins got ill, I didn't go to the hospital, he had one bout of pneumonia and the now-familiar remission, and Chas, who lives in a building behind my building, called raising money to get Perkins a color TV, since he had to stay in all the time, and I never gave it, I promised to, in the early autumn, and one mild afternoon I saw Perkins at Astor Place, looking all of his fifty-four years which he never had previously, he said, Call me sometime, and the next I heard it went into his brain and they brought him into St. Vincent's raving, Victor went four or five times, I said, My God, Victor, what do you say?

The thing is, Victor said, when he feels all right he doesn't feel as if he's dying, the worst thing is acting morbid and stricken about it. You just go have a normal conversation with him. But it's too late now because he isn't lucid for more than a few minutes during any given visit. At first he's his old self and then he babbles.

I never thought I'd be so chickenshit about anything.

But this new situation, with Paul, what does it mean? And with Gregory? Another thing about Perkins: he had, for a time, a comely Irish lover named Mike, a slender boy with soft brown eyes and a small wisp of a mustache, they were together for a while and then they weren't. Mike fucked everything that walked, one night we found ourselves using the toilet in Nightbirds when it was still an

PAN AM
TWA

afterhours joint and I let him piss in my mouth, then we screwed at my place the whole next day in every conceivable position. He called a few days later and warned me his doctor thought he had Hepatitis B. As it happened I'd just had a typhoid shot for my visa to Thailand and got a bad reaction; my pee turned red, then it passed on, and Mike phoned just before I left to say his results had been negative.

Mike moved to California and Hawaii for several months and when he came back he lived with Perkins again but soon after that he started looking spectral and then stopped going out and then everyone heard that he had it and a few months later everyone heard that he died. That was four years before Perkins came down with it and when Perkins came down with it he told everyone he was sure he got it from Mike, though how Perkins could be sure, since Perkins took it up the can as often as possible from anyone available, was a mystery. Yet he insisted that Mike had been the source.

Until now Mike has been the only person I know I've slept with who later died from it and I used to think that because I recovered from the typhoid shot, which I got after I slept with him, that meant I hadn't caught it from him, and I also rationalized that maybe Mike caught it in California or Hawaii and then gave it to Perkins when he moved back to New York, in which case Perkins's incubation period may have only been a year or two, or rather four years, I keep getting dates mixed up, I went to Thailand in '81 and I think I'd already stopped sleeping with Paul, so if I didn't get it from Mike possibly I didn't get it from Paul either. But with Mike I could only have been exposed once, and some people think that repeated exposure is necessary for the virus to take hold, so if it had only been Mike I could now feel fairly confident though how can anyone who ever did anything with anybody feel at all confident and with Paul, of course, the case is very different, his dong has been in every hole in my body hundreds of times squirting away like the Trevi Fountain, I've rimmed him too and once when he cut his finger chopping up some terrible cocaine he bought in the Spike I even sucked his blood.

Now, of course, everyone's conscious about the problem, but as somebody said in the paper the horses are out of the barn, how can you possibly know if, back in the days of unfettered casual screwing, someone you met by chance and screwed and never saw again wasn't a carrier? Not that I had so many in the last years, but they don't really know if numbers are important, even if I don't have it I probably have the antibodies and if I have the antibodies I'm probably a carrier. So if I do it with Gregory I risk infecting him. And then, I don't know about Gregory, eithei. He says he hasn't taken heroin in five years, but junkies who do actually manage to kick usually muck up several times before they get off it, maybe five years isn't so precise, in addition to that Gregory looks like a magazine cover and I can't imagine he hasn't satisfied all his sexual appetites regularly, in fact he's alluded to various dark periods of the past, hinted that when he used drugs he did some hustling here and there, he's so well spoken and smart it's hard to imagine him peddling his dick on the street but who knows what people will do. Anyway, I threw myself at him in less than a second after seeing that face and I'm shy, there must have been hundreds of opportunities. Thousands.

Victor says he'll go with me to see Paul.

I realize that I really am in love with Gregory.

These have to be peculiar times.

It would not be strange to get it and then to decide as Perkins did that this one particular person gave it to you, one out of ten or fifty or a hundred, maybe because that person made you feel something special, had done wonderful things in bed or got you to trust them physically and mentally as no one else ever had: Mike, for example, had miraculous talents because his sexual demands were flagrant and unyielding, he was socially genteel but I remember in the bathroom at Nightbirds and later too he talked dirty and tough, kneel down, bitch, suck that dick, and of course the pissing, which had introduced itself as an especially filthy surprise but the way he insisted on it made it seem like an ordinary thing people did. He was an incredibly complete fuck, he exhausted your imagination and wiped out your memory of other fucks, when Perkins remembered making love perhaps he only thought of Mike and things Mike did to him. You would naturally connect your most vivid memory of pleasure to infection and death because the others weren't remotely worth getting sick from, just pallid skimpy traces of sex crossed with thin trickles of "bodily fluids." If the two things had to be linked, better that a cherished image of sex connect with the transmission of the microbe.

In any case, if you had sex now it was a matter of deciding, even if you took elaborate precautions, whether the degree of risk involved—and who could calculate that?—was "worth it," whether your need for that kind of experience with another person outweighed, in a sense, your desire for survival.

When I think about Perkins in that fifth floor walk-up watching the color TV his friends gave him, I imagine him measuring out his life in half-hour segments, telling time by the flow of images and the chatter of voices, his thoughts melting into the TV. As he wasted away, the set continued entertaining him, keeping his mind off things. It showed him funny pictures that weren't really funny and brought him news of catastrophes that were somehow beside the point. The TV made his death feel vicarious and filled his bedroom with another world he could enter when this one had run its course. A quilt covered the bed, the same one he'd slept in with Mike, the room was big and chilly with a thin musty carpet covering the wood floor, brown velour drapes covered the arched windows. His bedside lamp had a pink shade, the square table near his pillows had pill bottles and a water glass on it. He didn't feel as though he were dying, Victor said, he just knew, intellectually, that his death would come sooner than later. Sooner than expected. But does anyone expect to die? Even when one is quite old, it must seem a fantastic event, if one is ninety, one can still imagine living, say, till ninety-five.

He is lying in the darkness of his own bedroom, a plywood cubicle within his vast loft, near the southern tip of the island. He's talking into his cordless telephone, which gives local calls the scratchy echo of long distance.

We live in large and small boxes in buildings on regularly shaped streets. We see each other seldom because we are busy. Nothing happens to us except dinner parties and visits to the dentist and work. Our lives have the generic flavor of deferred pleasure and sublimation until we fall in love or die.

M. is thirty-six, rich, successful. He's a closer friend than Victor but I haven't been in his apartment for years. When you're busy you use the telephone.

"Contamination," he says, through the phone crackle.

"Like water," I say.

"Water, blood, sputum, spit, urine, semen, any kind of fluid. It's all in the food chain," M. declares. "You have to imagine particles, like from Chernobyl, settling into the water table like—like little dissolving snowflakes. They sink into the ground when it rains, go into the water, everybody drinks it. Some people get a little bit, some people get a lot. Or maybe it gets eaten by a cow or a pig, it grows into grass and some *swines* store it up in their tissues, and then you pop into the local deli for a ham sandwich with a little mustard, on some nice rye bread, presto you've got AIDS."

And what if I die, right away instead of later on, if for instance I take the blood test, it's positive, I'll never finish *Burma,* I won't be leaving anything behind. Or just a few things, of no historical interest. On the immortality front I will fail, ashes to ashes, and no health insurance, I'll become a ward of the city and be put in one of those wards where the doctors and nurses shun you for fear of catching it, and none of your friends comes to the hospital. Libby would come, M. would come, Victor would come, my friend Jane would definitely come, but how would I die, what would I be like, and how lugubrious for them, if it's a big ward there's bound to be others dying in the same room, dying with the television on, perhaps they make them wear earphones, but when the ward got deathly quiet at night I'd hear the little bug noises in their earphones. Was that the point, to leave something behind, it's really a thick ambition, if you're dead what difference does it make. Of course they say it's why people have children, they can remember you for a time, though mainly they remember pain, pain from their terrible childhoods. Even if their parents loved them, it's usually so twisted it's as bad as hate, and even when it isn't, the other children torture you and make fun of all your little quirks and debilities, you try to escape into fantasies but those are poisoned from the very outset, while you're still in first grade they've already turned you into a monster, you spend your whole adult life trying to wipe out all the things they've taught you to do, trying not to hate yourself.

I never tell about my childhood because I only remember pain. And then I keep meeting people like Gregory who think they're as they are because of the father or because of the mother. He seems so clear about it, my father did this to me and my mother did that, therefore I am. I don't know what either of my parents did: my mother says she regrets slapping me too often and I can't remember ever being slapped. Maybe she remembers wrong. When you go into psychotherapy they teach you to invent false memories of childhood beatings and sexual abuse; people become addicted to these simple explanations of why they're monsters. And now everyone is going to die before they figure anything out. I'm going to die before I can be truly loved, I'll die with every sort of bitter memory of Alexis's coldness and Paul's faithlessness, though really that didn't matter with him, I'm not bitter against him, but why couldn't I have what I had with him with someone who loved me, and I'll die before I can make Gregory love me, I can see I'm fated to cash it in without a single memory of real happiness. What is real happiness, is it this business of living with another person, I never really lived with anybody, I thought no one could stand it. You think you'll have a long life, so you do everything at a snail's pace: before I tried to write *Burma* I tried to write a book about a family, one sister was a socialite, another was crippled in a wheelchair, the brother was a fag actor in off-Broadway, the parents had been murdered in their townhouse, I only wrote two scenes of that book, the sister in bed with her boyfriend and the brother getting drunk on the set of a soap opera, not bad, oh yes, and one scene with the sister racing through the townhouse in her wheelchair, she'd had special ramps built so she could get around. Before that I tried something like a love story based on me and that California surfer type I fucked a few times when I lived in Boston, a shoplifter. Nobody shoplifts anymore. I remember when everyone did it, it showed your contempt for the capitalist system. Everyone worships capitalism today, look at this obscene medical system, if Paul doesn't have insurance he's probably in a room full of other people's contagion, they say the patients with AIDS go into Sloan-Kettering perfectly healthy and pick up diseases in the waiting room, it's how Michael got pneumonia, I almost forgot about Michael, his apartment windows used to be right there, the windows still are there but he's dead.

Maybe I'm dying anyway, faster than others because I smoke so many cigarettes. I try and try quitting and nothing works. I can lay awake at night telling myself, You will not smoke a cigarette tomorrow, your body doesn't want you to smoke, when you go to the hypnotist he makes you close your eyes and tells you your brain is going down a steep flight of steps, that you're on an elevator going down, deep down into the hypnotic state, it sounds like a car salesman. And when you emerge from hypnosis, he says, You will have no desire for a cigarette, all cravings for a cigarette will have left your body, and whenever you feel a temporary urge for a cigarette you will tell yourself, "I need my body to live." The impulse only lasts for ninety seconds, he says; after ninety seconds you will no longer crave a cigarette. I ought to go back because I did stop for six hours, thinking the whole time, I'm a nonsmoker now, since telling myself "I'm a nonsmoker now" was one of the hypnotic suggestions, and even while I smoked the first ten cigarettes the same night, I thought, I'm a nonsmoker now.

They say if you're infected and have the antibodies you might not come down with the fatal syndrome, therefore you should build up your immune system, which I'm tearing down with cigarettes and alcohol, sometimes I drink nothing for weeks and then for reasons I've never figured out I'll get drunk at a party and then drunk again the following night, sometimes for as many as six or seven nights running, then stop again, though I never stop smoking, I wake up wanting a cigarette, it's crazy, but then again, Perkins went into AA two full years before getting ill, he stopped smoking at the same time, he began looking wonderful, his skin all clear, the bags around his eyes vanished, he'd always been youthful anyway, but then he became spectacular again, young again, and immediately got sick. And Michael, the same story exactly: he gave up drugs and alcohol and cigarettes, toned himself up at the gym, etherealized himself like some ideal sex object, but without screwing around because even then he was frightened of catching it, and perhaps a year passed before Michael's glands mysteriously swelled up, he woke one day in a high fever, they treated him at St. Vincent's for pneumonia, he recovered, then I saw him out and around, he said he felt normal and the only thing different was you suddenly know that anything can kill you. I despised Michael but near the end he wrote this hilarious story about assholes, laughing right to the grave about the whole business, which I can't help respecting, really, he died his own particular death without any pietistic nonsense or feeling of solidarity with anything, least of all the social contract, he'd had a good time while he was here, lots of laughs, plenty of weird scenes, his one full-length film which somebody somewhere has, Michael didn't want much in life besides kicks, I don't think death found him with a lot of plans pending for the future. Whereas Paul, this can't possibly feel natural to him, something further, quite a few things further were supposed to happen, he's always gotten acting work, always a play, a movie, something, never a starring part but it would have happened eventually, Michael had had plans once upon a time, but then his wife went through a windshield on the Ventura Freeway, after that Michael wanted a good time and eons of forgetfulness, but at the very least, he must have wanted to live. Life doesn't care about what anybody wants.

I see Gregory again, for five minutes, on his way into work. I'm walking along lower Broadway, deciding about shoes.

"I want to see you real soon," he tells me. "I'd really like you to see what I'm doing."

When he talks I go into a terrified ecstasy. I'm losing my will to this man, who embraces me on the corner of Prince and Broadway and purrs, "But mainly I want us to become very close." I've been walking along here thinking it might be the route he will take to the restaurant today. I'm not going to tell him about Paul, though I want to tell him everything I'm feeling and thinking. Not yet. If ever.

He has a beautiful smell, a faint animal funk mingled with some essential oil, opoponax or civit, in his fur-flapped hat he looks like an expensively bred, sleek creature, the thick nose a sexual mark, a carnal threat: and he looks as if he might dart away from me, slip out of my grasp, jump to something else like a fickle cat. He's interested in everything that doesn't interest me when I'm with him, little events in the street, what other people wear, how other people look, window displays, passing fashions, he dates everything, clocks everything, he seems obsessed with defining this minute, this period, this era, he savors details and tiny nuances, he knows about what's on television and all the new movies and every song that's played on the radio, his fixation with the inessential, the passing moment, also makes me feel he'll slink off to someone else, almost unconsciously, to whatever offers him a momentary pleasure, without obligations. I pretend an interest in his interests, wanting to seem modern, and in fact all this junk that he likes bores me silly. But I try seeing it through his eyes, and begin to learn what something will look like to Gregory. Magazine images start falling apart when I look at them, breaking themselves down into sex messages, sales points, prescriptions of what people are supposed to be, in this time, this place. He has more energy, more appetite than I do, as if the world were still offering him unlimited possibilities, endless options. As if he were born yesterday and still had a whole lifetime to make choices. His face lights up like a child's when he sees, for example, a stunningly well-dressed Puerto Rican girl.

Sunlight and Personality

SUZANNE JACKSON

In September 1979 I went to live with my brother and his wife. I lived with them for several years, although when I was living like that, I measured time differently; I can't explain how. I measured it in such a way that now, when I try to recall, I can't say how much time passed, but I believe it was several years. I lived with them first at my brother's request and then I stayed on, I suppose, because I wanted to, or, to put it another way, because I found I could not leave. My brother asked me to live with him and his wife because he felt obliged to help me. He had no way of knowing that I would be forced to stay as long as I did, such a long time. Still, he never complained and he made me feel more than welcome; he made me feel as if his house were mine. My brother is a very generous man.

I arrived at my brother's house on an unusually cold night, considering the time of year. To reach the house, I walked over a gleaming orange lawn where thousands of ice crystals reflected the house lights. When my brother opened the door to me, as he told me much later, he did not recognize me, but thought that I was someone else entirely. He thought I was his friend Roger Nance, whom I later met and who is a very nice man and worthy of my brother's devotion to him. When my brother told me this, perhaps four months after I had begun living with him, I realized that this confusion explained more clearly his immediate joy and enthusiasm upon seeing me. When he saw me on his doorstep he greeted me with a loud hello and shook my hand, at once communicating happiness and pride and deference and inner strength and weakness. I'm afraid my handshake did not communicate anything and this may have been the point at which he realized that I wasn't Roger Nance but another person. It wasn't really a handshake at all; it was more an extending of the hand that may have indicated passivity, possibly surprise. Surprise is what I felt when my brother shook my hand the way he did. But once I was inside the door the expression on my brother's face changed and although he still smiled, he narrowed his eyes as if he were trying to see more clearly and then widened them again and a look of calm spread over his features. I didn't know it at the time, but now, looking back on it, I believe it was at that moment, when he widened his eyes, that he actually recognized me as his brother and while he never told me what his deepest thoughts were at this moment of recognition, I can guess that his mind suddenly filled with memories, some harsher and some dimmer, of the time we had spent together in the past.

Soon he introduced me to his wife, Pam, whom I became very close to and loved very much. Pam and I were both feminine in that we didn't want anything specific in life. The kind of lovemaking we enjoyed together was usually oral, with some slow penetration. During the summer there were many warm sunny days where Pam and I would lay out on a sheet she had spread on the back lawn, naked and resting on our sides so that each one's mouth was at the other's sex organs for what seemed like hours. And then Pam might cradle me or I might kneel between her legs and rub the tip of my cock against her cunt lips which would feel like melted flesh. I still don't know if my brother knew I was fucking his wife. If he did he didn't care or he approved and if he didn't know then, in his mind, it wasn't happening. He never said anything about it to me. Certainly my presence didn't change things between him and his wife, or I believe it didn't, because at night I could hear them both moaning and Pam often cried out loudly or spoke a string of delirious and incoherent words.

But there were other days when Pam and I were alone in the house together (we were alone in the house almost every day except for Saturdays and Sundays when my brother was also there) when she would treat me in a very different way. On these days, even though she might embrace me, she would generally keep her distance. When she did approach me or pass me in some room or hallway, she would always look at me from the corners of her eyes with an expression that I can only describe accurately by calling it an expression of suspicion. On these days Pam would hardly say a dozen words to me. I never asked her or confronted her about this because I wasn't discontent; instead I spent most of my time in my brother's heated swimming pool. In the water I imagined myself disappearing, which was a feeling not unlike the feeling I experienced when I lay in the sun with my head between Pam's legs. I thought to myself: maybe I shouldn't be fucking Pam at all.

Usually at some point during the day, late in the day, my brother and I would reminisce about our childhood. We really didn't have many memories in common because we only spent about four years together, the years when he and his father returned to live with our mother. Our mother had married Carl's father in the decade after the war, but he left her soon after Carl was born, taking Carl with him. Two years later she had another child, me, by a man who she didn't marry. When I was about twelve Carl and his father returned to my mother and the four of us stayed together as a family until Carl left four years later. Then his father also left. And then I left, but only after my mother died in a fall from a building one year later. In common language, Carl is my half brother; in my private language I call him my brother.

One of the memories Carl and I had in common was trapping salamanders and frogs in a drainage ditch near the house. We also remembered the winding dirt roads that led to the Indian caves and a retarded boy named Sammy Tucker whose family tied him to the flat bed of a truck when they came to town. These conversations about our pasts were pleasant, but there were times when my brother would talk about something in his past, saying, "Remember when we . . ," and the memory would be foreign to me; often he would go into detail, but still I couldn't remember. Of course, I concealed my ignorance. I think these were memories of things he had done with other boys his age before or after we lived together or things he had done with his father. In many of our conversations we reconstructed for one another the house that we had lived in with our mother and Carl's father. Day after day we remembered the rooms, the windows, the furniture, the wallpaper, and all the inconsistencies, the places where the house had begun to deteriorate. There was one other important memory that Carl and I had in common: the memory of our mother's death and her burial. We each remembered this differently – me being close to her death and Carl being farther away. Carl told me he didn't hear about her death until a week after she had died. I remembered sending him the telegram and wondering if he would receive it. He attended the funeral with his father and I suspected that his father had followed him after he left our mother's house, but I didn't tell Carl this and he never said anything to confirm my suspicions. Carl said very little about the period of his life after leaving our mother's house.

Gradually the days when Pam and I made love grew fewer and the days when she said only a few words to me grew more frequent. Gradually also, her expression changed from one of suspicion to one of awareness, maybe complicity, and recognition. And when we did make love she would hold me very close, so close that

I sometimes imagined the surfaces of our skins breaking and the two bodies collapsing into one. But increasingly there were days where I lay on the grass in the backyard, or on a rubber float in the swimming pool, and listened to her movements inside the house. Now when I sank under the water I felt myself disintegrate and spread into unbroken time, into the time through which she passed inside the house (she passed through me), so that I existed for her as a measure of her movements.

There were other days when I would spend all day in the room my brother had given me. Inside the house I could hear Pam's movements more clearly. I closed my eyes or stared at a blank wall and listened. I tried to imagine how she used the house, what she did in it, what paths she chose to move from room to room, or move in a given room. There were also long periods of silence and during these I could not judge whether Pam was moving or doing something very very quietly, or not doing anything. I think there were times when she just sat down and didn't make a sound. These periods of silence were curious to me. Once, after over twenty minutes of silence, I called to Pam from my room and asked what she was doing; for a moment she continued to be silent, then she said, "Oh, nothing." The words were spoken in a voice that seemed to belong to another person, not Pam. It was a thin sound and reminded me of the sound wind makes when it moves over concrete or sand; a thin, whining sound. But it was not high-pitched like a whine, it was an even pitch. There was also in it, somewhere behind it, a vacantness like the dead noise or static that can come from a radio. But everything I've said about the voice is inadequate, it doesn't describe the voice; the voice was not quite like anything I've compared it to; the only accurate statement I've made about it was that it seemed to belong to another person, not Pam. I wanted to call to her again, but already she was moving from one room to another, and soon I became absorbed in the repeated sound of a knife slicing through some kind of meat or vegetable.

I began to spend more time in my room and I rarely went out in the backyard. When I wanted to leave my room to pass through the house for some reason, I waited and listened until I was sure that Pam wasn't in the areas that I would pass through; I waited until I heard her steps in a distant room and then carefully made my way out of my room and into some other part of the house without seeing her and without being seen by her. Once I adopted this strategy I never saw Pam during the days we were alone in the house together. The program worked so well that I soon came to believe that Pam was complicit in it and that she listened for me at the same moments I listened for her. Pam was, for me, a series of sound patterns growing louder or softer as she either moved closer to me or farther away.

One day I opened the door to my room and stepped out into the hall. I didn't see Pam anywhere. I walked down the hall to my brother's room, the room where he and Pam slept. I stood in the doorway of the room; I saw a bed to my left and a low dresser opposite the bed to my right; there was a large mirror attached to the dresser. I stepped into the room and shut the door, then I went to the bed and sat on it; I faced the wall and listened for Pam's footsteps or for the sounds of any other movements she might make. She was completely silent; she must have chosen to wait at the other end of the house. I rose from the bed and went over to the dresser where I stood looking at myself in the mirror. The reflection showed me from below my waist to my head. I looked at myself carefully: I was a young man, twenty-five years old. My eyes were perfect ovals pinched together at each end and the iris and pupil inside each were perfect circles; the eye color was green, suffused with gold and blue. The eyes were set on a perfectly straight line at either side of the nose, and they were framed by long dark lashes and dark eyebrows. The nose was small, with a thin, straight bridge and slightly flared nostrils. The lips were full and deep pink. The structure of the face was narrow with a smooth forehead and visible rounded cheekbones. Soft blond hair fell just past the ears and along the neck. My breathing was shallow and I felt a constriction in my throat and chest. Bright sunlight shone on me from two large windows in the room; it came in at my left side and illuminated my body and the mirror at the same time. As I unbuttoned my shirt, light seemed to radiate from my exposed skin, as if it were pushing through the thousands of pores in my skin. I was astonished by the beautiful figure that I saw reflected in the mirror. I closed my eyes against the brilliant light and retained the delicate reflected image of myself in my mind. I wanted to touch it and I slowly moved my fingers over the skin, which felt very smooth. I drew my hands from the curves at my hips and waist, over my belly and upward over my ribs and further upward until I felt the impression of two small swollen breasts. I pressed them in my hands and experienced a feeling like desire, or longing. Then the light from outside penetrated deep into my head and I felt the heat of a sensuous fever spread over me and I lost consciousness. I woke up later in my own room where Carl had moved me (he later said) after having found me half-naked on the floor of his room.

Apparently I was very ill. The doctors said I had been ill for some time with an internal infection that affected several organs. During the period of my confinement, Pam brought my meals and my medication to me in the room. I didn't leave the room for several months; I no longer greeted Carl at the door when he came home in the afternoons; instead he would come to me and sit on the bed or in the metal folding chair that Pam had brought into the room. He told me about the time I was sick just after he and his father had come to live with our mother. I said that I didn't remember much about it because I was in a fever. He said that everyone was afraid I was going to die because I was so frail and had lost over ten pounds during the illness. He said that he had felt indifferently towards me before the illness, but when, one day, our mother took him into my room and showed him my small pale body covered in sweat, he fell in love with me, in a certain way, and had continued to love me from that moment onward. He told me that he envied my having seen our mother's body after the accident; and, in fact, I did see them take the body from the cement and then later went to the morgue where I identified the body for the police. My brother asked me to describe my feelings at the times I saw the body. I told him this was impossible because some of them were now unthinkable. I had tried many times before – in attempts to cleanse my mind during periods of distress – but I had never been able to recall my feelings exactly. I told him the little that I did remember. He asked me to describe the body to him. I didn't understand what Carl wanted. He asked me again to describe the body.

I was looking for reasons to be happy. It was after midnight, and I was resting fitfully; I had slept for awhile, but then I woke up. In the dark I could feel my diseased body, its fever, and the pressure in my lungs. I was thinking about some minor experience in my life; I don't remember what it was, some small, unimportant experience, but for some reason I couldn't get it out of my mind. The same images and bits of conversation were repeating themselves in my head. Then I heard footsteps outside the door and the door opened. My brother and his wife came into the room. They must have thought I was asleep because they didn't say anything to me, but stood over me and looked at me; my brother lifted the blankets off me and they looked at my naked body. Either they believed I was asleep, or they knew I was pretending to be asleep and they were treating this false sleep as if it were real. They continued to be very quiet and soon covered me and they walked to the end of the bed. I kept my eyes closed. I don't know if I will ever understand what made them do it. It's not something someone needs to understand, but I think about it often, even now. I don't understand why I continued to pretend to be asleep. I didn't want to participate in their lives anymore, or I didn't want to be active. But that's not the reason I kept quiet.

Pam and Carl bent down to the floor; I heard them kissing. I knew their intentions from the beginning. Even though they didn't say anything and I didn't see them, I knew what was in their minds. I was breathing evenly, but because I was breathing through my mouth, each breath sounded difficult. I'm sure they could hear the breathing. They made love for a long time, maybe forty-five minutes or an hour, but it might have been shorter; to me it seemed much longer. During this time the sounds they made didn't vary, just the same sounds over and over. When they finally left it was getting light outside. I didn't sleep at all that night.

Carl began to stay home during the days, he said, because of my illness. I don't know if he had an arrangement with his boss or if he quit his job, or what. I didn't ask at the time and now, when I recall it, anything is possible. At first, Carl only stayed home two days a week, in addition to Saturdays and Sundays. He seemed to be helping Pam, who probably had harder days during my illness because she nursed me, in a way, and also took care of the house. But even when Carl began to stay home, only Pam brought my food and washed me and changed my clothes and the sheets. Then Carl stayed home every day of the week. He still only came to see me in the evenings, but he was in the house all day. I told Carl once that I felt guilty because I was such a burden to him and Pam, but he told me not to think about it that way, that what they were doing was only natural. I sometimes listened to the sounds that Carl made outside my room, but when I was awake I couldn't always trust that I was thinking clearly. My thoughts, although they were about the same things that they had always been about, were unreasonable; I believe they were ordered in a different way. I can't remember what I heard, but I knew that Carl was in the house during the days; both Pam and Carl had told me this.

I never left the room and got up from the bed only to use the bathroom. But there was one day when I did leave the room. It was late in the afternoon and I was sleeping. When I woke up I realized that I was very hungry. I waited for an hour thinking that

Pam would be in any minute with my food. Then I called Pam's name; it was the first time in several months I had raised my voice above a whisper. The sound that came out was weak, and I knew no one had heard it. I waited for three-quarters of an hour and still Pam hadn't come to my room. I felt it was time for Carl to come in for his usual visit, but he didn't come either. I was so weak that I fell asleep for ten minutes, and then I woke up. I decided that the only thing I could do was to try to get up and get some food. I couldn't understand why this was happening. I slowly got out of bed and walked to the door. I opened the door and I was overcome by a sickening smell. I fell to my knees and retched. The only thing I could think was that Carl and Pam were dead. I sat on the floor for a minute, and then I stood up again; I don't remember what I was thinking except that I believed that my brother was dead; but something else, some other thoughts, must have been going through my mind. I stepped out into the hall and realized that, yes, the smell was bad, but it wasn't as bad now as it had seemed at first. My first reaction had been so extreme because of the very sensitive condition of my nerves due to my illness and isolation. The air was thick and warm; an unusual feeling overtook me, but this time it wasn't nausea, it was closer to delirium; my head felt unbalanced, but not so much as to make me nauseous, the feeling this time was closer to euphoria. I no longer believed that my brother was dead. I walked down the hallway and then down another short hallway until I came to the living room area. I stopped at a point where I could see into the entire room. The air was so thick and sweet that I had to open my mouth to breathe. I tasted the sweet air; it was moist and it settled on my skin and in my mouth. I put one hand up to my cheek because already I was sweating. All the lights in the room and in the adjacent rooms were on, and I could see everything clearly. I saw everything simultaneous with smelling the air and tasting it and feeling the moisture on my skin. It is very difficult to describe what I saw. First, Pam and Carl were not dead, they were fucking on the couch; Pam was lying with her legs spread and her knees bent slightly, and Carl was on top of her pushing in a steady rhythm, not too fast and not too slow. I couldn't see Carl's face, but his back and the backs of his legs were covered with sweat. I could see Pam's face; her eyes were half-closed so that I saw part of the colored irises and the white on each side; the bottom part of her face was wet and her lips were pink and swollen. I have to describe the other things I saw in sequence, but actually I saw everything, including Pam and Carl fucking, virtually in a single instant; I did not see one thing first and another next and so on, but I will have to describe it as if I had. In my mind I remember it as one picture.

First, the room was a mess. I have already said that it smelled horribly. There were open bottles of liquor, some empty and some half-full. There were huge stains on the carpet. There was food on plates and on the furniture and the carpet. There was clothing everywhere; maybe half of Pam's wardrobe was in the room and one-quarter of Carl's. All the lights were on, including the track-lights above the couch which functioned as spotlights on Carl's body. The television was on, but the sound was turned down; it was tuned to a show that I didn't recognize. There were open magazines scattered around the room; most showed pornography – people tied up and gagged, and other things. I was beginning to understand what had happened. Carl hadn't stayed home from work to help Pam, but to be a part of everything that had happened here. Because of the smell (and, to some extent, the way the room looked) it was clear that this had gone on for a long time, probably for about four months, which was the time Carl had been off work, but possibly longer. Maybe it had been going on from the beginning (from the beginning of my illness which was nine months ago). I stood looking at the room for twenty minutes, and during this time neither Carl nor Pam noticed me, I'm sure of that. Their bodies were joined together in a combination or conjunction of right angles and forty-five-degree angles, and moved in a constant rhythm. I turned away and went back to my room. I was extremely weak due to hunger and the agitation of my senses. I lay on my bed with the lights out. I was grinding my teeth because of hunger and excitement. I hoped that Pam and Carl would realize that something was wrong, that they had forgotten the routine that previously had been maintained along with the disorder – the routine of feeding and caring for me, the sick person. Three hours later Pam did come into my room very quietly and set a tray of food and water next to the bed. I didn't move or make a noise, and she left as soon as she put the tray on the floor. Something must have gone wrong that day, but they hadn't abandoned me entirely.

My condition grew worse, but the doctors couldn't locate the infection. The days passed in the same way that they had before, with Pam bringing me food, etc., and Carl visiting me each day, late in the day. I was too weak to get up at all. After three months, during which the doctors didn't know if I would live or die (as Carl later told me), I was feeling much better. They gave Pam the credit for saving my life. I was grateful to her but I couldn't adequately express my gratitude. I noticed that she had a sore on her calf, just below the bottom of her dress. Once, when I was lying in bed and she was standing, I tried to touch it.

Because of the illness, the quality of my perceptions was changed. The illness had over-stimulated my senses, especially my sight and possibly the sense of touch. I don't know why these two were so greatly changed, because at the time, I considered these two senses remote from each other. My sickroom was unbearable now. I left the room in the morning and didn't return until the evening when it was time for me to go to bed. I suffered from insomnia for several months. Finally, I asked Carl for another room and he gave me the third bedroom, which was very comfortable, more comfortable than the other one, which reminded me of my fragile body.

After I had changed rooms I spent a certain amount of time in my room and a certain amount of time outside it. Carl still hadn't returned to work, and he was always in the house. He and I would have conversations similar to the ones that we used to have only in the late afternoons after he returned from work; now we talked like this at any hour of the day. Carl often commented on my light complexion and compared it to his darker skin. It was no mystery to me: we had different fathers. I looked at Carl when he talked to me, but for some reason was compelled to look away when I spoke to him. We talked about many things. Sometimes he would turn on the television and we might talk about that. So, in conclusion, I think that if I were to measure the hours I spent with my brother before, including the time we lived together as children, it would be the period I have just described (the period after my illness) that represents the most time I have spent with him.

Four Stories

JANE WARRICK

This is my husband. He is a strange man, always talking about beauty, he seduced me with his delicate, innocent ways. Sometimes I think he is more like a woman, his beard merely an obvious disguise. I met him by the river, or rather I noticed him there, doing what I now know to be characteristic – walking with his eyes closed. He thinks people don't notice, but I did, there was an odd look of exhilaration on his face. After that I saw him quite frequently, always in the same sort of places; large buildings after they had emptied of people, broad streets with pedestrians. He never seemed to see me and this I liked, it felt like a secret and at the time I was tired of people.

He never asks me questions about my past and sometimes when he makes love to me his mind wanders; once his eyes closed, his face took on that same look of exhilaration I first saw, and he began to hum. It was as though he'd gone away without effort or knowledge and it was because of me that it could happen. Often myself, I would see beautiful important things, fragments, scenes, I would feel anguish but without the pain. Once I saw an old Chinese man sitting on a structure of bamboo and bandages. I felt calmer, more quiet and awake than ever before. Sex became a journey for both of us, these wanderings were precious and we hardly ever mentioned them.

He's so horribly lonely. I feel it even in his enthusiasm. He keeps pushing himself in front of me, as though giving me the opportunity to touch him, and then fighting the intimacy in the coldest, most desperate way. It's as though I meant to take something from him. As though what I would take is that which makes him charming, clever, what he knows about himself when he enters a room, what he feels is the world when he lies down in the dark.

He talks too loudly, drawing my attention to him; he jumps up to get me a glass of water, summons the waiter, arranges the chairs, turns to me engagingly. "I was thinking . . . what you said . . . you're right . . . but explain the part about . . ." It's so odd, this presentation of himself, as though what I saw him to be was all this noise and action, this performance, as though without this there would be nothing. But he listens to my opinions and I can see he's stimulated.

Then there's a change; something behind his eyes closes. His sympathy is gone, he doesn't understand what I say, is distracted when I explain. His attention wanders, just a little, just enough to make me falter. And then: "I can see you're not sure . . . what actual evidence do you have, apart from your rather touching belief that this is so . . ."

Long ago I stopped trying to be close to him sexually; sex is a series of moves he undertakes with verve and executes with skill. There's no chance there. He prefers to watch me, when I'm dressing and putting on make-up, while he sits there fully clothed and ready to leave. He feels warm, protected; he's watching something intimate and murmuring under his breath, "such vanity."

I was courted by a strange boy when I was sixteen. His eyes shone with a light that was maniacal. I liked it. It made me feel like we were inhabitants of another world. Mother threw up her hands when she saw him. "I'm not going to leave," I told her, "I'm not going anywhere."

It wasn't really true, I planned constantly to leave, not with him but by myself. I wanted to live a different sort of life in another country. I longed to be able to get up in the morning and walk through foreign streets, hear a different language, smell different smells. I imagined being in a white room, full of sunlight, and silent like the grave.

I don't remember Father much, I was too young when he died. All I remember is when he'd come home after work, stand behind her while she was ironing, and wrap his arms around her.

"Stop it. I've got work to do," she'd say and look over at me, "you'll frighten the child." Then she'd shrug him off with that funny smile on her face.

She took me to work with her. I'd sit in the kitchen and watch her do the laundry.

"Damp down the sheets," she'd tell me, and I'd sprinkle water on them and roll them up tightly. She'd lift the iron off the stove, turn it over, and spit on it to see if it was hot enough.

In the evenings we'd play cards. She always won. I watched her as she dealt and although she never seemed to pay any attention she always knew what I had in my hand.

It's funny what you keep. I kept her glasses, even though there's something wrong with them. One day I caught myself doing something I realized I'd done before. I put the glasses on and found myself peering out of the window at the road. Just like she used to do. What is it she was looking for? I used to wonder. What did she expect to see that was different?

I stayed around the house. I always thought I'd leave immediately but I didn't. I'd spent so much time thinking I'd go, but now I found myself sitting by the fire and dreaming, as though it was still impossible.

I finally came here. I'm happy, but what I hadn't imagined was this vague sense of loneliness, cut-off, adrift from everything human and familiar. What I have is indescribable. Sometimes when I wake in the morning I feel an almost painful sense of exhilaration, of possibility. And look – what gifts, what beauty: a rented room in which the furniture hums with a sort of joy.

This is my house. It was once a barn. I knocked out the wall to put in the windows. I built the fireplace and it draws perfectly, a fact of which I'm very proud. In winter when I have guests I tell them, "I made that fireplace, look, it never blows back." Each time I say it I have the same sense of pleasure and achievement.

A friend lived here with me a long time ago, we'd go on long walks together and one year went away, to Italy. Our friendship lasted ten years. She had long dark hair which she'd brush every morning in front of the bedroom window. She died late one summer.

From the kitchen window I can see the sea. I spend a lot of time watching the water move.

I'll die here. One day, when the tide goes out, so will I. I love that thought and hold it close to me like a perfectly circular idea. The way something like that can fill you and nourish you like food is odd. So, too, is the way you can live intimately with someone, and yet, there will always be things about them that are unknown to you.

I like to work in the garden. In the spring of the year following my friend's death, when I was pruning the bushes beneath the windows, I found circles of her hair like little garlands. Every day she must have taken the hair out of the brush, twisted it around her finger, tucked in the ends, and then thrown it out of the window.

I hung one of the circles of hair on a nail above the fireplace. To remind me of all the things I didn't know about her.

6. Desire, Fetish, Commodity

Tea With Madeleine

VICTOR BURGIN

To start again. A train is stopping now at some nameless station and a little girl is turning to her brother in the carriage and is about to say: "Idiot! Can't you see we're at Gentlemen." This in reply to: "Look, we're at Ladies!" (At this point he rushes off down the corridor to pee – not so much because he has to, but rather to reassure himself it's still there.) Tea has now appeared. They look at each other and put it in their mouths. It is a Brief Encounter. *They look at one another and suffer. The lady behind the counter is "common" but speaks with a refined accent (the judgment of Celia Johnson's friend): she is of indeterminate identity and stands behind the bar, there, in the position of the* TREE. *Jack, meanwhile, finds it* occupé. *She, meanwhile, has bolted – rushing out to throw herself under the express; the body in pieces; but she doesn't do it. She goes back into the buffet. The last time that happened was the beginning of it all. The express roared through and she got a cinder in her eye; she went back into the buffet and he said, "I happen to be a doctor," and he got it out for her.*

Olympia's eyes are on the floor, waiting for Spalanzani to pick them up and throw them at Nathanael, who has just burst in. Coppola is hot-footing it through the other door with Olympia over his shoulder, sans *eyes of course. Nathanael is upset. It was Coppola who sold him the spyglass which he used to watch Olympia's room. He didn't know he had danced with such a doll. This is the end of* Casanova. *Outside the cinema it's pouring with rain, pissing down. I had a friend who was driving through a strange town in a rainstorm. He needed to pee, so he stopped the car when he saw a public convenience. It was pissing it down, so he dashed across the road and ran straight into the Ladies.*

Trevor Howard runs into Celia Johnson while she's out shopping and they go and have some tea together, and then they go to the pictures. But most of the time they are at the station and a train is always about to come in, either hers or his. They're always having to go, on different trains. He's closing the door behind him, standing up now. She's closing the door behind her and sitting down. And she's looking out of the window and dreaming. It's this phantasy about being young and free and together and they're in Venice, except she realizes it's just the canal with the willows near where she lives, and this is where she has to get off. Back to her husband and child. Love for duty's sake, says Kant, can be commanded; pathological love cannot.

Kant says she can't.

Tea With Madeleine

"Desire" and the "image" – two terms. And then a third term, the position from which I speak, the "man." Three terms then – "man," "desire," "image" – a triangle of terms where the consideration of one point moves me to the next.

To take the first – "man." "Male," and the opposing term which gives it its sense, "female," labels a body. The most important question asked of any of us is a question we do not, at the time, understand: "Doctor, is it a boy or a girl?" "Female" and "male" are anatomical terms. "Masculine" and "feminine" are sociological and psychological terms, whch designate gender roles and/or psychological characteristics along a spectrum between "active" and "passive." Social roles and psychology may be *assigned,* by convention and institutions, on the basis of anatomy, but they are not otherwise determined by anatomy.

If "*The* woman" does not exist, as Lacan puts it, striking out the definite article ("~~The~~"), then it follows that "*The* man" does not exist either. If I move now, therefore, from my first term, "man," to my second term, "desire," then I am allowed to do so, forming the expression, "man's desire," only if I strike through ~~"man"~~ – placing it, in Derrida's expression, "under erasure": I need the term in order to go on speaking, but it signifies the very concept of which my argument must be most suspicious.

Now to move to "desire." The term comes to us, in this context, from the French, *désir,* which in turn translates Freud's *Wunsch* (also, we might add, *Lust). Whose* desire? And for *what?* "Who," here already under erasure, is of course split: fundamentally, it is the *unconscious* subject that desires. "What," here, leads almost directly to the third term, "image" – "almost" directly, as desire is for an image only via the detour of an object. But the conscious object of desire is always a red herring. The object is only the representative, in the real, of a psychical representative in the unconscious (Freud's "ideational representative" of the instinct). In fact, desire *is* the instinct, as the Lacanians put it, "alienated in a signifier" – the *trace* of a primal, *lost,* satisfaction. The real object, present – most poignantly, the "love-object" – is "chosen" (does *choice* ever really come into it? – "*coup de foudre")* because something about it allows it

Desire comes uncommanded: "Love at first sight"; but, "Love is blind," sustained only insofar as we are mistaken about what it is we want. In Vertigo, *Scottie, an ex-detective, is hired by an old college friend to follow Madeleine, the friend's wife. He falls in love with her at first sight, in Ernie's Restaurant. But Madeleine is not the college friend's wife, she is an impostor, planted to deceive Scottie as part of a plot to kill the real wife. Later in the film, Scottie witnesses Madeleine's death. He has not fully recovered from the trauma of this event when he discovers Judy, a shopgirl who physically resembles Madeleine. But Judy (it is revealed to the audience but not to Scottie) is in fact the Madeleine with whom Scottie originally fell in love – it was not she but the* real *wife whose death Scottie witnessed. Throughout the film Scottie's desire is for an image, the truth of which is consistently denied to him. Image and truth only come together for Scottie at the end of the film, a coincidence which brings about the real death of the person he desired. (Incidentally, Scottie's love for Madeleine fulfills the conditions outlined by Freud in his 1910 paper, "A Special Type of Choice of Object Made by Men.")*

Her voice is distant. It's a little glitter in the darkness. The line crackles and the darkness is swept with snow. The glittering point disappears. Then it's black again. "Hello." The glittering again. She says – close to her is a man he does not know – "I love you." By the telephone is a printed message from the management. An adult movie in your room. Call the desk. They'll bill you seven dollars. The cables run in pipes. The bodies wait, entangled in the lines. There is nothing on the screen but snow.

There was an old Marx Brothers on TV. At the end, there's a huge society party held on a summer night in the grounds of some nob's estate. The lawns run down to the water's edge, the edge of the North Atlantic. And there, on a huge floating stage, is a symphony orchestra, playing for all it's worth. I don't remember how, but it slips its moorings (I suppose the Marx Brothers did it). Nobody in the orchestra notices – they're all too engrossed in their music; sawing and blowing, and the conductor flailing his arms like crazy. They float away. We keep cutting back, between scenes of the party – point-of-view shots from land. Each time, the orchestra is a bit further away, still floating, but quieter, smaller. Then just a spark in the blackness. Then nothing.

It's snowing again. Things were getting hot for Shklovsky. The Cheka were arresting members of the Socialist Revolutionary Party. So he fled to Finland, across the ice, at night, the blizzard lighting up his headlights. It's cold. So cold it freezes your nuts off and shrivels your prick to the size of a trouser button. The size of a pea. You might as well have a cunt between your legs. Shklovsky is crying. Damn. Her makeup is running. She'll look a

to represent the lost object, which is *irretrievably* absent. (Thus Freud identifies the structural unhappiness inherent in all sexual relationships; thus Lacan declares, "There is no sexual relationship" – no possibility of the *union* of mutually complementary beings, only the more or less happy *juxtaposition* of two island universes.) The lost object is something which – it is believed – will repair the rent which has opened up between the subject and the maternal body. (The breast is the prototype of all lost objects.) The "image" here, upon which desire turns, is a psychic image; it may be "visual," but it may equally be tactile, auditory, olfactory, kinaesthetic, gustatory . . ., or it may be a complex of various such images which coalesce through the agency of purely formal associations – for the Lacanians, "through the agency of the signifier." In the triad of terms making up the expression, "man – desire – image" therefore, "man" goes under erasure and "image" goes in scare-quotes. Thus we arrive at an inelegant but necessary deconstruction. ~~The~~ man('s) desire (in/for) the "image."

That's my first trip around the terminological triangle. I began by rejecting an essential "man," simply given in biology. Lacan refers to "he who finds himself male without knowing what to do about it." Over the last decade or more we have seen, in the feminist movements, "those who find themselves female" and moreover, at least in the sphere of political action, "knowing what to do about it." Insofar as the visual image has been seen to assist or incite the oppression of women, we have witnessed a women's *resistance* to the image. "*The* man" may be a fiction, but it is a fiction with real social effects. I believe the calculation of these effects cannot be made in advance of specific conjunctures; I do not believe in *lists* of "good" and "bad" images. No image, in and of itself, can be "sexist"; in and of itself it is a signifier, it is only when that signifier is articulated with others in complex discursive formations in a particular society at a particular moment that we can judge that the consequent meaning-effect/affect is, or is not, "sexist," *oppressive*. So I think the question of *contents* of the image is, in this context, a matter for political calculation rather than theoretical speculation. For me, theory comes in when we ask the question: "What is the *form* of visual imagery consequent upon the form of the construction of the fiction of *the* man?"

In social terms, "at street level," it seems quite obvious that men's desire often results in images which perpetuate the oppression of women. How is this fact to be articulated with the theoretical insight that *the* man – the putative "author" of these images – is a fic-

mess if she ever gets there. She peers into the blizzard trying to pick out the glittering light at the edge of the ice. Distant. A little glitter in the darkness.

It's too hot in this cafe in the hotel in Warsaw. An extravagant display of long-stemmed chrysanthemums shields the pianist from his audience. I Fall in Love Too Easily. *The dress looks like silk. Tight. The sleeves are slashed. Her face is angular; the nose prominent. She is leaving the table she shares with an older woman.* Love For Sale. *Now she is returning, striding past the chrysanthemums, through the thick smoke of cigarettes.* Don't Blame Me. *One foot rests squarely on the ground; the other, arrested in forward motion, touches the ground only with the tips of the toes.* 'Round Midnight. *Western journalists and businessmen circulate amongst the women who lounge in the couches in the bar, dipping into their purses for lipsticks and currency-conversion tables. Room numbers are noted. Framed in the doorway. Blonde, darkening towards the roots. Rouge, blending into white. Green eyes. Yellow light in the corridor. Yellow walls. Yellow dress. Yellow carpet.*

In a dim yellow puddle of light. On the aeroplane. She was reading. A large man's bulk leans over her, his voice dragging in time with the dull grind of the engines: "You have *to be negro, with hair like that." She says: "I want to be alone. I'm sorry. I'm reading." The book resting against her thighs is by Virginia Woolf. In* A Room of One's Own, *she argues that writing is not "spun in mid-air by incorporeal creatures" but is produced by real individuals in specific material circumstances. Women (like working-class men, also) have had only very limited access to the means of literary production: an appropriate education, publishing houses, uninterrupted periods of leisure, and so on, . . . and on, and on, his dull voice dragging along with the sound of the engines.*

I. Sleep. A woman, a beautiful actress, bends over a child in a taxi. They are in a train. Departure is imminent. The woman's face, in close-up, is heavily caked in makeup, not adequately masking open pores. "You're *not my mummy!" I get off the train and run down the platform. I am in Chicago. I must find the airport. How did I come to be so far from home? I must find my way back before it is too late.*

Julia Kristeva admonishes me: "Woman, as such, does not exist!" I have my fourth glass of white wine over the white cliffs of Cape Farewell, the southernmost tip of Greenland. The cliffs rise to eleven thousand feet. Beyond the cliffs, the ice cap begins. In Milan, in the hot summer of 1972, at the conference, JK wore a white dress; when she spoke, someone in the audience released a white bird. It's said that, because of his wartime heroism, Kennedy never doubted his masculinity. I pick up Nothing Sacred *and begin reading about Lulu. I am. Enraptured. The thought occurs, "I wish I could*

tion (just as Barthes reminds us that the author of a novel is as much a fictional character as the other characters we construct at the instigation of the text)? Here, again, we must begin with Freud – with the concept of psychic bisexuality. The question of precisely how "men" and "women" emerge from an initially undifferentiated pre-Oedipal sexuality has provoked storms of confusion, and biologism is the port in which many seek shelter. To deny that biology *determines* psychology is not however to deny that the body *figures*. In certain religions, men wear a lock of hair long, so that when they die God may grasp it in order to lift them into heaven. Lyndon Johnson is supposed to have said: "If you've got them by the balls, their hearts and minds will follow." As a male, *the* man has me by the penis.

The body *figures*, is *represented*, in psychic life. In male psychic life these representations turn between the poles of having/not having the phallus. This is so for the female too, but the male has the means of representing the phallus, as an integral part of his body, in the form of the penis. Male desire, insofar as it leaves its trace in the image, is premised on castration anxiety. I believe we must truly "return to Freud" here in taking the idea of castration quite literally. I believe Lacan's emphasis on the metaphorical nature of the penis/phallus, a greater emphasis than is to be found in Freud, perhaps allows us to see the woman better at the cost of rather dimming our view of the man. Julia Kristeva has spoken of Don Juan as representing the unrestrained masculine libido, endlessly bent on conquest. But we can interpret Don Juan's behavior another way: the most poignant moment for Don Juan is not the *invasion* of the woman's body, but its *investigation*. The most poignant moment for Don Juan takes place, we might say, between the bedroom door and the bed – it's the moment of undressing, it is Don Juan's disappointment at the answer to the question, "what does *this* woman's body look like?" which hurls him onto the *next* woman in this "endless metonymy" (we might say, "endless monotony") of desire. If we did not lack, says Lacan, we would not desire. If the woman's body did not lack, Don Juan would be happy with "This sex which is not Don Juan." I'm reminded here of an antique Roman wall painting of Pan unveiling the body of a sleeping maiden, only to discover that he's uncovered a hermaphrodite. The author of the book in which I saw this image commented that such paintings were intended as a joke – but we may remember that where there is a joke there is a repressed wish. For me, this painting is the very *emblem* of men's desire as inscribed in the image.

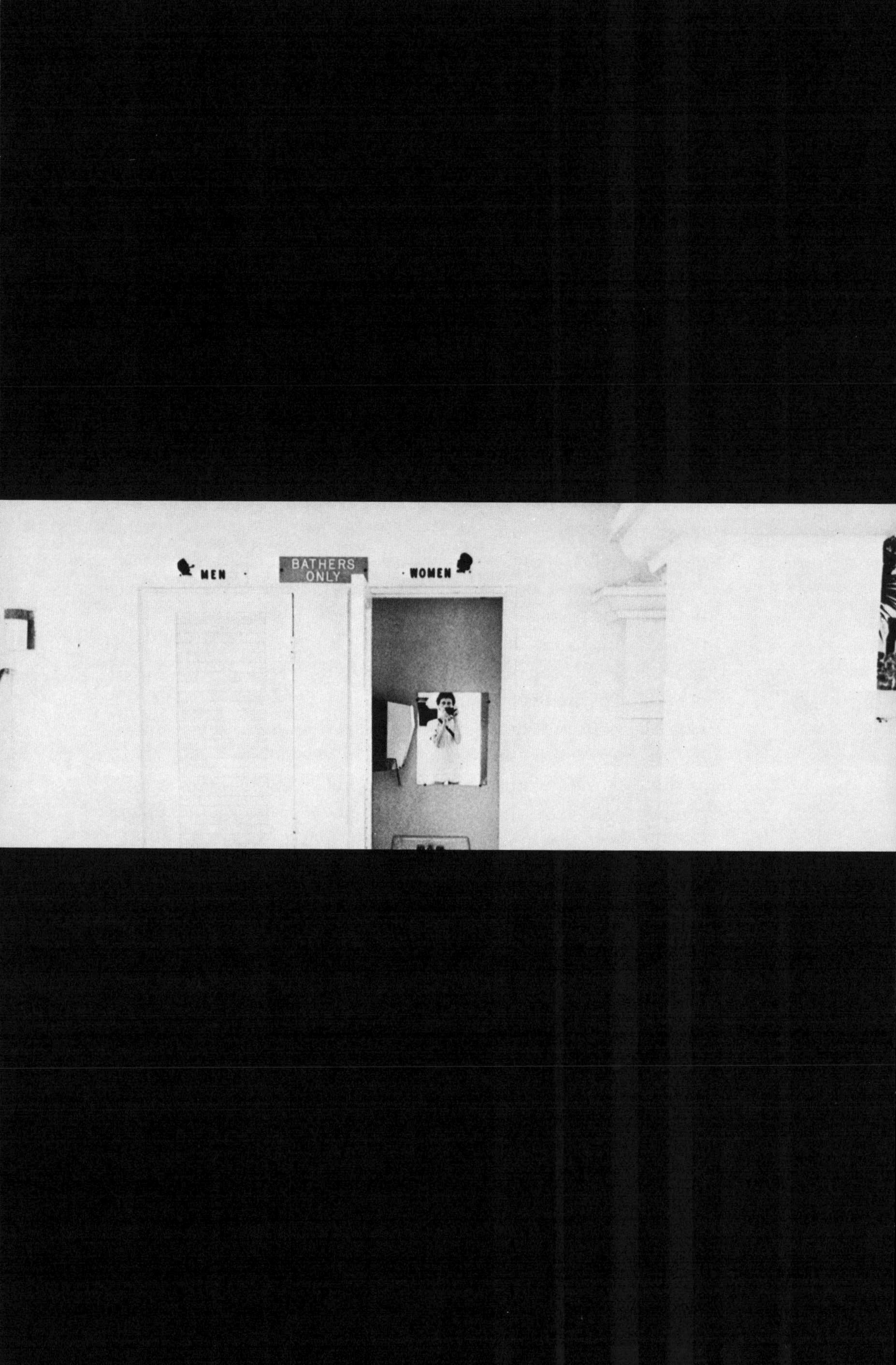
MEN
BATHERS
ONLY
WOMEN

Man's desire in/for the image is lodged under the sign of *fetishism*. The fetish is that fragment which allays the fetishist's castration anxiety by serving as a reassuring substitute for that which he construes as "missing" from the woman's body. Laura Mulvey has remarked on the universal tendency of men to fetishize the entire body of the woman – an attempt to make the totality represent the part which is "lacking." In this connection we might remember the ancient prototype of this perfect woman, Zeuxis' painting of Helen of Troy: commissioned to paint the likeness of Helen, the most *perfect* woman (and in the absence of the original), Zeuxis assembled a composite figure of the best individual features of the most perfect females in the land. The body of the "perfect" woman is a paradox, it is that of which every fragment is a totality.

Man's desire is, most fundamentally, in and for that which can be *seen*. If the penis serves as privileged signifier of the phallus, we are told by several writers, it is because it is *visible*. For example, Freud and Lacan apart (looking now for a woman to speak), Catherine Johns, in her book on the erotic imagery of Greece and Rome, remarks: "The vulva is rarely seen: its situation makes it invisible in any normal position even to its owner. . . ." But I'm made to think of that mainstay of the pornographic photographic genre, the masturbating woman. There she is, eyes closed, touching herself, all laid out for the male voyeur: he sees her, she doesn't see him. But what he cannot see, and never will see, is what *she* is seeing with her closed eyes. We're reminded again that to say "image" is not necessarily to say "visible." We might judge then that the Judy Chicagos – those who would make a meal of the visible vulva – are already working on the side of *the* man in privileging the visible; and, of course, this is indeed the theme of much feminist argument, for example, that of Irigaray: that which is on the side of the woman privileges such things as touch, and scent, above the visual; all those things we experience in "extreme close-up," where vision blurs, where form separates, fragments, dissolves, and spreads. Cameo of mother and child, certainly, but this is not only a female province. Men may not become mothers (Little Hans's fantasies apart), but they have all been children. (I'm stating the obvious to remind us of Kristeva's position, with its stress on a *shared* pre-Oedipal experience, as against that of Irigaray, with its assimilation of the pre-Oedipal to a "woman's language" premised on the woman's body; for Kristeva, as for Freud – albeit the intent may be different – the "feminine" is an attribute of both women *and* men.)

Whether or not we want to accept the idea that the visual is a male domain, it does not help the worker in the visual arts industry to be

have written this." The plane bucks, alarming me. I look to the steward. Mummy does not return my gaze, he is looking elsewhere and smiling; I know I am safe. It is then that it occurs to me, "Perhaps I would have had to be a woman to write like this." It's theoretically unsound, but it's out. It was then that Julia Kristeva snapped at me.

"What's wrong with you?" asked Wanda.

I pointed to the mirror.

"Ah, yes, how beautiful," she cried. "What a pity we cannot keep this moment." "And why not?" I replied. "Wouldn't any painter, even the most famous, be proud to immortalize you with his brush? . . . I am seized by all the shivers of death and nothingness at the dreadful thought that this extraordinary beauty, these marvelous features, these eyes with the strange green fire, this demonic hair and all the splendor of this body, risk being lost to the world . . . But the hand of the artist must rescue you from all that. It must not be that, like us, you disappear entirely and definitively, without leaving a trace of your existence. Your image must survive when you yourself shall be long fallen into dust; your beauty must triumph over death." (Sacher-Masoch, Venus in Furs)

It is the woman's body which reminds men of death. Kristeva says it's not the woman who is repressed under patriarchy so much as maternity – that reminder of the blind continuity of the species at the expense of the individual me. *Besides, I don't want my mother to become someone else's mother – so I'm jealous of the child my lover wants. The periodic fluctuations of the woman's body remind us of the organic, of change – birth, growth, death, birth . . . Men would repress all this in the interests of sustaining the illusion of their own immortality. Liquidity, shape-shifting,* all *change, must be subject to the strictest control.*

The image *is on the side of the feminine. Polysemic. Swept away along streams of associations it provokes but does little to control. "Text" is its pilot (Barthes: "anchorage"). The image is potentially frivolous. It wanders. A "serious" book is one which contains no pictures (and where the words do not seek to "paint" pictures). "Thinking in pictures . . . is unquestionably older than (thinking in words) both ontogenetically and phylogenetically. . . ." (Freud). The image is on the side of the pre-Oedipal. The word stands to it in the relation of the Law – words added to an image always have an air of paternal guidance and/or reproval.*

But there is another way of looking at this. We must be suspicious of this appealing assimilation of image to liberty and word to prison. Patriarchy depends on its divisions. First: the *woman/*the *man. But* the *image/*the *text is just such a form of patriarchal organization. Just as, in patriarchy, the concept of* the *woman is the repository of that "feminine" which a man must*

offered early retirement in lieu of a progressive visual art practice. One direction in which the idea of a "feminine language" (Kristeva's sense) has led has been into an emphasis on the *trace* (in terms of Peircian semiotics, the "indexical" sign – particularly, here, the indices of the fetishized aspects of visual art), it is the trace of the *Artist,* this Other source of imaginary plenitude, this punctual guarantee of authenticity, this Being who does not lack. Another sort of response to the primacy of the visual – other than the attempt to find visual equivalents, or analogues, of primarily nonvisual experiences – has been the response of "troubling" vision, the attempt to undermine its apparent certainties. We can think here of cubism, with its unsettling of classical, single-point-of-view perspective; or of Russian futurist photography, which attempted to "defamiliarize" the visual world by offering, literally, a "new angle" on things. Or again, there has been the practice of intruding words into the space of the image. In all of these cases however, the disturbances are local and temporary, or may be otherwise contained: the representational jumble of a cubist picture is ordered by a formalist logic and held within a single (often golden) frame; new angles on things are only new for as long as they are new; and the words which appear on advertisements do not, simply by their presence, destabilize régimes of the publicity image.

At this point, my speech – having begun, perhaps, on the side of the hysterical – is now becoming more historical. I am also an "artist" – if that means anything at all in this post-Derridean context, it means someone (and he or she is of course far from being alone in this) who must draw practical lessons from theory. If, in order to produce anything, women artists had to wait until the vexed theoretical question of woman's relation to castration had been finally resolved, it would suit men very well – this is a small corner of the marketplace, and no stallholder welcomes increased competition. Paradoxically, it is within this same marketplace that we must peddle our politics (as I've said elsewhere, a "politics of representation" rather than a "representation of politics"). The application of theory in forging a strategy is a wager the outcome of which cannot be certain. How *are* we to avoid the imitation of the fetish?

Structurally, fetishism is a matter of separation, segregation, isolation; it's a matter of petrification, ossification, glaciation; it's a matter of idealization, mystification, adoration. Greenbergian modernism was an apotheosis of fetishism in the visual arts in the modern period. For a long time, Western art aspired to the condition of

evict from himself in order to become the *man, so the concept of* the *image is made up of that which must be expelled from the text in order that the word may become* Law. *To demand that the image be liberated from the word therefore is to make a gesture whose implicit essentialism exacerbates the problem it seeks to cure.*

Is she boring him? She takes a sip of her tea and then changes the subject. When she tells her dealer she intends moving, he says, "Good. That apartment was bad for your image – it wasn't an artist's *place." So there it is, confirmed. She always suspected that her refusal of* that *otherness had contributed to her lack of commercial success. The image of the* Artist *had always stood beckoning in the wings of her imaginary. How tempting to go on stage as that character. Reviving the pleasures of her art-student days, she would entertain critics and curators in her* Studio. *It would be dirty and exciting, showing them things there. Sketches pinned roughly to the walls, paint-caked pallets, oil-soaked rags – the smell of turpentine. (The smell of the makeup, the pinups on the walls of her adolescent bedroom.) All the chaotic paraphernalia of creativity her visitors desire. But the apartment/office from which she works resembles any other – no* sign *of a revolution of the spirit, no coquettish display; hence, low sales.*

He swallows his coffee and wipes his mouth, disappointed that breakfast is over. He often goes to bed looking forward to breakfast. Lunch is a guilty evasion of the day's work. Dinner too often a defiantly excessive solace for the shame of the day's failures. But breakfast is a feast of the innocent. He prefers to take this pleasure alone, but this is the only time he can fit her into his day. The "Garden Café" of her hotel overlooks a carpark, in what is known as a "hooker's district." On the walls are many bad lithographs (obviously from the same hand) in which a variety of domestic flora lounge unhappily in badly-drawn planters. She lounges unhappily opposite him. He shouldn't have said that about her apartment, why was he getting at her?

As she leaves the restaurant he glances at her again. She does not appear to see him. Amongst her symptoms: all the people she sees seem like wax figures; in a bunch of flowers she can only see one flower at a time. She will scatter the nosegay of narcissi on the black waters of the bay. He will descend into that darkness beneath the bridge, where she floats like Ophelia, for love of the face he glimpses just below the surface, believing it to be that of someone other than himself. Throughout the film they will miss each other, or they will miss their trains, waiting until the last possible moment, until they can't wait to go any longer. Then, finally, each will be lost to the other, closing their respective doors behind them.

nonsignificance. "Content," said Greenberg, "is something to be avoided like a plague." Strong words; *anxious* words. The art-object was to signify nothing; that is to say, it must not serve in the place of something which is absent *as the signifier of that absence* but rather it must serve, like the fetish, to *deny* that absence. The modernist art-object denies that there is anything lacking in the field of vision, it represents a canonized empiricism which seeks to cover over the activity of the unconscious in the visual field. The more recent lurch towards expressionism has changed nothing. Today's expressionism, in the wake of modernism, is the obverse face of the same coin, the flip side of the long-playing record of fetishism in the visual arts. The fulfillment of lack is now guaranteed by that mythic Other-who-does-not-lack, locus of fertility, the *Genius.* The artist here figures both as phallic mother and as infant *(in-fans* – "without speech"). It is *his* trace which is left on the canvas – it's not really a metaphor to say that the recent market for freshly-done expressionism has been dealing in shit. From "this object does not lack," we moved to "this artist, whose trace this is, does not lack" – either way, there's no *difference.*

Fetishism denies, "disavows," difference. To do so it presents a *fragment* as self-sufficient. To move against fetishism in visual art is to move "beyond its fragments," beyond its divisions: division of form from content (political subject matter can be fetishized just as much as can be the avoidance of any subject matter whatsoever); division of the private from the social (which after all only maps the division of family life from work in industrial capitalist societies, including those in the East); division of the word from the image (I've written at length elsewhere about what a complete nonsense *that* is); division of the masculine from the feminine in the interests of producing "men" and "women"; division of theory from practice; division of the inside of the institution from its outside (for example, the almost complete isolation of art-historical and critical discourse from the wider analytical discourses – including psychoanalysis and semiotics – surrounding them).

This breaking down of divisions is not a unifying, ecumenical movement – not a denial of difference by other means, not just another road to fetishism. It is in the interest of showing the *meaning* of sexual difference as, precisely, a *process of production;* as something mutable, something historical, and therefore something we can do *something* about.

What is Poetry to You?

CECILIA VICUÑA

In the house of prostitution.

We arrived early one afternoon to interview the girls. At first, they rejected the idea of taking part in the film, didn't want to be seen in it. Many were housewives and mothers and had to conceal the kind of work they did. Nevertheless, when we explained that the film was about poetry, not prostitution, and that all sorts of people – scientists, workers, students – were interviewed too, they agreed to a taped interview, as long as we didn't photograph their faces or talk about their profession.

(Verbatim transcript)

What is poetry to you?

I think that poetry is what each one of us feels inside herself, that lovely thing you have inside, for me, that's poetry. I haven't read much poetry, but that's what I feel, for me, that's poetry, what you feel for everyone you love, the tenderness a mother feels for a child, or let's say, when a woman's in love; she feels that tenderness, yes, it's like a love affair, something like that.

That's what I think.

At least when you look at a flower, inside you feel you want to pick it, like when you have a child and you feel tenderness for that child, for me that's poetry, the inner tenderness you have hidden inside, in the depths of your soul, like the birds, like the tenderness Doña Cecilia felt for the birds over there yesterday, poetry's just like that, the pleasure of seeing those helpless creatures. All that is poetry. Or when you start to watch a stream running and see the purity of the water, for me that is such a natural thing, such a pure thing, and I feel that as something very beautiful.

Do you think that poetry is something written?

No. Inspired.

How do you mean, inspired?

. . . Well, no, because poets, when they're going to write a book about poetry, they get inspired first, don't they? By somebody, a tree, a person, a plant, a flower, that's what I think, the idea I have about it. For me poetry is something very beautiful, very important, above all very fundamental in a person's life, in a human being's life . . . a faraway part, where there aren't any roaring noises of cars, just trees and animals, and if I'm inspired, I'll get a great poem out of it, to write it or tape it, but here in the middle of all this, no, because right now all I think about is money.

But there can be poetry in that, too?

That, too, sure, there can be poetry in everything, even in the feeling, more than anything, and in every act we commit, carry out, think, and desire, can't there? And even in sex there can be poetry, too, yes. Mmmmm.

How do you mean?

For example, I'm doing it, making love with a man, I can be inspired and get a poem out of it, out of what I did, in that moment, of course . . . I've said . . .

You mean, when you like it?

Well, no when I like it and when I don't.

Even when you don't like it?

Of course, it can be a feeling, something deeper. I say that because I feel it, you know? I've felt it and I've experienced it . . .

Then you actually have the power, each time you make love . . .

. . . It can become sublime and beautiful, because, besides, you're making a sacrifice, that sacrifice can inspire you, you can be inspired by anything, by a sacrifice, by an emotion, a moment of happiness, everything, whether you like it or not.

Does that happen often?

Not always, it's something very special.

But do you try to make it happen?

No, I don't try. It just comes to me. Yes, it comes alive inside me and it happens.

But, by trying you can make it happen?

But, by trying for it, every human being, we all have the capacity to make what we want happen, don't we? What happens is that we don't really set out to do it, because all us human beings have the mental, spiritual, and moral capacity to be, if we want, for example, if you want to be a great artist, a great actor, or writer, if you set out to do it, you're sure to do it, because if you feel it with that mental capacity, you'll do it. Pain and suffering are the most beautiful experiences a human being could want, experience costs so much, doesn't it? So the person who hasn't suffered or felt pain, I think, doesn't have the same inspiration as someone who's suffered.

(Translation by Anne Twitty)

Transcendent Anti-Fetishism

ROSS BLECKNER

Latent in every man is the venom of amazing bitterness, a black resentment, something that curses and loathes life, a feeling of being trapped, of having trusted and being fooled, of being helpless prey of impotent rage, blind surrender, the victim of a savage, ruthless power that gives and takes away, enlists a man, then drops him, promises and betrays, and crowning injury, inflicts on him the humiliation of feeling sorry for himself and of regarding this power as intelligent, sentient being, capable of being touched . . .

In each of us this venom is always ready to pullulate in secret, to permeate the organism, darken the sun, change true to false and false to true, an hour into eternity, and to turn all thoughts into the fuel of a somber force consuming indiscriminately our flesh, our reason, talents, and instincts and sometimes even the self-love which is all powerful in man.

Paul Valéry

Paul Valéry was among the turn-of-the-century misanthrope artists and intellectuals who were anxious to get their cultural turmoil and personal angst into a logical order. They found this order in language, the disjunction of symbols manifesting itself in surrealism. With the symbolic order of language, they mapped their reality, their word-and-deed-signifiers, on linguistic charts – the chart, a labyrinth, a point of entry into the latent, the loathing, the onerous and dark. The symbols that were the expression of particular desires carried the tension and power of their discoveries. More than anything, this tension sought its credibility in its logic, but a logic that was transparent. The signals, contained in the symbols that they uncovered, were translucent.

The texts of these artists and intellectuals were analogous ones, their thoughts being the analogues. They gave contradictory questions elementary form. Why this and not that? And then? Why do I need desire to do what I do? Either or, or either this or that? They used an ambiguous, contradictory model of consciousness to understand these questions: they used the model of the dream, the structure of desire that precedes formalizing constraints. This could only have been done by locating themselves at the juncture of memory and language, where dialectical impulses and disparities such as physiological/psychological, natural/cultural, could be examined.

Artists have always sought the language by which they could validate their experience vis-à-vis the things that they put into the world. Art theory has developed out of the problem of locating the coordinates of perception in consciousness, and the art object has been assigned meaning to the degree that an individual consciousness could establish beauty, and/or enjoyment, in the formally entrancing object. This view assumes that there are certain characteristics intrinsic to the objects under scrutiny. But what is really intrinsic is only the linear transference between things that we "know." They then enjoy the benefit of the doubt, and are epistemologically convincing.

In order to reconcile the object with what we in fact do know and feel, it has been necessary for many artists to take the emphasis off the continuous repetition of autonomous moments in the world of feeling and to root these moments in a larger psychological, social, and political reality, meaning by "reality" the authority that an artist has over (and then through) his or her production. This process becomes the translucent symbol of thinking, for "everything about thought is psychological, only the pattern of thought is logical."[1] The work gropes for a meaning that implies a form, a signifier, a substructure with a psychological correlative. Recently many artists have used such axiomatic language to talk about their production. This is discourse, not a stab in the dark. When work addresses desire, and the object made is the function of this desire, the artist works with very little formal "margin." In such a constricted, specific area the possibilities are taut, and categorical terms like "deconstructed," "minimal," and "conceptual" seem empty.

Although a psychoanalytic model is useful because it furnishes plausibility for a cultural model, it is more useful in its approach to the questions of why we do what we do. We are invited to look into desire through the dream, that primary tool for understanding all that is disguised, substitutive, and fictive. We do this not by concentrating on the dream account. Analysis attempts to substitute

1. For a discussion of "the deconstructed object," see Marcia Hafif, "Beginning Again," *Artforum* 17, no. 1 (September 1978): 34-40.

this text, "the primitive speech of desire," for the literal text, the formal account; it does this by moving from one meaning to another, so that it is not desires that are placed at the center of the analysis so much as the form they take, their content (abstractions), and their implications.[2] The symbol becomes the image embodied in the object, and "the vicissitudes of meaning can be attained only through the vicissitudes of instinct" (Freud).

"Desire is always extraterritorial-deterritorialized-deterritorializing. It passes over and under all barriers, and the work of the artist is constantly to be tearing down systems which reify desire, which submit the subject to the social and familial hierarchy."[3] As Poincaré says somewhere, the work of the artist, like that of the inventor, is not to exploit the useless possibilities, but to exploit the useful ones, which are, by far, in the minority: "To invent is to discern, to choose."

The consciousness of desire, the "psychologized object," belongs to the areas of meaning that come under the unified questions: How do desires achieve speech? How do desires make this speech fail? And why do they themselves fail to speak? The investigation of these issues, involving perception in its broadest sense, is the content of art. Little has been said of the psychologized object, and the terms that have been used to designate it as such have been misleading, attaching to it the incorrect attributes of the anthropological, the primitive, and the fetishistic. Resulting from a vast array of psychological variables, and involving itself in fundamental problems of consciousness, the psychological object goes beyond these things and attempts to delineate a place, locating an origin and human intention and going from the ideational to the notional.

In his essay for the catalogue of the exhibition *Pictures* (held at Artists Space, New York, 1977), Douglas Crimp addressed this issue, but misrepresented the struggle by which objects become mediated, resonant, "distanced"–the coefficients of experience, perception, and memory. Assigning an object-image a linguistic or characterological texture does not mean that the object-image functions merely as a sign, or, inversely, that it denies the function of

2. See Paul Ricoeur, *Freud and Philosophy: An Essay on Interpretation,* trans. Denis Savage (New Haven: Yale University Press, 1970), Book II, Part II, especially "The Analogy of the Work of Art," pp. 163-177.

3. Félix Guattari, "Anti-Oedipus: Psycho-Analysis and Schizo-Analysis. An Interview," *Semiotext(e)* 2, no. 3 (1977): 77-85.

the signifier.[4] The message remains fixed in its function as a relayer of action, from which detachment, as a symbol of communication itself, is impossible. "Intensity of feeling does not necessarily correlate with validity of conclusions."[5] A fetish implies a temporary resolution of contradictions intrinsic to the problem of differentiation (this is not you/this is not me); it indicates an arrested development, stagnant and inert. To fetishize is to reify, which makes the object opaque, distant, alien. The fetishizing process operates restrictively at the level of displacement, vacillation, and passivity. To fetishize is to trivialize the palpability of the experience of the object.

On the other hand, psychological and cultural distance is established from a primary drive through mediation (or reflection-imagination-investigation) and objective break. *It* is not you/*it* is not me, but *it* comes with you (the artist): hence, there is a humanizing condition, albeit a tragic one, that engenders the contradictory nature of social relations – the giving up, the transitional. The object negotiates its reality through particular desires, a libidinal cathexis, and not a descriptive encoding.

The transitional object is of interest to us when it becomes an anti-fetish, a force that functions symbolically or multiply ("schizophrenically"), when it evokes characteristics that can be understood in terms of our models, our instinctual desires, and our limited category systems (memory). Thus the great artistic battles are always those that are waged with the self, and they find their fruition in the disparity between things. Power and powerlessness, the cultural and the social, excitation and boredom: instead of providing clear emblems, such dichotomies emphasize the problematic. Otherwise, unreflective insights or narrative passages that are beholden to the hierarchy that they parody (like puns) point without describing, and deprive the object of its symbolic function.

> *A madman who imagines himself a prince differs from the prince who is in fact a prince only because the former is a negative prince, while the latter is a negative madman. Considered without their sign, they are alike.*[6]

4. See Douglas Crimp, "Pictures," in the exhibition catalogue for the show of the same name at Artists Space, New York, 1977.
5. Sigmund Freud, *Three Essays on a Theory of Sexuality* (1908), *Standard Edition,* vol. 7, trans. James Strachey (London: Hogarth Press, 1953).
6. Jacques Lacan, "The Function and Field of Speech and Language in Psychoanalysis," in *Écrits: A Selection,* trans. Alan Sheridan (New York: W. W. Norton & Co., 1977), p. 109, n. 52; Lacan is quoting an aphorism of Lichtenberg.

The problem of artistic creation is the problem of madness and death. The psychological object is verifiable to the extent of its capacity to remodel the means of access it offers the superego for the relief of certain symptoms and inhibitions. Capacities tell us what is possible, and each must also include a conception of purpose: each is a capacity *for*. The capacity of a person or his creation to influence social existence is a power, and the question of consciousness is understood only insofar as we are able to avoid enslavement or subjugation, whether by our ideological models (accumulated meaning), or by an institution.

In turning to a psychoanalytic model for the structure of signification in artistic production, it seems appropriate to engage an exegesis of the intrasubjective symbolic function, one made possible by hermeneutical interpretation rather than by the traditional psychoanalytic theory of aesthetics. By turning to the psychodynamic and mythical tensions, we get away from the more restrictive, unreconstructed Freudian models that predicate the communication of desire on sublimation and "regression in the service of the ego."[7]

The extraction of the symbolic form distilled into the dream text, or the thought text understood as language, and so interpreted, seems more apt than Freud's model of the artist's world view as an expression of fantasy. "The symbolic function presents itself as a double movement within the subject: man makes an object of his action, but only in order to restore to this action in due time its place as a grounding. In this equivocation, operating at every instant, lies the whole process of a function in which action and knowledge alternate."[8]

What gives rise to a psychological object is an intentional structure that consists not in the relation of meaning to thing, but an architecture of meanings in relation to each other. The texture of these interrelations is what makes interpretation possible, although the texture itself is made evident only through the actual movement of interpretation. Art, like language, presents a map of possibilities located in memory and experience; it struggles to go from lesser to greater consciousness (understanding), so that the possibilities can, through signification, congeal into a text that can be seen, discussed, and interpreted. The artist, exercising a so-called

7. Sigmund Freud, *The Interpretation of Dreams* (1900). *Standard Edition*, vols. 4 and 5, trans. James Strachey (London: Hogarth Press, 1958).
8. Lacan, "Function and Field," p. 73.

doxalethic function[9] (the license to violate reality-testing temporarily), interprets one archeology and substitutes for it the object text, by "the calculus of the thought content of desire," or what desire would say were it to speak without restraint or inhibition.

Consider Lacan: "We always come back, then, to our double reference to speech and to language. In order to free the subject's speech, we introduce him into the language of his desire, that is to say, into the *primary language* in which, beyond what he tells us of himself, he is already talking to us unknown to himself, and, in the first place, in the symbols of the symptom."[10] Or Ricoeur: "Too often it has been said that imagination is the power of forming images. This is not true if by image one means representation of an absent, or unreal thing, a process of rendering present – of presentifying – the thing over there, elsewhere, or nowhere. . . . The imagery of sensory perception merely serves as a vehicle and as material for the verbal power whose true dimension is given to us in the oneiric and the cosmic."[11] As Bachelard noted, the poetic image "places us at the origin of articulate being . . . it expresses us by making us what it expresses."

This verbal or visual image, which runs through the representation, is symbolism:

> *Symbols occur when language produces signs of composite degree in which the meaning, not satisfied with designating some one thing, designates another meaning attainable only in and through the first intentionality. . . . Far from lending itself to formalization, it is a relation adhering to its terms. I am carried by the first meaning, directed by it, toward the second meaning; the symbolic meaning is constituted in and through the literal meaning which achieves analogy by giving the analogue. In contrast to a likeness that we could look at from the outside, a symbol is the very movement of the primary meaning intentionally assimilating us to the symbolized, without our being able to intellectually dominate the likeness.*[12]

Thus the psychological object differs from the deconstructed minimal object, which is, by reduction, an affirmation, a statement asserting something of something. The psychological object is a

9. For a discussion of doxalethic function, see Donald M. Kaplan, "Reflections on Eissler's Concept of Doxalethic Function," *American Imago* 29, no. 4 (Winter 1972): 353-376.
10. Lacan, "Function and Field," p. 81.
11. Ricoeur, *Freud and Philosophy*, p. 15.
12. Ibid., pp. 16-17.

negation, separating something from something (me from you, me from myself), it has what Brecht describes as an "estrangement effect." It is the result of negative capabilities and, although didactic, it is not intellectually dominated, or intellectually dominable.

> *The situation in which language today finds itself comprises this double possibility, this double solicitation and urgency: on the one hand, purify discourse of its excrescences, liquidate the idols, go from drunkenness to sobriety, realize our state of poverty once and for all; on the other hand, use the most "nihilistic," destructive, iconoclastic movement so as to* let speak *what once, what each time, was* said, *when meaning appeared anew, when meaning was at its fullest. . . . We have not finished doing away with* idols *and we have barely begun to listen to* symbols.[13]

Prometheus:

> *In those days they had eyes, but sight was meaningless;*
> *Heard sounds, but could not listen; all their length of life*
> *They passed like shapes in dreams, confused and purposeless.*
> *Of brick-built, sun-warmed houses, or of carpentry,*
> *That had no notion; lived in holes, like swarms of ants,*
> *Or deep in sunless caverns; knew no certain way*
> *To mark off winter, or flowery spring, or fruitful summer;*
> *Their every act was without knowledge, till I came.*
> *I taught them to determine when stars rise or set—*
> *A difficult art. Number, the primary science, I*
> *Invented for them, and how to set down words in writing—*
> *The all-remembering skill, mother of many arts.*
> *I was the first to harness beasts under a yoke*
> *With trace or saddle as man's slaves, to take man's place*
> *Under the heaviest burdens; put the horse to the chariot,*
> *Made him obey the rein, and be an ornament*
> *To wealth and greatness. No one before me discovered*
> *The sailor's waggon—flax-winged craft that roam the seas.*
> *Such tools and skills I found for men . . .*[14]

Prometheus accomplishes all this by using the stolen gift of fire. By presenting—and representing—new modes of production, he leads man into a period of self-liberation, providing the crucial

13. Ibid., p. 27.
14. Aeschylus, *Prometheus Bound and Other Plays,* trans. Philip. Vellacott (Harmondsworth, Eng.: Penguin Books Ltd., 1961), p. 34.

contribution in the transition of infantile man into a state of civilization and productivity. His narcissism, his audacity, his manipulation of reality causes him to be chained to a rock for thirty thousand years, while a vulture tears at his liver. The themes of aggression/submission, power/powerlessness, love/hate, and control/being controlled, are salient throughout the myth.

Do we control or are we controlled by what we see? Does our reality induce images or is an image a design that we use to map our reality? Does experience take a back seat to the reality of images (things), or can the experience of images inform the internalization of our reality? Is our real trivial, or do our representations of it trivialize it?

When we are conditioned (through simulation and displacement), when we use other than ourselves to record, when we get it through the media and popular culture, we are talking icons and signs and not perceiving forces and flows. As in religion, this reality is of things above, looking down, and it "blind[s] us to other realities, and especially the reality of power as it subjugates us. [Its] function is to tame, and the result is the fabrication of docile and obedient subjects."[15] If reality strikes us as a cultural, and not a psychological dynamic, then our representations of it are as docile as the forms by which we receive it (as itself). We are placated by merchandising techniques that validate these forms. Identity with these images – which are more real than our memories, which seem to be more personal only because we are the result of them – certainly does nothing to establish a critical relationship with them. Impoverished object relations always result in the fetish. Creation of the self is only possible at the moment of division from (or contact with) the other. One experiences self in relation to what is not self. The struggle for differentiation is a critical struggle, and when the transition cannot be made, when there is total cultural amalgamation, we only know ourselves through culture's fabrications. Or, what we internalize is only a composite of history's ideological misinterpretations.

People then seek their object relations through the emblems of the culture, and things like television, stars, doctors, and mechanical gadgets take on monumental significance. What is crucial about the symbol (as communication, inquiry, discourse, notion, and not

15. Mark Seem, "Introduction," in Gilles Deleuze and Félix Guattari, *Anti-Oedipus: Capitalism and Schizophrenia,* trans. Robert Hurley, Mark Seem, and Helen R. Lane (New York: The Viking Press, 1977), p. xx.

as a universal sign in the Jungian sense), or about the text, is that it is a critical embodiment of desire that does not reiterate and is not beholden to a codified, generalized model of meaning. "Libido is primarily object-seeking rather than pleasure-seeking."

The sign represents primary intentionality; whether it be the retinal registration of images, more expressive forms of representation, or patterning, all function only at the level of discharge. They are easy because they operate at the lowest level of psychic tension, ventilation. They point to ready solutions and pat formulas. Just as speech desires reply, even if it implies nothing, even if it denies the evidence, even if it is intended to deceive, the discourse represents the existence of the communication that constitutes truth. A reaction is not a reply.

Pre-logico-symbolic thought, attempting the reconciliation of the irreconcilable, avoids problems of the tragic, of the deadly consequences of "I" versus other, of difference and of contradiction. The infant "I" fears the death that separation denotes. The transitional "I" is physically charged by confronting threatening psychodynamic challenges. The reconstruction, in psychodramatic terms, of fragmented memory, of partial objects, takes place in an ambiguous region, where signification is the function of symbolic intentionality. The notion stops before the idea, or begins after the idea, and is not categorical. This is a restless state where no image is satisfactory. There is overlap, contradiction, and ultimate entropy.

Vito Acconci, for example, has continually employed notional categories of memory to signify fundamental desire/need discrepancies that the "I" might undergo in transition or in relation. The tension between attraction and repulsion: one is always a comment on, and reflection of, the other, in a going *toward.* Reality does not *come* in one way or another; instead the contradictions that constitute the tension between different cathected states evoke our memory of this tension. Our images are transitive as well as transitional, for going toward something indicates the passage from a lesser to a greater knowledge and awareness: "Knowledge comes about insofar as the object known is within the viewer."[16]

Desire is a perpetual effect of symbolic articulation. The reality that an artist ascertains through his work, the degree to which it is

16. An aphorism of Thomas Aquinas.

there within him, within his memories, grids the chart for the negation of external control. The giving up of infantile notions of value, which is understood in terms of something being pleasurable or unpleasurable, and the transition to the renunciation of the passive love object, move the understanding of value to control,[17] control being the strength or weakness that one has in his productions (how much he is willing to relinquish), as a way of renegotiating a relationship to autonomous objects. External control (the parent) is superseded by self-control (relations with the self/other). The essence of mobility is the ability to go from the one to the other.

The idea of self-control involves elements of mastery. Thus we get out of ourselves by and through the control we have over ourselves and our work (production). Our production indicates a going toward something else; it signifies the dynamic relation of something with the outside without codifying that relation. We get out of ourselves by going into ourselves and evoking the dialectical tension of this symbolic discourse. Obsessiveness and ritual are the meaningless activities that support empty gestures and decorative repetition. The notional space in which delusion, madness, and death are ferreted out in reality-testing is the place where symbols are taken in, and where they are issued as communication itself.

The psychological image, like the dada and surrealist literature and art that predates it, destroys, by calling our attention to the differences between the superficial and the symbolic. It demystifies our reactions to the formalized logic which aestheticizes superficiality. It is not so much the actual structures that we create, but the memories of psychological variables that characterize our desire to make structures. By synthesizing the dramatic aspects of our existence, the artist does not attempt to cosmeticize radical linguistic and psychological models. Instead, these insights are put into another form, the notion form or the chart form. Such systems proceed by, as it were, entering into the same maze, but at different points. Ultimately, all the questions are the same.

This view implies a declaration of principles, of social reality, of vision, of differentiation, of transition, passage, and memory. It is puzzling because it asks and answers questions in no particular order or way. It is a black pool, reflective, translucent, taut, associative, ambitious, and evocative. It is also a trap that is critical of its capacity to trap, to fool, to evoke.

17. Edith Jacobson, *The Self and the Object World* (New York: International Universities Press, 1964).

The Paintings are Dead

DAVID SALLE

1. The paintings are dead in the sense that to intuit the meaning of something incompletely, but with an idea of what it might mean or involve to know completely, is a kind of premonition of death. The paintings, in their opacity, signal an ultimate clarification. The paintings do this by appearing to participate in meaninglessness.

2. The movement towards meaning contained in the uses of the subject matter is a sign of the approach of death. It is the viewer's will to make sense which brings the paintings down (as the hunter brings down the bird). This is similar to the mechanism of man's inquiry into his own nature which brings about his undoing in Greek tragedy.

3. I'm interested in work which makes you think that you're going to have to keep paying out the rest of your life.

4. The works are connected to the erotic life in more than just subject matter. They align themselves with the state of being in love; there is nothing more involved in prefiguring its own end than love and sex. Each new affair, each new fixation already contains the fantasy of the next – of the bittersweet sensation of bringing this affair to an end and, more importantly, of surviving it, and being able to recreate it mentally; to exist in the perfect tense by seeing the object of a fixation recede in the distance; becoming fragmented and untrue.

5. The way this art works is to make you want it to disappear so that you can mourn its loss and love it more completely.

6. The operative method of the work is like the spurned lover, clinging to someone or something when no longer wanted. These paintings are to life as the overzealous lover is to the loved.

7. The paintings measure our feeling that images control our lives. The images in the paintings take over our own because of their similarity – much the way commies took over government jobs by infiltration through the subtle ways they understood what was required to fulfill those jobs – because of their sensitivity to "modes of presentation."

8. To redeem the present tense time of looking at them, the pictures have to disappear from that time – recede into the distance. The work has to go away (reject the present) in order to redeem the present from a meaningless "looking at something." This is connected to loving someone who is nothing. A beautiful paradox – to love something or someone whom you know to be nothing, or of doubtful existence. There is a way in which that knowledge fuels the love and allows it to be a record of futility.

9. Connection making is seen as replication or renewal for the soul. We pursue metaphor to understand the first thing compared. What we love most is for something to be "put into words."

10. I am interested in infiltration, usurpation, beating people at their own game (meaning scheme). I am interested in making people suffer, not through some external plague, but simply because of who they are (how they know).

11. I am interested in the elevation of the arbitrary and contrived to the level of the ineluctable; not ineluctable in the sense of some higher purpose, but just arbitrary and inevitable at the same time.

12. I am interested in the pictures' ability to make felt a "you" addressed by the picture . . . an idealized nonexistent "you" which nonetheless takes on a certain credibility. The pictures' strength is in making the real "you" congruent with the "you" addressed by the picture by a process of complicity – which becomes surprising in this case because, paradoxically, it is what we expect a picture to do anyway.

13. The pictures present improvised views of life – normalized, but, in fact, as it is never seen. The pictures imitate life to find a way out of it.

On Line

PETER HALLEY

Suddenly, in sixties art, images of circles began to appear. There were Noland's targets, the circular arrangements of Smithson, the ring-shaped configurations of Morris and Serra. The sixties assigned to this impetus to the circle the meaning of unity – the circle was held to be an orb, an image of completeness, a sign for unity. But the appearance of these circle motifs represented something more complex. In almost every instance, the center was empty. The character of these circle-images turns out to be not solid but linear. This art announced that, from that time on, line was to turn back in on itself, that the linear had ceased to cut its way through the undergrowth of Nature, that the linear was complete, and that henceforth line would flow into line in endless circularity.

The Interstates. They wind majestically through the cities – elevated disinterestedly on pale concrete piers. They course through the open land, bridging chasms, leveling hills, skimming over swamps. Along these routes, advertising is prohibited, and all buildings have been removed. The broad right-of-way is landscaped with well-kept lawns and orderly rows of trees, as befits a ceremonial site.

They span the nation along evenly spaced north-south and east-west routes. The north-south routes are labeled I-5 to I-95 in intervals of ten, while the east-west routes are numbered I-10 to I-90. A third digit prefix is added to the code to denote the interaction of the Interstate with the city (as a beltway, a by-pass, or a business district extension). The system makes of the country an all-encompassing Cartesian grid. It is our greatest monument to the linear.

From the 1860s to the 1920s, art heralded the coming of the linear universe. First in Manet, then in Gauguin, then in Matisse, drawing was freed from the confines of *chiaroscuro*. Drawing was freed – and line was freed to become a pictorial force that demonstrated the role the linear was coming to play in the social. Then in cubism and neoplasticism, the linear universe was described as well established: in cubism the real gave way to the vector and was replaced by the diagrammatic. Neoplasticism then described the apotheosis of the linear in all its glory.

Behind the wheel: it is to be at the altar of the linear. Hands grasping the cool plastic of the linear made circular. Eyes on the road. Following not only the road, but the cool geometry of the lines that divide the road into lanes. At nightfall, the landscape and even the road gradually disappear, and we are left only with this display of linear signs glowing in phosphorescent paint under the headlights. On the road. It is said for us to be the greatest feeling of freedom. But the feeling is really that of oneness. On the road, behind the wheel, hurtling down the highway, there is a feeling of unity with the formal power of the linear. It is our theater of the philosophic.

In the city, on the other hand, we feel overwhelmed by the complexity of these linear networks. The street, of course, is also an artery of circulation. Its efficiency is enhanced by the system of traffic lights that use colored signs to cause the stream of cars to ebb and flow. But the street is also a roof covering another massive network of circulation that runs below it. Below, there are pipes carrying water, sewage, and gas. There are wires that carry electricity, telephone lines, and cable television. There are tunnels for subway trains and underpasses that carry still more automobiles. It is this bundling of the linear, this creation of parallel systems of circulation, that characterizes modernity.

There has developed a formal pattern universal to this system. It is the formalism of the cell and the conduit, the formalism of plugging in. The 747 pulls up to the gate and immediately technicians appear with hoses, electric lines, and ramps connecting the plane to conduits from which flow fuel, electricity, baggage, and passengers. The patient in the hospital is hooked up to oxygen and to an I.V., while the office worker is hooked up to a computer terminal. At home, we plug in for everything that used to be natural, be it wind, light, heat, or water.

The cell. Its ubiquity reflects the atrophy of the social and the rise of the interconnective. At the same time that the advent of piped-in "conveniences" has made it *unnecessary* to leave the cell, it has also made it *impossible* to leave the cell. One finds oneself stuck at home waiting for a phone call; instead of entering the social, one must stay within the cell to communicate with someone else. Or one stays at home to watch something on television, in order to be entertained or informed by human beings. One enters another cell, the automobile, to travel from the cell – and the automobile too is increasingly being outfitted with communications equipment to make it a desirable place in which to remain.

The mechanism of cell conduit, while universal, is hidden. The automobile may travel from destination to destination along various routes of circulation, but only when it stops at a gas station does it plug in. Filling up, that minor task, is actually the essential part of the system. Similarly, in the home, the conduits are hidden, ignored, not noticed. Plumbing is sealed in the walls, electrical sockets are placed inconspicuously in baseboards, heating systems are in the basement.

This is a realm without absolutes. The linear networks contain cells, but the cells also contain linear networks in endless progression. The airliner is a cell, but it contains miles of wiring and tubing. The home is a cell, but within the home are to be found machines with their own networks of circuitry.

In the 1920s, the idea of linear abstraction was at its height. Linearity was a goal, an ideal that could only be fully expressed in a work of art, whether painting, sculpture, or architecture. But today the closure of the linear universe has long since been achieved. Linearity has now abandoned abstraction and taken on the mantle of the diagrammatic. Today linearity backtracks and seeks to appropriate for itself the trappings of the old reality of specificity. This is the impetus behind the diagrammatic representation of video games and computer graphics, airport signs, and the smile-have-a-nice-day symbol of the seventies.

New York is the quintessential city of the heroic era of linear conquest. With its strictly gridded and numbered streets, New York insists constantly on the Cartesian quality of its plan. The lines of its great skyscrapers surge transcendentally into the air in defiance of gravity. The networks of conduits tunnel far underground, then rise giddily into the air. (The elevator, that vertical road, is a key element of this spatiality.) The ground line of the earth is ignored. The linear structures expand in three dimensions with Dionysian frenzy.

In Los Angeles, as well as in other cities of the suburban era, the linear no longer struggles defiantly against the forces of gravity and topography. The grid simply spreads horizontally, two-dimensionally, casually, almost naturally over the landscape – like Borges's ideal map that covers the landscape itself (as cited by Baudrillard).

The semiconductor chip conforms to this same model of two-dimensional planar circulation. Gradually, just as the social has been transferred onto this schema of highways and malls, so is memory and knowledge being transposed onto these miniature circuits.

The shopping center, the strip center – it has abandoned the city and the town and clings to the circulatory system of the highway. But the shopping center itself is also a model of circulatory efficiency. It is placed adjacent to the highway, which has already gathered a vast flow of cars from many tributaries. Its huge parking lot, many times larger than the shopping area itself, is easily negotiated by means of a well-designed system of circulation, with one-way signs, turn-off lanes, and multiple entrances onto the road. In back, the plate glass, supergraphics, and planters give way to cinderblock, long rows of loading docks, and dumpsters. Here, goods are received from the same system of highways and access roads that supplies the customers. Consumer and producer arrive along the same pathways and are then split into separate routes of entry. The goods are fed in from the back, where they are easily unloaded onto raised platforms that match the height of the trailers of the giant delivery trucks. The goods are then unpacked and distributed onto shelves and racks. Meanwhile, the customer is fed in from the front and is guided to aisles which are a continuation of the circulatory model of the highway's lanes. Finally, the shopper is channeled into a line which leads to the cashier and the only exit.

MacDonald's and other fast-food stores also obey this circulatory imperative. Their exterior circulation is like that of the shopping center. They have easy access from the road and ample parking. Moreover, here one can even choose to "drive thru" – thus minimizing the interruption to one's linear peregrinations. Inside, the arrangement of the tables mirrors that of the parking lot outside. Customers are channeled into lines as they enter; then, as they reach the counter and the cashier, they are met with their food channeled from the sophisticated factory-like production mechanism on the other side. After leaving their tables, the customers are encouraged to combine their waste by dumping their trays into formica-covered, woodgrained trash bins with the words "thank you" on them.

The stimuli of the modern world – sounds and sights – are reproduced and distributed through endless systems of linear technology. (The more intimate senses were long ago excluded from this order.) Stereo and video are recorded onto tape, that opaque blackish substance that symbolizes the intransigent, incomprehensible linear time of this universe. Computers and record players use flat disks whose spiral roadways reflect the circularity of their contents. All visual and aural information – speech over the telephone, the television picture, computer data – is encoded into lines of electronic information. The linear becomes language. The arcane discipline of electronic circulation now guards the gates of the senses.

The proliferation of the computer is the development that most insures the closure of this system. In the computer, we see physically affirmed, as if by an independent source, all the assumptions of linear thought. Conversely, the computer ignores all utterances not made according to the rules of its own linear code. With the advent of private computer use, the computer becomes an oracle of instruction in the structures of the linear. It gives instruction in how to write and how to conduct business – but according to its own linear rules. It is even deployed to indoctrinate children into the ways of the linear. Further, as greater and greater amounts of society's information (both financial and intellectual) are stored in computers, even the reluctant are coerced into dealing with the computer and its pattern of thought.

Color and drawing. They are the watchwords of a certain kind of formalism in the visual arts. The emphasis on drawing reflects the modern omnipresence of the linear, but the importance given to the role of color also has a meaning. Color in modernism is sometimes seen as a means of enacting an ideal of hedonistic release – of the freeing of the bourgeois sensibility from the constraints of morality and the symbolic. But this emphasis on color reflects the crucial role that color plays in the realm of the linear. In the planar universe, only color is capable of coding the linear with meaning:

colored lines on maps distinguish the character of highways. Wires are colored to mark their purpose. In hospitals, one can even follow colored bands on the floor through labyrinthine corridors to one's destination.

The linear world has its own kind of space and time. Virilio has analyzed the transition from geopolitics to chrono-politics. Distance between places is now measured in time spent in the linear networks of transportation. But matrices of streets, hallways, corridors, and elevators also alter the space and time of the social. In the city, two individuals may live a few feet apart in adjacent apartments, in adjacent buildings, on the same floor, without ever meeting or even considering each other's existence. Space here is stretched by distance in three dimensions as well as by the distance-value of various barriers such as walls, doors, and elevators.

In the sixties, the astronauts' purpose was to orbit the earth, to inscribe a circle through the heavens around the planet. It was a great public spectacle and an event of great ritual significance. In their reflective silver suits and gleaming capsule (an archetypical cell with only the most limited maneuvering capacity and a tiny window), their epic flights announced the closure of the linear for all humanity to see (on television): the linear and the abstract would now circumscribe the natural. The speculative tradition of Descartes, Kant, and Hegel had remade the world. It was as if the magic of the shamans had been proven all-powerful, and the shamanistic recipes had banished the mysteries of Nature for good. The system had become closed, had become a massive machine for reproducing its own assumptions, had reached in the orbital model a condition of stasis.

Casual Imagination

JUDITH BARRY

In literature, indeed, even the great criminal and the humorist compel our interest by the narcissistic self-importance with which they manage to keep at arm's length everything which would diminish the importance of their ego. It is as if we envied them their power of retaining a blissful state of mind—an unassailable libido-position which we ourselves have abandoned.

The great charm of the narcissistic woman has, however, its reverse side; a large part of the dissatisfaction of the lover, of his doubts of the woman's love, of his complaints of her enigmatic nature, have their root in this incongruity between the types of object-choice.[1]

The activity of shopping directly engages the shopper in the generation of a complex narrative all her own. In a sense she is the protagonist of the detective story, following her own desire as she moves through the store, but not to the scene of the crime. Access to her desire is so difficult, so mysterious. . . . Hence the difficulty for each of us in finding out what really interests us.

If woman is enigmatic, it is because she has reasons—good ones—for hiding herself, for hiding the fact that she has nothing to hide . . .[2]

Shopping is marked by a series of exchanges, of looks and projections, in an environment that is deliberately mazelike, composed of inhabitable space that is only corridors. Pedestrian space as such for resting, occupying in groups, and sitting down does not exist. All of this space is filled with items to purchase, and with the application of Bauhausian principles to store design, the architecture itself has been completely effaced.

In one sense the architectural plan could be said to describe the nature of human relations since it marks the elements it recognizes—the walls, doors, windows, and stairs, which both divide and selectively re-unite inhabited space.[3]

1. Sigmund Freud, *On Narcissism: An Introduction* (1914). *Standard Edition,* vol. 14, trans. James Strachey (London: Hogarth Press, 1953), p. 89.
2. Sarah Kofman, "The Narcissistic Woman: Freud and Girard," *Diacritics* 10, no. 3 (Fall 1980): 36.

3. There are severe methodological problems in treating architecture and human relations as part of the same textual system, in addition to the collapsing of class and ideology into the

By the end of the fifteenth century, the madonna and child had become earth-bound. These figures are more than the subject of the picture – they *are* the picture, they fill it completely. A look at the floor plans for villas of the period reveals a tendency toward the same corporeality. It is difficult to tell which parts of the building are enclosed and which are open; the relationship between all the spaces is similar throughout. The chambers, gardens, loggias, and courts all register as walled shapes – they add up to fill the site. Doors and stairs are used only to connect adjacent rooms. This plan shows that there was no qualitative distinction between the way through the house and the inhabited space within it. In these villas, household members had to pass through room after room to conduct their business, with the effect that every activity was liable to be interrupted unless definite measures were taken. Similarly, as we know from the writings of Castiglione, Erasmus, and Cellini,[4] social contact in the villa was normal and privacy/solitude the exception. Rarely is architecture mentioned specifically in the writings of this period and there is a predominance of figure over ground. These figures occupy the room, but there is no indication of what these rooms were actually like.

Department stores are transparent so that nothing interferes with the shopper's vision. While space planning has remained quite rigid over the last forty years, display techniques have continued to improve, particularly in relation to the variety, wattage, and mood of the lighting utilized. In addition, total environments are often built entirely of transparent materials, creating a phantasm (phantom) of set design.

Consider the difference in the utilitarian design of the supermarket versus the department store. The supermarket has high shelves and straight aisles allowing for the maximum amount of goods to be presented in a minimum amount of space.

The man with the proper imagination is able to conceive of any commodity in such a way that it becomes an object of emotion to him and to those whom he imparts his picture, and hence creates desire rather than a mere feeling of ought.[5]

assumed transparency of architecture, but since I set out to describe *how* the commercial space, specifically the department store, is mediated by the television commercial, I had to propose a relation. In this sense this article might be considered a textual reading of the spaces buildings occupy and the social relations within them. I found Robin Evans, "Figures, Doors and Passages," *Architectural Design* 48, no. 4 (1978): 267-278, extremely useful in formulating some of these relations.

4. See Castiglione, *The Courier;* Cellini, *Autobiography;* Erasmus, *Epistolai.*

5. Walter Dill Scott, *Influencing Men in Business* (New York: The Ronald Press, Co., 1911; enlarged ed., 1928), p. 131.

Can we say that buildings accommodate what pictures represent – the social relations of a particular period in history? Can we generalize about these relationships by examining the plans, photographs, and paintings of an epoch for characteristics which might allow for or provide insight into the ways in which people occupy space?[6]

After about 1650, a radical reorganization took place in home design. Entrance halls and back stairs combined to create a network linking the rooms of the entire house. Every room had a door or a passageway into the hall. At first, the corridor was installed parallel to the connecting room, but gradually it replaced the adjoining door completely. This parallel division functioned to give the family direct access to one another and also served to keep the servants in the adjacent area: an area that was not thought of as a place, but as an activity – a corridor, a passageway. This innovation mirrored the increasing desire for privacy and a simultaneous strain on the relations between the classes. The compartmentalized building was organized as a thoroughfare, because movement was the only thing that could give it coherence.

Private life, thrust into the background in the Middle Ages, invades iconography, particularly in Western painting and engraving in the sixteenth and above all the seventeenth century.[7]

The corridor had another effect: as a thoroughfare it was able to draw rooms at a distance closer, but only by disengaging those close at hand. The corridor facilitated communication, particularly speed, but diminished contact. Privacy and uninterrupted solitude could not be secured.

The family, which had existed in silence but "did not awaken feelings strong enough to inspire the poet or artist," became a concept. This powerful concept was formed around the conjugal family, as opposed to the "line" – that of parents and children, and the specific relation between them that the concept of childhood refined.[8]

As the events of the seventeenth century were displaced onto the nineteenth, the body was conceptualized differently. It lost its carnality and was seen as spiritual otherness – just as the telling of

6. Evans, "Figures, Doors and Passages," p. 274.
7. Philippe Ariès, *Centuries of Childhood: A Social History of Family Life*, trans. Robert Baldick (New York: Vintage Books, 1962), p. 347.
8. Ibid., pp. 339-364.

sexual thoughts, desires, and transgressions became part of confessional discourse. Consider the famous Pre-Raphaelite painting by William Morris, the bohemian English designer, in which his wife Jane is the subject of his representation of Guinevere. There the body becomes the site of an invisible occupant. The objects surrounding her and the space they mark are stand-ins for her spiritual presence.[9]

The old code of manners was an art of living in public together. The new code emphasized the need to respect the privacy of others.[10]

The matrix of connected rooms was appropriate to a society that valued carnality, recognized the body as the person, and experienced gregariousness as habitual. The corridor plan, which completely replaced the Renaissance villa plan, signified the drastic separation of those three functions. What was previously united under one roof was now institutionalized as consumption, production, and distribution in distinct parts of the city. The corridor plan was also appropriate to a society that found carnality distasteful, that separated the body, dividing it into a multitude of discourses, and that regarded privacy as habitual.

The design in the mind of the architect belongs to an order of eternal truth which the actual building expresses in material stuff.[11]

Prior to the sixteenth century, no buildings existed that contained a stage and an auditorium with spectator seating. In his Gran Teatro delle Scienze, Giulio Camillo (ca. 1475-1544) hoped to construct a model theater that reversed the relationship of spectator to audience. Originally, Camillo had thought to use the metaphor of the human body as a microcosm of the universe in order to illustrate his memory system, but later he chose instead the ancient metaphor of the world as a great theater.[12]

May we not regard every living being as a puppet of the gods, which may be their plaything only, or may be created with a purpose.[13]

9. Evans, "Figures, Doors and Passages," p. 274.
10. Louis Sebastian Mercier, *Les Tableaux de Paris* (Paris: Gustave Desnoiteres, 1853), p. 19.
11. Frances A. Yates, *Theatre of the World* (London: Routledge & Kegan Paul, 1969), p. 191.
12. Ernst Curtius, *European Literature and the Latin Middle Ages,* trans. Willard R. Trask (Princeton: Princeton University Press, 1953), pp. 138-144.
13. Plato, *The Laws of Plato,* trans. Thomas L. Pengle (New York: Basic Books, 1980), Section I, line 644d, pp. 24-25.

Camillo was attempting to combine the form of the encyclopedia with the Ciceronian mnemonic method of visual "loci" for the retention of knowledge or orators. The art of memory was associated with images. Pictures were believed to signify an ultimate reality which words could not represent. In one hour, by occupying the center of the stage, the scholar could master the universe which the theater reconstructed through a Vitruvian ordering of the planets in conjunction with elements from Christianity, Neoplatonism, Hermetics, and the Kabala. Along with the memory theater came the conviction that man could grasp and hold the greater world – of which he, man, is the image – through the power of his imagination. Imagination became man's highest power and he could obtain the world beyond appearances by holding onto significant images.

Before the invention of printing, oral memory became codified into rules. According to Cicero, the invention of the art of memory rested on Simonides's discovery of the superiority of the sense of sight over the other senses. "Simonides," says Plutarch, "called painting silent poetry and poetry painting that speaks." Poetry, painting, and mnemonics were seen as intense visualization. By the Middle Ages the art of memory had been dropped from rhetoric and degraded as a memory aid for a weak man who had to use corporeal similitudes to retain his spiritualness.[14]

All the world's a stage,
And all the men and women, merely players.[15]

In the late sixteenth century, Andrea Palladio designed the Teatro Olimpico in Vicenza, based on a reconstruction of a Vitruvian theater. Its proscenium represents the stylized facade of a two-story palace and, as in the traditional Roman theater, it has five doorways, three in the back and one on each side. What is most unusual about the theater is its use of stage design in perspective (the contribution of Vincenzo Scamozzi, who completed the theater after Palladio's death) to give the illusion that the five doorways on the twenty-foot stage empty into the street. It might be interesting to consider the relationship of the use of perspective and its representation in the theater to the development of the Enlightenment city.

14. See Frances A. Yates, *The Art of Memory* (London: Routledge & Kegan Paul, 1966), pp. 129-159, and Douglas Radcliff-Umstead, "Giulio Camillo's Emblems of Memory," *Yale French Studies,* no. 47 (1972): 47-56.
15. William Shakespeare, *As You Like It,* ed. Richard Knowles (New York: Modern Language Association, 1977), Act 2, Scene 7, lines 147-148.

The first boulevard was designed by Sebastiano Serlio in 1507 for an Ariosto play; the illusion of the boulevard existed before the boulevard. Many of the ways in which perspective might be utilized were formulated by men who today we would call military strategists (although at the time there was no such profession – hence the term "renaissance man"). Theater for the "renaissance" mind represented imagination in space, not fiction. Early plays were often historical tableaux performed in the palace.

Serlio's five books of *Architettura* did more to turn the theater in the direction of the frenetic expansion of Vitruvius's remarks about changing scenes. With Serlio's illustration of the comic, tragic, and satiric, the art of theater was identified with the art of changing perspectives. The audience looked at a "picture theater," a window, where the "renaissance" developments in optics and mechanics as well as perspective could be displayed.[16]

In one sense, perspective could be seen as taking over the function of the occult memory art, displacing perception and emotion onto a kind of mechanics. Perhaps this can best be expressed by comparing the medieval street, meandering and crooked, with a limited vista and haphazardly erected buildings which had grown up organically along the arteries of the town, with the boulevard based on perspective, imposing order from a fixed plan, demonstrating the illusion of harmony, and having a view as though there could be a window on the world.

Perspective had become a methodology, among other things, a way of methodologizing the imagination.

Walter Benjamin quotes Georg Simmel: "Interpersonal relationships in big cities are distinguished by the marked preponderance of the activity of the eye over the activity of the ear. The main reason for this is the public means of transportation. Before the development of buses, railroads, and trams in the nineteenth century, people had never been in a position of having to look at one another for long minutes or even hours without speaking to one another."[17] For Benjamin, this situation is not a pleasant one.

Before the institution of the arcades in Paris in the mid-nineteenth century, pedestrians were literally pushed out of the way on the boulevards by the fast-moving carriages of the royal

16. For a discussion of perspective and optics in relation to the construction of the theater, see Yates, *Theatre of the World*, pp. 112-135.
17. Walter Benjamin, *Charles Baudelaire: A Lyric Poet in the Era of High Capitalism*, trans. Harry Zohn (London: New Left Books, 1973), p. 38.

and the wealthy. Although the arcades represented the increasing commercialization of public space, they also responded to a need, providing a thoroughfare and a vista for the pedestrian. The arcades, at least, provided a shop window on the world. The harnassing of private-sector values to create a passageway that was public (but which in fact was private) helped to generate a new subject – the *flâneur*. He felt more at home strolling in the interiorized miniature city than within his own four walls. The arcades, like the boulevards, also shared a militaristic function, for while they were not too wide to effectively blockade, they could be shut against the "rabble." However, unlike the boulevards, they did not allow for a mingling among classes; rather, they encouraged a new form of spectatorship to become normal. Not only was there a predominance of the eye over the ear, but the lack of allowable contact and the separation between the classes made this voyeurism the only form of communication that was acceptable. The world of experience was becoming the imagination.

The *feuilleton* section of the newspapers created a market for another kind of speculation: anthologies of literature designed to be sold in the streets. First came the portraits, or "physiologies," then came the *feuilleton* section itself with its short, gossipy witticisms, large ads, and serialized novels. The *feuilleton* linked together the phantasmagorica of Parisian life. It set a standard of value by providing relief from the tedium of an increasingly fragmented yet mundane existence. In the newspaper, scattered, illogical events from day to day had no underlying connection except contemporaneity.

Here the [masses that crowded through the arcades] appear as the asylum that shields an asocial person from his persecutors.[18]

If the *flâneur* is an unwitting detective it accredits his idleness. In Alexander Dumas's serialized novel *Mohicans de Paris,* the hero searches for adventure by following a scrap of paper which he gives to the wind to play with. But, no matter which trail he follows, each leads him to a crime. The increasing need to narrativize daily life, to imbue its fragmentation with meaning while simultaneously laying the foundation for what would lead to information theory and surveillance technology, is reflected in Benjamin's

18. Benjamin, *Charles Baudelaire*, p. 38.

remark that it was the detective story that was most emblematic of the fabric of Parisian life in the nineteenth century. Yet it was not only the detective story, but the *flâneur* and other participants who contributed to this narrative of city life. In his quest for the fantastic, this idler was fascinated by social situations within which he could imagine himself. Imagination was reaching beyond the world of appearances to a private, self-contained world where the subject was supreme. This was imagination free from images, unbound by conventional memory practices. The printed page made memory unnecessary and provided an audience, a shared practice where this constant desire, the telling and retelling – even if it couldn't be expressed by touching or conversation – found other means of expression, as a history, a poem, a private discourse, or a secret.[19]

Life before the seventeenth century was lived in public, either in the streets (outside of the small, one-room dwellings that housed all but the wealthy), or in the "big" house that fulfilled a public function. This was the only place where friends, clients, relatives, servants, protégés, and workers (the same people who would have spent their early years in the one-room dwelling) could meet and talk. These visits were not simply either professional or social: there was little distinction between the categories.

The traditional ceremonies which accompanied marriage . . . afford further proof of society's rights over the privacy of the couple. . . . Privacy scarcely ever existed when people lived on top of one another, masters and servants, children and adults, in houses open at all hours to the indiscretion of callers.[20]

In discussing newspaper ads in the mid-nineteenth century, Benjamin complained that the ad took up more space and was better designed than the copy around it, so that even when the product was criticized in an editorial, the effect was negligible. Advertisements, shorter news items, serial novels, and a decrease in subscription rates began to alter the way in which newspapers were consumed. Suddenly, to be out of date was to be out of fashion – a sin. The news items caught on because they could be employed commercially. *Reclamés*, independent notices masquerading as news items, referred to products that were advertised in the paper.

19. See Michel Foucault, *The History of Sexuality*, Vol. 1: *An Introduction*, trans. Robert Hurley (New York: Pantheon Books, 1978), and *The Archaeology of Knowledge*, trans. A. M. Sheridan Smith (New York: Pantheon Books, 1972).
20. Ariès, *Centuries of Childhood*, p. 405.

Although they were denounced as irresponsible and deceptive, their use underscored the increasing connection between advertisements and paper sales. These short news items and different typefaces allowed the papers to have a different look every day, predisposing their daily purchase, and making them appropriate complements to the newly defined cocktail hour – the ultimate in nonserious gossip that had become institutionalized in the cafés.

Deception had come under criticism in other public forms, particularly in the diorama where it was charged that Daguerre's sorcery "carried the viewer away to Switzerland, the land of yearning, and the effort was so perfect that a sentimental Englishwoman believed she had reached the valley of Chamonix, the destination of her consolatory escape from the metropolis – or at least she owned to being truly enchanted."[21] This observation is typical of spectator responses to the diorama in that it explicitly links the power of the imagination and the impression of reality with sorcery and witchcraft. By 1889, when Anton von Werner's memoirs were published, the issue of deception as ethics was directly addressed. Werner compiled a mass of testimony by domestic and foreign colleagues, all of them confirming that the art of deception was "done for its own sake, and not – to deceive."[22]

Just as the changing face of the paper predisposed the pedestrian stroller to purchase it, so too the daily change in advertisements enticed the stroller into the new department stores. Already the stroller in the arcades appreciated the displays in the store windows. As Baudelaire remarked, "They gave the *flâneur* somewhere to rest his eyes." (Even as late as dadaism, Marcel Duchamp noticed the relation of the avant-garde to the practice of the consumer – that the product of the avant-garde was to have the same characteristics of planned obsolescence/mass production as the products of mass consumption while simultaneously allowing the producer/artist to register shock at being reduced to a machine.[23]) The spectacle of looking, along with the accumulated skills of set design, painting, and lighting were employed to transform the stroller into a shopper and the arcade into a department store. "The intoxication to which the *flâneur* surrenders is the intoxication of the commodity around which surges the stream of customers."[24]

21. Dolf Sternberger, *Panorama of the Nineteenth Century* (New York: Urizen Books, 1977), p. 11.
22. Ibid., p. 34.
23. Discussed in Manfredo Tafuri, *Architecture and Utopia: Design and Capitalist Development* (Cambridge, Mass.: MIT Press, 1976).
24. Benjamin, *Charles Baudelaire*, p. 55.

By the early 1890s many people who, perplexed by the changes taking place in American life, began to turn to the political and economic writings of Ruskin and Morris, but also of Carlyle, Kropotkin, Tolstoy, and others who wanted to turn back the course of industrial development. All of these authors argued that first it was important to create a humane society; only then could satisfactory products be made. Versions of this society varied but in most of them the division of labor was minimal, wealth came directly from the land, and craftsmen, not artists or machines, made the everyday goods. The model of the ideal citizen in this felicitous state was the medieval artisan. He was a member of a society of equals, and he was free to work as he wanted, unencumbered by abstruse ideas about what "art" was.[25]

Baudelaire saw his existence outside conventional society, as a *bohème,* all the more heroic because it was so "*ordinaire.*" His poem, "Le vin des chiffoniers," details the way in which the poet derives his heroic subject from the refuse of society: it is a chronicle of the ragpicker. "Here we have a man who has to gather the day's refuse in the capital city. Everything that the big city threw away, everything that is lost . . . he catalogues and collects . . . he collects like a miser guarding a treasure the refuse which will assume the shape of useful or gratifying objects."[26] This same mythical projection extends to the consumer who was presented with the possibility of heroism by adopting the images of commercial products. As Charles Perrier said in criticism of Courbet's painting, "Nobody could deny that a stone-breaker is as worthy a subject in art as a prince or other individual. . . . But, at least, let your stone-breaker not be an object as insignificant as the stone he is breaking."[27]

Realism in art became the protest – and yet the paradigmatic expression – of an increasingly bourgeois society. Even though realism attempted to forsake all idealism to depict reality, it still frequently repeated Jean-Jacques Rousseau's ideas about the intuitive grasp of truth that the uncorrupted man, as represented by the peasant, embodied. The bohemian spirit, constructed in opposition to the bourgeois spirit, had an ambivalent relation to and was part of the bourgeoisie: the differences were complementary rather than exclusive. Nowhere is this clearer than in the work of Baudelaire who, "having failed to create a politics of his own, brought to perfection the attitude of stifling contempt for the world, making

25. David Handlin, *The American Home: Architecture and Society, 1815-1915* (Boston: Little Brown Co., 1979), p. 442.
26. Benjamin, *Charles Baudelaire,* p. 79.
27. Quoted in Linda Nochlin, *Realism* (Harmondsworth, Eng.: Penguin Books, Ltd., 1971), p. 35.

the city mere decoration for a private drama."[28] With the growth of the department stores, which presented vast panoramas for gazing, the *flâneur* was free to pursue his private drama indoors. (Certainly, not being able to buy must have made it all the more enticing.) Not only did this roving spectatorship focus "pleasure" – within proscribed, rigid ways along "memory paths"[29] – but the bourgeoisie fulfilled the aims of the revolution by providing it in the form of the mass and the anonymous crowd, the perfect correlative to privacy, collectivization, and individual fantasy.

In the early nineteenth century, the subject matter of salon painting was considered important as it expressed the cultural values of the ruling class (which until the first French revolution had been totally based on court life). After the middle of the century (and during the short-lived Second Republic), advertising in stores and newspapers might be seen as taking over much of this function, particularly among the bourgeois and peasant classes. Artists had already begun to construct an aesthetics in opposition to the academic salon style, as can be seen by tracing the acceptance of the work of Manet, Courbet, Daumier, and Millet. Subject matter had become increasingly unimportant in conventional terms; gone were the representations of "noble" subjects in historical settings with all the trappings of wealth.[30]

Not only that, but a different attitude, best expressed by Kant in his *Critique of Judgment,* fostered the popularization of art as an *experience* – taking it away from the educated class, where a certain amount of erudition was required to "read" the salon paintings, and "making it available to everyone."[31] The quality of the work of art could only be known by a personal experience of that quality and that experience could only be achieved by placing oneself in the right relationship to the work under consideration – by adopting the right attitude.

28. Benjamin, *Charles Baudelaire,* p. 14.
29. Term used by Freud to describe the way in which events are inscribed within memory. See especially "Project for a Scientific Psychology" (1895), where, despite the neurophysiological orientation, Freud attempts to account for the way in which memory trace follows one route in preference to another.
30. See Nochlin, *Realism,* and Sternberger, *Panorama,* pp. 111-129.
31. Kant continued his investigation of synthetic propositions in the realm of aesthetics: that all judgments of aesthetic criteria are based on subjective states and not on rationally applied criteria, and that these judgments are not only based on personal taste, but can claim universal truth. Clement Greenberg is perhaps the best known critic espousing this formalistic (because it takes into consideration only the intrinsic qualities in the work of art) viewpoint. This view has been attacked in recent years for its failure to be historically specific, for its reduction of all art to a celebration of the senses, rather than allowing for the real network of complex relations situating the work of art within culture to be exposed (T. J. Clark).

It might be argued that advertising effectively assumed the functions of salon painting for the newly emergent bourgeoisie. Salon painting, with its emphasis on legible signs, was already a kind of advertisement for the aristocracy. This "advertising" was also aided by the widespread acceptance of a Kantian-based aesthetics, since it was this aesthetic that could be incorporated into the practice of advertising and made to place the spectator in the "right relationship" to the newly discovered commodity. Did advertising facilitate an aesthetics which had come to be based as much on taste as is fashion, and which was also bound up with the notion of the "masses" in Marx's sense as well as Rousseau's natural man?

It doesn't take much acuteness to recognize that a girl who at eight o'clock may be seen sumptuously dressed in an elegant costume is the same who appears as a shop girl at nine o'clock and a peasant girl at ten.[32]

The bohemian was about to become the "anti-hero" of the mid-nineteenth century. For with his ability to empathize with both the organic and inorganic as the source of his inspiration, the poet enjoyed the incomparable privilege of being both himself and someone else, as he saw fit, like a roving soul in search of a body – even if that body became an "old boudoir full of faded roses" or a "forgotten Sphinx that in some desert stands."[33]

In the broader context of a burgeoning commercial culture, the foremost political imperative was what to dream.[34]

As Victor Hugo said, "A street, a conflagration, or a traffic accident assemble people who are not defined along class lines. They present themselves as concrete gatherings, but socially they remain abstract – namely, in their isolated private interests. Their models are the customers who, each in their private interest, gather at the market around their common cause."[35] Hugo wrote this to explain, in part, the failure of the "mass" to solidify into a political body. For Benjamin, it was monstrous that private individuals could cluster around their private interests.[36]

32. Benjamin, *Charles Baudelaire,* p. 28.
33. Ibid., pp. 55-56.
34. Stuart Ewen, *Captains of Consciousness: Advertising and the Social Roots of Consumer Culture* (New York: McGraw-Hill Book Co., 1976), p. 109.
35. Benjamin, *Charles Baudelaire,* p. 62.
36. Ibid., p. 68.

. . . it was enough in some areas of Paris to be seen dressed like a worker to risk being executed on the spot.[37]

Yet, increasingly this historical period was marked only by private interests (expressed by all classes in their imaginative fantasies), in the construction of the bourgeois family (both divided and contained by housing), and even in the "collectivization" of the commune movement.[38] So it is not surprising that the "cube of the individual" became the basic building block of modern architecture,[39] or that advertising came to represent what was valuable in a culture for the majority of its people.

I am proposing that just as there is a relation on many levels between the *flâneur* and the bourgeoisie, so too, there is a complementary relation between "realism" in art, the adoption of the "transcendental subject" in aesthetics, and the increasing importance of advertising – particularly as an expression of "social" reality, of the way in which the imagination can be made to stand-in for experience.

Considering the quantitative possibilities of mass production, the question of "national markets" became one of qualitatively changing the nature of the American buying public. In response to the exigencies of the productive system of the twentieth century, excessiveness replaced thrift as a social value. It became imperative to invest the laborer with a financial power and a psychic desire to consume.[40]

The wife's service was becoming one of directing the consumption by her selection of the goods and services that society was producing.[41]

The modern housewife is less of a routine worker and more of an administrator and enterpriser in the business of living. Homecraft had passed into self-determination. The woman could work out an economic plan of life in which family resources are utilized to buy the best possible combination of satisfactions for today and the best sequence of satisfactions for the future. Women as portrayed by ads in the 1920s were the repositories of choice and freedom that mass-produced goods were said to encompass. Women were in-

37. T. J. Clark, *The Absolute Bourgeois: Artists and Politics in France, 1848-1851* (Greenwich, Conn.: New York Graphic Society, 1973), p. 14.
38. In this sense the commune movement can be seen as further dissipating the clammy heat of intimate relations begun before the institution of the bourgeois family.
39. For instance, see Le Corbusier at Algiers, particularly the Obus plan.
40. Ewen, *Captains of Consciousness*, p. 25.
41. Ruth Lindquist, *The Family in the Present Social Order: A Study in the Needs of American Families* (Chapel Hill: University of North Carolina Press, 1931), p. 14.

vested with a high degree of political and social determining power—a formation that linked the expanding commodity market with the political climate born out of suffrage.[42]

In 1852, as the Second Republic came to a close, Aristide Boucault opened the first department store in Paris. Based on an understanding of customer psychology, the department store flourished by supplying a desire that a customer "didn't know she had until [she] entered the premises."[43] Department store practices were bound up with a recognized philosophy clearly articulated: clear pricing on goods, unlimited exchange, free access to the store, and quality items at lower prices due to added bargaining power. In addition, exploration of the store was encouraged: free libidinal access, including touch. Before the advent of the department store, even in the arcades, stores were still within the domain of the home. Browsing was discouraged. It was morally incumbent on the customer to purchase once she entered the family-run store. The use of glass in the arcade show windows was crucial for the development of display techniques. For not only did it frame and present the goods, but in the reflected light it collapsed the image of the gazing spectator onto the displayed items. In *Bonheur des dames,* Émile Zola characterizes Mouret, the department store proprietor, as successfully combining financial daring with artistic panache. For instance, Mouret created a white linen display so dazzling that, as Zola said, it made "the December skaters look black" by comparison.

The presence of female shop assistants served to change shopping from a dreary, solemn occasion to an enjoyable activity. Management responded to the attention by adopting sophisticated employment schemes; even so-called shop mashers were employed, attractive young women meant to entice male shoppers to the store. Often they were peasant girls, trained in the stores in the fine arts of Salesmanship, Manners, and Style. These women also served another function by bringing the peasant class within the consumer fold.[44]

Industry could sell to the masses all that it employed the masses to create . . .

42. Benjamin R. Andrews, "The Home Woman as Buyer and Controller of Consumption," *Annals of the American Academy of Political and Social Science* 163 (May 1929): 42.
43. Alexandra Artley, *The Golden Age of Shop Design: European Shop Interiors* (New York: Whitney Design Library, 1976), p. 14.
44. For a discussion of how this practice continues today, see Rachel Grossman, "Women's Place in the Integrated Circuit," *Radical America* 14, no. 1 (January-February 1980): 29-49.

The time has come when all our educational institutions . . . must concentrate on the great social task of teaching the masses, not what to think, but how to think, and thus to find out how to behave like human beings in the machine age.[45]

The department store provided a safe arena for the new work of the bourgeois woman in the home – consuming – by giving her an institution to which she could go unchaperoned. Department stores could not be dens of vice, like the tavern, for what woman of good breeding would risk her reputation? Instead, they were based on the baroque idea of the palace, and the woman was often handed over to the gentleman proprietor, who took the place of her father or husband.

What is most needed for American consumption is training in art and taste in a generous consumption of goods, if such there can be . . . Advertising, whether for good or ill, is the greatest force at work against the traditional economy of an age-long poverty as well as that of our own pioneer period; it is almost the only force at work against puritanism in consumption. It can infuse art into the things of life; and it will . . .[46]

Early department stores were constructed around a gallery utilizing an atrium and skylights to maximize the availability of light to the multiple tiers. Palatial in design and elegance, they differed considerably from most department stores today with their self-effacing fixtures and invisible walls. Early department stores presented a simulation of the glamor and glory of the court, now available to everyone. Their ornate balconies, crystal chandeliers, and grand staircases provided both an efficient flow of pedestrian traffic and unlimited visual access: to see and to be seen. Shopping had become the grand activity – the merchant's court.

The essence of the commodity structure is that the relation between people takes on the character of a thing and thus takes on a "phantom objectivity," an autonomy that seems strictly rational and all embracing to conceal every trace of its functional nature: the relation between people.[47]

45. Edward A. Filene, *Successful Living in the Machine Age* (New York: Simon and Schuster, 1931), p. 157. Filene was a Boston department store merchant who became the "mouthpiece" of American industry.
46. Leverett S. Lyon, "Advertising," in *The International Encyclopedia of Social Sciences*, ed. Edward R. A. Seligman (New York: Macmillan Publishing Co., 1930), vol. 1, p. 475.
47. Georg Lukács, *History and Class Consciousness*, trans. Rodney Livingstone (Cambridge, Mass: MIT Presss, 1971), p. 45.

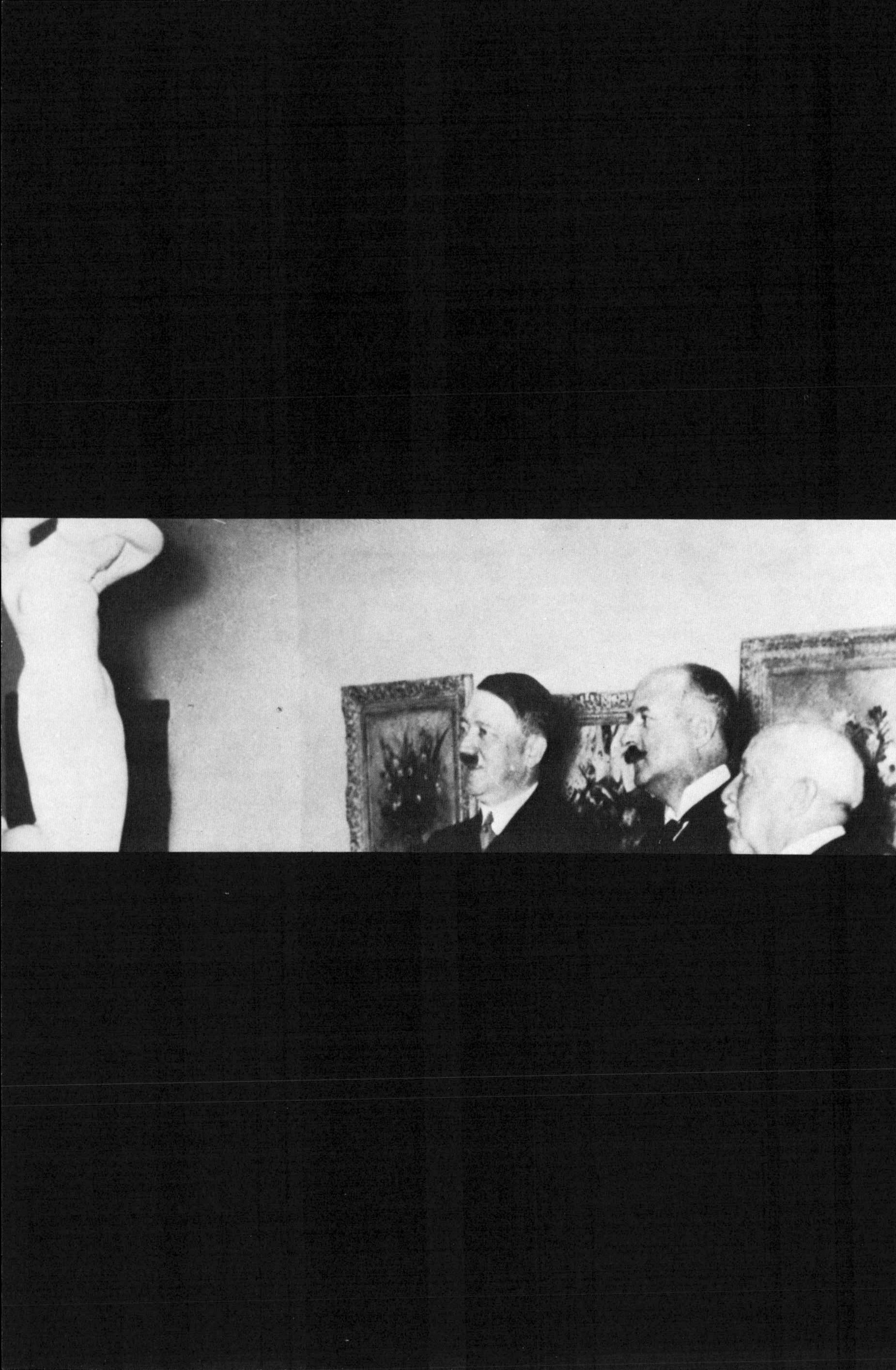

Shopping creates a particular subject within an activity that is complexly coded. Of course, there are psychoanalytical concepts that would be applicable, although it has not been my intention to apply them in so preliminary an article. Shopping functions as both a means to something and as an end in itself. It is located as a reward, as a pleasurable activity encompassing so much that is considered desirable in the culture within which we live. Shopping as an activity is relatively recent. As work became less a matter of accumulated skill and more a question of loyal diligence to task, consumption was depicted as the way in which diligence could be objectified. By smoking a pipe or looking a certain way, people could accumulate the social appearance necessary in a world which placed decreasing value on creative skill. Creative skill came to be located in the act of consuming. "They must consume to be healthy."[48]

There is no one who escapes shopping's primarily bourgeois dictum, an activity that bears the trace of yet another bourgeois activity of exchange: "the baby's cry answered by the breast . . . where the non-specific demand of the baby, the cry," forever gets the same response, the breast – the ultimate pacifier. "Rather than merely answering the generalized request for love, the mother's response satisfied the need by provoking and reducing the excitation to a particular zone of the body . . . The desire that the 'lost object' causes . . . is at once unconditioned in that virtually any object will suffice, and conditioned in that the object must gratify a particular zone."[49]

Shopping is an activity that consists of predictable yet indeterminant activities, where, as in the cinema, what we go to see, what we experience over and over again, is our own desire.

A signifier is what represents a subject. For whom? – not for another subject, but for another signifier.[50]

Television commercials are viewed on TV sets in the home. Shopping takes place in a space specifically constructed for that purpose. Just as theaters are constructed to make possible specific spectator relations with the film, stores are constructed to produce specific subject-effects in the consumer. These, of course, are quite different

48. Ewen, *Captains of Consciousness*, p. 38.
49. John Brenkman, "The Other and the One: Psychoanalysis, Reading *The Symposium*," *Yale French Studies*, no. 55-56 (1977): 418.
50. Jacques Lacan, *The Four Fundamental Concepts of Psycho-Analysis*, ed. Jacques-Alain Miller, trans. Alan Sheridan (New York: W. W. Norton & Co., 1978), p. 198.

from the spectator subject-effects produced through the cinematic institution, although there are also a number of parallels. In fact, early shopping malls were often built around movie theaters.[51] However, we cannot make the comparison "film is to theater structure" as "television commercial is to shopping structure." The shopper in the store is not stationary, but is constantly moving, and there is usually not an actual film or TV commercial with which to enter into an identificatory relation. During Macy's promotional week, designers were spotlighted in monitors in front of their respective departments. This practice was discontinued when the department managers noticed that the shoppers who watched the videotape no longer felt the desire to browse in the department where the videotape was playing.

All of this leaves to the side the fact that while the cinema subject is passive and the shopping subject is constituted as active, and both reflect a private subject involved in a private activity, the spectator sits and the film does its work, the shopper moves and the store comes to life.

When the shots of a TV commercial are considered in relation to the store, rarely do they represent diegetically the mall or store complex, so already we are not speaking of a denotative relation, but of several referential and discursive interactions.[52] The department store and the television commercial need the spectator/shopper to "come to life." Both exploit the mechanisms of identification often associated with, and in some relationship to, the cinematic institution. And while the specific nature of these relations has yet to be articulated, nonetheless, they too create an effect such that all traces of their respective discourse are erased.[53]

51. David Horn, "A Moving Picture Theatre and a Shopping Center," Ph.D. dissertation, University of California at Berkeley, 1930.
52. Much of the recent film theory has tended to collapse these two registers. For discussion, see in particular Christian Metz, "Metaphor/Metonomy, or the Imaginary Referent," and Bertrand Augst, "Metz's Move," both in *Camera Obscura*, no. 7 (Spring 1981). "Métaphor/Métonomie, ou le référent imaginaire," was first published as the fourth section of *Le Signifiant Imaginaire: Psychanalyse et cinéma* (Paris: Union Générale d'Editions, 1977). To quote Augst: "The danger of confusing the discursive and the referential concepts is in fact implicit in any form of enunciation because 'the associations between referents . . . can always be stated, and once they are, they in turn become the principle and the driving force behind various discursive sequences which may be codified to varying degrees. Conversely, the associations which appear in discourse always suggest the existence of parallel associations between the corresponding referents'" (p. 38).
53. I am referring to the denotative nature of the film as well as the psychical effects (subject-effect) produced within the subject as s/he watches a film in the theater. See in particular Jean-Louis Baudry, "The Ideological Effects of the Basic Cinematographic Apparatus," first published in English in *Film Quarterly* 28, no. 2 (1974-75): 39-47; Christian Metz, "The Imaginary Signifier," published in French in *Communications*, no. 23 (1975): 3-75, published in English in *Screen* 16, no. 2 (Summer 1975): 14-76; Jean-Pierre Oudart, "Cinema and Suture" and Stephen Heath,

The commercial often utilizes a "musical" format where the diegetic rules which control the logic of the narrative are suspended, creating a thirty-second world in which there is perfect resolution: the commercial, more than other conventional Hollywood genre, allows for the willful suspension of belief in favor of a continuity carried through the music. The store also seeks to create a situation where realism might be suspended. In its maze-like corridors is constructed an imaginary space where nothing interferes with the shopper's perceptions, not the past, not other memories; there is only *now.* And credit, which has been instantly available since 1882, allows for immediate possession.

The store engages the shopper in a process of self-fetishization, a continuous repetition of an activity whose "aura" is its power as an image which attracts and transforms.[54] There are certain specific features of the psychological process of shopping that might allow us to say this – such as the primary and secondary narcissism that is clearly involved, or the fetishization of objects which take the place of or stand for our desire (recalling Freud's dictum that associations take place along proscribed paths: the inscription of the "plan").

But if the woman fetishizes herself, is her recovered unity re-experienced as an adult "mirror-phase"? Surely, she does not regress to the pre-symbolic. Or, is there someone else on the other side of that mirror? Fashion for women revolves around these issues. How can she gain access to this Other? How does she "misrecognize" herself? Fetishism is a broad term that can be applied to the "everyday" as well as the psychoanalytical. I am using it here as both the "process of fetishism" where different objects are substituted for desire, as well as fetishism as "nosography" where objects are tied to other objects, including, of course, the subject herself.

What must be continually kept in mind is that the concept of fetishism in psychoanalysis is bound up with questions of sexual difference and disavowal.[55]

"Notes on Suture," both in *Screen* 18, no. 4 (Winter 1977-78): 35-76. I am arguing that in a related yet different way the relations between the consumer and the "shopping institution" are such that these complex relations appear to be transparent, anonymous, invisible, and yet natural.

54. See, in general, Guy DeBord, *Society of the Spectacle* (Detroit: Black & Red, 1977).

55. See Jacqueline Rose, "The Cinematic Apparatus: Problems in Current Theory," in *The Cinematic Apparatus*, eds. Teresa De Lauretis and Stephen Heath (New York: St. Martin's Press, 1980), pp. 172-186. Basically Rose argues that the concepts of the "imaginary," "disavowal," "fetishism," and so on only have meaning in relation to "sexual difference." See also "The Cinematic Apparatus as Social Institution: Interview with Christian Metz," *Discourse*, no. 1 (Fall 1979): 7-38.

The image/object is a mixture of what is present and also at the same time what is absent – of fulfillment and lack. In a commercial this same operation is at work when the image of the product and the product itself are associated. In the store you have a real material – the product for sale – *used* to represent something else. A fiction has been generated elsewhere, yet the material of the signifier appears to remain within the real space of the store, while in the TV commercial you are faced with what is unreal, because the material of the signifier is not completely real, but is absent. There is a slippage between the referential and discursive levels. As Christian Metz has said, the material signifier is much more unreal in film (and commercials), which makes the belief in the diegesis of the film (or commercial) all the more real (in cinematic terms).[56]

The concepts of mass production/efficiency and product differentiation through advertising removed to some extent the analyzable signifier that Jean-Louis Baudry describes in "Author and Analyzable Subject," replacing it with other signifiers not as specifically tied to an "author."[57] Mass production and product differentiation were germaine to the construction of the consumer-subject. As mass production took the value of an object away from its producer-author, it had to be given value through product differentiation. Advertising tries to place the consumer in the "right relation" to the product. A product which initially is perceived as having no meaning must be given value by a person or an image of a person who already has meaning for us. Television commercials, like ads, invite us to freely choose ourselves in a way in which we have already been constructed. Roland Barthes characterized the hermeneutic code, the code of expectations, as a proposition of truth articulated like a sentence.[58] In this sense, "truth in advertising" can be seen not as a movement by irate citizens to clean up the ad business, but as part of a public relations campaign which attempted to legitimize the advertising industry's own concept of truth as honesty; and as identified with a concept of reality whose naturalness disguises the ideological material of the cultural message – making it appear self-evident.[59]

56. Metz, "The Cinematic Apparatus," p. 17.
57. Translated by Bertrand Augst and Johanna Drucker in *Apparatus*, ed. Theresa Hak Kyung Cha (New York: Tanam Press, 1981), pp. 67-83. See Metz's response in *L'effet cinéma* (Paris: Editions Albatross, 1978), pp. 51-78.
58. Roland Barthes, *S/Z*, trans. Richard Miller (New York: Hill and Wang, 1974), pp. 84-88.
59. See James Rorty, *Our Master's Voice: Advertising* (New York: The John Day Co., 1934).

Most television commercials revolve around a sentence (slogan) articulated through partial representations, utilizing the principles of montage. It is the particular aptitude of filmic images to maintain some kind of diegetic continuity that has allowed the television commercial to continue in the tradition of Kuleshov's experiments – pushing to extremes the possibilities for associations between images.[60]

Baudry describes Chanel and her suits as creating for the buying public a neurosis that is identifiable. Chanel's company makes a perfume which is advertised in a similar premise. The glamorous and recognizable star's face (Catherine Deneuve) is associated in the space of the print ad with the bottle of perfume. But perhaps the most slippery signifier of them all is the television commercial where an undulating, vaporous, and sexual shape, changing its colors from green to blue and gold, spends twenty-five seconds before our eyes only to be at last identified as the bottle of Chanel No. 5 perfume. The subject as author-producer is analyzable in brand names, designer jeans, and even in department stores themselves: the Sak's woman and the Macy's woman.

The commodity's value is not so much the unmediated relation between a need and the object's inherent qualities, but the effect of those underlying intersubjective, symbolic libidinal relations on the consuming subject, which determines the relation of subjects to objects in general. As Lacan has said, history in psychoanalysis is an open interplay between the events in a subject's life – her or his history – and the history that the subject makes of these events. Narrative is not simply the expression of an already formed ideology, but the very form that ideology takes.

It is, of course, in making sense, in naturalizing the discontinuities, the ruptures in the social fabric that ideology takes on its "always-already" formed characteristics. Floyd Dell, a libertarian historian of the 1920s, saw modernity and mass production machinery as establishing family life on the basis of romantic love because it changed the fundamental character of the productive relation that had characterized the patriarchal formation.[61] Businessmen had a different view that of the reconstitution

60. For a discussion of Kuleshov's experiments, see Jean Mitry, *Esthétique et psychologie du cinéma*, vol. 1 (Paris: Editions Universitaires, 1963), pp. 283-295.

61. Floyd Dell, *Love in the Machine Age: A Psychological Study of the Transition from Patriarchal Society* (New York: Farrar and Rinehart, 1930).

of the declining pre-industrial patriarchy into a recomposed conception of authority. There was still Mom-and-Dad-and-the-Kids, the family romance, but the link between them was thoroughly externalized as the bourgeois family became the site of leisure and consumption.[62] I would argue that the power of this history-making ability, as it mediates the relation between this subject and her/his objects in the imaginary/symbolic realms (as those relations have been constructed in Western metaphysics) is bound up with questions about representation itself – within historical formations preceding psychoanalysis.[63]

How can one trace back a concept as poorly defined as "imagination" within the "world of experience," retrospectively, into a mythical past?

The store is the plane upon which the subject and object are united in a real sense. It is tempting to map a Lacanian reading onto the construction of the shopping subject. Certainly you could argue that the S/s, the repressed signifier that turns out to be an endless chain of associations, occurs in this activity.[64] Even though the objects themselves lie outside the discursive system, and there is not, as is implied, a one-to-one correspondence between these operations and the referent, they have come to represent – they stand for – what they signify. We do not buy a pair of jeans, we buy an image of a pair of jeans, in a different way than we buy an egg, or maybe even a brown, fertile egg. We buy how this image will make us feel – an image that places us in the "right relationship" to these feelings. Fredric Jameson characterizes the space of the imaginary as an ambiguous redoubling, a mirror reflection, an immediate relation between the subject and its other in which each term passes immediately and is lost in a play of reflections such that the frag-

62. For example, the significance of youth is central here both as signaling a change in production values (strength to run a machine and work versus accumulated skill) as well as shifts in authority. Age becomes a detriment – compulsory retirement. See Max Horkheimer, "The End of Reason," *Studies in Philosophy and Social Science* 9 (1941): 366-388.
63. Throughout this article I have been referring to the construction of the bourgeois family so that I could begin to discuss the construction of the consumer. This argument, such as it is, suffers from the lack of a theory of the subject articulated within the frame of what could be called the "social imaginary," to use Marx's term. And even though this "montage" is not linear in a usual sense, this chain of "facts" spanning the last four hundred years has been reconstructed from the perspective of the present, and shares in the problems of a historicizing methodology.
64. Lacan adopts Saussure's linguistic description of the sign to generate his re-reading of Freud "that the unconscious is structured like a language." S/s, signifier over signified, with the bar containing in the form of its barrier the idea of a repression of the signified such that a symptom is a signifier whose signified is repressed from consciousness. This is particularly apparent in Freud's case histories, such as "The Rat Man" (1909). This repressed signified can be seen as an endless chain of repressed signifiers because signifiers always refer to other signifiers, and because in Lacan's formula for metaphor the replaced signifier doesn't vanish, but slips below the bar to function in an associative chain marked by nodal points (Lacan, *Écrits*, pp. 148-152). For it is the structure of metaphor (as read by Lacan) that makes symptoms possible.

mented subject becomes re-united in the object.[65]

The decentered subject – unlike the transcendental subject, who was idealized by Kantian metaphysics, and unlike the bourgeoisie, for whom the avant-garde was this idealized subject – was ready for reflection. Advertising has always been involved in the production of an image of resolution that cannot be accomplished in social life. The aura of television in the private sphere is the fetishization of the image itself. The television set is the mediator between the image and the producer of the image, the spectator. Ultimately, it is the image that becomes the locus of value.

Since pseudo-experience is not gratifying as experience, we find our pleasure in its pseudo-ness, in the process of image-making, of technological manipulation. This is why contemporary advertising no longer glorifies the product, but glorifies the system, the corporate image and advertising itself.[66]

We take our pleasure in the technology of fantasy, through the deliberate fake-ness of special effects. Consider the fetishistic aspects of fantasy as portrayed in television ads for FIAT and PEPSI, both heavily dependent on special-effects magic. The denotative structures of both ads are extremely different: FIAT is basically narrative (an episodic syntagma to use Metz's terminology), while PEPSI is nonnarrative (a parallel syntagma). The relation constructed with the spectator through the special effects involves her or him in both avowal and recognition and denial and repression. As Metz says in his essay "Trucage et cinéma," "[A special-effect shot] can pull its illusion out of the hat, while simultaneously displaying its capacity to astonish the senses."[67] This process occurs along with the more "ordinary" mechanisms already operating through the TV commercial and its signifiers.

Since the mid-1970s, a revival has been taking place in downtown San Francisco department stores. There has been a return to the baroque palace construction of the mid-nineteenth century. Yet, now there is a twist, for the shopper is not naive; the shopper knows that the recaptured glory that the store attempts to pass onto its customers – as it dispenses with its own self-effacement – is not the revival of the beaux-arts tradition, but the analyzable subject of the store itself, as author-distributor, permanently on display in the building.

65. Fredric Jameson, "Reification and Utopia in Mass Culture," *Social Text* 1, no. 1 (Winter 1979): 130-148.
66. Shierry Weber, "Individuation as Praxis," *Critical Interruptions*, no. 1 (1980): 34.
67. Christian Metz, "Trucage et cinéma," in *Essais sur la signification au cinéma*, vol. 2 (Paris: Klincksieck, 1972), pp. 173-192, my translation.

7. Mass Culture and the Structure of Fantasy

Dean Martin / Entertainment as Theater

DAN GRAHAM

The star is wheeled out in a child's wagon by one of the rainslicked and white-booted chorines as, eyes drawn and cigarette dangling from mouth, he drawls:

EVERY TIME IT RAINS IT RAINS *BOURBON*
FROM HEAVEN . . .

"I got picked up the other night on suspicion of drunk driving," Martin admits. "The cop asked me to walk a straight line and I told him not unless you put a net under it."

He comes to a dead stop, now starting, staring directly into the camera, his gaze unilateral with that of the audience transfixed by their screens as if, stoned – perhaps in half-conscious parody designed to mirror the viewer's stupor and occasional embarrassed awareness – he has only then become aware that he is, in fact, on the air. Shaking himself self-consciously, he asks, "How long I been on?"

How true is that public image of stiff stupor and slap-happy sloth that Martin projects? According to the star, the public has stereotyped him as a boozer because of his lackadaisical physical appearance and he just decided to go along with it. Actually, the actor is known in fan magazines as but a moderate drinker. ("I drink moderately," a TV quip goes. "In fact, I keep a case of Old Moderately in my dressing room.")

Walter Kerr writes about a dance team appearing on TV when "16 to 18 beats in the act, a swift flow of words, blocked out in capital letters, suddenly divided the screen, moving with resolute importance from right to left across the dancer's feet. We were getting a news bulletin *without* interrupting the program . . . The message turned out to be inconclusive." All this ingenuity, Kerr protests, simply serves to call attention to the medium – a mechanism indifferent in fact to the "content" of the dance itself. It simply threw together two pieces of information at the same time, neither one worthy in itself of the viewer's undivided attention. It would seem the medium regards itself transparently; as a stretch of neutral material extending a certain length of time which can be used to occupy a vacuum tube as long as nothing else is occupying it. It has no particular identity as either entertainment or information. Television, frequently accused of "using" its viewers and thereby holding them in contempt, demonstrates here contempt for itself.

What Martin *does* "expose" is an easygoing contempt for the medium of TV. He boasts of preparing a one-hour show in only four hours: "All I have to do is read some cards and sing four or five songs; if you can't do that in a day, you're stupid and don't belong in the business."

All the dialogue is written out on prompting or "idiot" cards and a favorite Martin "bit" is to be caught staring blindly into the camera attempting to make sense out of the material on the cards. At other times, it is all too obvious that he is reading his supposedly impromptu remarks. After a particularly stumbling effort, he confides in an awkward aside to the home audience his problem. (But, one can ask, is this, too, spelled out on the cards and rehearsed prior to performance?)

Dean has introduced the first of his "myth status" guest stars, Orson Welles:

> ORSON WELLES: *Dean, I'd like you to try something.*
> DEAN MARTIN: *I'll try anything once.*
> ORSON: *I think the people would like to hear you do a Shakespeare reading.*

We are "in" – knowing his "drunk" is an act – as Dean, lax, knowing (or a knowing of his writers') without knowing what is happening, reads in an unmodulated ellision, without allusion . . . Sometimes things – words – slide a bit *too* far or too easily . . . without pausing for the expected laughs that come with understanding to sink in . . .

As Orson Welles is an institution and also something of a "father figure," all that's required is to play the obvious:

> DEAN: *Oh,* (aside to audience) *this guy's kiddin' me.*
> ORSON: *But, you've read Shakespeare.*
> DEAN: *I've read the book, but I don't know who wrote it . . . my audience doesn't understand Shakespeare.*
> ORSON: *I'll translate . . . just pick up the book and read any passage.*
> DEAN: *This is stuff to read.*
> (Dean reading): *Ho there serving wench, fetch me a succulent morsel of food that has had its feathers plucked by a flaxen-haired damsel.*
> DEAN: *Now what does that mean?*

ORSON: ONE CHICKEN DELIGHT TO GO!
(Dean reading): *See how she leans her cheek upon my hand that I might touch her cheek and she in turn may place her hand upon my gamlet.*
ORSON: SOCK IT TO ME, SOCK IT TO ME!
DEAN: (following after the applause and a cut in the videotape): *Here's a guy had on my show last year* (this was probably taped at an earlier time and Dean's "lite" singsong in the second, segued section is a little off, that is, "too" pronounced), *a Broadway actor and he does – ah – marvelous impressions of a chicken and I've asked him to do it again for us tonight – ladies and gentlemen, Jack Guilford.*
(to music Jack Guilford enters and gives an imitation of a clucking chicken; the audience responds laughing)
DEAN: (having by this time tipsily reentered the stage): *Jack, do your impression of a goat.*
JACK: Well, Dean, actually tonight I would like to do something a little less frivolous; I would like to take the opportunity to talk about a serious thing, about a minority that has no civil rights – this group can't vote in most states – I speak of the gigolos . . .

Dean rides loosely out mounted on horseback like his next guest, John Wayne, both wearing cowboy duds. The camera pulls back, revealing the stage bare without frivolous scenery. The two actors circumscribe in tandem the fundamentals of TV "guestshot" dialogue: how nice it is to be on the show again, the making of Wayne's last movie, the outdoors, the country – that is, America, generally. John discusses what's wrong and what's right about America, about the importance of supporting the boys in Vietnam, while Dean listens briefly before riding off *sans* comment to leave his guest "room" to do his "bit." A solid, self-conscious six minutes worth until the solitude is broken for a commercial message.

Who is the *real* Dean Martin? His supposed stupor replete with jarring silences is a deliberate, but awkward concealment, calling attention to the duplicity of his role playing. The combined lack of grasp of the script role (the "real" Dean Martin presumed drunk and misunderstanding the nature of the character proscribed for him by the lines) give him an odd self-consciousness. The audience is never "taken in" by the myth of "Deano's" "personality"; instead it is made aware that this is but an artifice – the sustaining scaffold necessary to support the premise of the show; the complicit knowledge shared in by Martin's audience and reinforced with allusion to "idiot" cards and other self-conscious humor is the structural pivot on which the show totteringly balances.

Martin's stumbling style of acting finds a striking precedence in playwright Bertolt Brecht's conception of the actor: "He should strike people as 'jarring.' But it wouldn't be his way of acting that would jar, but he himself . . . he would be accused of being too self-conscious . . . He who is showing should himself be shown."

Brecht's theater similarly intended to display the self-mechanism of its structure. Like the revelation of the "idiot" cards in the Martin show, Brecht desired that his audience be aware of the literal machinery of the ropes, flues, and lighting apparatuses "shown openly as mechanical means" so that the exposure produced "a very brilliant illumination of the stage (since a half-lit stage makes the spectator less level-headed by preventing him from observing his neighbor and in turn hiding him from his neighbor's eyes) and also making visible the sources of the light."

Andy Warhol, like Brecht before him, has used the mechanism of film with lassitude to eliminate the conventional complicity of audience identification with the protagonists. The film version of Ron Tavel's *The Life of Juanita Castro* "distances" its lax "action" from the audience as the actors read their lines lulled on bleachers and photographed throughout from the identical off-center oblique angle reversible with the experience available to members of the audience averting their eyes from the screen to observe the equally "spaced" reaction of the rest of the audience. Warhol has noted that these earlier films "were made to help the audience get more acquainted with themselves." The reason for this is a paraphrase of Brechtian logic: "Usually when you go to the movies, you sit in a fantasy world, but when you see something that disturbs you, you get more involved with the people next to you. Movies are doing a little more than you can do with plays and concerts where you just sit there. I think television will do more than movies." (It's still too formal, though, to *really relax* at an Andy Warhol movie.)

Peter Townsend of the rock group, Who, would split the screen into horizontal and vertical motions in analysis of the audience/performer relation: "The audience is schizoid . . . they're sensitive in that they're open to media . . . open to media distorters like grass, like booze, like all these things . . ." So when the play catches them, they are in this flux and in order to hit them "you've got to move with them on the same plane . . . this isn't to say you're going down to anything . . . up and down – it's a question of a vertical thing, and when you're making a performance, it's not vertical."

Jean-Luc Godard's *Contempt,* with Brigitte Bardot, also dedicated to the great BB (Bertolt Brecht, not Brigitte), plays constantly with self-reference as the props and technical scaffolding of a movie being made as we are watching is included within the terrain of its own making. Like the physical appearance in the film of Bardot, the film shows its own "backside." Its mood runs parallel to the "Martin Show," inducing a nauseous, lush languor which, expressed in the film's music and scenery, provides undercurrents of a false romantic pastoral. And when the film's antihero, Bardot's movie husband Paul, insists on wearing his hat while in the tub, he is "just imitating Dean Martin in *Some Came Running.*"

Dean Martin's contempt for the "reality" of his image is only one manifestation of a widespread trend in television. In recent years actors have appeared in roles as "themselves" doing commercials. It is assumed that, since everybody knows it is a commercial, what they say isn't important. They're, in fact, not "really being themselves" at that moment. The "personality" projected is different from the one we know which erodes into a depersonalized, self-contemptuous, hollow substitute. Actors become things that can be bought, used, monopolized – their "validity" placed in parentheses; just as in Brechtian dramaturgy.

The popular view is that a television show is a mechanical, prearranged, readily manipulatable thing. Slabs of entertainment are indifferently strung together in a tedious continuum for anyone wishing to waste his time. It exposes not only the actor or action, but itself as a medium for self-alienation.

(A cut in the videotape . . .) Caterina Valente and Dean Martin standing, dressed completely differently from their appearance a split-second ago in the "go-go" set, but still croonin'/cooing. Dean, looking to the side (actually directly at Caterina's front-side or "tits") – that is to say, facing the camera/audience as Caterina stands slightly to the rear of the host (so she can direct herself both to him *and* to the viewers) centers his attention to fix his charm only on the lovely lady as he sings, "*You put a spell on me.*" His relation to the audience is peculiar – they are peering as he is leering (but is it all fantasy?): the song comes to a conclusion and he turns to meet the gaze of his viewing confidants with a fishy wink of complicity.

It's expected. There is always a conventional dialogue between two principles playing stereotyped roles – with a third element acknowledged to be present – never denied: the viewer. Dean's complicit awareness of this third element is often used as a prop; it is assumed in the conversation that this third man is listening. However the third presence doesn't always have to be the viewer, but shifts fluidly to surrogates, an unseen cameraman Dean knows, the studio audience, or Dean's wife watching at home. For example: one "bit" (standard to the point of redundancy for the series of shows) involves Dean alone in an intimate setting with his "ole" buddy, Ken, who is there ostensibly to play the piano while the star croons and mugs sentimental/drunk tunes for his home audience . . . but the next moment Ken is turned into a prop as we find Dean dead drunk, propping himself as he is talking/sputtering sloppy attention at Ken, confiding seeming confidences, then the next second Dean has turned away from Ken and seems to be talking to a viewer at home; the audience's status (and involvement) has suddenly flipflopped from disassociated voyeur to that of listener or "dumb" prop.

This dumb-show is clearly fake; at first perception it appears to eliminate all pretense, all "distance," but in fact it makes the spectator all the more aware of the conventionalization of television's image of "intimacy" – that the "real" Dean Martin (his television persona) is but a media fabrication. This certain self-consciousness of the audience is most pronounced when Dean is "leveling" – speaking "just between us." When Dean talks directly to the camera (perhaps confusing it in his "drunken" state with the person he has been talking to), when he is "alone with" his male guests, or "alone" differently, with his female guests, or when he addresses his "embarrassed for him" intimates, us, we are made aware of the pseudo-intimacy of the medium, its multilevels of "distancing."

Contempt begins and ends with moving camera shots of the movie being made within it observed in its mechanics. The final scene shows Paul saying goodbye to *his* director (of the interior movie) and then standing by to watch the filming of a scene in this movie while Godard (himself the *real* director of *Contempt* which *we* are presently watching) has put himself also into this shot, as the director's assistant who is setting up the scene. We the viewers are, like the interior crew making the movie (including Godard), acting out our mechanically conditioned responses through our repeated exposure to the medium in which we are the manipulated semi-participants. Godard's *Contempt* cameraman passes across the film-within-a-film director's camera and crew, turning 180° to the reverse back-side, camera-view facing over the precipice out where there is nothing to look at but the horizon line separating blue Mediterranean sea from blue Mediterranean sky.

Dean biding "bye" to his home audience, the camera pulls back and our view opens further; now we perceive the technicians pulling out the plugs and hear the clicks as the lights are turned out—the show is over (this is "dead air"). We become aware of an incredible, inexplicable time or generation gap, for the image we are currently seeing is evidently after the fact, although live, as we are still there watching.

Here in Lower Manhattan's "loft" district, I am looking for some sort of nightclub, "Cerebrum." Coming upon the correct number, I ring, pushing the door open upon the answering buzz to find myself in a small, dark cubicle. I can't *feel* a door (visions of some remote Charlie Chan movie dance in my head). Suddenly, a panel slips back, and I am confronted by a mini-skirted young lady who asks if she might help me. "Yes." I am to remove my hat and coat; having done this, to remove my shoes and follow. My guide leaves me here to the charge of a second girl who wears a flowing diaphanous robe. Her name is Denise, and she has been instructed to take me to Platform Four. As I observe her unclothed body beneath the thin robe, she chats politely, handing me a canvas bag and a white robe, and announcing that I am to take off any and all clothes I might wish. "Certainly," she addresses me, "you'd be much more comfortable without your coat, vest, tie, and shirt."

Denise having left, I squat down on the platform, which has a small square in the middle containing several plugs into one of which a large, round light is plugged. Rock music pours into the room and, from the two projection rooms, slide images are simultaneously sprayed onto the walls. I feel suddenly out of place.

Denise again emerges to bring me a device upon which one can draw patterns then to be projected. As I doodle with the toy, some voices reach me; various hippie couples are led in. A threesome emerges—they seem quite relaxed already; perhaps they had come stoned. Observing each group as individuals disrobed and dressed in the diaphanous habit, I now am somewhat embarrassed, uncomfortably aware of my underclothes lying just beneath the thin veneer. (It occurs to me that usually we are embarrassed if our behavior is being observed by people who are not part of the situation, while an individual who glories in such observation is ordinarily condemned.)

Guides hand each group a toy—a *prop*—to be played with. It seems quite bland. Balloons are brought and a couple begins to pat one about—until it bursts. Just then I become aware; I (we?) am to be the player in the drama and not merely one of the audience. The props are brought to me so that I might play myself.

The atmosphere, which once seemed bland, slowly begins to change. Each person is starting to relate to his or her partner and to the guides. Now another guide enters and, propping herself, kneels by me with a small bowl. She removes a white lotion (baby cream?) and then starts to massage (I see, the medium is the massage) my hand. At first I am unresilient, but then begin to ply *her* hand with the lotion. Couples begin putting the stuff on hands, arms, and faces to feel and touch. We are inside our skins, not merely looking out at an illusion of ourselves. As more props are brought in and are related to, we relate to our own bodies and to those of our neighbors. There is no need to relate or project to the others our experiences. Nothing is happening on stage and we are not being used by the performers; we ourselves are on stage. We are our own entertainment tonight (if "stoned," "living" our fantasies) as we are here.

One of the attractive girls on the platform across from me walks onto my platform. "Join me with the others," she says. We lie beneath an opened parachute given to "us" earlier, feeling the cool air of its movement. I feel part of a warm humanity. "Why have you been sitting alone all evening?" the girl asks. There is no "distance" here. The free-floating mood changes as all couples return to their platforms. A fog appears from beneath the platform and fills the air. Then the fog disappears and into the clear space the guides bring strawberries soaked in wine. I am "together." Alive, calm as the music stops.

Pathetic Readings

WILLIAM WEGMAN

My name is Bill Wegman. W-e-g-m-a-n. Perhaps you have heard of me. Some of you are new to this part of the country. I myself am a relative newcomer to this part of the country. Like many of my friends, I was trained in the East, and then moved away only to return again.

I can see by the looks on your faces that many of you are surprised that I have an Eastern background. Don't act so surprised. After the show I hope to be able to meet and talk with you . . . If any of you are interested, I would like to meet with you and talk with you. But, before we begin with the show, I would like to say a few things that I have written down beforehand . . . to acquaint you with some facts about me that perhaps you are confused about or have never heard before.

I can see by the looks on your faces that many of you are confused by the new video movement from the technical standpoint. It's really simple; don't be confused. It's just like regular network television except stripped to the bare essentials. But I don't want to bore you with a lot of technical jargon. Often when highly specialized and trained professionals get together they tend to get overly involved in this kind of talk and forget the layman entirely. Please stop me if I unconsciously slip into this habit. Nevertheless, I know that there are some of you here who are interested in technical talk and for those that are, if you are, you, please, will remain, er . . . I can perhaps talk more about that after the show.

Umm . . . moving along to . . . Perhaps many of you know, have noticed that I use a Sony 3600 VTR as my basic workhorse. Before that I used the old CV type, if any of you are old enough to remember the old CV type, and before that I used a Craig machine. But unlike the big networks, I only have one camera, a Sony AVC 3200. When I converted from CV to AV, I was forced to use a different cable connecting the recorder to the camera. Otherwise it wouldn't work.

Visitors to my studio in the past have remarked about my unusual monitor. I guess I have gotten so used to it, it has no real effect on me. The connector on the back of it is so different, I had to hunt all over town for the right plug. It takes a plug with eight sharp blades at the end of it. The blades go into the input in the monitor. Following the black cable along until we reach the other end of it, we find a plug with eight pins rather than blades . . . pins rather than blades. The configuration is the same, but it looks different. When I switched from CV to AV I was forced to rewire the cable, and it took almost the whole day to do. Switching from CV to AV wasn't as easy as I had hoped. In the beginning I couldn't get used to it. It looked different. You see, with AV you get a sharper picture, and it took a while to figure out how to tone down the sharpness. I learned to adjust the focus and the F-stops on the camera lens to attain the degree of focus and depth of field I had gotten used to with CV. After a while, it didn't matter any more.

Audiophiles in the audience have perhaps detected, perhaps you have noticed that I use an electrovoice R15 microphone as my basic workhorse in the sound department. There's nothing flashy or fancy about it. It's just a very good durable high quality dynamic quality good durable microphone. Unfortunately the jack at the other end of it didn't match up with the input in my 3600. I had to snip off the original plug and solder a mini to it. [Pause. Soldering sounds.]

My father taught me to solder when I was a boy, when I was a kid. When I was a kid, to make a little extra money on the side, we sold newspapers or shined shoes. I sold newspapers down by the post office. One of the boys down there, Limpy Tim we called him, because of the limp, his limp, shined shoes. But nevertheless we were best of friends. So naturally, I was taken aback when he told me he wanted to sell his shoeshine kit for a quarter. He said he needed the money right away. Why, he wouldn't say. He sold the kit to little Joey. Joey was a sickly little boy. Joey was sick, but when he saw the kit his eyes lit up. When he brought the kit home, he asked his mother if they had kits in heaven. She didn't know what he meant. She thought about it for a while and remembered reading in the Bible somewhere about heaven being cheerful and without hunger. She told Joey that when he got better they would take a trip to the country. Then Joey's eyes grew dim. He looked queer. He dropped the kit and died. Limpy Tim brought the quarter to the newspaper office. With tears in his eyes he asked the man, take down the following: "Of scarlet fever, little Ted, aged three. One brother left to mourn him dead. Funeral tomorrow at eleven." Ted had died in Tim's arms. The news traveled fast. All the boys on the post office block chipped in to reclaim Tim's shoeshine kit, and with our meager earnings, bought flowers for the funeral.

My father taught me all I know about electronics, so I don't know too much about electronics. After the funeral, he took me down to the basement in Massachusetts. We were living in Massachusetts at the time. He took me down to his workshop area, to show me the Jacob's ladder. It was terrifying. He saw that I was frightened so to comfort me he began, "You know my son, I know how you feel. I once lost a friend's brother when I was young like you. His name was little Jim. Poor little Jim. One day I brought him this Jacob's ladder because I knew how much he liked it. Jim was very sickly, very sick. He was sick, but when he saw the Jacob's ladder, his eyes lit up. He asked me if they had a Jacob's ladder in heaven. I thought I knew what he meant, vaguely. I remembered reading in the Bible about heaven being cheerful and without hunger. I told Jim that when he got better, we could take a trip to the country. Then Jim's eyes grew dim. He dropped the ladder and died. This is the first time I've been able to bring myself to touch this thing since then. I'm going to give it to you." "No thanks, Dad," I said. "I want to learn how to solder." Later I was to meet someone who later became my wife who had a summer job as a solderer at Ray-O-Vac. Strange how fate moves us. Now you know why I mention soldering and the cables and me doing it by myself. Married men in the audience will know how it feels to have to learn something technical from their wives.

I know that some of you have been flown here from another country, and you might have trouble relating to these kinds of relationships, because your background is so different. You come from a whole different . . . culture. Don't get blackballed into thinking that you're not. Everything is different here. [Excerpt from radio newscast in Spanish, signature tune, etc. . . .] And yet, in many ways we have much in common. We all share an enthusiasm for the video medium. Otherwise we wouldn't be here. [Radio excerpt, weather forecast, in Spanish.] I don't think there is a soul in this room, no matter what their backgrounds are, who can't feel pity and feel real sad about, for the parents of poor little Jessie.

The cottage was a thatched one, the outside old and mean
But all within the little cot was wondrous neat and clean.
The night was dark and stormy, the wind was howling wild,
As a patient mother sat beside the deathbed of her child.
A little worn-out creature, his once-bright eyes grown dim:
It was a collier's wife and child, they called him little Jessie.

And oh! to see the briny tears fast hurrying down her cheek,
As she offered up the prayer, in thought, she was afraid to speak,
Lest she might waken one she loved far better than her life;
For she had all a mother's heart, had that poor collier's wife.
With hands uplifted, see, she kneels beside the sufferer's bed,
And prays that He would spare her boy, and take herself instead.

She gets her answer from the child; soft fall the words from him:
"Mother, the angels do smile and beckon little Jessie,
I have no pain, dear Mother now, but oh! I am so dry,
Just moisten poor Jessie's lips again, and, Mother, don't you cry."
With gentle, trembling haste she held the liquid to his lips;
He smiled to thank her as he took each tiny, little sip.

"Tell Father when he comes from work, I said goodnight to him,
And Mother, now I'll go to sleep." Alas! poor little Jessie!
She knew that he was dying; that the child she loved so dear
Had uttered the last words she might ever hope to hear.
The cottage door is open, the collier's step is heard,
The father and the mother meet, yet neither speaks a word.

He felt that all was over, he knew his child was dead,
He took the candle in his hand and walked towards the bed;
His quivering lips gave token of the grief he'd feign conceal
And see, his wife has joined him – a stricken couple kneel;
With hearts bound down by sadness, they humbly ask of Him
In heaven once more to meet again their own poor little Jessie.

I don't think, uh . . . now if I have done no more than to . . . give you some idea about . . . clear up some of the confusion . . . If I have accomplished no more than to kindle a flicker of pain and sorrow from your bosom for the pathetic waifs I have . . . whose stories of their brief lives I have retold the story of . . . have given you whatever small insight into the new video movement at all, then I am deeply moved and rewarded. [Pause] As of now, I am emotionally exhausted and drained physically. The pressure on me has been great. I don't think that I'll have the strength to meet you and talk afterwards, but perhaps some other time when, when we meet again. Goodnight and thank you all for coming.

Beyond Chiffon: The Making of *Storme*

MICHELLE PARKERSON

Actually, my mother (a devout Catholic) supplied the inspiration for this film.

Martin Luther King was still alive. I was twelve and trying to mind my own business when I emerged from the bathroom at a hapless moment. In the next room, my mother brimmed over the phone about a show she had seen the night before at Washington, D.C.'s famed Howard Theater. Destiny placed me in earshot of the open door at the exact moment my mother chattered, "Chile, the men dress like women and the one woman even dresses like a man! Between the feathers and gowns, I couldn't tell who was who. . ."

In short order, my mother spotted me eavesdropping on her indiscretion and quickly slammed the door. That moment forever sparked my interest in the Jewel Box Revue.

Twenty years later, I find myself producing a documentary on the history of the Revue as told through the fascinating story of its host, Miss Storme DeLarverie. *Storme: The Lady of the Jewel Box* is currently in production for public television. In recent years, PBS has spearheaded the national broadcast of several films on gay and lesbian history, among them: *The Times of Harvey Milk, Before Stonewall,* and *Silent Pioneers. Storme* will profile an era, a woman, and an integral part of the black lesbian and gay experience.

"America's Most Unusual Show" was often billed as "Twenty-Five Men and a Girl." From the mid-fifties to late sixties, the Jewel Box Revue ran a headlining tour of the black theater or "chittlin" circuit which consisted of the Apollo in New York, Baltimore's Royal Theater, the Uptown Theater in Philadelphia, Washington, D.C.'s Howard Theater, and the Regal in Chicago.

For many black Americans, the Jewel Box was our first public exposure to gay life and the Revue was frequently featured in the black press on the entertainment pages of *Afro-American, Jet, Hue,* and *Ebony* magazines. The Jewel Box changed and shared marquees with the great celebrities of the day: Dinah Washington, Sammy Davis, Jr., the Supremes, Lionel Hampton, Ray Charles . . .

The Jewel Box Revue was a unique female impersonation show boasting elaborate costumes, lavish production numbers, and the foremost "femmepersonators" in the nation. Miss DeLarverie, performing in male drag, served as stage manager and M.C. of a glittering evening of original comedy, music, mime, and dance. This was no drag show. The Revue was the first commercially successful and integrated impersonation show to play American stages and nightspots.

The chorus members and featured performers of the Revue were consummate entertainers, artists skilled in the discipline of illusion. Today, the term "female impersonator" conjures confused notions of transvestites/transsexuals or weary images of overdone men lipsynching various and sundry versions of Diana Ross, Tina Turner, Barbara Streisand, and Patti LaBelle. Whether camp or sleaze, these generic divas pull off the worst impressions of the worst sexist stereotypes. Far beyond typical "queen" or "butch" personas, a woman named Storme DeLarverie and the talented men of the Jewel Box embodied the *art form* of impersonation. And, as Miss DeLarverie states in the film, "we did it with respect and we did it with dignity."

Storme DeLarverie brought a distinctive style and fashion sense to the mystique of male impersonation – à la Harry Belafonte. "In those days," she said, "men's jackets were loose, but the pants were skin tight . . . so if I opened my jacket, the dirt was out." She amassed an enviable wardrobe of tailored suits, formal and sportswear, that would dwarf the pages of *GQ*. She was a favorite subject of photographer Diane Arbus, best known for her candid portraits of the unusual.

At sixty-six, Miss DeLarverie lives and works in New York City as a bodyguard. When she speaks or when, on that rare occasion, she sings, her rich contralto rises.

Born in 1920 in New Orleans, Storme DeLarverie grew up the fiercely independent child of interracial parents. Storme was reared around music and show business, working circuses and later singing with big bands before joining the Revue. Like most women, she juggled several roles while with the Revue – stage manager, musical arranger, mother to the chorus, and master of ceremonies.

The Jewel Box showcased the talents of black and Hispanic men like Doodi Daniels, Mel Michaels, Billy Daye (who did a flawless vocal impression of Billie Holiday), and Joe Pheasant, a Native American. Along with white cast members like Robin Rogers (with a five-octave range) and Lynn Carter (whose Pearl Bailey impression floored Pearl Bailey), the Revue thrived and traveled in a social malaise of segregation and McCarthyism. Though it had a dedicated gay following, the show played largely to mainstream audiences. Its demise in the early seventies was prompted by violent homophobic boycotts staged by black nationalist groups which claimed the Jewel Box undermined the black male and the black family, and promoted homosexuality in the black community.

The grandeur of the Jewel Box Revue was conceived by Florida entrepreneurs Danny Brown and "Doc" Benner, who transformed the femme impersonation showcase of Miami's Club Jewel Box into a touring cabaret. From 1932 to 1973, the Jewel Box presented the highest standards of impersonation immortalized in Shakespearian theater and the Chinese opera, as well as the rituals of Africa and the Middle East.

The Jewel Box was the forerunner of *La Cage aux Folles.* It is mythologized in the Broadway smash *A Chorus Line* and recently has been noted in bestsellers like Ted Fox's *Showtime at the Apollo* and Mary Wilson's autobiography, *Dreamgirl: My Life as a Supreme.* Some of the original Jewel Box members have lost contact or changed lifestyles. Some have fallen to AIDS. But in the many hours of archival research, conversation, and filming, one fact remains: Miss DeLarverie and the Jewel Box Revue were one of a kind.

I never saw the Revue, but the times, the people, and the show itself are vividly present in my mind's eye. In a sense, *Storme: The Lady of the Jewel Box* is a coming-out for me as a black lesbian filmmaker, because the subject deals overtly with the gay and lesbian experience.

Though funding plagues most independent productions, particularly the films and videos of black women, the fundraising process for *Storme* has also been difficult because of the subject of the documentary. Female impersonation, and definitely the less explored area of male impersonation, are not topics of priority in this neoconservative age. Social services and support for the arts have been drastically cut in the Reagan years and grants and endowments tend to reflect the interests and biases of the ruling administration. To my surprise, the project received a substantial grant from the Corporation for Public Broadcasting, a federal agency which administers the Public Broadcasting Service. But fundraising continues even as production ends and post-production begins.

There is a "soft politic" to the history and human chronicle of *Storme,* but much of the political work has taken place behind the camera. During a five-day shoot in October, the film crew was a capable blend of technicians reflecting a wide variety of races, gender, and sexual preferences. While filming in New York's liveliest women's bars, a lot of consciousness-raising happened under the guise of location scouting and hanging lights.

Further, the principals of the Jewel Box, now in their fifties and sixties, are a generation removed from the fervor of today's lesbian and gay activists. One of the major challenges inherent in this project has been translating the realities of the pre-Stonewall years and the revolutionary importance of the Jewel Box Revue in the proud, post-Stonewall eighties.

During the making of *Storme,* two incidents stand out. As preproduction research intensified, I joined film researcher Isaac Jackson at a major archive of black culture, hoping to locate press clips and other references to the show. After a white librarian ran out of leads, she referred us to an older, black staff member. His smile turned to a shocked expression as we asked for his assistance in finding material on the Jewel Box. "Do you know what that was?" he asked incredulously. "Oh, it was a fabulous company of female impersonators!" I replied. "We're doing a film on it for PBS." The man left abruptly and just as suddenly returned with a small stack of index cards from the reserved collection. "I don't know why people have to bring out the worst in black folks for public display!" he said, reluctantly handing us the references. This took place in a public library.

On another occasion, I was screening an excerpt of *Storme* during a college lecture tour. A middle-aged black woman, mother of three, recalled excitedly how everybody in her neighborhood – straight and gay – came out to see the Jewel Box when it hit town. "Now *that* was a show!" she said.

Somewhere between the bitterness and the nostalgia, there's a film. These reactions typify the resistance and the welcome *Storme: The Lady of the Jewel Box* will encounter as the film premières in festivals and screenings across the country.

Perhaps it's impossible to think one short film can bridge a chasm of ignorance and repression. But you've got to start somewhere.

Thoughts on Women's Cinema: Eating Words, Voicing Struggles

YVONNE RAINER

Polemics and manifestos having always served as sparkplugs to my energies and imagination, I've been surprised when, following their publication, such statements were taken with what seemed to be excessive seriousness. Thus, in the mid-sixties, when I said "no" to this and "no" to that in dance and theater, I could not foresee that these words would dog my footsteps and beg me to eat them (or at least modify them) for the next twenty years. Such may be the case with my more recent stance toward/against/for narrative conventions in cinema. Raised as I have been with this century's Western notions of adversarial aesthetics, I continue to have difficulty in accommodating my latest articulation of the narrative "problem"– i.e., according to Teresa De Lauretis's conflation of narrativity itself with the Oedipus complex, whereby woman's position is constantly reinstated for the consummation or frustration of male desire. The difficulty lies in accommodating this with a conviction that it is of the utmost urgency that women's voices, experience, and consciousness – at whatever stage – be expressed in all their multiplicity and heterogeneity, and in as many formats and styles – narrative or not – from here to queendom come and throughout the kingdom. In relation to the various notions of an avant-garde, this latter view, in its emphasis on voicing what has previously gone unheard, gives priority to unmasking and reassessing social relations, rather than overturning previously validated aesthetic positions. My personal accommodation becomes more feasible when cast in terms of difference rather than opposition and when the question is asked: "Which strategies bring women together in recognition of their common *and* different economic and sexual oppressions and which strategies do not?" The creation of oppositional categories of women's film or video, or, for starters, film *and* video, begs this question.

For what it's worth, here is a list of useless oppositions. Documentary vs. fiction. Work in which the voices carry a unified truth vs. work in which truth must be wrested from conflicting or conflicted voices. Work that adheres to traditional codes vs. work in which the story is disrupted by stylistic incongruities or digressions (Helke Sanders's *Redupers,* Laura Mulvey and Peter Wollen's *Riddles of the Sphinx).* Work with a beginning, middle, and end vs. work that has a beginning and then turns into something else (Marguerite Duras's *Natalie Granger).* Work in which the characters run away with the movie vs. work whose characters never get off the ground (Rabina Rose's *Nightshift).* Work in which women *tell* their herstories (Julia Reichert and Jim Klein's *Union Maids)* vs. work in which they parody them (Ana Carolina's *Hearts and Guts).* Work that delivers information in a straightforward manner (Jacki Ochs's *Secret Agent*) vs. work in which information accrues slowly, elliptically, or poetically (Trinh Minh-ha's *Naked Spaces).* Work in which the heroine acts vs. work in which she does nothing but talk (my *Journeys from Berlin/1971).* Work in which she triumphs vs. work in which she fails (Valie Export's *Invisible Adversaries).* Work in which she is a searcher or dominatrix (Bette Gordon's *Variety,* Monika Treut and Elfie Mikesch's *Seduction: The Cruel Woman*) vs. work in which she is victim (Lynne Tillman and Sheila McLaughlin's *Committed).* Work whose heroines you like (Connie Field's *Rosie the Riveter,* Julie Dash's *Illusions)* vs. work whose heroines repel you (Doris Dorrie's *Straight to the Heart,* Chantal Akerman's *je, tu, il, elle).* Work in which you nearly drown in exotic signifiers of femininity (Leslie Thornton's *Adynata*) vs. work whose director can't figure out how to dress the heroine, so removes her altogether (my *The Man Who Envied Women).* All of these films share a potential for political purpose and historical truth.

I could go on *ad infinitum* with these divide-and-conquer oppositions. There is one other example that I'm not going to give equal footing with the others but will mention in passing only insofar as it bears a deceptive resemblance to the others: films in which the heroine marries the man vs. films in which she murders him. We have only to look in vain for recent films by women that end in marriage to realize what a long way we've come, give or take the baby. Marriage at the beginning maybe, but at the end – never. I challenge anyone to name one in recent memory. Murder, on the other hand, is a different story. As Joan Braderman pointed out last spring at the "Gender and Visual Representation" conference at the University of Massachusetts, in the past ten years a substantial number of women's films have been produced that focus on a murder of a man by a woman or women. To name a few: Akerman's *Jeanne Dielman,* Marlene Gorris's *A Question of Silence,*

Dorrie's *Straight to the Heart,* Sally Heckel's *A Jury of Her Peers,* Margaretha Von Trotta's *Sheer Madness.*

The phenomenon of man-murder in women's films points to the problematic of representing men. Do we wreak revenge on them (if for no other reason than the cinematic sway they have held over us for so long), turn the tables on them, turn them into celluloid wimps, give them ample screen time in which to speak self-evident macho bullshit, do away with them by murder within the story, or eliminate them *from* the story to begin with? Do we focus on exceptional men who escape the above stereotypes, or do we weave utopian scenarios in which men and women gambol in egalitarian bliss? Lynne Tillman and I pondered the question of whether it is politically useful to allow ourselves to be fascinated with men in our films even as we discussed the strange fascination with the 1986 World Series that had befallen the two of us along with every woman we know.

Following one screening of *The Man Who Envied Women,* a well-known feminist who subscribes to Lacanian psychoanalytic theory asked me why I hadn't made a film about a woman. I was flabbergasted, having been under the impression that I had done just that. But she, taking the title literally and taken in by the prevailing physical presence of the male character, had discounted the pursuing, nagging, questioning female voice on the soundtrack. By staying out of sight my heroine is never caught with her pants down. Does this mean the film is not *about* her?

It's also been noted that my female characters are not heroines. I would qualify that: my heroines are not heroic. They are deeply skeptical of easy solutions and very self-critical, constantly looking for their own complicity in patriarchal configurations. But neither are they cynical or pessimistic. The moments I like best in my films are those that produce – almost simultaneously – both assertion and question. Early on in *The Man Who Envied Women,* the assertion that women can't be committed feminists unless they give up men is uttered as part of a conversation, overheard by a man in the foreground, by a woman who is testing her female companion by quoting yet another woman whose relationship to the speaker is not identified and who never appears. The two speakers are also anonymous and are never seen again once this scene is over. I, the director, am not trying in this scene to persuade my audience of the rightness or wrongness of the statement. What is important is that *it be given utterance* because, in our culture, outside of a convent, giving up men freely and willingly – that is, without the social coercion of aging – is a highly stigmatized act or downright taboo. The linkage of giving up men, in this scene, with commitment as a feminist, however, is distanced and made arguable through the device of having the spectator become an eavesdropper on the conversation along with the foregrounded male character, then distanced once more through quotation. "*She told me,*" says this minor, will-o-the-wisp heroine, "that I would never be a committed feminist until I give up men."

Whether an utterance comes across as feminist prescription, call-to-arms, or problem-articulated-ambiguously-to-be-dealt-with-or-not-later-in-the-film is always on my mind in the collecting, mounting, and framing of texts. If the experience of watching certain kinds of social documentaries is like watching the bouncing ball come down at exactly the right moment on the syllables of the familiar song, watching a film of mine may be more akin to "now you see it, now you don't." You never know when you're going to be hit on the head with the ball, and you aren't always sure what to do when the ball disappears for long stretches of time.

Which brings me to what might be called a method of interrogating my characters and myself when I set out to make a film. Thinking about this has been facilitated by rereading Bill Nichols's essay, "The Voice of Documentary," which poses certain questions that are relevant to both fiction and documentary. To what degree are we to believe a given speaker in a film? Do all the speakers convey a unified vision of a given history? Do the speakers emerge as autonomous shapers of a personal destiny or as subjects conditioned by the contradictions and pressures of a particular historical period? To what degree does a given film convey an independent consciousness, a voice of its own, probing, remembering, sustaining, doubting, functioning as a surrogate for our own consciousness? Do the questioning and believing of such a film question its own operations? Does the activity of fixing meaning in such a film refer to relations outside the film – "out there" – or does the film remain stalled in its own reflexivity? Is reflexivity the only alternative to films that simply suppose that things were as the participant-witnesses recall or state them, or as they appear to the spectator, in the case of fiction films?

Finally: Should a film whose main project is to restore the voice and subjectivity of a previously ignored or suppressed person or segment of the population, should such a film contain argument, contradiction, or express the director's ambivalence within the film either directly, through language, or indirectly, through

National

stylistic intervention? Obviously, we can't afford to be prescriptive about any of this.

My own solution runs to keeping an extradiagetic voice, a voice separate from the characters and story, fairly active in every scene. It need not take the form of a narrating voice, although it often does. Sometimes it takes the form of a *Tyl Eulenspiegel*-like disruption, as when an anonymous woman enters the frame just before a troubling bit of sexual theory is enunciated, peers into the camera lens, and asks all the menstruating women to leave the theater. Sometimes it operates like a kind of seizure, producing odd behavior in a given character, as when the analysand in *Journeys from Berlin* speaks in baby-talk. Often it comes across in reading or recitation, which has the effect of separating the voice of the character from that of the author of his or her words.

At this historical moment we still need to search out and be reminded of suppressed histories and struggles: housewives, prostitutes, women of color, lesbians, Third World people, the aging, working women. The methods of representing these histories is a separate and equally important issue. I see no reason why a single film can't use many different methods, which is something I've been saying for years but didn't come close to realizing until *The Man Who Envied Women.* In this film, fictional and documentary modes come into play more fully than in any of my previous work, offsetting the calculation of my still-cherished recitations and readings with the immediacy of dramatic and documentary enactment. These last are, admittedly, the strategies that offer the spectator the most powerful sense of the real. But reality, as we so well know, always lies elsewhere, a fact that we nevertheless endlessly seek to disavow and from which we always retreat. I shall continue to remind us of that disavowal by challenging reality's representational proxies with assorted hanky-panky. I hope others continue to do likewise and otherwise.

Discordant Views

SILVIA KOLBOWSKI

Suspended action, excessive display, repetitious posturing: representations of women in the advertising print medium generate the most diffident of responses: flipping through the pages of a magazine or newspaper, each image/slogan registers no more than a pale imprint as it dissolves into the next. The woman viewer – finding identification or exclusion – is recruited into impassive complicity with the rendered positions. The male viewer routinely gazes with flippant acceptance of status quo assumptions, framed as though by a mirror.

As this myriad of images increases, an accretion through time of minor variations in style and motivation, it takes on the quality of an immovable support, a purposeful prop.

In the past few years, photography critic Carol Squiers has addressed the reading of mass media imagery in the form of critical thematic exhibitions. Each exhibition is composed of several hundred magazine tearsheets, montaged in specific groupings – chains of images, as it were, on gallery walls.[1] In her statement for the exhibition *Design for Living*, curated for the photography room at P.S. 1 and shown during the spring of 1984, Squiers writes:

> *The recumbent woman, in particular, has become popular in the '80s, laid out across one magazine page after another, propped up on useless arms or merely sprawling in ungainly positions on couches, beaches, and studio floors, powerless and immobile.*[2]

A design for living: woman's frozen sprawl is the timeless, essential prop for man's contextual, temporal pose. His pose – whether polo-playing in Ralph Lauren or cradling the tools of his trade on a *New York Times* cover – tells "a predictably different story," of an upright, subjective relation to power. Her suspended-action pose, a leap out of time, camouflages her static role as prop.

1. This same format – a grouping of tearsheets methodically laid out on gallery walls – has been used by Squiers previously in five other exhibitions: *In and Out of Power* (1982), *Making News: Black Americans in the '60s* (1983), *Men* (1983), *Women of Distinction* (1983), and *All God's Creatures* (1983).
2. Exhibition statement, *Design for Living*.

Magazine closed, "ungainly" sprawl hidden and gaze redirected, women go on with their lives. But is this balance so easily regained? Can *She* simply pick herself up at will and feign misrecognition: "This is not woman, this is mere representation"? Or would this detachment simply root her more firmly in her "invisible support for masculine representations"?[3]

Luce Irigaray, a French psychoanalytic theorist who has written much on the subject of woman's reflective, specular qualities, believes that woman is never far from her position as mirror for the masculine. Woman is the producer of comfort and reassurance. Formed at the congruence of patriarchal – social, linguistic, and historical – lines, woman seems to be inextricably caught in this web. Yet Irigaray does locate a potentially critical space for the woman, a space which does not relegate her to the position of outsider searching in a vacuum for a new self, but which leaves room within the existing structure for difference:

> *Going back into the house of the philosopher . . . making hay* [faire le noce] *with the philosopher also presupposes maintaining what in the mirror cannot reflect itself: its tarnish, its brilliance, thus the dazzle, the ecstasies. Matter for reproduction, mirror for duplication, the wife of the philosopher will also have to ensure that guarantee of a narcissism often extrapolated in a transcendental dimension. Certainly without saying it, without knowing it.*[4]

Women may unwittingly "maintain" or lend themselves to this insidiously invisible support. But the act of lending, as opposed to a *giving* nature, implies an exchange. And it is in the very suffocating proximity to this guarantee of masculine narcissism that the space for difference can be constructed.

For women to enter into a cultural/political critique requires an immersion in a duplicitous system which purports to create a place for the woman, while making of her a reflecting pool of masculine modes. But with this immersion comes "the rejection and putting outside of what resists transparency," what resists invisibility.

3. Elizabeth L. Berg, "The Third Woman," *Diacritics* 12, no. 2 (Summer 1982): 15. In this case, Berg is paraphrasing Luce Irigaray.
4. Luce Irigaray, "Questions," in *Ce sexe qui n'en est pas un* (Paris: Minuit, 1977), p. 147, as quoted in Berg, "The Third Woman," p. 15. I use Berg's own translation of this quotation. Since this article was written, a translation of Irigaray's book has been published, in which a slightly different version of this paragraph can be found: *This Sex Which Is Not One*, trans. Catherine Porter (Ithaca: Cornell University Press, 1985), p. 151.

"Thus the woman critic," writes Elizabeth Berg, "must continue to function as a support for man's representation of himself, yet all the while maintaining what exceeds that masculine self-portrait: that is to say, *the trace of the material support itself.*"[5] This requires looking through or to the side of the blinding light of the mirror, and focusing on its "tarnish" and "dazzle," on that structure which, as Berg notes, both makes possible *and* disrupts representation.

Squiers's curatorial format in *Design for Living* seems to mirror the above formulation. The exhibition is comprised of a compilation of hundreds of photographic media images and their accompanying copy texts, uncropped and unmarked, except for the succinct statement at the head of the show which explicitly points to general male/female stereotypes and their differing relations to power.

These unmarked images are marked by the effect of frozen montage. Squiers "curates"[6] a chain of images which is organized in such a way as to highlight the structure of each advertisement or article format. Layers of meaning within individual pages are cast in a different light by their proximity to disparate or similar representations on the same walls. While the curator does not alter the individual images/advertisements in any way – she could be said to act out a traditional femininity in her support of a presentation – she plays an active role in producing a different narrative or story. The images may speak for themselves, and therefore speak the language of "invisible" masculine hegemony, but by paring down the mass of images, marking out an area of focus, and making the reading of individual images and copy contingent on context, Squiers outlines the "traces of the material support" of phallocentrism. Consider one of the groupings:

In an opening image for a *New York Times Magazine* article entitled "Life with Leona," a resplendent Leona Helmsley lies recumbent on a plush bed in hotel surroundings – her/his hotel – gaze and arms extended upward to meet the camera-view angled overhead, while next to her a black chambermaid, with head and eyes lowered, leads away two plump pillows. To the right of this image is an advertisement for Johnny Walker Black whiskey, depicting

5. Berg, p. 15 (my italics).
6. For specific discussions of how Squiers's curatorial strategies differ from more traditional approaches, see Kate Linker, "Multiple Choice" (review) in *Artforum* 12, no. 1 (September 1983): 77, and Abigail Solomon-Godeau, "'In and Out of Power' at P.S. 1" (review) in *Art in America* 70, no. 3 (March 1982): 142-143.

four images: a woman in black fur, a (black) oilwell field, a black Rolls Royce, and a Johnny Walker Black bottle label. The copy line for this advertisement reads "Success is often measured by how deeply you're in the Black." Next to this a *New York Times Magazine* cover image of author Alice Walker "Telling the Black Woman's Story," which leads to an advertisement for the sunny Bahamas, where a couple of smiling white tourists stand against a brilliant blue sky, their arms encircling a native Bahamian woman, illustrating that "It's Better in the Bahamas." One might even consider another advertisement, located near these images, as related to this group: a very "Extravagant" pair of black shoes displayed against a brilliant skyblue background, openings encircled by metal chains.[7]

A chain of meanings can be discerned here. For example, the servitude of blacks tied to that of women, the happy bedding down of women with conservatism, the reduction of enchainment to decor and accessory – where stepping out means stepping on – and patronization with a smile, among other readings.

Or another arrangement: in a high-fashion layout, a woman clothed in underpants kneels on a bed and displays her face on the screen of a television monitor facing the reader by looking directly into the video camera she holds in front of her face. By this action the camera lowers her gaze, which is ostensibly involved in an act of narcissism, and places it on the screen as the object of the viewer's gaze. Near this image Squiers has placed an advertisement for a gold watch; the page frames a closely cropped image of a woman's face looking down with parted lips at her hands as they tie a man's shiny shoe. She does not look at what her hands are doing, but rather at the gift received in exchange for her services – the other gleam, of the gold watch encircling her wrist. An image of a woman selling a watch next to one of a woman watching her sale.

Also in this vignette is a fashion photograph of a woman wearing a diamond watch and bracelets on one wrist, while the other hand holds a torn photograph of half of the model's face in front of it to form a "complete" face with a tear down the middle. Here representation seems to be both equated with and separated from the "real" body, a revealing point of view in that the rent produced

7. The color relationships between advertisements are intentionally emphasized in this exhibition layout. As Squiers notes in her statement: "Color and form in photographs serve a crucial function in conveying the message of stereotype, throughout the exhibition photographs are 'matched' to show how the aesthetics of the photograph help create a sense of continuum – the continuum of stereotype – fashion into politics, politics into warfare, warfare into aesthetics."

by the photograph marks the inaccessibility of a purely real body, or, for that matter, of an original image. While the lived experience of the male or female body undeniably differs, perhaps radically, the experience of the body is always interwoven with its representation in culture. There is no clearcut distinction between the body in the bedroom or boudoir and its imag(in)ed version.

But all that glitters in this ad is gold – the glimmer of a radical construction of sexuality is overshadowed by the redundancy of the two objects posed – model and jewel form the more explicit equation.

It would seem that these juxtapositions point to the price the woman pays for being well kept: she is pinned down by a visualizing economy which runs the gamut from overt media scenarios of violence in which she plays the pampered object of a crime, to the most oblique constructions, equally implicit of violence. In fact, representation's woman appears to thrive on violence.

The particular meaning inferred from these groupings have in a sense been orchestrated by Squiers. But although a very active position has been taken by the curator, this grouping would not be out of place in the ordinary pagination of a mainstream magazine. Squiers's composition merely has the bad taste to point a finger.

Accusation is the resistant victim's strategy. And rather than act as the guarantor of the masculine gaze, Squiers demands that we look differently. The language of serious business plays with the spaces between commonplaces and "high" art, between high fashion and the necessities of life, between "warfare" and "aesthetics,"[8] and *Design for Living* plays the game of serious business on its terms – but from a distance. The close scrutiny of magazine-scale layouts often degenerates into passive absorption of isolated details – a kind of losing sight of where one stands. But the insistence of this exhibition on contextualized readings generates a larger view – not a view which projects a detached, floating figure looking down at broad con-figurations and obliterated detail, but rather, a point of view which is closer to a "listening with [the] body,"[9] a different kind of "distraction," terms which filmmaker/writer Marguerite Duras uses in describing the relation between the oral and visual scenarios of her film, *India Song:*

> *If the oral scenario stated, for example: "Anne-Marie Stretter enters the private drawing room, looks out at the garden," then Delphine*

8. See statement, note 7.
9. Marguerite Duras, "Notes on *India Song,*" *Camera Obscura,* no. 6 (1980): 43.

Seyrig in fact entered and looked at the garden. But at the same time she was listening to what was said about what she did. *She therefore entered* less, *looked at the garden less, but by the same token listened* more. *What was lost of her entrance and her look was compensated by the words, which expressed it at the same time as she did. The words, the oral scenario, were to be eliminated in the editing and Delphine was to remain alone to effect the entrance and the look at the garden. But the result was there: Delphine's distraction, due to her listening with her body, is part of the film.*[10]

The female viewer of advertising and journalism's representations must gaze as though without a body. Not listening to "what is said about what she does," she mechanically performs in the narrow space afforded her. The pleasure marked out for her within the confines of consumption and the consumption of the image, delimits an acknowledgment of the body which pays the violent price of this enactment.

Duras's distracted looker sacrifices a certain attentiveness to seamless narration, to "realism," in order to hear the voice which described her actions before/as she performs them. The "look" which she loses is not so much her subjective gaze, as much as it is her "looked-at-ness." What remains is an attention to culture's unquestioned formulas and, as in *Design for Living*, a distinctly critical focus on the female body.

Squiers's curatorial "voice" in *Design for Living* resonates an "unspeakable" text throughout the exhibition. This voice does not let "truth" speak for itself, knowing that this truth will have a masculine, dominant voice. Rather, it leaves room for the female viewer/reader to find a voice which might skirt these truths. Squiers fingers those in power through, as I noted above, a strategy of presentation, or "display." The act of display is one which is comfortingly familiar to women. But, strangely enough, Squiers uses the familiar to find the unfamiliar—a critical space for women within phallocentric discourse.

Irigaray writes of "mimetism" as a way out for women from the unavoidability of masculine codes: "mimetism, the role historically assigned to women—that of reproduction, but deliberately assumed; an acting out of role-playing . . . which allows the woman . . . the better to know and hence to expose what it is she mimics."[11]

10. Ibid.
11. Mary Jacobus, "The Question of Language: Men of Maxims and *The Mill on the Floss*," in *Writing and Sexual Difference*, ed. Elizabeth Abel (Chicago: University of Chicago Press, 1980), p. 40.

To play with mimesis is, therefore, for a woman, to attempt to recover the place of her exploitation by discourse, without letting herself be simply reduced to it. It is to resubmit herself . . . to "ideas," notably about her, elaborated in/by a masculine logic, but in order to make "visible," by an effect of playful repetition, what should have remained hidden: *the recovery of a possible operation of the feminine in language. It is also to "unveil" the fact that, if women mime so well, they do not simply reabsorb themselves in this function. They also remain elsewhere.*[12]

Squiers repeats – in a gesture of display – an act already performed: the public has already been exposed to these photographs before, in a different context, one which does not allow for a response or, for that matter, a careful reading. She takes "what should have remained hidden," even within explicit photographic and textual scenarios, and makes it difficult to ignore.

Covering almost the whole of one of the four walls of the exhibition – and punctuated by a clipping entitled "Women at War" – is a combination of advertisements or fashion layouts depicting model women, and articles covering war, nuclear weaponry, politics. In one advertisement, a woman – literally in the hands of a man who fashions her look, designer Bill Blass – is admonished by two ordered lists, "What I like and don't like so much in a woman," in which woman's socialized predictability is chastised, re-ordered. In another layout a woman's face is posed in contemporary makeup: traditional makeup markings – the hyperemphasis of features so that they may take the place of an erroneous absence (of the penis)? – are displaced on the face and re-colored so as to produce "bruises" and tasteful wounds, her face spotlighted, as though in the midst of interrogation. Nearby, a model's wrist is held in the grip of a Doberman's teeth, and a man attempts to break into a fashion scenario. In this image the women are shown resisting – after a fashion. One woman leaves through the window, while the other one leans against the door, closing out the intruder. But the scene is clearly a traditional reenactment, of a traditional pleasure, wherein the models are going nowhere, frozen in their positions.

12. Luce Irigaray, "Pouvoir du discours, subordination du féminin," in *Ce sexe qui n'en est pas un* (Paris: Minuit, 1977), p. 78, as quoted in Jacobus, "The Question of Language," p. 40 (my italics). Irigaray's "elsewhere," a concept she uses in several of her essays, seems to have something in common with Duras's "distractions" or "listening with the body." I use Jacobus's translation here. A translation of this whole essay can be found in the recently published *This Sex Which Is Not One*, pp. 68-85 (see note 4).

The commonplaces of feminine victimization are placed next to their counterparts – overt discussions of violence, the world events of imperialism and warfare, waged and precipitated by those in power. An article in this section is entitled "Is the Nuclear Threat Manageable?" Implicit in the inclusion of such articles in this exhibition is not a search for answers to such questions, not simply a liberal strategy of highlighting the tragedy of their necessity. Rather, Squiers questions the positioning of power and powerlessness – our "proper" places. Busily living out their "pleasure," women are made "manageable," and thus lose their defenses against repressive order. Squiers points to the question of pleasure and locates it within the *un*natural, the social – a realm from which the biological never escapes. This feminine pleasure has a hollow resonance, as though ricocheting in a vacuum.

Having been taught to speak softly, critical femininity finds a strident whisper. In *Design for Living,* like a relentless murmur running throughout, another, different voice can be discerned.

Remote Control

BARBARA KRUGER

A well-oiled bicep fills the screen and flexes to the strains of the already-ancient *Purple Rain.* The bicep is sort of an orange color and, in this extreme close-up view, totally unrecognizable as a swatch of human anatomy. It mobs the viewing aperture and looks like a cross between a slab of fatty bacon and a piece of kryptonite approaching its melting point. It is then quickly replaced by a talking roll of toilet tissue which pleads with members of a family to "touch" it. The rotund glob of needy, animated paper gives way to an "anchorman," a somber talking head who reports a catastrophic plane crash. We look at images of emergency medical teams packaging the dead in yellow body-bags. The runway is littered with blood and spare body parts. This segment is immediately followed by a shot of a kitten in sunglasses propped under a beach umbrella.

As this clashing litany suggests, television is the most relentless purveyor of the messages that constitute and perpetuate our severely fragmented public consciousness. It slices our attention span into increments too infinitesimal to get up and measure. Spending a large part of our lives planted in front of a piece of talking furniture, we are held hostage by the pleasure of the cutting and the repetition, by a kind of intermittent fascination which is facilitated by the relief we feel in numbness and which has the feel of the erratically riveted wonderment experienced by infants. That television's parade of segments follow one another but do not "go together" does not seem strange or problematic to its viewers. Seen cinematically, these disjunctions might appear as affronts to narrative or as some kind of "kooky" avant-garde collage.

Television tells us not of *a* vision, but of visions. It evades singularity and loiters amid the serial, the continual, the flow. Its interest in storytelling is peripheral yet promiscuous. For although a large portion of broadcast time is given over to Hollywood-style filmic drama and the familiar closure of storytelling, television, perching in our living rooms like a babbling, over-controlling guest, is deeply embroiled in the authoritative declarations and confessionals of direct address. The cinema frames and brackets particular incidents and in doing so reveals its connections to painting and photography, while television seems to emerge via the coupling of new picture and computer technology with the chattering of radio. As film's anecdotal accountings necessarily speak of the past, television's direct address inhabits the present. The "nonfiction" genres (news, sports, talk shows) that use direct address also appropriate the stuff of events almost instantaneously and play them back with the relentlessness of an avenging mirror. And because all this combined with ads, sit-coms, soaps, game shows, and docudramas looks like what we've come to think of as life, its simulation grants it perpetual license. Blurring the distinction between the thought and the act, between imagination and experience, TV's constant broadcast alleviates the truth of its special sanctity and sprinkles it on everything that moves.

Perhaps the most obvious feature of any rhetoric of realism is its offering of assurance: its suggestion that "yes, this is the way things are." The illustration of the seemingly real lets us know where we stand, what side we're on, and who's winning. As long as sides are being taken and good battles evil, as long as stories are climaxed and laws enacted, we can continue to think that we're in the neighborhood of ethics, principles, and truth.

We look at television. Its delivery of conventional narrative via soap operas, sit-coms, and miniseries comforts the viewer with the re-creation of prosceniumlike space and the proposal of the real. It returns our look via a cast of miniature characters who declare, tease, and sing themselves into our lives. Left without a singular, continuous script, but bombarded by short quasi stories and subjects without predicates (and vice versa), we search for sustained narratives and their attendant realism. But we find only segmented smidgens that "make sense," that supply us with our need for order and control. We sit and watch the little people. We hear voices. They give us "the news."

Direct address dominates the proceedings and lets the viewers think they know who's doing the talking and to whom. We know when Dan Rather is going to break the bad news and we're not surprised when we're contradicted by a talking tub of margarine or seduced by a roll of toilet paper. We know TV meant what it said when it announced "You Are There." We know that we have received orders not to move and that we're learning to walk in place at the speed of light.

Direct-address television (most notably the news) recognizes the audience and treats it to a sort of rampant discursiveness that depends on the amplification of the crisis, the catastrophe, the event. If the American government can allude to its role in the field of "crisis management," then perhaps it can be said that the media partakes of a kind of "crisis construction." Spewing out an event a minute, news broadcasts jump from the Mediterranean to Detroit, from famine to a puppy's plaintive cry for "Kibbles and Bits." We keep up with current events.

But what is an event? A gesture framed, a statement repeated, an image reproduced, a shot fired? What happens when details are bracketed and actions extracted from the horizontal expanse of lived time and stacked to form a reconstruction of the real? Events are literally created for the media, from miniseries, whenever hostages are taken, to the structural embroilments of diplomacy and the aesthetic formalities of summit meetings and state visits. These terse docudramas are stuffed into the nightly news broadcasts, which are then generously spiked with a dollop of "natural disaster" footage. While the former remind us of the strong government leaders who are taking care of both business and us, the latter – the meteorological mishaps, the "acts of God" – give airtime to our Ultimate Leader and handily distract us from what his lieutenants down here on Spaceship Earth are really up to. So while wars are fought over bruised egos and saved faces, we are treated to major coverage of natural calamities, of that which seems beyond "man's" control and through which we all suffer together. Cameras stalk the globe sniffing out clumps of "natural" morbidity ripe for representation. Broadcast worldwide, these become symbolic of "universal suffering," elicit sympathy and some money to alleviate a fraction of the problem, and are quickly forgotten, supplanted by the next atrocity in another exotic "elsewhere."

Deciphering who's really who in TV's world of substitutional histories and circuitous ventriloquisms is a game that hardly anyone wants to play. Things are accepted at face value, at the surface of the screen, because the audience thinks this scrim of fascination is all the medium has to give. And this scrim is usually more than enough. Offering itself up as a rest stop for wandering eyes, the tube offers a parade of personalities masquerading either as other personalities or merely as themselves. Neither real nor illusory, they appear and disappear at the flick of a switch, controlled by some remote idea of what is fit for the moment or what might be better.

In a recent episode of *Miami Vice* directed by its star Don Johnson, America's newest national treasure, a retired army man is exposed as a major drug-dealer busy distributing a product left over from his days in Vietnam: killer heroin contaminated by wood alcohol. It seems the captain was shipping the drug back from Nam in the body-bags of dead combatants, and the alcohol had been used to preserve the corpses. And who portrays this "pig," this necromonster whose office walls are lined with photos of Richard Nixon and Henry Kissinger? Why, none other than G. Gordon Liddy, of *Watergate,* the miniseries that thrilled and entertained us over a decade ago. Considering *Vice*'s proclivities toward embroidering the seamier (as in Versace) side of life, the mind boggles at the casting possibilities to come: Robert Vesco as a smuggler hot into stuffing toot up the innards of lava lamps to be sold on the tonier boulevards of New York and L.A., and Chuck Colson as a dealer-turned-born-again-Christian hawking courses on how to get rich quick by buying real estate for no money down.

This human exchangeability was the subject of a recent installment of *Amazing Stories,* Steven Spielberg's ongoing joke on and homage to the cute joys and even cuter tribulations of life in the good old U.S. of A. "Remote Control Man," directed by Bob Clarke, tells the story of a poor schnook who is victimized by the entire kit and caboodle of his traumatic domestic life and turns for solace to (surprise!) his TV. His nagging wife gets pissed off, so she sells the TV for a new pair of pumps and all hell breaks loose. In the usual whiz-bang sci-fi manner, the husband winds up with a spectacular replacement, a video appliance that makes the term "state of the art" seem archaic. Propped up in his chair, remote-control device grasped tightly in his chubby little hands, the schnook is able to zap his family into scores of character mutations and to fill his house with a veritable army of TV celebs. Bounding out of the screen at the speed of light, they nudge, cajole, and crusade their way into his domain, making his delirious family squabbles seem like a slow day at the library. Barbara Billingsly, recreating the role of June Cleaver, makes his breakfast, and his son is transformed into Gary Coleman. Richard Simmons, Lyle Alzado (the Hulk), and Ed McMahon are but a smidgen of the onslaught that converts what he thought would be heaven into a semi-living hell. In response to the schnook's frantic questions as to why this star-studded gang is occupying his living room, the grinning celebs reply, "What are you asking me for? I'm just a character on TV! I'm not real." "Don't be such a wimp." "Turn on to people, not to the boob tube. Turn on to your wife and kids."

So what are Spielberg and Co. trying to tell us? That the characterological simulations of television must be dislodged? That the rhetoric of the real must be reestablished amid the morass of electronic duplications? That we should abandon the dictates of our favorite light source and return to the clumps of figures that constitute our notion of the family? Of course this is being suggested, but with the full understanding that almost nothing short of nothing can treat the heavy dose of fascination that grips so many of us. And so, the folks of Amblin Entertainment figure, why not go through the motions and make like you're going for the apple pie?

The ventriloquistic capabilities of television reach their literalized apex in *Puttin' on the Hits,* a show in which contestants are judged on their lip-syncing prowess, their looks, and their "originality." The latter category is a particularly poignant one, since most of the contenders appear as carbon copies of their favorite rock star, not only replicating the attire and gestures, but also miming the voices of their idols. Out of their open but mute mouths spring the vocal virtuosities of Prince, Sade, Bruce, and dozens of other current and nostalgic divinities. Bounding across the stage, the contestants act out in front of millions of viewers what was once relegated to the mirrors of teenagers' bedrooms, private arenas where air guitars and sultry poses reigned supreme. *Puttin' on the Hits* stages the charged bonding of uncritical appropriation with exhibitionism, and grants its practitioners the right to make spectacles of themselves while making believe they're someone else.

This ventriloquism coupled with narrative rearrangement recently played havoc with scads of pirated videotapes of the movie *Rambo* that were smuggled into the Middle East and subtitled in French and Arabic. For along with the translation came the erasure of all references to Vietnam and the Soviet Union. The whole story was transformed to the Philippines circa 1963, where Rambo is busy rescuing POWs held by the Japanese. Sylvester Stallone's daftly rabid red, white, and blue-ism remains visually intact, but the muscle-bound hulk's rants are now accompanied by a contradictory text which propels his story to another time and another place.

This cavalier mixing and matching of pictures, words, char-

acters, and personages foregrounds video's chameleonic flexibility. Through rapidly spreading technology, video is able to be adapted to the needs not only of its authors and distributors, but ultimately those of its domestic spectators, as well. Thus, video's lure is not only the promised pleasures of fascination, but also those of alteration, of "creativity." Planted in our own cozy "home box offices," we not only receive the prepackaged masquerades and lip-syncs of network TV, but can also partake of our own brand of substitution, time-shifting, editing, and dubbing. This puttering and hobbyism can be seen as an alleviation of the viewers' passivity, a way of allowing us some control over the image and words of corporate culture. But these are simply rearrangements of prescribed images, or, when the footage is one's own, simply private, undistributed gestures. The power of the corporate network is its ability to multiply and project its desiring voice into the larynx of its viewers and, with a few exceptions, to marginalize and make absent what it finds undesirable and unprofitable. Whether this business-as-usual can be interrupted by the supposed freedom of visual and vocal choices granted to us by the new video and cable technologies remains to be seen. And if we, the ventriloquistic dummies, really do start to talk back, will we merely end up selling Charmin to each other?

Girl/boy crime-busting duos have sleuthed their way through decades of black-and-white mystery films and color caper movies and are now a staple of prime-time TV programming. From *Mr. and Mrs. North* in the 1950s to *Moonlighting* in the 1980s, the genre has functioned not only as a pleasurable mix of sneaking and sexing, but also as a succinct barometer of the dispensations of the duo: of what is shared and who is slighted and how all this defines the division of labor. Early examples of the genre required the couple to be hitched, exceptionally solvent, and unusually susceptible to the scenes of crimes. In this way, *Mr. and Mrs. North* is clearly the antecedent of *Hart to Hart,* in which Jennifer and Jonathan Hart (Stephanie Powers and Robert Wagner) mate matrimony with material witnesses and seem to attract ulterior motives like crawlies to a roach motel. Swatched in glamorous expenditure and showering one another with "dahlings," they crime-bust their way from continent to continent via private jet, just one of the perks supplied by Hart Industries, a corporation of whose manufacture and services we know nothing. Consisting of plush offices and far-flung subsidiaries, the company is evacuated from the site of actual labor and appears as a model of today's nearly intangible service industries. We never see Jonathan "on the job," and although Jennifer floats through her various hobbies with grace and virtuosity, she (along with Max the butler and Freeway the dog) is seen as just another corporate perk, a reward that Jonathan treats with respect and humor.

The generically structured corporation whose nonspecificity seems suspect also surfaces in *Scarecrow and Mrs. King*. Our suspicions are confirmed when we discover that Lee Stetson (Bruce Boxleitner) and Amanda King (Kate Jackson), who are ostensibly employed by Federal Films, are actually federal agents pitted against the various evil empires that threaten the American government. If all this weren't enough of a throwback to the fifties, Amanda is ensconced in a little white-picket-fenced number in the D.C. suburbs which she inhabits with her mom and two kids, who have no idea that she lives a vicarious double life. And although she handles her assignments with decisiveness, she is generally sketched as an able but befuddled puritan, a ditzy housewife with weird hours. And, of course, she and Lee barely brush up against one another.

If *Hart to Hart* and *Scarecrow and Mrs. King* suggest that Jennifer and Amanda's deductive prowess exists only through the largess of corporate and government sanction, the more recent examples of the genre focus on independent women who make it their business to own their own business. But regardless of their investigative acumen, they still rely upon and enjoy the company of men as both partners and "fronts." In *Remington Steele,* Laura Holt (Stephanie Zimbalist) uses the name and body of Steele (Pierce Brosnan) to establish the credibility of her sleuthing venture (which once again is housed in the omnipresent plush offices). Though she engineers most of the goings on, she frequently defers to Steele in order to perpetuate her fabulation of noncontrol. The series also suffers the affliction that strikes all current examples of the genre: the postponement of the couple's sexual pleasure in order to fan the viewer's desire. This season Laura and Steele actually do embrace and kiss, but their relationship remains one of conversational seductions and competitive prowess. Pitting Steele's smooth demeanor and lightning command of movie trivia against Laura's entrepreneurship and enlightened bachelorettehood, the series renders a "battle of the sexes" in which the warriors seem to be driven to distraction by their attempts to pelt each other to death with candy kisses.

But this battle of the bon mots reaches truly pleasurable new heights in *Moonlighting,* in which Maddie Hayes (Cybil Shepherd) and David Addison (Bruce Willis) enter into hand-to-hand combat in the war of the words. As in *Remington Steele,* the woman runs the shop (once again the proverbial plush offices), and takes on David as a partner in the Blue Moon detective agency, which is overstaffed with a flock of loitering misfits. Although these peripheral characterizations are witty and well drawn, the real pleasures of the show are the intricate idiosyncracies of its scenario and the wonderfully smart rapid-fire repartee that runs relays between David and Maddie's mouths. Willis's David is that charming kind of fast-talking gorilla to whom some women spend their entire lives trying to build up an immunity, while Shepherd's Maddie is effective in a wonderfully played and constantly perturbed but ladylike sort of way. But although capable of silencing David's rants with haughty aplomb, she all too frequently is scripted to appear at a loss for words, responding instead with adorable gruntlike musings and grimaces which dishevel her lovely visage *just* enough. Aside from this very unfortunate convention, *Moonlighting* is chock-full of cute minitransgressions: smallish formal innovations which define its difference from the usual hack products that dominate prime-time TV. A recent episode sported a pretitle sequence in which Maddie and David addressed the audience and acknowledged that they had received a great deal of mail questioning when they were going to get it on or at least kiss. David wanted to do it right then and there, but Maddie insisted that it wasn't in that week's script and she couldn't possibly indulge in such unscripted pleasures. This portrayal of a female character as unable to proceed without the sanctions of the usually male-manufactured text was excruciatingly on the mark, but was depicted in a painfully uncritical manner. Nevertheless, the extension out of the narrative was a nice formal device and served to foreground the abstinence that stalks the genre. Some episodes of *Moonlighting* hopscotch from color to black-and-white and back, while others raise the meandering delights of the detective saga to new levels of lovable silliness.

The changes that the crime-busting mode has undergone over the past forty years show us how visual and literary forms develop in little fits and stops and starts. These alterations are both the impetuses for and the results of the times in which they were produced. If Maddie and David are the current "state of the art," then hopefully we can look forward to a future where the pleasures of verbal and sexual reciprocity flood prime-time television; where the role of the sexy, devil-may-care, fast-talking but affectionate asshole can be filled by either sex; and where it is easily understood that two equally gregarious assholes are not only better than one but can solve the crime in half the time.

Certain songs have a kind of hook that coaxes us into a hazily pleasurable, looplike rift between nostalgia and futurology. Certain magazines have a kind of hook that couples a seemingly endless variety of sameness with a trashy veneer of disbelief. From the *National Enquirer* to its upscale relations, *People* and *Us,* these publications emit a relentlessly ridiculous yet compelling rendition of information and its relationship to "celebrity." This magazine format has also invaded television, emerging in the form of newslike presentations and lifestyle shows. The most persistently visible examples of the genre, and not coincidentally those with the biggest hooks and the most juice, are *Entertainment Tonight* and *Lifestyles of the Rich and Famous,* which light up American homes with their baroquely unbridled reports from the end of the rainbow.

While *Entertainment Tonight* focuses on the processes of production and the business of show business, *Lifestyles of the Rich and Famous* sloppily paddles through the extremities of reward, through the acquisitions that accumulate after the deals are made, the public delivers its verdict, or the family delivers its inheritance. Bellowing at the top of his lungs, Robin Leach dominates the proceedings with his sideshow bark and his "If-this-is-Tuesday-it-must-be-Belgium" travel agenda. Rushing from Wayne Newton's lavish spread to Adnan Khashoggi's birthday party to Valerie Perrine's jaunt through the South of France, Leach lets the audience in on the stuff they will never forget: that money can buy you love, and that the best things in life are never free.

Like *Dynasty* and *Dallas, Lifestyles* works hard to delineate the difference between having and having not, but television's penchant for evacuating meanings and roughing up the mechanics of transference and identification plays havoc with the viewer's actual positioning. We can observe the proceedings with distanced amusement, giggling at its excesses and possibly resisting its almost undeclinable invitations. Or we can project madly onto the mélée, perhaps believing that if we use the right bubble bath or drive the right car then, poof!, we're Alexis or Adnan. Through these tenacious transmissions, voyeurism's rewards are presented not as ditzy fabulations but as the real stuff of our lives. Convincing us that seeing is not only believing but becoming, *Lifestyles'* flamboyant flaunting of baubles and bucks seems to efface rather than enhance the difference between rich and not. So, after a hard day's work, couch potatoes are snappily transformed into duchesses and dreamboats as the hard reality of our everyday labor (or lack of it) is handily dematerialized. Everybody's an executive adrift in their own inner space, suctioned up by the powerful seductions of managerial power and perks.

Entertainment Tonight breaks down this seduction a bit by focusing on the work that paves the way for reward and on the actual mechanics of profit and loss. Perched on contempo chairs that float in a space that resembles a black hole furnished by Conran's, the duo in charge (Robb Weller and Mary Hart on weekdays, Weller and Leeza Gibbons on weekends) spout a tidy continuum of juiced-up reportage. From a relatively detailed accounting of the government's attempt to curtail the distribution of critical documentary films to the latest industry gossip on Mike the dog's next career move, the presentation zigzags wildly between earnest liberal exhortation and fan-mag gush. But framing this narrative lowdown is a constant numerical barrage of box office statistics, celebs' birthdays, and audience demographics, which, although informational in their foregrounding of market valuations and career longevity, soon become, through their perky yet trancelike recitation, almost pataphysical if not downright otherworldly. If *Lifestyles* cultivates the rich terrain of the spectators' inner space, then perhaps *Entertainment Tonight* is claiming the turf of numerical capital as its outer space. Could it be just a coincidence that Weller and Hart and Gibbons affectionately allude to their cozy little mothership as "ET"?

Unlike *Lifestyles'* frenzied myopia, *ET*'s long view goes a short way to expose the underpinnings of America's love affair with power and celebrity. But these meager efforts are hardly enough to break the spell. Together with *Lifestyles'* and Leach's newest entry, *Fame, Fortune and Romance, Entertainment Tonight* reminds its viewers to sit back, relax, and live the fantasy – to blast off into an outer and inner space where living well is the best revenge.

The Perfect Tense

RICHARD PRINCE

It started out when she gave him a home. Really the first he'd ever had. The first rooms he could go to when it was time to go home. It's what she provided, and to go home is what he had always wanted.

He had always wanted to go back to a room where he could lie on a couch and watch TV, and in the TV he could put a video movie. She gave him these things. She gave him what he wanted and had never had. And what happened was, in the end, she wanted to kill him for what she had given him. "I'm sorry," she said, "it happened and you happened in it. If I had seen you one more time on the couch watching movies I would have killed you. I wanted to kill you. I'm sorry, but that's what I felt." I'm sorry, too. That's what he said. He said it to himself. He said too he was still glad; it didn't matter that she felt those "things" turned him into half a person.

"I liked coming home and doing nothing," he said. "I didn't want to come home and talk about the day and I didn't want to talk about us or our relationship. I didn't want to argue or sit across from you at the table and end up staring and saying nothing. I didn't want to go out later to dinner or a club. I didn't want to read a book or the paper. I didn't want to have sex. I didn't want excitement. And I didn't want to be exciting.

"I needed a chance. I needed to know what that sensation of normalcy is. I needed to know how the other half lives."

A lot of people wish they were someone else. And some of us would like to exchange parts with other people, keeping what we already like and jettisoning the things that we can't stand. Some people would like to try to change places, just for a day, with maybe someone they admire or even envy, to see what it would be like, to see if it would be what they'd always heard it would be. There are those too who are quite satisfied with themselves and never think about such things as another person's blessings, and it seemed appropriate to someone like him that these satisfied ones were the ones that he most wanted to be like and exchange with and try to take the place of.

He could never imagine what it must be like to spend an entire day without ever having to avoid a mirror. And where he lived, he made sure, never had a reflection, and any surface that did so got dulled or rubbed out, and any surface that became stubborn and kept its polish got thrown in a bucket.

When he went out, to the outside, he would make sure to take care of all of what was him, and be aware to resist and turn away from even a frame of glass, something as common as a darkened window. Uninhibited unconsciousness was something uninheritable, like a nameless form of new life, something not learned . . . a kind of anomalous gracenote.

This type of character or "component" (as he came to call it) was one of his wishes . . . a surprise he had asked for on every one of his last thirty-three birthdays . . . and although the chance of receiving such a gift was next to under the well, it became a habit, an attitude . . . a toll to be paid, like: sure, make the bet, why not . . . wishful thinking cost about as much as the chances of getting it anyway.

His inability to come to terms with the order of his physical demands wasn't, as one would assume, eccentric, or even dangerously whimsical. He had justifiable reasons, and asking for deliverance, however unanswered, was, he felt, strict and necessary clockwork.

Mostly he wasn't sure (a question of sorts) how long he could continue to walk around with the feeling of blood on his hands.

He used to live in the West Village in New York on Eleventh Street near the southwest corner of Hudson Street. And even in a part of the city where a lot of men were incredibly handsome, he was more. His looks had the *call,* they exploded the bill for what was generally considered classical or godlike, and what was usually said about them was something like: "How can that be?"

He had heard this many times and as many times as he had, he still took it badly . . . sort of seeing his luck as a curse, something thought up on purpose, a bone pointed at him by an unknown tribe for reasons he felt unfair. He was being punished for existing as he was, and what was left of his life came to be lived as a version of one, like a shadow (a life as subtle as a detail), always making sure never to be tagged or named good guy or bad guy.

The self-casting, this assumed state of invisibility, was the ready way he figured to avoid embarrassment and showdown. Being what many people imagined as the most handsome man in the world was

من قبل

not at all the adventure it was rumored to be. Privacy in public, at least in the city, was something to be negotiated. The constant fingering and targeting was never as harmless as gossip or whisper, and what most people tolerated as "dirty laundry" he rightly feared as a possible (at any time) lynch mob free-for-all.

He had spent most of his adult life in an urban surrounding, where pedestrian relationships had come to be seen as modern dance. He would say he was a solo performer, an independent, someone who ramrodded more than walked . . . and if his move wasn't exactly in a straight line, he'd come about as if in a sail race and return from where he began . . . usually his home, go inside, stay, and not come out for a week.

He wasn't a martyr. He wasn't someone who felt sorry for himself and walked around with his head down willingly. Eye contact was supposed to be natural and welcome, and having to wear dark glasses as one would wear a pair of shoes wasn't for him jazzy or cool or soulful.

The turning of heads or the useless effect of stopping traffic was like confronting his peers as a set of exposures. People froze and anticipated, as if the sight of his presence was religious in nature. It was scary. Really a fright. He was better than Christ, he was physically perfect.

He came to refer to his condition as his *surface,* and his surface was a sign of an emotion that the literal could be as true, perhaps truer than the symbol. I mean the man could breathe, and unless he died and came to be known only through a photograph, then one would have to concede that the tables had turned.

His literalness was what was real. This was what he wore on his hands. He was a carrier, maybe the only one, an everpresent reminder that proportion and line and beauty did not necessarily exist only in an impression or form or idea. This was what all the blood was about, and this revelation and the seriousness of it weighed an amazing ton.

His delusion was his stake, a kind of wager in trying to control his own destiny. At least to some extent he thought that if he kept himself behind the camera, determining the direction of how and where he looked, and sharpening his attention on only those areas specifically set aside by his own absence, then perhaps he wouldn't have to live it, in order to have any memory of it.

He liked to call his relationships with what he saw and what he knew, playing the Tom-Tom. A kind of dumb pun on the peeping one. The play was more aggressive than passive and the take more staring than ogling. And the nice thing about it was he never expected the scene through the keyhole to provide him with even a glimpse of what might be making him tick.

The first thing he wanted from Jack was Jack's toothbrush. The toothbrush was black. He wasn't aware they made the tool in that color, and thought maybe Jack had the thing custom-built.

It didn't have any writing or brandname. The cleaning part was thick and blonde, like the horsehair of an old-fashioned shaving brush. It had a reddish-orange tip at the heel for the gums. The thing ended in a little hang, not quite a curlique, but longer than most he had seen.

What is essentially a readily available, purposeful article, to suddenly become a designer accessory . . . to have it so thought about, manipulated, and arranged, so that its presence could operate next to other forms and lines and colors, was, for a few seconds, shocking, hard to imagine, hysterically seductive, something he wanted right away so he could have it when the initial blast of its look wore off.

He knew this was going to sound idiotic, but when he was standing there, staring at the thing, he thought about New Guinea and the tribesmen there and about how their history functions around memory and how, for them to remember something, they have to either see it or touch it, and what popped into mind was, forget about the memory, just steal the damned thing so he could have it for his own.

I mean he didn't want to kiss it or give it a hug . . . or pass it on, or tell anybody about it. It wasn't like a covering up, or anything perverse or secret. It was crazy, the thing made him go up a wall. It nailed him when he walked in. He became shellshocked. His mood became awful. It was like his friend Jack had this piece of ass, he wanted to sit on it, couldn't . . . and sat around wondering, withdrawn, trying to figure out how this guy had it so together.

Anyway, a greedy little thief is what he wanted to be, but somehow he got bonged on the head by maybe the clearest form of involuntary sympathy he'd every comprehended. Lungs, heart, liver, kidneys . . . the whole thing, they were all in on it. No matter how much he tried to steal it, all the outer commands were put upon by this inordinate amount of love for their friendship. It was strange.

He picked it up and put it back. He watched it settle into its monogramed tray (the tray was molded, and the brush laid horizontally in the mold).

He wanted what was Jack's but couldn't have it. He had done it in the past, to other people . . . stolen what was theirs, but now it became clear that the level of indulgence that he was used to couldn't make it this time and instead he'd have to let it go and resist what was tempting and think about someone else first.

The love was abnormally mental. The manifestation was new, different . . . the clarity wasn't anything about control and certainly nothing about guilt. Being the center of the meditation and all the other stupid survival tactics that kept him single got hung out to dry so to speak. White trash smartens up. Something like that. An abreaction. A catharsis. A dissolution. It didn't matter, as long as his history got traded off for a new one.

The familiarity of love would probably have its own contempt, but he knew it couldn't be anywhere near the kind of loathing you can feel from smelling your own arse.

It was settled. Jack came first. He brushed his teeth with the blasted fucker and spit the paste and blood right into the mirror.

The first time he saw her, he saw her in a photograph. He had seen her before, at her job, but there she didn't come across or measure up anywhere near as well as she did in her picture. Behind her desk she was too real to look at, and what she did in daily life could never guarantee the effect of what usually came to be received from an objective resemblance. He had to have her on paper, a material with a flat and seamless surface . . . a physical location which could represent her resemblance all in one place . . . a place that had the chance of looking real, but a place that didn't have any specific chance of being real.

His fantasies, and right now the one of her, needed satisfaction. And satisfaction, at least in part, seemed to come about by ingesting, perhaps "perceiving," the fiction her photograph imagined.

She had to be condensed and inscribed in a way that his expectations of what he wanted her to be (and what he wanted to be too) could at least be possibly, even remotely, realized. Over-determination was part of his plan and, in a strange way, the same kind of psychological afterlife was what he loved, sometimes double-loved, about her picture.

It wasn't that he wanted to worship her. And it wasn't that he wanted to be taxed and organized by a kind of uncritical devotion. But her image did seem to have a concrete and actual form . . . an incarnate power . . . a power that he could willingly and easily contribute to. And what he seemed to be able to do, either in front of it or away from it, was pass time in a particular bodily state, an alternating balance which turned him in and out and made him see something about a life after death.

Their inability to recognize one another was one of the principal reasons why they were together. Their relationship never went (and probably couldn't go) anywhere. And since neither one of them would take responsibility for what some say was both their faults, the possibility of their condition continuing seemed certain.

The best thing that could be said for their situation was that it lacked urgency. And, if nothing else, they could always pretend to envy their relationship for its own sake. Theirs was a relationship (like intelligence and taste) that couldn't be taught. There was nothing professional about it. It existed only by virtue of themselves and hadn't any need for comment or critique.

One was crazy and plotted the demise of the other. And the other had no desire to separate from the one who plotted. Both thought it better to stick around to see which one would wreck himself first. The risk was part of it, why they kept it up, but to find out what would happen afterwards, after ignoring their instincts, was the real reason they adapted to the possibility of suffering. (Not necessarily a pleasant experience, but one that assured the absence of progress.)

Like all great amateurs, they thought in literal or pragmatic terms and had little use for poetry or drift. They were great at refusing to focus on anything other than the part of the road where they found themselves standing.

Having fun? They weren't sure.

It wasn't a misunderstanding about the feeling or a difficulty about how it could be appreciated. Nothing about shame or like, hey, is this allowed, should we really be feeling this good? Nothing like that or stupid or anything. Just more like they were so keyed up on having Sex and being Serious, that the amount of time funning never seemed sufficient or quite substantial enough for them to form any kind of reasonable opinion about what fun was supposed to be anymore.

They wanted to be flexible. They wanted to be able to say, yes, we've participated, we're acquainted with the emotion and have a pretty fair idea of how and why it exists, but aside from appearing happy, there was, in practice, only a slight commitment, with most of that energy protecting their reservation and skepticism.

They understood too though, if fun was rejected publicly, others might point to them and say their preoccupation with S&S made them dark and square and something to be turned out. So if they knew they could trust you, that's when they'd come out and just say it, point blank . . . "Okay off with it. If it was up to us we'd rather have no part of fun."

They felt the sudden flux, an inflation, transitory . . . like being in love. A kind of swelling from fever. And if it wasn't too much to ask, all they wanted to do was move at a reasonable pace, sounding along at a nice kind of idle . . . so maybe they could get on with their work and their lives.

Fun was too unpredictable. "Much too much," they would say. Another feeling that comes and goes . . . an unsatisfactory rupture in what would have otherwise been a fine and steady day.

For them funning seemed to be another kind of pressure. An obligation they had come to expect as part of the routine. Something to be taken in doses. Part of the checks and balances. The good with the bad. Another factor to figure in what was prescribed to produce a healthy equilibrium.

It was suggested too that fun existed on the same coin as guilt and if the pleasure of its purpose wasn't occasionally tossed and allowed to be "called" in the air . . . then the game could never begin and sides could never be taken.

"Lighten up," was what they heard. "Don't be such stones."

They'd hear the dig out doing the shopping. Hear it in the supermarket. Sometimes right in the middle of the week. They would try to smile and sparkle and move down the aisle. One foot in front of the other. They tried. They stepped. They remembered to participate.

They did their bit and acted the part that was called for. Parts of the mood came back, like a view lit up by lightning. Slowly, carefully, as if egged on by some invisible sidekick, they managed to tickle themselves. And if not exactly to death, then to an acceptable titter and gaffe.

Luckily for them, their own inclusion in having the requisite gullibility, simplicity, and tolerance for repetition made some of life's little jokes impossible to grow out of.

Magazines, movies, TV, and records. It wasn't everybody's condition but to him it sometimes seemed like it was, and if it really wasn't, that was alright, but it was going to be hard for him to connect with someone who passed himself off as an example or a version of a life put together from unmediated matters.

He had already accepted all these conditions and built out of their givens, and to him what was given was anything public and what was public was always real. He transported these givens to a reality more real than the condition he first accepted. He was never too clever, too assertive, too intellectual . . . essentially too decorative. He had a spirit that made it easier to receive than to censor.

His own desires had very little to do with what came from himself because what he put out (at least in part) had already been out. His way to make it new was *make it again,* and making it again was enough for him and certainly, personally speaking, *almost* him.

He liked to think of himself as an audience and located himself on the other side of what he and others did . . . looking back at it, either by himself or with a group, hoping to exchange an emotion that was once experienced only as an author . . . an exchange he willingly initiated for reasons he felt necessary . . . necessary because he knew if he didn't make the switch, from author to audience, he knew he could never say, "I second that emotion."

Being the audience, or part of one, was for him a way to identify himself physically and a way to perceive rather than affect . . . a way to share with others in what might be described as a kind of impossible or promissory nonfiction. A way to see or realize what essentially was a surface with public image, a surface that was once speculative and ambitious, as something now referential and ordinary. Referential because the image's authority existed outside his own touch and ordinary because their frequency of appearance could be corroborated by persons other than himself.

"You don't have to take my word for them," he would say, as if defending against a cross-examination . . . "These pictures are more than available, and unless you've been living in an alley, inside an ash-can, wrapped up in a trash liner (with the cover closed), chances are better than even, you've seen them too."

He's a thief. He steals. But he's generous.

"Without lifting a finger," he says . . . like a slogan, something he repeats so often it sounds like a law.

He goes to church and steals candles. He never panics. He's selective. He knows which ones to take.

"Not the ones already lit. They've been spoken for. Their history has been signed by whoever made the flame, and I'm afraid their light is to be respected. There are lines that cannot be crossed, and this is one of them. Their light is an offering, a kind of ceremonious consultation between an image and his maker."

About her, she didn't steal. She raised her arm and asked permission.

"Would you mind if I steal candles like you do?"

"Not at all," he said.

He hung up the phone and never spoke to her again. As far as he's concerned their affair is over, finished, impossible, and stupid to begin again. She occasionally calls but he screens the calls. She should have known not to ask. There are things a thief doesn't ask permission for, and two of them are approval and a blessing.

It was too bad. She thought the stealing was some kind of party. A birthday. She went to church. She made a wish. She took a breath. And made it dark.

He doesn't pray and he doesn't wish either. But now every once in a while he lights a candle for her, hoping it will be the one she takes. It's not what he wanted, but it's what he has, and the matter between what he's got and what he doesn't is something that he finds painful to separate.

Perhaps even now his attempt at lighting a candle is more a settlement than a put down. A coming to terms with cutting her off . . . a gesture for forgiveness. And when he wants to admit it, a try at least at sharing what he steals . . . a way, his way, to stay for her, wanted and remembered.

Bibliography

This bibliography is intended as a suggestion of further reading in the general area of recent artists' writings and of additional writings by the artists included in this collection. The citations are selected in most cases and many shorter periodical publications or reprinted texts are not cited. This bibliography was compiled by Russell Ferguson, Susan Rosenberg, and Brian Wallis.

Anthologies and Critical Writings

Art-Rite, no. 14 (Winter 1976-1977). Issue on artists' books.

Benamon, Michel, and Charles Caramello. *Performance in Postmodern Culture.* Madison, Wis.: Coda Press, 1977.

Cardoni, Edmund, ed. *Blatant Artifice.* Buffalo, N.Y.: Hallwalls, 1986.

Cave Canem: Stories and Pictures. New York: Cave Canem Books, 1982.

Ess, Barbara, and Glenn Branca, eds. *Just Another Asshole, no. 6.* New York: Just Another Asshole, 1983.

Franklin Furnace, New York. *Franklin Furnace Archive Artists Book Bibliography.* 3 vols. New York: Franklin Furnace, 1977-1979.

Guest, Tim, and Germano Celant. *Books by Artists.* Toronto: Art Metropole, 1981.

Independent Curators Incorporated, Washington, D.C., and New York. *Artists Books USA: A Traveling Exhibition.* Exhibition, April 1978–March 1980. Catalogue essay by Peter Frank and Martha Wilson.

Institute of Contemporary Arts, London. *Issue: Social Strategies by Women Artists.* Exhibition, November 14–December 21, 1980. Catalogue; preface by Sandy Nairne, essay by Lucy Lippard.

Jacobs, Jessica, ed. *Word Works Too.* San Jose, Calif.: San Jose State University, 1975.

Kostelanetz, Richard, ed. *Essaying Essays.* New York: Out of London Press, 1975.

Kostelanetz, Richard, ed. *Breakthrough Fictioneers.* Boston: Something Else Press, 1973.

Kruger, Barbara, ed. *TV Guides: A Collection of Thoughts About Television.* New York: Kuklapolitan Press, 1985.

Lewis, Rebecca. "Spreading the Word (s and Images)." *Afterimage* 12, no. 1-2 (Summer 1984): 7.

Linker, Kate. "The Artist's Book as an Alternative Space." *Studio International* 195, no. 990 (1980): 75-79.

Long Beach Museum of Art. *Remembrance of Things Past.* Exhibition, November 23, 1986–January 18, 1987. Catalogue edited by Lane Relyea.

Lyons, Joan, ed. *Artists' Books: A Critical Anthology and Sourcebook.* New York: Peregrine Smith Books in association with Visual Studies Workshop Press, 1985.

McCaffery, Larry, ed. *Postmodern Fiction: A Bio-Bibliographical Guide.* New York: Greenwood Press, 1986.

Milazzo, Richard, ed. *Beauty and Critique.* New York: Mussman Bruce Publishers, 1982.

New Langton Arts, San Francisco. *Image/Word: The Art of Reading.* Exhibition, October 8–November 2, 1985. Catalogue essay by Barrett Watten.

Owens, Craig. "Earthwords." *October,* no. 10 (Fall 1979): 121-130.

Peskin, Nancy, ed. *Angle of Repose.* Buffalo, N.Y.: Hallwalls, 1986.

Phillpot, Clive, ed. "Words and Wordworks" issue. *Art Journal* 42, no. 2 (Summer 1982).

Prince, Richard, ed. *Wild History.* New York: Tanam Press, 1985.

Printed Matter Catalogue 86/87. New York: Printed Matter, Inc., 1986.

Robertson, Jack. *Twentieth-Century Artists on Art: An Index to Artists' Writings, Statements, and Interviews.* Boston: G.K. Hall, 1985.

Sondheim, Alan. *Individuals: Post-Movement Art in America.* New York: E.P. Dutton and Co., Inc., 1977.

Tannenbaum, Barbara. "Artists' Books: A Chronology of Secondary Sources." *The Flue* 3, no. 1 (1982): 20-21, 24-25, 28.

Wallis, Brian. "An Absence of Vision and Drama/On Lynne Tillman, Kathy Acker, Gary Indiana, and Richard Prince." *Parkett,* no. 5 (1985): 63-74.

Wallis, Brian. "Mindless Pleasure: Richard Prince's Fictions." *Parkett,* no. 6 (1985): 61-62.

Williams, Reese, ed. *Hotel.* New York: Tanam Press, 1980.

Writings by Artists in *Blasted Allegories*

Acker, Kathy. *The Childlike Life of the Black Tarantula.* New York: TVRT Press, 1975.

Acker, Kathy. *The Adult Life of Toulouse Lautrec by Henri Toulouse Lautrec.* New York: TVRT Press and Printed Matter, Inc., 1978.

Acker, Kathy. *New York City in 1979.* Top Stories, no. 9. Buffalo, N.Y.: Hallwalls, 1979.

Acker, Kathy, and Robert Kushner. *The Persian Poems.* New York: Bozeau of London Press, 1980.

Acker, Kathy. *Great Expectations.* New York: Grove Press, Inc., 1982.

Acker, Kathy. *Hello, I'm Erica Jong.* New York: Contact II Publications, 1982.

Acker, Kathy. "Impassioned With Some Song We." *Artforum* 20, no. 9 (May 1982): 66-68.

Acker, Kathy. *Implosion.* New York: Wedge Press, Inc., 1983.

Acker, Kathy. *Algeria: A Series of Invocations Because Nothing Else Works.* London: Aloes Books, 1984.

Acker, Kathy. "The Following Myth of Romantic Suffering Has to Be Done Away With (from Scenes of World War III)." *Bomb,* no. 9 (Spring-Summer 1984): 80-83.

Acker, Kathy. "Models of the Present." *Artforum* 22, no. 6 (February 1984): 62-65.

Acker, Kathy. "Realism for the Cause of Future Revolution." In *Art After Modernism: Rethinking Representation,* edited by Brian Wallis. New York and Boston: The New Museum of Contemporary Art and David R. Godine, 1984, pp. 31-41.

Acker, Kathy. *Don Quixote.* New York: Grove Press, Inc., 1986.

Acker, Kathy. "Empire of the Senseless." *Bomb,* no. 9 (Spring 1987): 58-63.

Acker, Kathy. "Male" (from the novel *Empire of the Senseless). Between C and D* 3, no. 2 (Spring 1987): 19-23.

Anderson, Laurie. "Confessions of a Street Talker." *Avalanche,* no. 11 (Spring 1975): 22-23.

Anderson, Laurie. *Notebook.* New York: The Collation Center, 1977.

Anderson, Laurie. "Autobiography: The Self in Art." *LAICA Journal,* no. 19 (June-July 1978): 34-35.

Anderson, Laurie. "From Americans on the Move." *October,* no. 8 (1979): 45-59.

Anderson, Laurie. *Words in Reverse.* Top Stories, no. 2. Buffalo, N.Y.: Hallwalls, 1979.

Anderson, Laurie. "Dark Dogs, American Dreams." In *Hotel,* edited by Reese Williams. New York: Tanam Press, 1980, pp. 107-131.

Anderson, Laurie. *United States.* New York: Harper and Row, 1984.

Baldessari, John. *Ingres and Other Parables.* [n.p.]: John Baldessari, 1971.

Baldessari, John. "I Will Not Make Any More Boring Art." In *Essaying Essays,* edited by Richard Kostelanetz. New York: Out of London Press, 1975.

Baldessari, John. *Fable.* Hamburg: Anatol AV und Filmproduktion, 1977.

Baldessari, John. *Close-Cropped Tales.* Buffalo, N.Y.: CEPA Gallery, c1981.

Barry, Judith, and Sandy Flitterman. "Textual Strategies–The Politics of Art Making." *Screen* 21, no. 2 (Summer 1980): 35-48.

Barry, Judith. "Women, Representation and Performance Art: Northern California." In *Performance Anthology,* edited by Carl E. Loeffler and Darlene Tong. San Francisco: Contemporary Arts Press, 1980, pp. 439-462.

Barry, Judith. "Building Conventions." *Real Life Magazine,* no. 6 (Summer 1981): 33-35.

Barry, Judith. "Space Invaders or The Failure of the Present." In *The Un/necessary Image,* edited by Peter D'Agostino and Antonio Muntadas. New York: Tanam Press, 1982, pp. 80-82.

Barry, Judith. "Public Fantasy." In *Artists' Architecture.* London: Institute of Contemporary Arts, 1983, pp. 86-89.

Barry, Judith. "Vamp r y." In *Just Another Asshole,* no. 6, edited by Barbara Ess and Glenn Branca. New York: Just Another Asshole, 1983, pp. 17-18.

Bleckner, Ross. "Disavowal and Redemption: An Ideology of Exhaustion and Renewal." *Effects,* no. 1 (Summer 1983): 15.

Bogosian, Eric. "Fascination." *Real Life Magazine,* no. 7 (Autumn 1981): 32-34.

Bogosian, Eric. *In the Dark.* New York: Wedge Press, Inc., 1983.

Bogosian, Eric. "Notes for a Play (The New World." In *Just Another Asshole,* no. 6, edited by Barbara Ess and Glenn Branca. New York: Just Another Asshole, 1983, pp. 23-24.

Bogosian, Eric. *Drinking in America.* New York: Vintage Books, 1987.

Burgin, Victor. *Thinking Photography.* London: Macmillan Publishers, Ltd., 1982.

Burgin, Victor. "Some Thoughts on Outsiderism and Postmodernism." *Block* 11, no. 6 (1985-1986): 19-26.

Burgin, Victor. *Between.* Oxford and London: Basil Blackwell, Ltd. and Institute of Contemporary Arts, 1986.

Burgin, Victor. *The End of Art Theory: Criticism and Postmodernity.* Atlantic Highlands, N.J.: Humanities Press International, Inc., 1986.

Casebere, James. *In the Second Half of the Twentieth Century.* Buffalo, N.Y.: CEPA Gallery, 1982.

Cha, Theresa Hak Kyung. *Etang.* Berkeley: Lane, 1979.

Cha, Theresa Hak Kyung, ed. *Apparatus.* New York: Tanam Press, 1980.

Cha, Theresa Hak Kyung. "Exilée Temps Morts." In *Hotel,* edited by Reese Williams. New York: Tanam Press, 1980, pp. 133-189.

Cha, Theresa Hak Kyung. *Dictee.* New York: Tanam Press, 1982.

Cha, Theresa Hak Kyung. Untitled. In *Fire Over Water,* edited by Reese Williams. New York: Tanam Press, 1986, pp. 209-225.

DeJong, Constance. *Modern Love.* New York: TVRT Press, 1977.

DeJong, Constance, and Philip Glass. *Satyagraha: M.K. Gandhi in South Africa, 1893-1914.* New York: Standard Editions, 1980.

DeJong, Constance. "In Between the Dark and the Light (Television/Society/Art: A Symposium)." *Artforum* 19, no. 5 (January 1981): 25-29.

DeJong, Constance. *I.T.I.L.O.E.* Top Stories, no. 15. Buffalo, N.Y.: Hallwalls, 1983.

DeJong, Constance. "Twice Told Tales." In *Five,* edited by Anne Turyn. Top Stories, no. 23-24. Buffalo, N.Y.: Hallwalls, 1986.

Fiengo, Robert. "On Trace Theory." *Linguistic Inquiry* 8 (1977): 35-61.

Fiengo, Robert. *Surface Structure.* Cambridge, Mass.: Harvard University Press, 1980.

Graham, Dan. *Articles.* With notes by R.H. Fuchs and afterword by Benjamin H.D. Buchloh. Eindhoven: Municipal Van Abbemuseum, 1977.

Graham, Dan. "Art in Relation to Architecture, Architecture in Relation to Art." *Artforum* 17, no. 6 (February 1979): 22-29.

Graham, Dan. "Funk: Political Pop." *LAICA Journal,* no. 22 (March-April 1979): 27-33.

Graham, Dan. *Video–Architecture–Television: Writings on Video and Video Works, 1970-1978.* Edited by Benjamin H.D. Buchloh. Contributions by Michael Asher and Dara Birnbaum. Halifax and New York: The Press of the Nova Scotia College of Art and Design and New York University Press, 1979.

Graham, Dan. "*The Destroyed Room* of Jeff Wall." *Real Life Magazine,* no. 3 (March 1980): 4-6.

Graham, Dan. "BowWowWow (The Age of Piracy)." *Real Life Magazine,* no. 6 (Summer 1981): 11-13.

Graham, Dan. "The End of Liberalism." *ZG,* no. 2 (1981): 6-8.

Graham, Dan. "Not Post-Modernism: History as Against Historicism, European Archetypal Vernacular in Relation to American Commercial Vernacular, and the City as Opposed to the Individual Buildings." *Artforum* 20, no. 4 (December 1981): 50-58.

Graham, Dan. "The End of Liberalism (Part II)." In *The Un/necessary Image,* edited by Peter D'Agostino and Antonio Muntadas. New York: Tanam Press, 1982, pp. 36-41.

Graham, Dan. "Theatre, Cinema, Power." *Parachute,* no. 31 (June-July-August 1983): 11-19.

Graham, Dan. "Signs." *Artforum* 19, no. 8 (April 1984): 30-43.

Gray, Spalding. "The Farmer's Daughter." In *Wild History*, edited by Richard Prince. New York: Tanam Press, 1985, pp. 203-220.

Gray, Spalding. *Swimming to Cambodia*. New York: Theatre Communications Group, 1985.

Gray, Spalding. *Sex and Death to the Age of 14*. New York: Vintage Books, 1986.

Halley, Peter. "Against Post-Modernism: Reconsidering Ortega." *Arts Magazine* 56, no. 3 (November 1981): 112-115.

Halley, Peter. "Beat, Minimalism, New Wave, and Robert Smithson." *Arts Magazine* 55, no. 9 (May 1981): 120-121.

Halley, Peter. "Ross Bleckner: Painting at the End of History." *Arts Magazine* 56, no. 9 (May 1982): 132-133.

Halley, Peter. "Nature and Culture." *Arts Magazine* 58, no. 1 (September 1983): 64-65.

Halley, Peter. "The Crisis in Geometry." *Arts Magazine* 58, no. 10 (Summer 1984): 111-115.

Halley, Peter. "The Frozen Land." *ZG*, no. 12 (Fall 1984): 16.

Halley, Peter. "After Art." *New Observations*, no. 27 (1985): 11-13.

Halley, Peter. "Notes on Nostalgia." *New Observations*, no. 28 (1985): 3.

Halley, Peter. "On Line." *New Observations*, no. 35 (1985): 8-10.

Halley, Peter. "The Deployment of the Geometric." *Effects*, no. 3 (Winter 1986): 17.

Halley, Peter. "Essence and Model." In *Beyond Boundaries*, edited by Jerry Saltz. New York: Alfred van der Marck, 1986, p. 121.

Hatch, Connie. "The Desublimation of Romance." *wedge*, no. 6 (Winter 1984): 20-23.

Heap of Birds, Edgar. *Sharp Rocks*. Buffalo, N.Y.: CEPA Gallery, 1986.

Hill, Candace. "Notes." In *Issues: Social Strategies by Women Artists*. London: Institute of Contemporary Arts, 1980, n.p.

Hill, Candace. *Fire Escape Scrolls*. New York: Appearances Press, 1982.

Hill, Candace. *Evening Tomorrow's Here Today Since the Hornet Flies I Triangle*. New York: Wedge Press, Inc., 1983.

Holzer, Jenny. *Diagrams*. New York: Jenny Holzer, 1977.

Holzer, Jenny. *A Little Knowledge Can Go a Long Way*. New York: Jenny Holzer, 1978.

Holzer, Jenny, and Peter Nadin. "Living." In *Hotel*, edited by Reese Williams. New York: Tanam Press, 1980, pp. 84-106.

Holzer, Jenny, and Peter Nadin. *Eating Friends*. Top Stories, no. 7. Buffalo, N.Y.: Hallwalls, 1981.

Holzer, Jenny, and Peter Nadin. "Eating Friends." *Cover*, no. 6 (Winter 1981-1982): 14-16.

Holzer, Jenny, and Peter Nadin. *Eating Through Living*. New York: Tanam Press, 1981.

Holzer, Jenny. "Survival Series." In *Just Another Asshole*, no. 6, edited by Barbara Ess and Glenn Branca. New York: Just Another Asshole, 1983, p. 74.

Holzer, Jenny. *Truisms and Essays*. Halifax: The Press of the Nova Scotia College of Art and Design, 1983.

Holzer, Jenny, and Mike Glier. "Trust Visions." *New Observations*, no. 20 (1984): 23.

Indiana, Gary. "Black Moon." *Bomb*, no. 1 (Spring 1981): 24-25.

Indiana, Gary. "The Family Dog . . . Chapter One, Pillow Talk." *Bomb,* no. 4 (1982): 48-50.

Indiana, Gary. "Une Semaine de Bonté." *Bomb,* no. 6 (1983): 50-53.

Indiana, Gary. *Shanghai.* New York: Wedge Press, Inc., 1983.

Indiana, Gary. "The Hidden Anguish of the Mousketeers." *Bomb,* no. 9 (Spring-Summer 1984): 76-79.

Indiana, Gary. "Scar Tissue (Games from Other Games)." *New Observations,* no. 26 (1984): 2-5.

Indiana, Gary. "American Express." In *Wild History,* edited by Richard Prince. New York: Tanam Press, 1985, pp. 94-105.

Indiana, Gary. "Burma." *ZG,* no. 13 (Spring 1985): 14-15.

Indiana, Gary. "The Cabbage Patch Massacre." *New Observations,* no. 31 (1985): 23.

Indiana, Gary. "The Role of My Family in the World Revolution." *wedge,* no. 7-8 (Winter-Spring 1985): 26-29.

Indiana, Gary. "A Pathetic Waltz." *Bomb,* no. 26 (Summer 1986): 34-37.

Indiana, Gary. "At Night" (from the novel *Burma). Between C and D* 3, no. 2 (Spring 1987): 29-34.

Indiana, Gary. "Endless Lunch." *Bomb,* no. 23 (Winter 1987): 50-51.

Indiana, Gary. *Scar Tissue.* New York: Calamus Press, 1987.

Jackson, Suzanne. "Five Things (after whose destruction A. will be free)." *wedge,* no. 7-8 (Winter-Spring 1985): 86-89.

Jackson, Suzanne. "Painted Desert." In *Tourist Attractions,* edited by Anne Turyn and Brian Wallis. Top Stories, no. 25-26. New York: Top Stories, 1987, pp. 70-73.

Kolbowski, Silvia. "Virgin Territory: Gilbert and George's 'Modern Faith.'" *Afterimage* 11, no. 4 (November 1983): 12-13.

Kolbowski, Silvia. "All Things Being Equal." *ZG,* no. 12 (Fall 1984): 5.

Kolbowski, Silvia. "Representation's Reproduction." *wedge,* no. 6 (Winter 1984): 62-67.

Kolbowski, Silvia. "Sa(l)vages of Femininity/Domestic Salves." *wedge,* no. 7-8 (Winter-Spring 1985): 94-103.

Kruger, Barbara. "Work and Money." *Appearances,* no. 7 (Spring 1972): 30.

Kruger, Barbara. "She Makes the Wrong Choices." *Tracks* 2, no. 2 (Fall 1976): 39-40; 3, no. 1-2 (Spring 1977): 137-140; 3, no. 3 (Fall 1977): 99-100.

Kruger, Barbara. "Four Poems." *Tracks* 3, no. 1-2 (Spring 1977): 130-136.

Kruger, Barbara. *Picture/Readings.* New York: Barbara Kruger, 1978.

Kruger, Barbara. "Game Show." *Real Life Magazine,* no. 2 (October 1979): 5.

Kruger, Barbara. "Irony/Passion." *Cover* 1, no. 1 (May 1979): n.p.

Kruger, Barbara. "Devils With Red Dresses On." *Real Life Magazine,* no. 4 (Summer 1980): 24-25.

Kruger, Barbara. "Sculpted in Marble Next to the Sparkling Pond." *Effects,* no. 1 (Summer 1983): 6.

Kruger, Barbara. "Utopia: The Promise of Fashion When Time Stands Still." In *Just Another Asshole,* no. 6, edited by Barbara Ess and Glenn Branca. New York: Just Another Asshole, 1983, pp. 75-76.

Kruger, Barbara. "Cumulus . . . From America." *Parkett,* no. 1 (1984): 81-84.

Kruger, Barbara. "Incorrect." *Effects,* no. 2 (1984): 18.

Kruger, Barbara. "Great Balls of Fire!" *Parkett,* no. 11 (1986): 111-124.

Kruger, Barbara. "Dictation." *New Observations,* no. 44 (1987): 10-11.

Lawson, Thomas. "Every Picture Tells a Story Don't It?" *Real Life Magazine,* no. 2 (October 1979): 10-12.

Lawson, Thomas. "The Uses of Representation: Making Some Distinctions." *Flash Art,* no. 88-89 (March-April 1979): 37-39.

Lawson, Thomas. "Going Places." *Real Life Magazine,* no. 3 (March 1980): 12-13, 19.

Lawson, Thomas. "Too Good to Be True." *Real Life Magazine,* no. 7 (Autumn 1981): 2-7.

Lawson, Thomas. "Conflicting Panaceas." *Cover,* no. 6 (Winter 1981-1982): 34.

Lawson, Thomas. "The Dark Side of the Bright Light." *Artforum* 21, no. 3 (November 1982): 62-66.

Lawson, Thomas. "Last Exit: Painting." In *Art After Modernism: Rethinking Representation,* edited by Brian Wallis. New York and Boston: The New Museum of Contemporary Art and David R. Godine, 1984, pp. 153-165.

Lawson, Thomas. "Toward Another Laocoon, or, The Snake Pit." *Artforum* 24, no. 7 (March 1986): 97-106.

Levine, Sherrie. Untitled. New York: Sherrie Levine, 1977.

Levine, Sherrie. "Art Work." *ZG,* no. 11 (Summer 1984): 14.

Levine, Sherrie. "A Simple Heart (After Gustave Flaubert)." *New Observations,* no. 35 (1985): 15-19.

Mueller, Cookie. "San Francisco Bay 1967 Near Easter All True." *The World,* no. 34 (1981): 21-25.

Mueller, Cookie. "Theatre." *Bomb,* no. 2 (1981): 2.

Mueller, Cookie. "The Third Twin." *The World,* no. 34 (1981): 38-39.

Mueller, Cookie. "A True Story About Two People." *Bomb,* no. 1 (Spring 1981): 29.

Mueller, Cookie. "Baltimore 1969." *Bomb,* no. 4 (1982): 62.

Mueller, Cookie. "Brenda Losing/Valerie Losing 2." *Bomb* 1, no. 2 (1982): 34.

Mueller, Cookie. "The Mystery of Tap Water." *Bomb,* no. 6 (1983): 27.

Mueller, Cookie. "Route 95 South. 1969." In *Just Another Asshole,* no. 6, edited by Barbara Ess and Glenn Branca. New York: Just Another Asshole, 1983, pp. 103-106.

Mueller, Cookie. *How to Get Rid of Pimples.* Top Stories, no. 19-20. Buffalo, N.Y.: Hallwalls, 1984.

Mueller, Cookie. "Six Stories." In *Wild History,* edited by Richard Prince. New York: Tanam Press, 1985, pp. 152-175.

Mullican, Matt. "Untitled." In *Documenta 7.* Kassel: Documenta, 1982, vol. 1, p. 383, and vol. 2, p. 232.

Nadin, Peter. "Lyrics of Ten Songs." In *Just Another Asshole,* no. 6, edited by Barbara Ess and Glenn Branca. New York: Just Another Asshole, 1983, pp. 107-108.

Nadin, Peter. "Songs." *Real Life Magazine,* no. 10 (Summer 1983): 7-9.

Nadin, Peter. *Still Life.* New York: Tanam Press, 1983.

Nadin, Peter. "The Live Pool." In *Wild History,* edited by Richard Prince. New York: Tanam Press, 1985, pp. 50-69.

Nadin, Peter. "Poems from *Still Life.*" *New Observations,* no. 28 (1985): 16-17.

Nadin, Peter. "The Ownership of Land" and "Dr. M.T.'s Waiting Room." *Effects,* no. 3 (Winter 1986): 112.

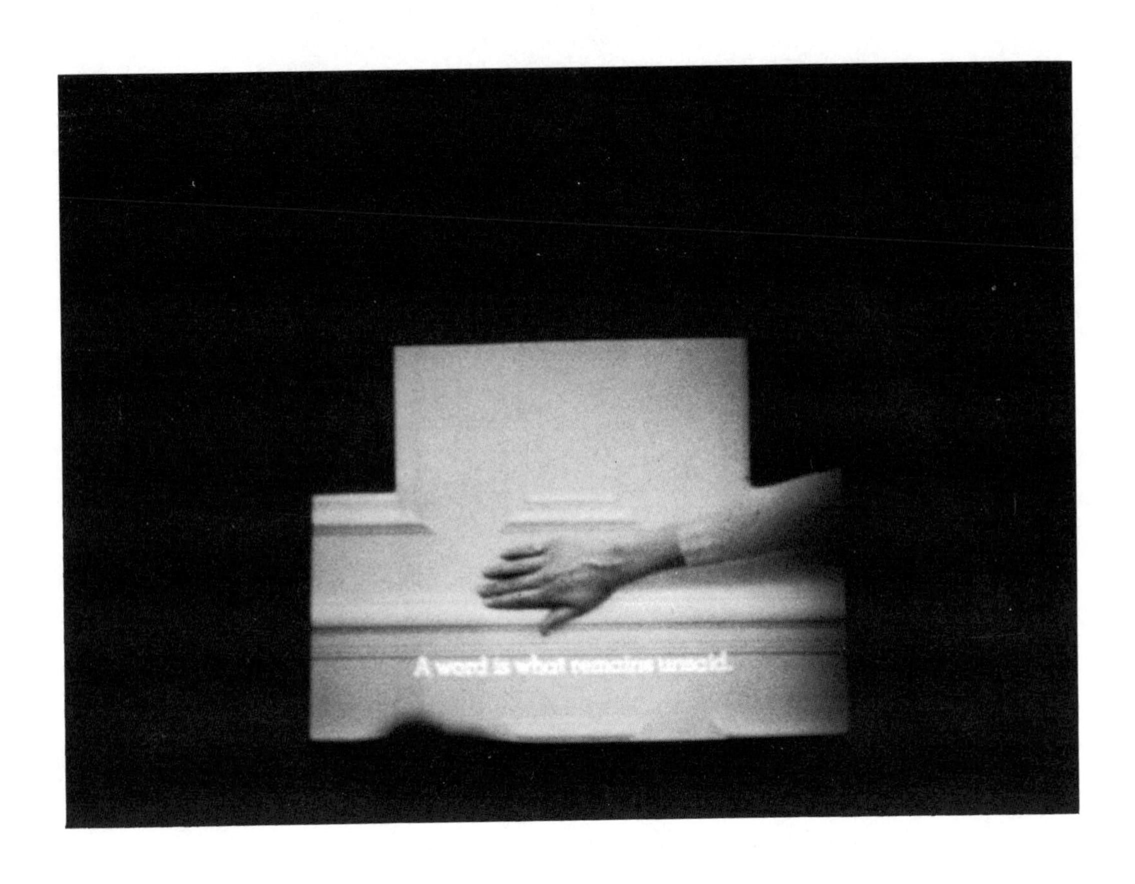
A word is what remains unsaid.

Nauman, Bruce. Untitled. *Criss Cross Double Cross,* no. 1 (Fall 1976): 18-19.

Piper, Adrian. "Three Models of Art Productive Systems." In *Conceptual Art,* edited by Ursula Meyer. New York: E.P. Dutton and Co., Inc., 1972, pp. 202-203.

Piper, Adrian. *Talking to Myself: The Ongoing Autobiography of an Art Object.* Hamburg: Hessen, 1974.

Piper, Adrian. "Notes on the Mythic Being" In *Word Works Too,* edited by Jessica Jacobs. San Jose, Calif.: San Jose State University, 1975, n.p.

Piper, Adrian. *Talking to Myself/ Parlando a me stessa.* Bari, Italy: M. Bonomo, 1975.

Piper, Adrian. "Some Reflective Surfaces." *Studio International* 192, no. 982 (July-August 1976): 22-23.

Piper, Adrian. "A Tale of Avarice and Poverty." *WhiteWalls,* no. 14 (Autumn 1976): 8-19.

Piper, Adrian. "Notes on the Mythic Being: I/You(Her)." In *Individuals,* edited by Alan Sondheim. New York: E.P. Dutton and Co., Inc., 1977, pp. 267-269.

Piper, Adrian. "Political Self Portrait #2." *Heresies* 2, no. 4 (1979): 37-38.

Piper, Adrian. "Five Other Features That are a Dead Giveaway." In *Events: Fashion Moda–Taller Boricua, Artists Invite Artists.* New York: The New Museum of Contemporary Art, 1980, p. 47.

Piper, Adrian. "Food for the Spirit." *High Performance* 4, no. 1 (Spring 1981): 34-35.

Piper, Adrian. "It's Just Art, April 1980." *High Performance* 4, no. 1 (Spring 1981): 36-37.

Piper, Adrian. Untitled. In *The Art of Memory/The Loss of History.* New York: The New Museum of Contemporary Art, 1985, pp. 34-35.

Prince, Richard. "Eleven Conversations." *Tracks* 2, no. 3 (Fall 1976): 41-46.

Prince, Richard. "Author's Note." *WhiteWalls,* no. 2 (Winter-Spring 1979): 2-5.

Prince, Richard. "From *Moving by Wading More Than Swimming.*" *WhiteWalls,* no. 4 (Summer 1980): 2-3.

Prince, Richard. "Menthol Pictures." *Real Life Magazine,* no. 4 (Summer 1980): 29-31.

Prince, Richard. *Menthol Pictures.* Buffalo, N.Y.: CEPA Gallery, 1980.

Prince, Richard. *Menthol Wars.* New York: Richard Prince, 1980.

Prince, Richard. "Primary Transfers." *Real Life Magazine,* no. 3 (March 1980): 2-3.

Prince, Richard. *War Pictures.* New York: Artists Space, 1980.

Prince, Richard. "The Thomas Crown Affair." *wedge,* no. 2 (Fall 1982): 16-17.

Prince, Richard. *Pamphlet.* Lyon, France: Nouveau Musée, 1983.

Prince, Richard. *Why I Go To the Movies Alone.* New York: Tanam Press, 1983.

Prince, Richard. "Anyone Who Is Anyone." *Parkett,* no. 6 (1985): 67-70.

Prince, Richard. "The Bela Lugosi Law." In *Wild History,* edited by Richard Prince. New York: Tanam Press, 1985, pp. 116-127.

Prince, Richard. "Jokes." In *Five,* edited by Anne Turyn. Top Stories, no. 23-24. Buffalo, N.Y.: Hallwalls, 1986.

Rainer, Yvonne. *Work: 1961-72.* Halifax and New York: The Press of the Nova Scotia College of Art and Design and New York University, 1974.

Rainer, Yvonne. "Letter Utterings." *Heresies,* no. 2 (May 1977): 25.

Rainer, Yvonne. "Working Title: Journeys from Berlin/1971." *October,* no. 9 (Summer 1979): 81-106.

Rainer, Yvonne. "Looking Myself in the Mouth." *October,* no. 17 (Summer 1981): 65-76.

Rosler, Martha. "Losing . . . a conversation with the parents." *Criss Cross Double Cross,* no. 1 (Fall 1976): 9-10.

Rosler, Martha. "She Sees in Herself a New Woman Every Day." *Heresies,* no. 2 (May 1977): 90-91.

Rosler, Martha. "The Private and the Public: Feminist Art in California." *Artforum* 16, no. 1 (September 1977): 66-74.

Rosler, Martha. *Service: A Trilogy on Colonization.* New York: Printed Matter, Inc., 1978.

Rosler, Martha. "For an Art Against the Mythology of Everyday Life." *LAICA Journal,* no. 23 (June-July 1979): 12-15.

Rosler, Martha. *Social Works.* Los Angeles: Institute of Contemporary Art, 1979.

Rosler, Martha. "Know Your Servant Series #1." *Impressions,* no. 24-25 (Spring-Summer 1980): 14-15.

Rosler, Martha. *3 Works.* Halifax: The Press of the Nova Scotia College of Art and Design, 1981.

Rosler, Martha. "Notes on Quotes." *wedge,* no. 2 (Fall 1982): 68-73.

Rosler, Martha. "Some Contemporary Documentary." *Afterimage* 11, no. 1-2 (Summer 1983): 13-15.

Rosler, Martha. "Lookers, Buyers, Dealers, Makers: Thoughts on Audience." In *Art After Modernism: Rethinking Representation,* edited by Brian Wallis. New York and Boston: The New Museum of Contemporary Art and David R. Godine, 1984, pp. 311-339.

Rosler, Martha. "Video: Shedding the Utopian Moment." *Block* 11, no. 6 (1985-1986): 27-33, 36-39.

Salle, David. "Jack Goldstein: Distance Equals Control." In *Jack Goldstein.* Buffalo, N.Y.: Hallwalls, 1978.

Salle, David. "New Image Painting." *Flash Art,* no. 88-89 (March-April 1979): 40-41.

Sekula, Allan. *Photography Against the Grain: Essays and Photo Works, 1973-1983.* Edited by Benjamin H.D. Buchloh. Halifax: The Press of the Nova Scotia College of Art and Design, 1984.

Sekula, Allan. "The Body and the Archive." *October,* no. 39 (Winter 1986): 3-64.

Smithson, Robert. *The Writings of Robert Smithson.* Edited by Nancy Holt. New York: New York University Press, 1979.

Sundiata, Sekou. "Pop Life." In *Tourist Attractions,* edited by Anne Turyn and Brian Wallis. Top Stories, no. 25-26. New York: Top Stories, 1987, pp. 74-76.

Tillman, Lynne. *Weird Fucks.* New York: privately published, 1980.

Tillman, Lynne. "Words Without Images." *Bomb,* no. 4 (1982): 52.

Tillman, Lynne. "Twisted Intentions." *Bomb,* no. 6 (1983): 36-37.

Tillman, Lynne, ed. *Critical Love. New Observations,* no. 26 (1984).

Tillman, Lynne. *Madame Realism.* New York: The Print Center, 1984.

Tillman, Lynne. "AKA Mergatroyde." *New Observations,* no. 31 (1985): 3-6.

Tillman, Lynne. *Haunted Houses.* New York: Poseiden Press, 1987.

Tillman, Lynne. "Madame Realism Saw This in *The Wall Street Journal.*" *New Observations,* no. 44 (1987): 6.

Tillman, Lynne. "Madame Realism's Imitation of Life." In *FAKE*. New York: The New Museum of Contemporary Art, 1987, pp. 45-48.

Trinh T. Minh-ha. "The Plural Void: Barthes and Asia." *Sub-Stance* 11, no. 3 (Winter 1982): 41-49.

Trinh T. Minh-ha, ed. *She, the Inappropriate/d Other*. Special issue of *Discourse*, no. 8 (Winter 1986-1987).

Trinh T. Minh-ha. "Questions of Images and Politics." *The Independent* 10, no. 4 (May 1987): 21-23.

Turyn, Anne. *Real Family Stories*. Top Stories, no. 13. New York: Top Stories, 1982.

Turyn, Anne. "Idioglossia." In *Wild History*, edited by Richard Prince. New York: Tanam Press, 1984, pp. 17-28.

Turyn, Anne. *Missives: Dear Pen Pal, Dear John, Lessons & Notes, Flashbulb Memories, Photographs*. New York: Alfred van der Marck Editions, 1986.

Vicuña, Cecilia. *Precario/Precarious*. New York: Tanam Press, 1983.

Vicuña, Cecilia. "Palabrarmás." In *Fire Over Water*, edited by Reese Williams. New York: Tanam Press, 1986, pp. 5-37.

Warrick, Jane. "Some Photographs and Brian." *Bomb*, no. 4 (1982): 26.

Warrick, Jane. "The Children's Stories." *Bomb*, no. 8 (1983-1984): 26-28.

Warrick, Jane. "Rooms." *Bomb*, no. 13 (Fall 1985): 76-77.

Watney, Simon. "Never-Never Land: An Examination of the Case for the Impossibility of Children's Fiction." *Screen* 26, no. 1 (January-February 1985): 86-89.

Watney, Simon. "Katharine Hepburn and the Cinema of Chastisement." *Screen* 26, no. 5 (September-October 1985): 52-62.

Watney, Simon, and Jo Spence, eds. *Photography/Politics 2*. New York: Methuen, Inc., 1987.

Watney, Simon. *Policing Desire: Pornography, AIDS and the Media*. Minneapolis: University of Minnesota Press, 1987.

Wegman, William. "Shocked and Outraged as I Was, It Was Nice Seeing You Again, or, Mrs. Burke, I Thought You Were Dead." *Avalanche*, no. 2 (Winter 1971): 58-69.

Wegman, William. *Everyday Problems*. New York: Brightwaters Press, 1984.

Wegman, William. *$19.84*. New York: CEPA Gallery, 1984.

Williams, Reese. *Past Trial Nearer*. New York: Reese Williams, 1978.

Williams, Reese, ed. *Hotel*. New York: Tanam Press, 1980.

Williams, Reese. *Figure Eight*. New York: Tanam Press, 1981.

Williams, Reese. *A Pair of Eyes*. New York: Tanam Press, 1983.

Williams, Reese. *Heat From the Trees*. New York: Benzene Editions, 1984.

Williams, Reese. "Conditions of Sensuous Perception." In *The Art of Memory/The Loss of History*. New York: The New Museum of Contemporary Art, 1985, p. 13.

Williams, Reese. "Gift Waves." In *Wild History*, edited by Richard Prince. New York: Tanam Press, 1985, pp. 6-14.

Williams, Reese, ed. *Fire Over Water*. New York: Tanam Press, 1986.

Wojnarowicz, David. "Cutting Through the South." *Zone*, no. 2 (Summer-Fall 1977): 74-77.

Wojnarowicz, David. *Sounds in the Distance*. London: Aloes Press, 1982.

Wojnarowicz, David. "Monologues for the Stage from *Sounds in the Distance*." *Bomb*, no. 8 (1983-1984): 56-57.

Photo Credits and Captions

The photographs reproduced in this catalogue have been selected by Barbara Bloom, with the assistance of Karen Marta, Gilles Peress, Nan Richardson, and Brian Wallis. The following is a list of descriptive captions, keyed to page numbers, and citing acknowledgment for the right to reproduce these images. In most cases, reproduction rights have been provided by the original photographers or their agents. The editors and publishers wish to thank the photographers, agencies, and institutions for their generous assistance and kind permission to reproduce these photographs.

Half-title, Peter DeLory, *Andy Ostheimer Reading, Ibiza, Spain,* 1976 (courtesy the photographer and The Minneapolis Institute of Art, Gift of Frank Kolodny); ii, Josef Koudelka, *Untitled, France, 1976* (Magnum Photos, Inc.); x, Margaret Bourke-White, *Mr. Karl Lisso, Leipzig's city treasurer, and his wife and daughter (Red Cross uniform) took poison as American tanks rolled into the city,* 1945 (Margaret Bourke-White, LIFE Magazine, ©1945 Time, Inc.); xviii, above, below, and center right, Bourke-White, *Dr. Karl Lisso . . .,* 1945, details; xviii, center left, photographer unknown, *Scene in Russian Revolution, July Troubles in Petrograd,* 1917 (The National Archives, Washington, D.C.); 8, anonymous Japanese postcard; 8, below, photographer unknown, *Franco at his desk,* 1936, detail (Ullstein Bilderdienst, Berlin); 16, above, Rembrandt van Rijn, *The Mennonite Clergyman Ansio and his Wife,* 1641, oil on canvas, detail (Staatliche Museen Preussischer Kulturbesitz, Berlin); 16, center, Barbara Bloom, *Street Scene, Tokyo,* 1986 (courtesy the photographer); 16, below, Erich Salomon, *Sir Austen Chamberlain Stresemann Briand, Lugano,* 1928, detail (Magnum Photos, Inc.); 24, above, Ralph Steiner, *After Rehearsal: Lee Strasberg and Morris Carnovsky,* 1936 (courtesy Prakapas Gallery, New York); 24, below, Erich Salomon, *Elks Dinner, Mayflower Hotel,* 1932, detail (Magnum Photos, Inc.); 32, left, anonymous Japanese advertisement; 32, right, Gothard Schuh, *Morra-Spieler, Tessin,* 1920s, detail (Kunsthaus, Zürich); 40, above, Jalon Angel, *Marzo,* 1939, detail (collection Christina Zelich); 40, below, René Burri, *São Paulo,* 1960 (Magnum Photos, Inc.); 48, all, Josef Koudelka, *Roumania,* 1968 (Magnum Photos, Inc.); 56, above, Gothard Schuh, *Cancan im Tabarin, Paris,* 1936 (Kunsthaus, Zürich); 56, below, Brassai, *A Fortuneteller in her Wagon, Boulevard Saint-Jacques,* 1933, detail (private collection); 64, above, Raymond Depardon, *Freedom Heals, Italy, 17 December 1980,* detail (Magnum Photos, Inc.); 64, center, Gilles Peress, *Harvest, Brittany,* 1972 (Magnum Photos, Inc.); 64, below, Gilles Peress, *Same location seven years later. All the men are dead. All the farms are sold,* 1979, detail (Magnum Photos, Inc.); 72, all, Margaret Bourke-White, *Dr. Karl Lisso . . .,* 1945, details; 80, all, Robert Smithson (courtesy the estate of the artist); 88, anonymous print, "Evolution"; 96, anonymous print, "Greek statuary"; 104, above left, Paul Citroen, *Im Theater,* 1929 (private collection); 104, above right, anonymous UFO photo; 104, center left, anonymous newsphoto; 104, center right, anonymous newsphoto; 104, below left, Michelangelo Antonioni, *Blow Up,* 1966, film still, detail (The Museum of Modern Art, Film Stills Archive); 104, below right, anonymous Dutch advertisement; 112, photographer unknown, *Franco at his desk,* 1936 (Ullstein Bilderdienst, Berlin); 120, Jean-Luc Godard, *Alphaville,* 1965, film still; 128, Marc Riboud, *Wuhan, 1971* (Magnum Photos, Inc.); 136, Barbara Bloom, *Mubarek,* 1984 (courtesy the photographer); 144, anonymous newsphoto; 152, Susan Meiselas, *Burning Somoza, Nicaragua,* 1979 (Magnum Photos, Inc.); 160, Barbara Bloom, *Shop Window, Cairo,* 1984 (courtesy the photographer); 168, anonymous Japanese advertisement; 168, inset, Margaret Bourke-White, *Dr. Karl Lisso . . .,* 1945, detail; 176, Josep Sala, *Untitled,* © 1940, detail (collection Sala family); 176, inset, Henri Cartier-Bresson, *Leghorn, Italy,* 1932 (Magnum Photos, Inc.); 184, Gilles Peress, *Godard at screening of* Detective, *Palais Festival, Cannes,* 1985, detail (Magnum Photos, Inc.); 184, inset, Raymond Depardon, *Freedom Heals, Italy, 17 December 1980,* (Magnum Photos, Inc.); 192, René Burri, *São Paulo,* 1960, detail; 192, inset, Jean-Luc Godard, *La Chinoise,* 1968, film still; 200, anonymous advertisement, detail; 200, inset, Gilles Peress, *Beggars, Teheran, Iran, 1980* (Magnum Photos, Inc.); 208, both, Micha Bar-Am, *Egyptian POWs, Yom Kippur War,* 1973 (Magnum Photos, Inc.); 216, Margaret Bourke-White, *Dr. Karl Lisso . . .,* 1945, detail; Laszlo Moholy-Nagy, *At Coffee,* n.d. (The Museum of Fine Arts, Houston, Museum Purchase with funds provided by Max and Isabell Herzstein); 232, Piet Zwart, *Teller im Seifenwasser,* 1931 (private collection); 240, Ralph Steiner, *After Rehearsal . . .,* 1936, detail; 248, Barbara Bloom, *Two Watches,* 1985 (courtesy the photographer); 256, Barbara Bloom, *Chanel Chanel,* 1983 (courtesy the photographer); 264, anonymous postcard; 272, Jean-Luc Godard, *Deux ou trois choses que je sais d'elle,* 1966, film still (The Museum of Modern Art, Film Stills Archive); 280, anonymous postcard; 288, Charles Harbutt, *Two Chairs, Stephentown, Massachusetts,* 1969 (courtesy the photographer and Archive Pictures Inc.); Margaret Bourke-White, *Dr. Karl Lisso,* 1945, detail; 304, Victor Burgin, *Olympia,* 1982, detail (courtesy John Weber Gallery); 312, Barbara Bloom, *Fascination,* 1985, detail (courtesy the photographer); 320, Robert Doisneau, *Sidelong Glance,* 1948, detail (Rapho/Photo Researchers, Inc.); 328, Stephen R. Brown, *PLO Soldier with Pistol and Artillery Shell, July 1982,* detail (courtesy the photographer); 336, anonymous French advertisement, detail; 344, anonymous fashion photo, detail; 352, photographer unknown, *Adolf Hitler Attending a Berlin Art Exhibition,* 1939, detail; 360, Robert Welch, *Shipyard, Harland and Woolf, Belfast, Northern Ireland,* ©1900 (collection Gilles Peress and Nan Richardson); 360, inset, television still representing Margaret Bourke-White photograph (photo: Barbara Bloom); 368, anonymous newsphoto; 368, inset, television still, PIA jetliner (photo: Barbara Bloom); 376, Henri Cartier-Bresson, *Peking, 1949* (Magnum Photos, Inc.); 376, inset, television still, atomic bomb test (photo: Barbara Bloom); 384, anonymous advertisement; 384, inset, television still, Chinese acrobats; 392, Paul Senn, *Trade Union Meeting,* 1941 (private collection); 392, inset, television still, Eve Arnold photograph, 1980 (photo: Barbara Bloom); 400, anonymous postcard, Hong Kong Space Museum, detail; 400, inset, television still, Barbara Bloom, *The Diamond Lane,* 1981 (photo: Barbara Bloom); 408, anonymous newsphoto, detail; 408, inset, television still, *Charlie's Angels* with Arabic subtitles, 1984 (photo: Barbara Bloom); 416, Peter DeLory, *Andy Ostheimer Reading, Ibiza, Spain,* 1976 (courtesy the photographer and The Minneapolis Institute of Art, Gift of Frank Kolodny); 432, Jean-Luc Godard, *La Chinoise,* 1968, film still.

Reprint Sources

David Wojnarowicz, "Sounds in the Distance," selection from *Sounds in the Distance* (London: Aloes Press, 1982); Laurie Anderson, "Words in Reverse," selections from *Words in Reverse* (Buffalo, New York: Hallwalls, 1980; *Top Stories,* no. 2); Robert Smithson, "A Tour of the Monuments of Passaic, New Jersey," published as "The Monuments of Passaic," *Artforum* 6, no. 4 (December 1967): 48-51; Anne Turyn and Robert Fiengo, "If Only," from *Remembrance of Things Past,* edited by Lane Relyea (Long Beach, California: Long Beach Museum of Art, 1986), pp. 39-41; John Baldessari, "My Files of Movie Stills," in *Carnegie International Exhibition 1985* (Pittsburgh: Carnegie Institute, 1985), pp. 91-93; Jenny Holzer, "Truisms," from *Truisms and Essays* (Halifax, Nova Scotia: The Press of the Nova Scotia College of Art and Design, 1983); Allan Sekula, "Reading an Archive," excerpted from "Photography Between Labour and Capital," in *Mining Photographs and Other Pictures, 1948-1968* (Halifax, Nova Scotia: The Press of the Nova Scotia College of Art and Design and the University College of Cape Breton Press, 1983), pp. 193-202; Adrian Piper, "Ideology, Confrontation, and Political Self-Awareness: An Essay," *High Performance* 4, no. 1 (Spring 1981): unpag.; Martha Rosler, "Constructing a Life," in *Documenta 1982* (Kassel: Documenta, 1982), vol. 2, pp. 234-235; Thomas Lawson, "Spies and Watchmen," *Cover,* no. 3 (Spring-Summer 1980): 16-17 (this text was originally accompanied by a photograph); Eric Bogosian, "In the Dark," selections from *In the Dark* (New York: Wedge Press, Inc., 1983); Spalding Gray, "From *Swimming to Cambodia,*" excerpted from *Swimming to Cambodia* (New York: Theatre Communications Group, 1985), pp. 22-33; Simon Watney, "The Rhetoric of AIDS," published in a slightly different version in *Screen* 27, no. 1 (January-February 1986): 72-85; Edgar Heap of Birds, "My Past, My People," selections from *Sharp Rocks* (Buffalo, New York: CEPA, 1986); Theresa Hak Kyung Cha, "Clio/History," excerpted from *Dictee* (New York: Tanam Press, 1982), pp. 23-41; Candace Hill, "Evening Tomorrow's Here Today Since the Hornet Flies I Triangle," *wedge,* no. 3-4-5 (Winter-Summer 1983); Cookie Mueller, "My Bio: Notes on an American Childhood, 1949-1959," *Bomb,* no. 11 (Winter 1985): 88-89; Constance DeJong, "Modern Love," from *Modern Love* (New York: Standard Editions, 1977), pp. 3-35; Kathy Acker, "Russian Constructivism," from *Don Quixote* (New York: Grove Press, 1986), pp. 41-59; Lynne Tillman, "For the Future," from *Haunted Houses* (New York: Poseidon Press, 1987), pp. 132-148; Gary Indiana, "Burmese Days," *Bomb,* no. 9 (Spring 1987): 52-53; Victor Burgin, "Tea with Madeleine," *wedge,* no. 6 (Winter 1984): 40-47; Ross Bleckner, "Transcendent Anti-Fetishism," *Artforum* 17, no. 7 (March 1979): 50-55; David Salle, "The Paintings Are Dead," *Cover,* no. 1 (May 1979): unpag.; Peter Halley, "On Line," *New Observations,* no. 35 (1985): 8-10; Judith Barry, "Casual Imagination," *Discourse,* no. 4 (Winter 1981-1982): 4-31; Dan Graham, "Dean Martin/Entertainment as Theater," in *Dan Graham: Articles* (Eindhoven: Stedelijk Van Abbemuseum, 1977), pp. 41-46; William Wegman, "Pathetic Readings," *Avalanche* (May-June 1974): 8-9; Yvonne Rainer, "Thoughts on Women's Cinema: Eating Words, Voicing Struggles," *The Independent* 10, no. 3 (April 1987): 14-16; Silvia Kolbowski, "Discordant Views," *Parachute,* no. 40 (1985): 18-20; Barbara Kruger, "Remote Control," *Artforum* 24, no. 3 (November 1985): 7; 24, no. 5 (January 1986): 11; 24, no. 7 (March 1986): 11; 24, no. 9 (May 1986): 14; 25, no. 1 (September 1986): 10-11; Richard Prince, "The Perfect Tense," selections from *Why I Go to the Movies Alone* (New York: Tanam Press, 1983).